KIYOHIKO AZUMA

YOTSUBA&!

11

CONTENTS

#76 YOTSUBA& ·······! 187

#75 YOTSUBA& FRIENDS 149

#74 YOTSUBA& CAMERA 121

#73 YOTSUBA& PICKING CHESTNUTS 093

#72 YOTSUBA& BUBBLES 059

#71 YOTSUBA& PIZZA 025

#70 YOTSUBA& UDON 003

YOTSUBA&!
KIYOHIKO AZUMA

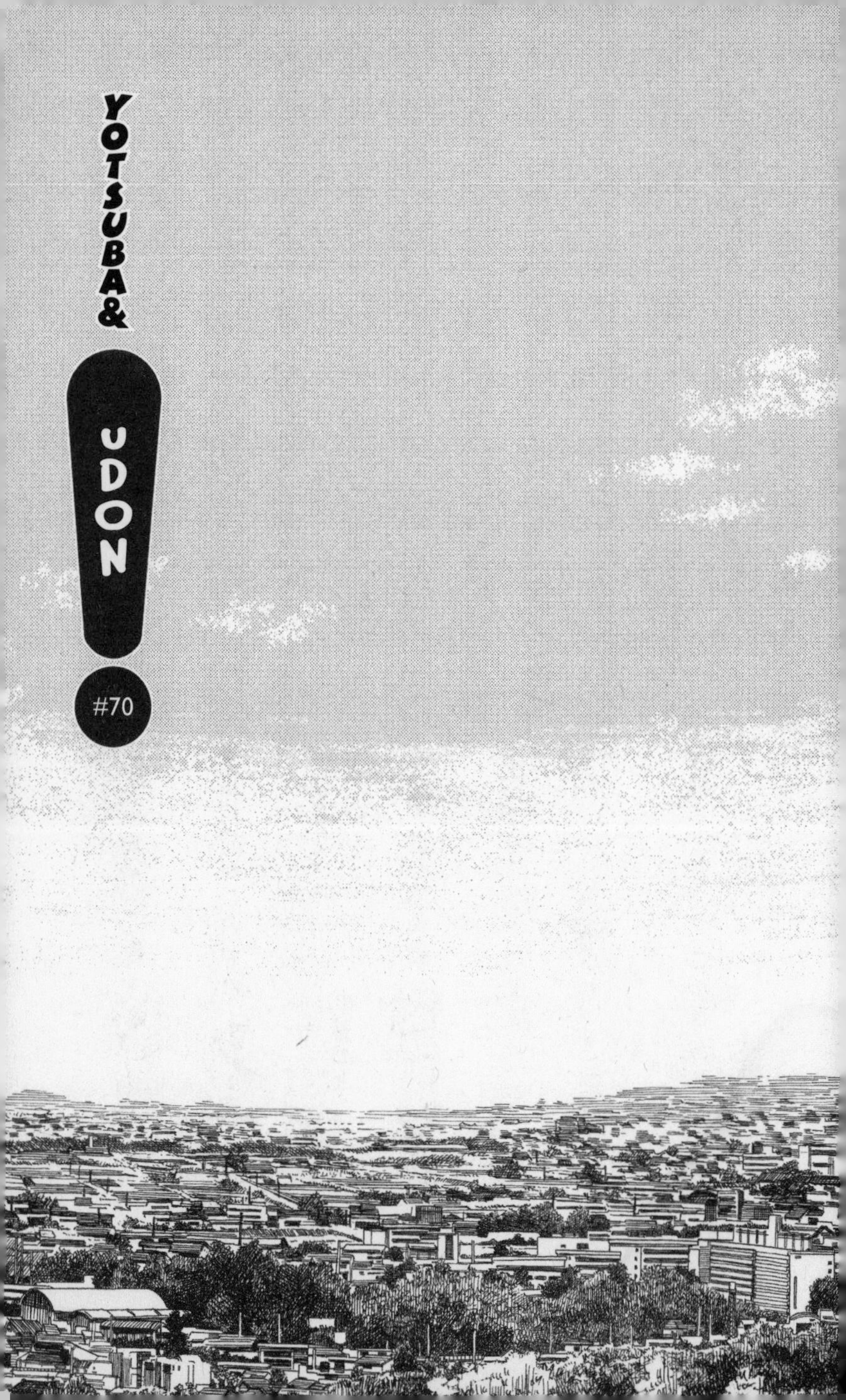
YOTSUBA&
UDON
#70

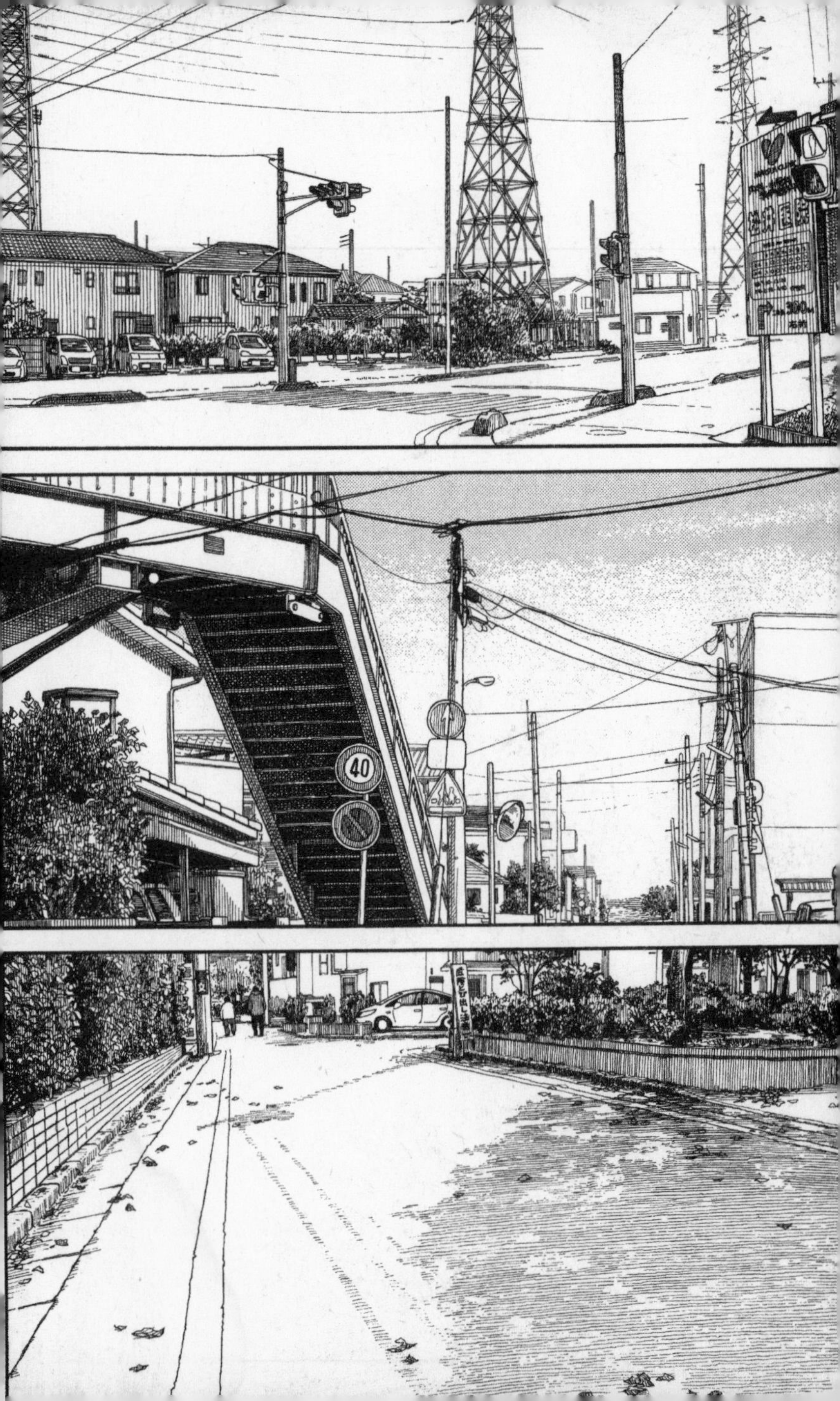

300m
40

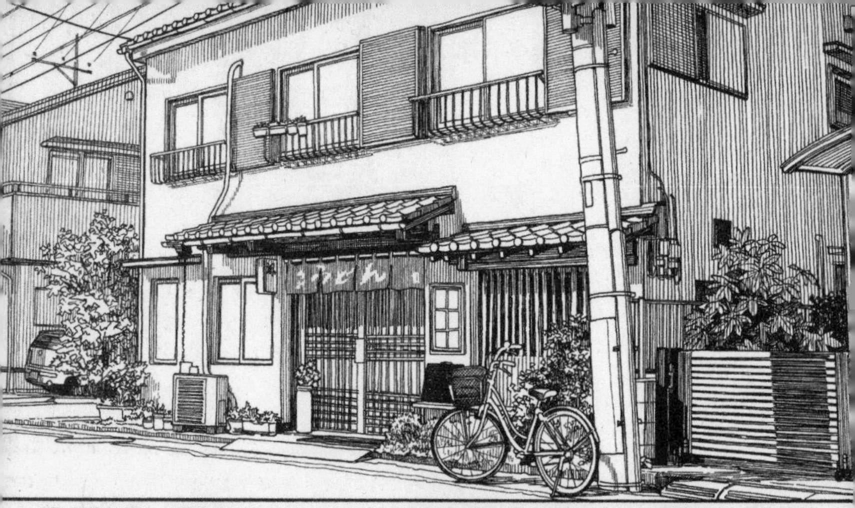

SIGN: TEMPURA FEST — SHRIMP TEMPURA UDON ¥850, VEGETABLE TEMPURA UDON ¥800

BANNER: HANDMADE UDON

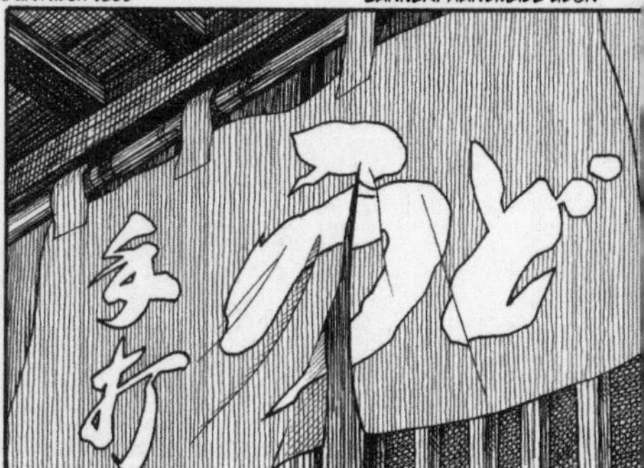
手打
うど

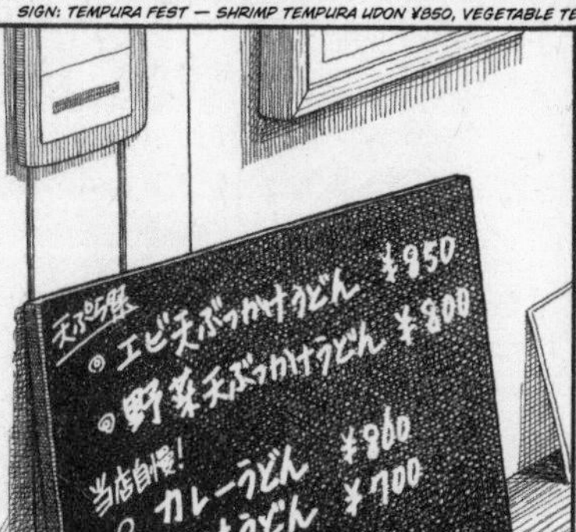
天ぷら展
◎エビ天ぶっかけうどん ¥850
◎野菜天ぶっかけうどん ¥800
当店自慢!
○カレーうどん ¥800
○肉汁うどん ¥700
本日のおすすめ
月見うどん ¥750

SIGN (CONT.): COOK'S FAVORITES! — CURRY UDON ¥800, MEAT BROTH UDON ¥700 / TODAY'S SPECIAL — TSUKIMI UDON ¥750

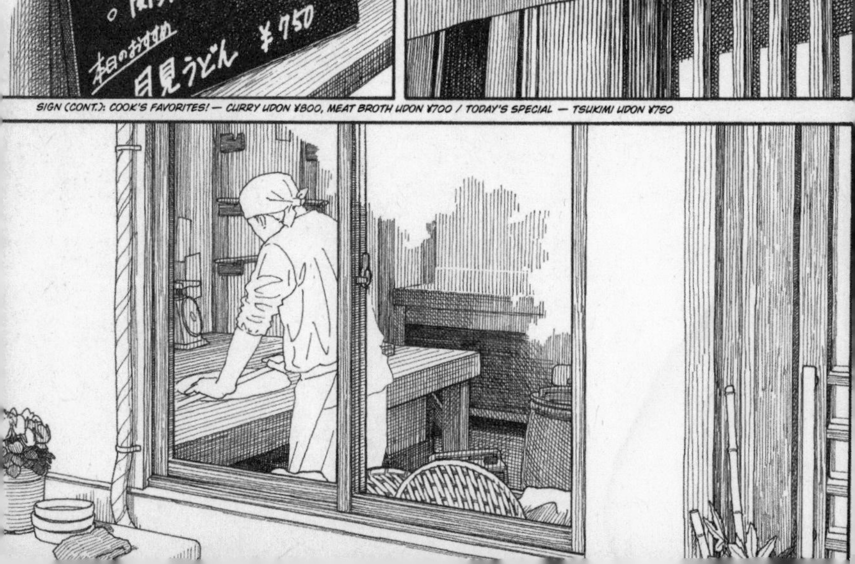

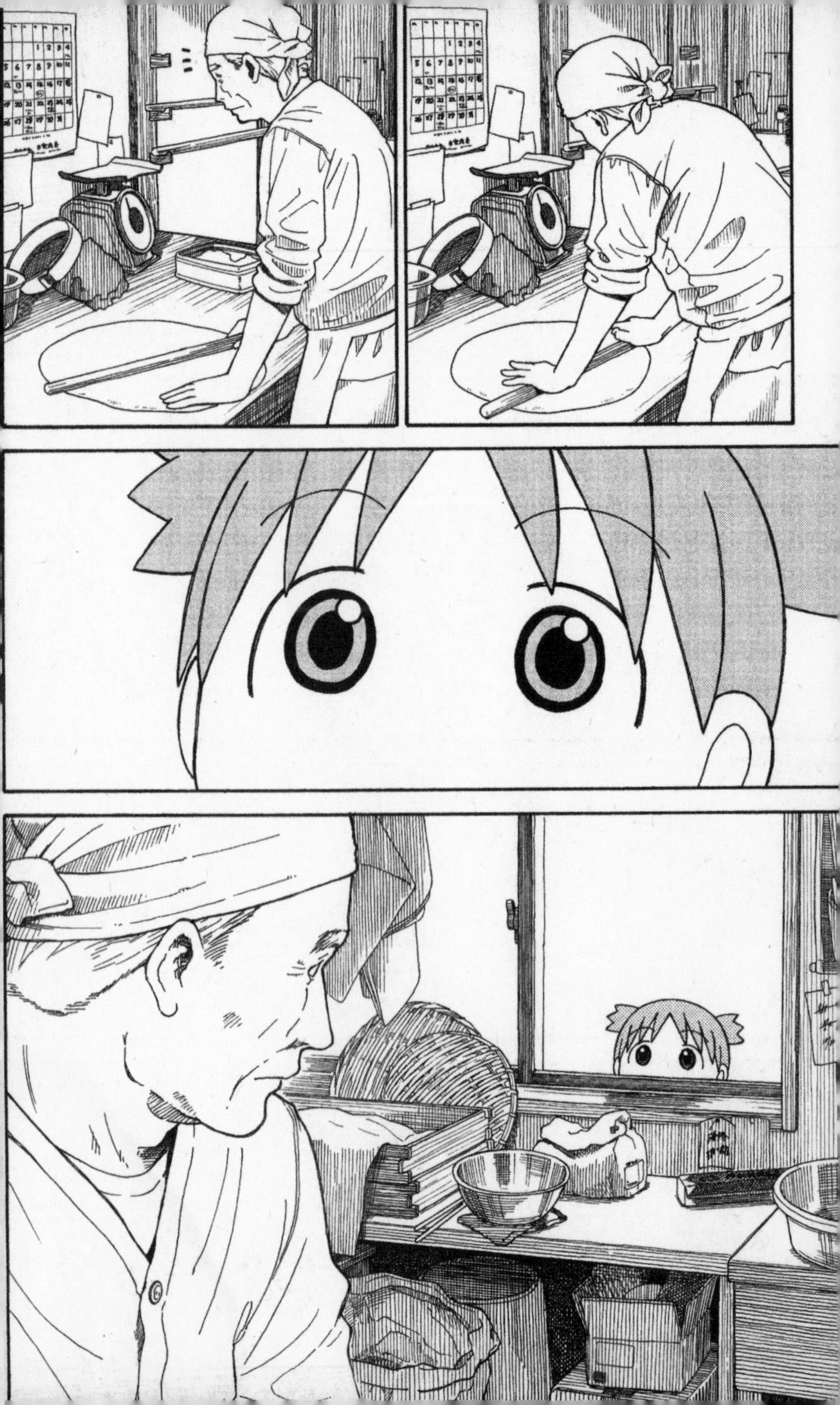

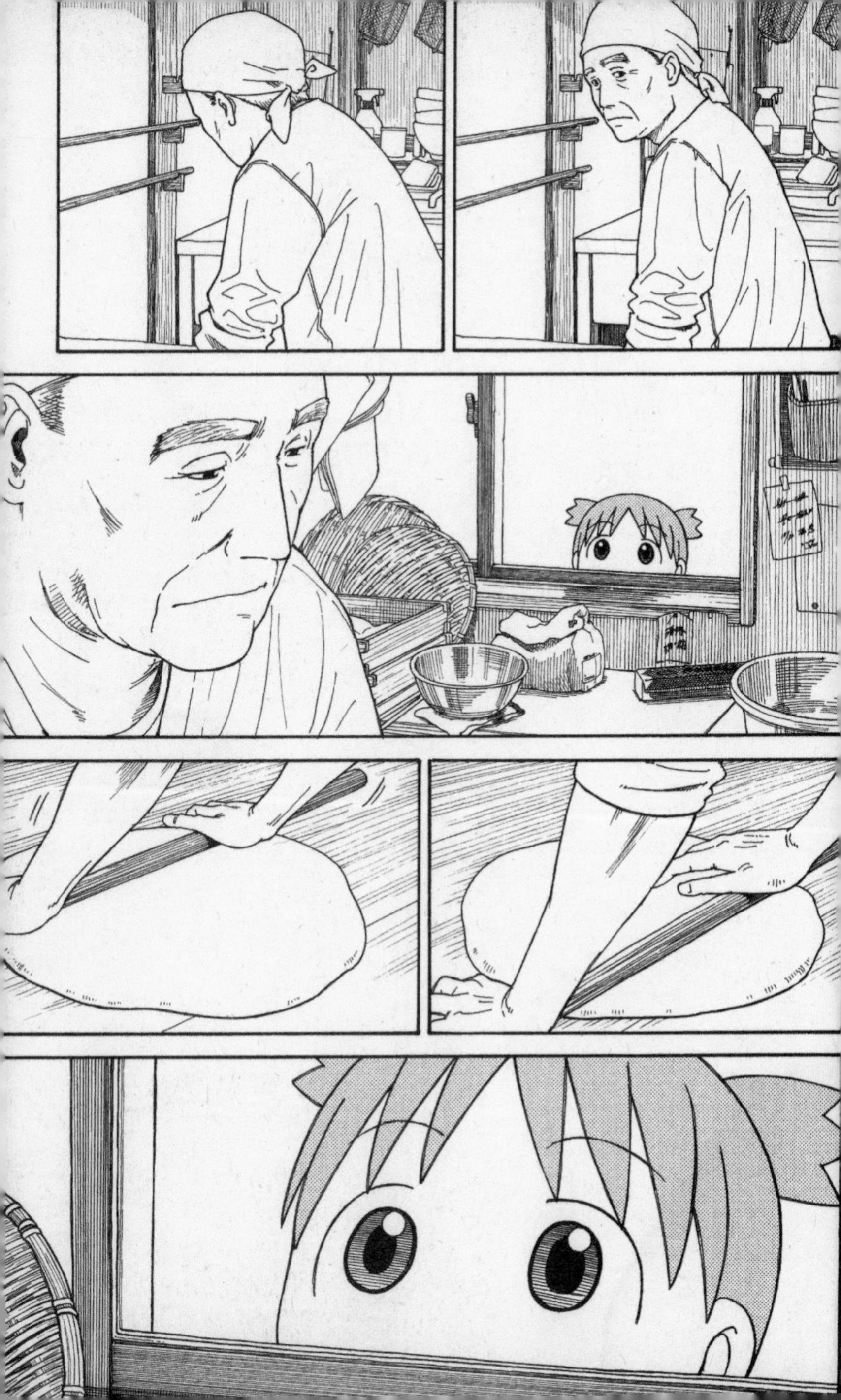

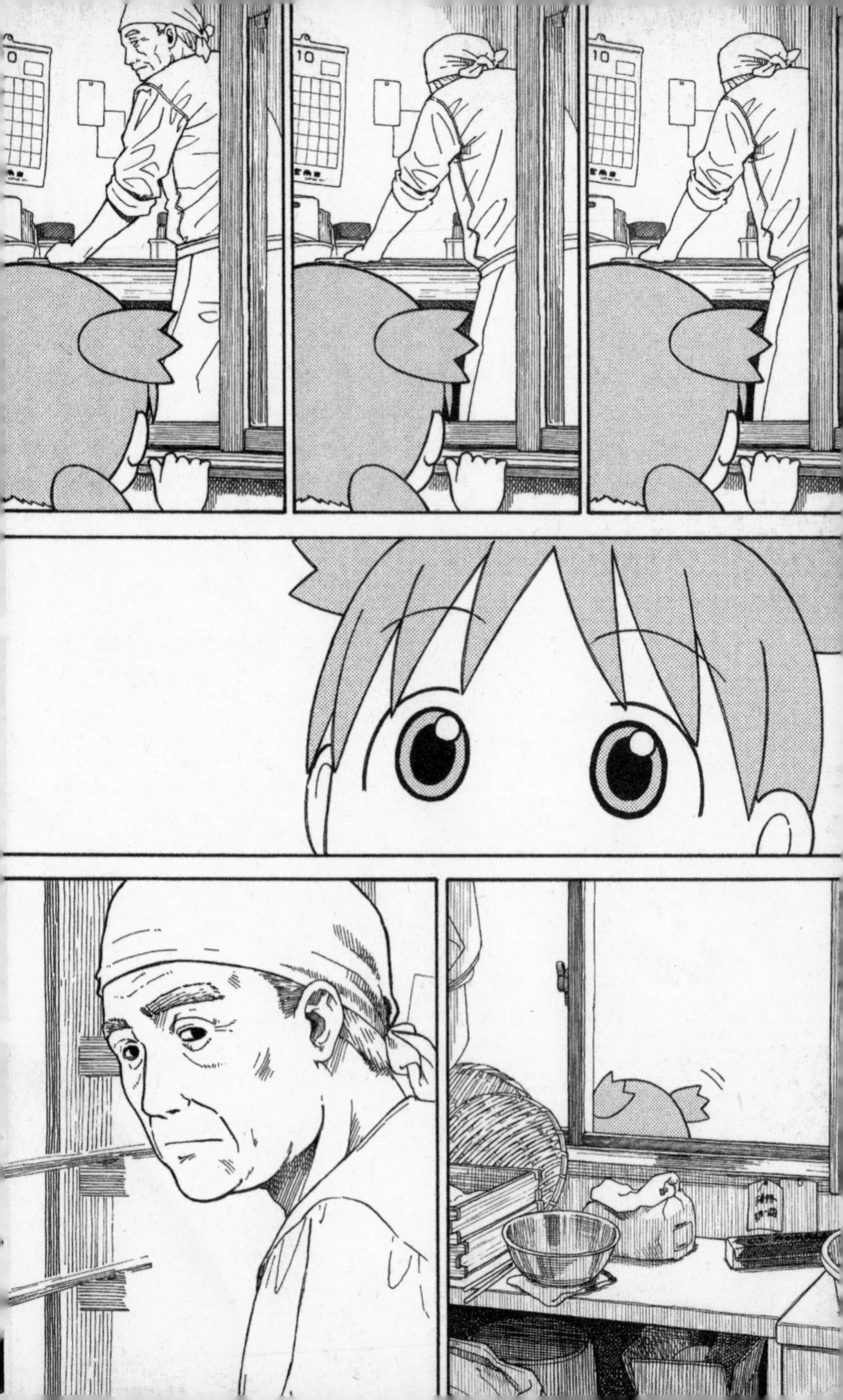

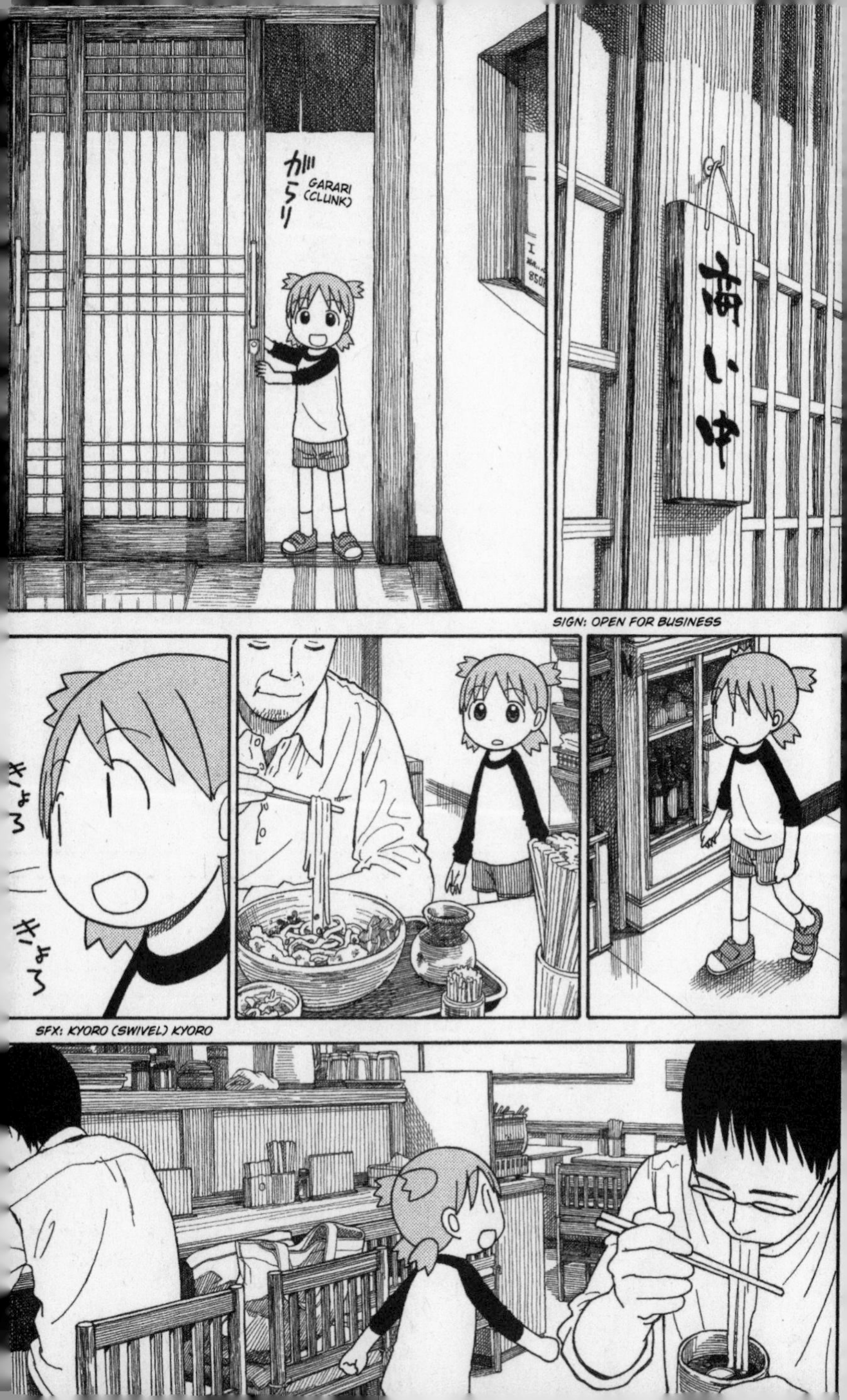

商い中
SIGN: OPEN FOR BUSINESS
ガらり
GARARI (CLUNK)
きょろ きょろ
SFX: KYORO (SWIVEL) KYORO

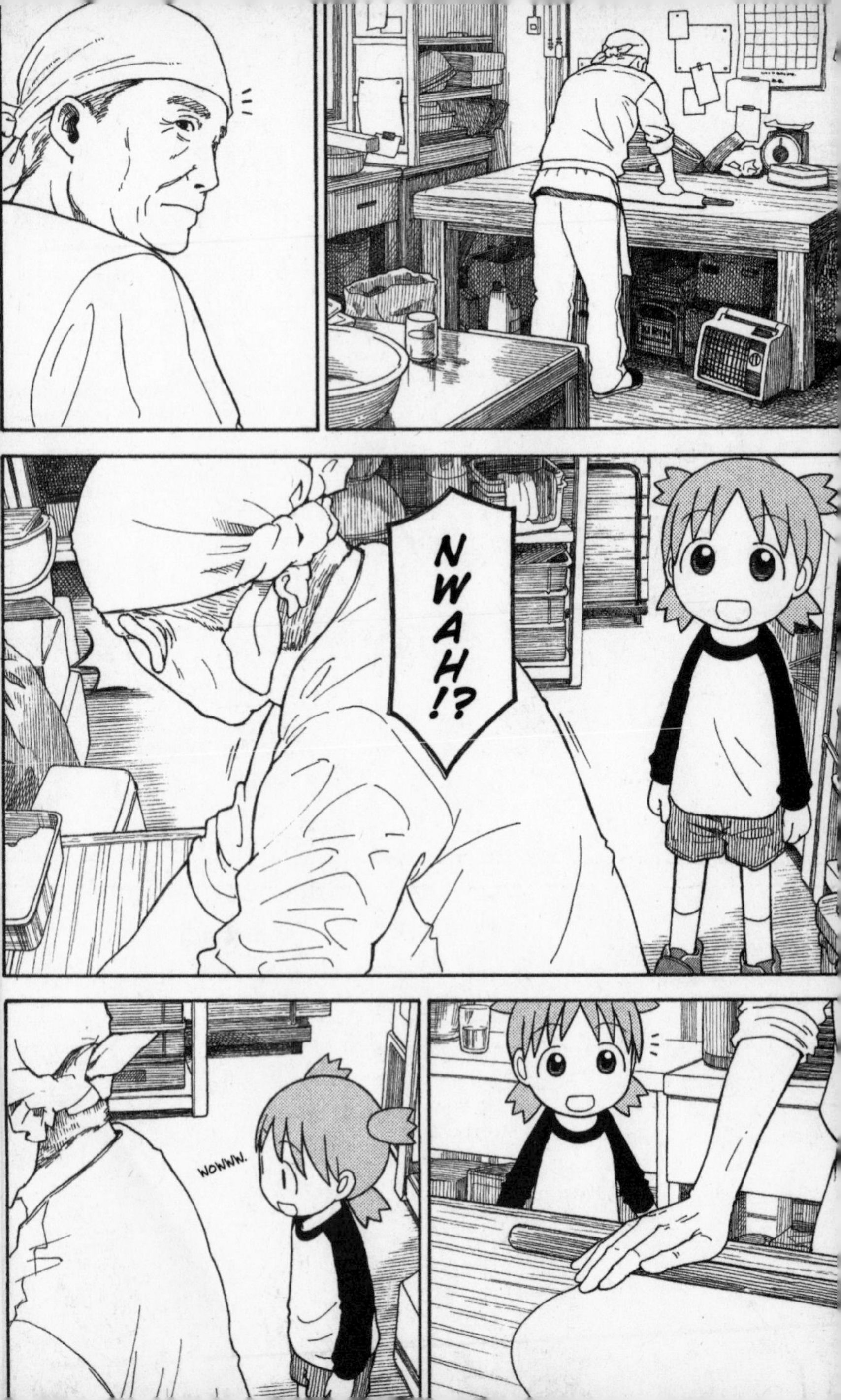
NWAH!?
WOWWW.

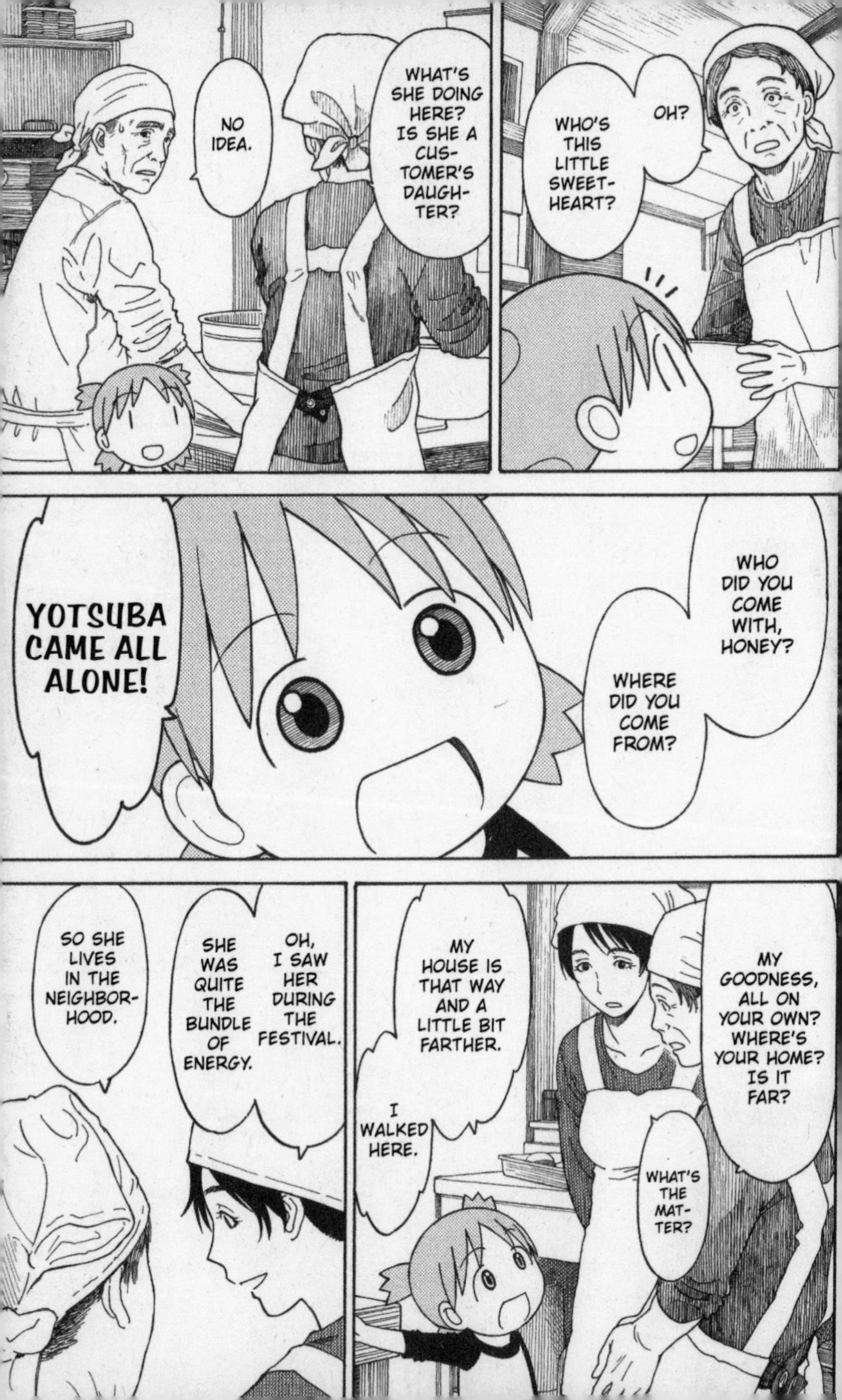
OH?
WHO'S THIS LITTLE SWEET-HEART?
WHAT'S SHE DOING HERE? IS SHE A CUS-TOMER'S DAUGH-TER?
NO IDEA.
WHO DID YOU COME WITH, HONEY?
WHERE DID YOU COME FROM?
YOTSUBA CAME ALL ALONE!
MY GOODNESS, ALL ON YOUR OWN? WHERE'S YOUR HOME? IS IT FAR?
WHAT'S THE MAT-TER?
MY HOUSE IS THAT WAY AND A LITTLE BIT FARTHER.
I WALKED HERE.
OH, I SAW HER DURING THE FESTIVAL.
SHE WAS QUITE THE BUNDLE OF ENERGY.
SO SHE LIVES IN THE NEIGHBOR-HOOD.

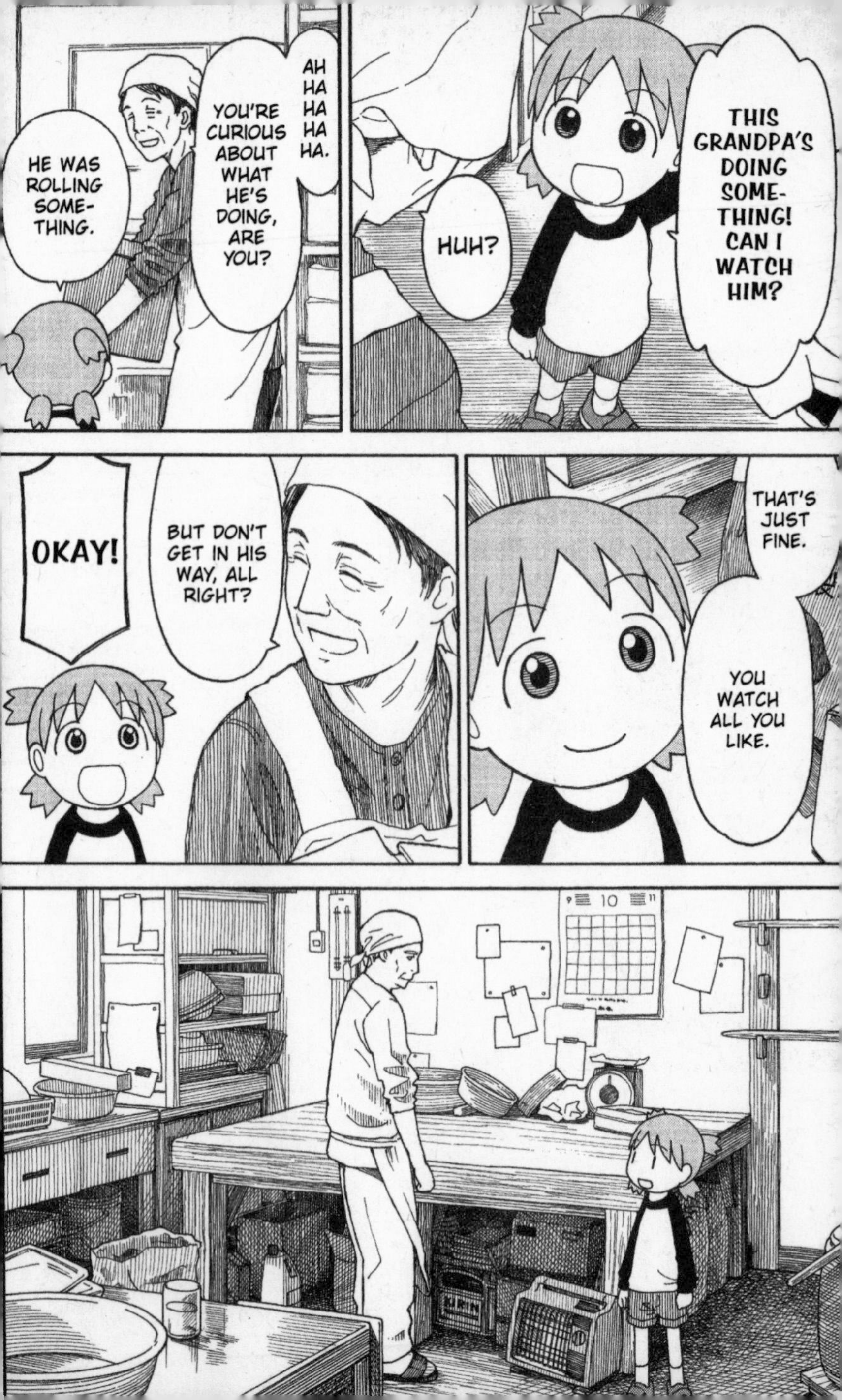
THIS GRANDPA'S DOING SOME-THING! CAN I WATCH HIM?
HUH?
AH HA HA HA HA.
YOU'RE CURIOUS ABOUT WHAT HE'S DOING, ARE YOU?
HE WAS ROLLING SOME-THING.
THAT'S JUST FINE.
YOU WATCH ALL YOU LIKE.
BUT DON'T GET IN HIS WAY, ALL RIGHT?
OKAY!

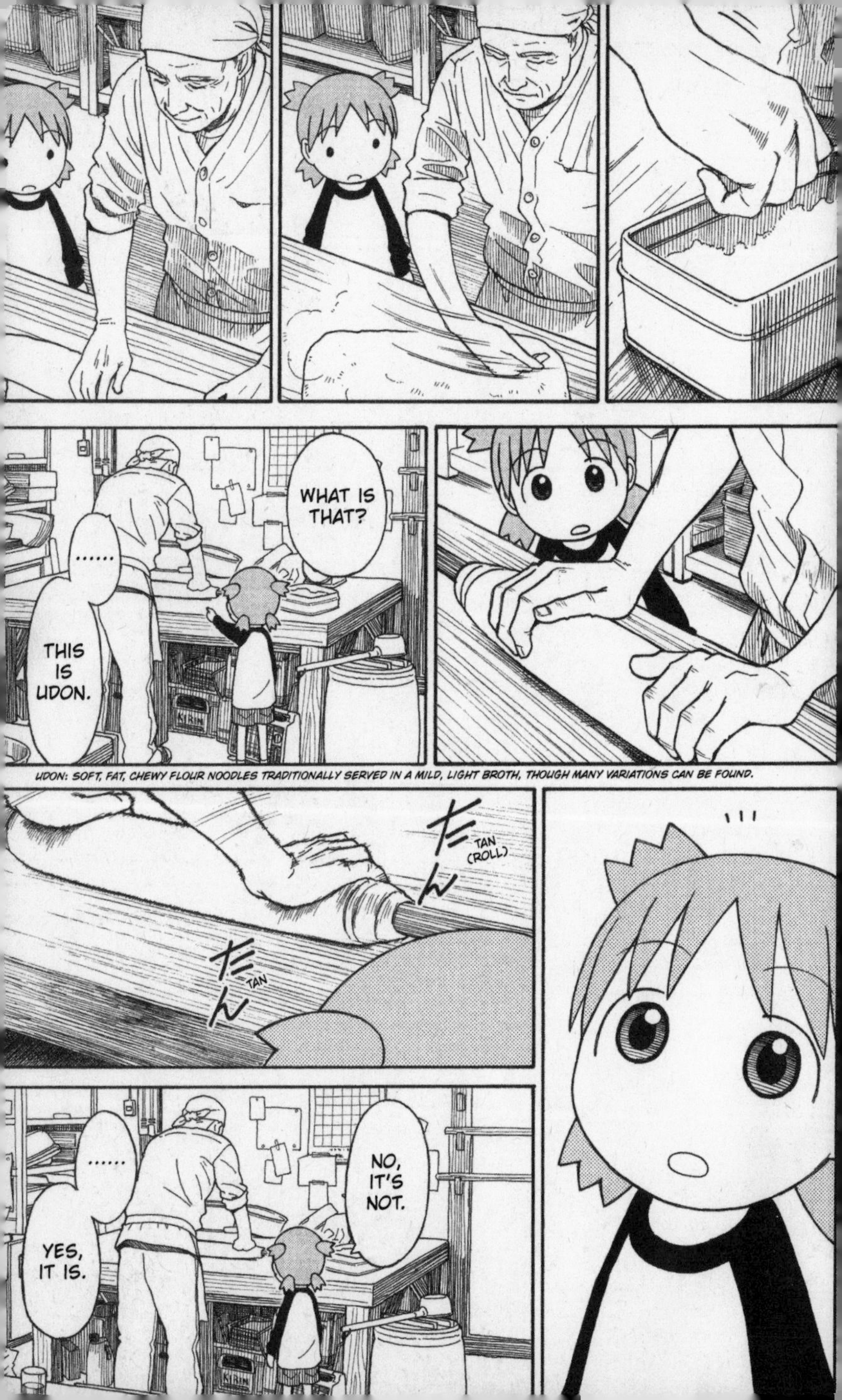
WHAT IS THAT?
......
THIS IS UDON.
TAN (ROLL)
TAN
NO, IT'S NOT.
......
YES, IT IS.
UDON: SOFT, FAT, CHEWY FLOUR NOODLES TRADITIONALLY SERVED IN A MILD, LIGHT BROTH, THOUGH MANY VARIATIONS CAN BE FOUND.

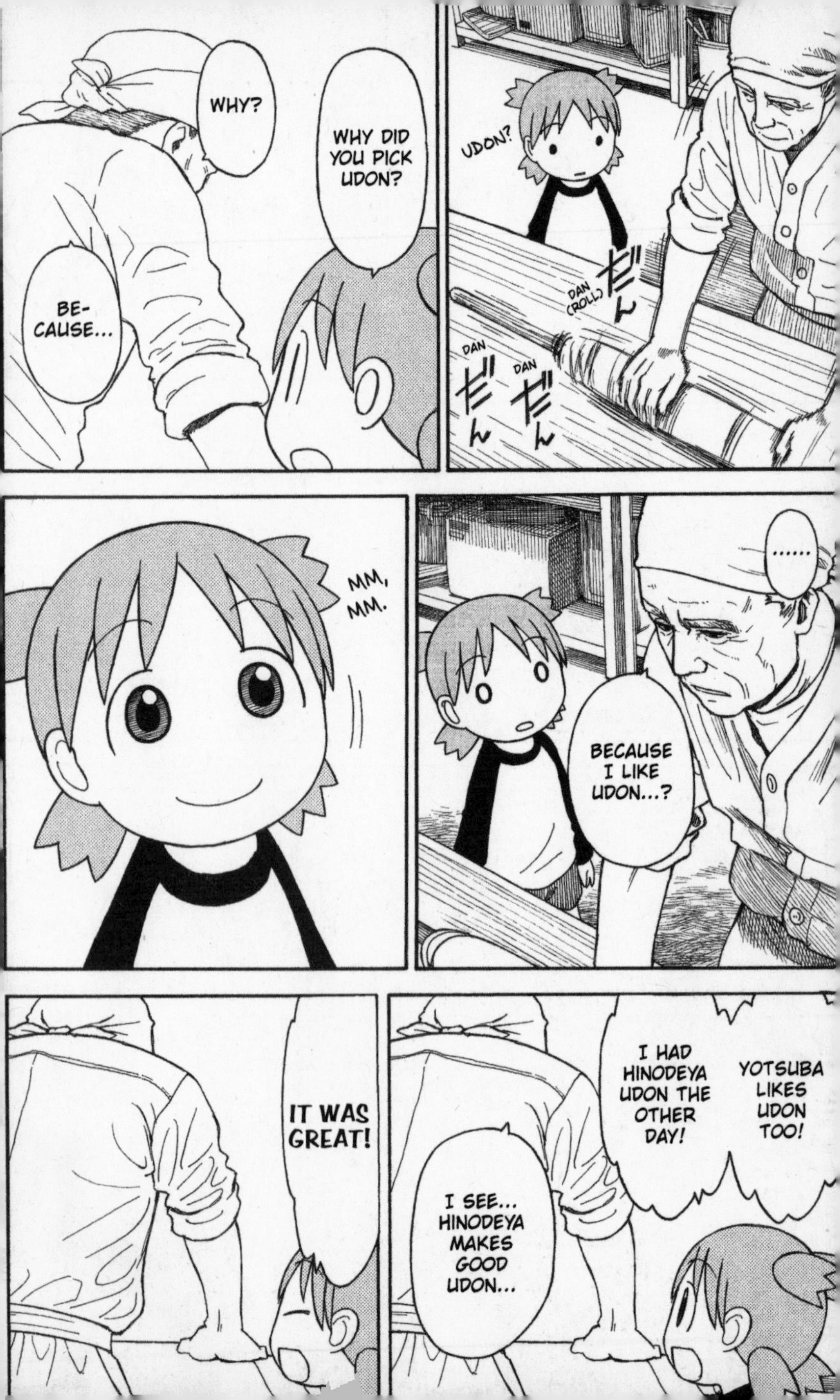
UDON?
DAN (ROLL)
DAN
DAN
WHY?
WHY DID YOU PICK UDON?
BE-CAUSE...
......
BECAUSE I LIKE UDON...?
MM, MM.
YOTSUBA LIKES UDON TOO!
I HAD HINODEYA UDON THE OTHER DAY!
I SEE... HINODEYA MAKES GOOD UDON...
IT WAS GREAT!

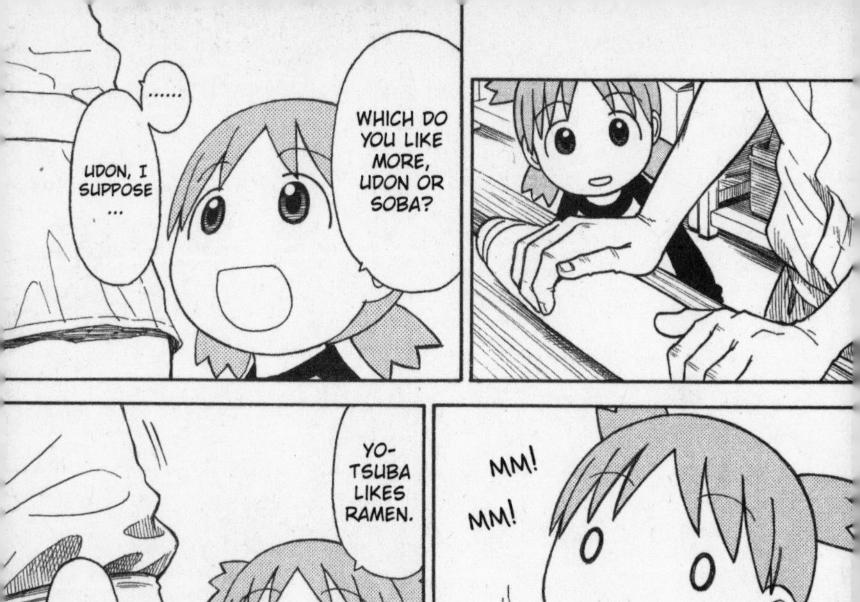
WHICH DO YOU LIKE MORE, UDON OR SOBA?
......
UDON, I SUPPOSE ...
YO-TSUBA LIKES RAMEN.
I SEE...
MM!
MM!
IS THAT KONTOTSU FLAVOR?
YOU MEAN TON-KOTSU?
NO, IT'S NOT.

TONKOTSU: A CREAMY, HEAVY RAMEN BROTH MADE FROM PORK BONE (FROM WHICH IT GETS ITS NAME) AND FAT.

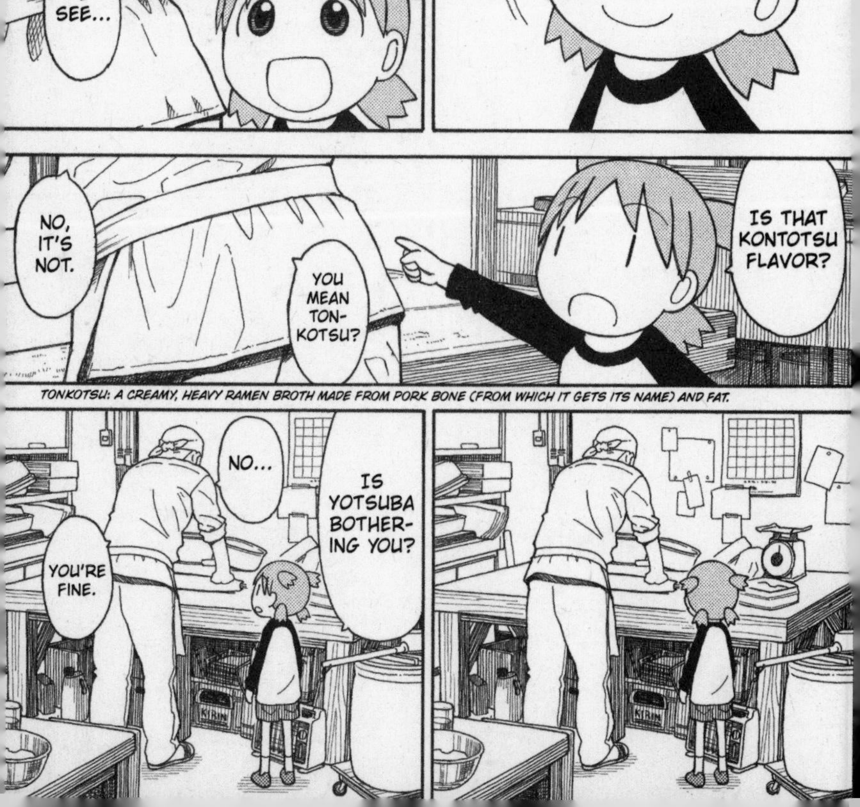
IS YOTSUBA BOTHER-ING YOU?
NO...
YOU'RE FINE.
KIRIN

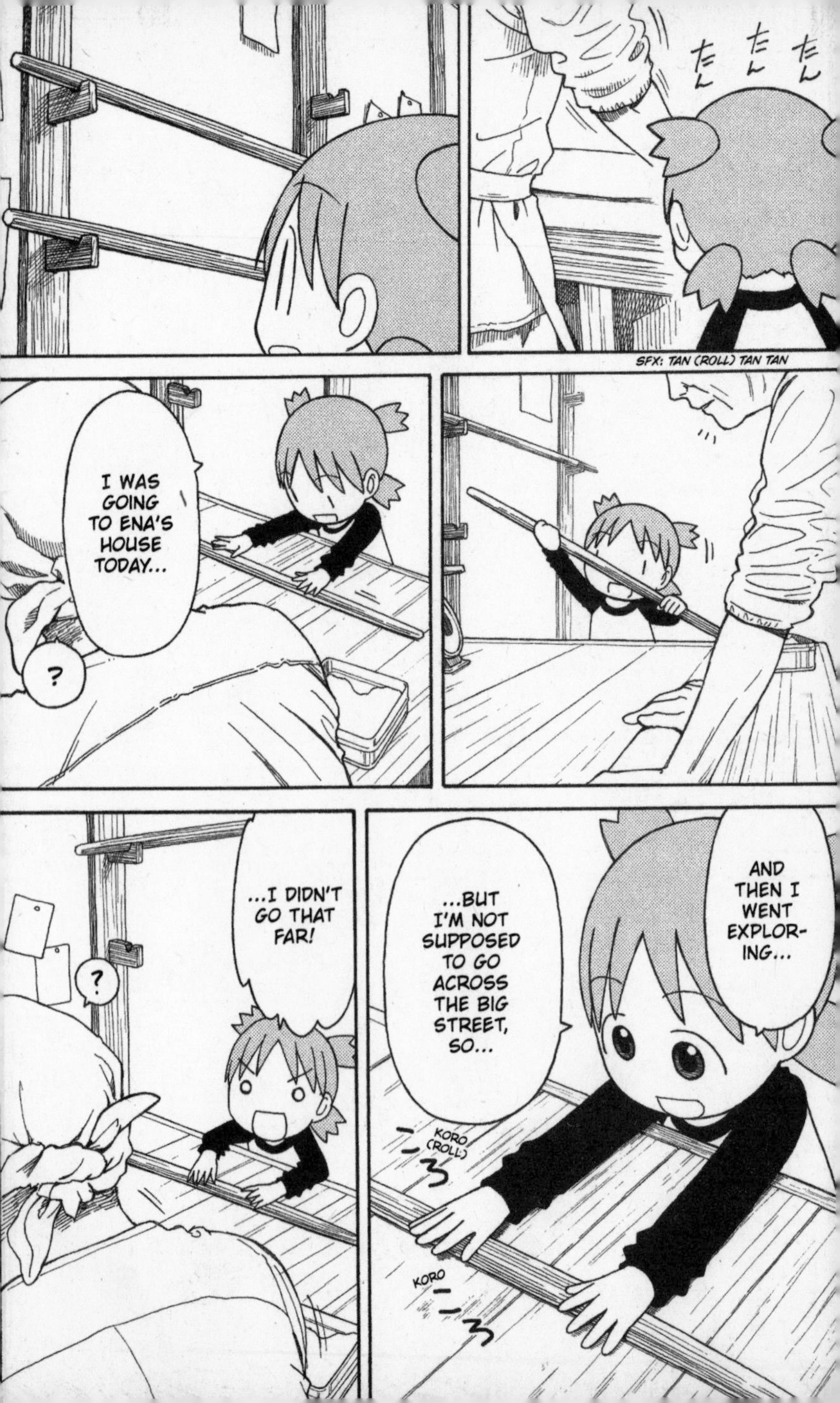

たん たん たん
SFX: TAN (ROLL) TAN TAN
I WAS GOING TO ENA'S HOUSE TODAY...
?
AND THEN I WENT EXPLOR-ING...
...BUT I'M NOT SUPPOSED TO GO ACROSS THE BIG STREET, SO...
KORO (ROLL)
KORO
...I DIDN'T GO THAT FAR!
?

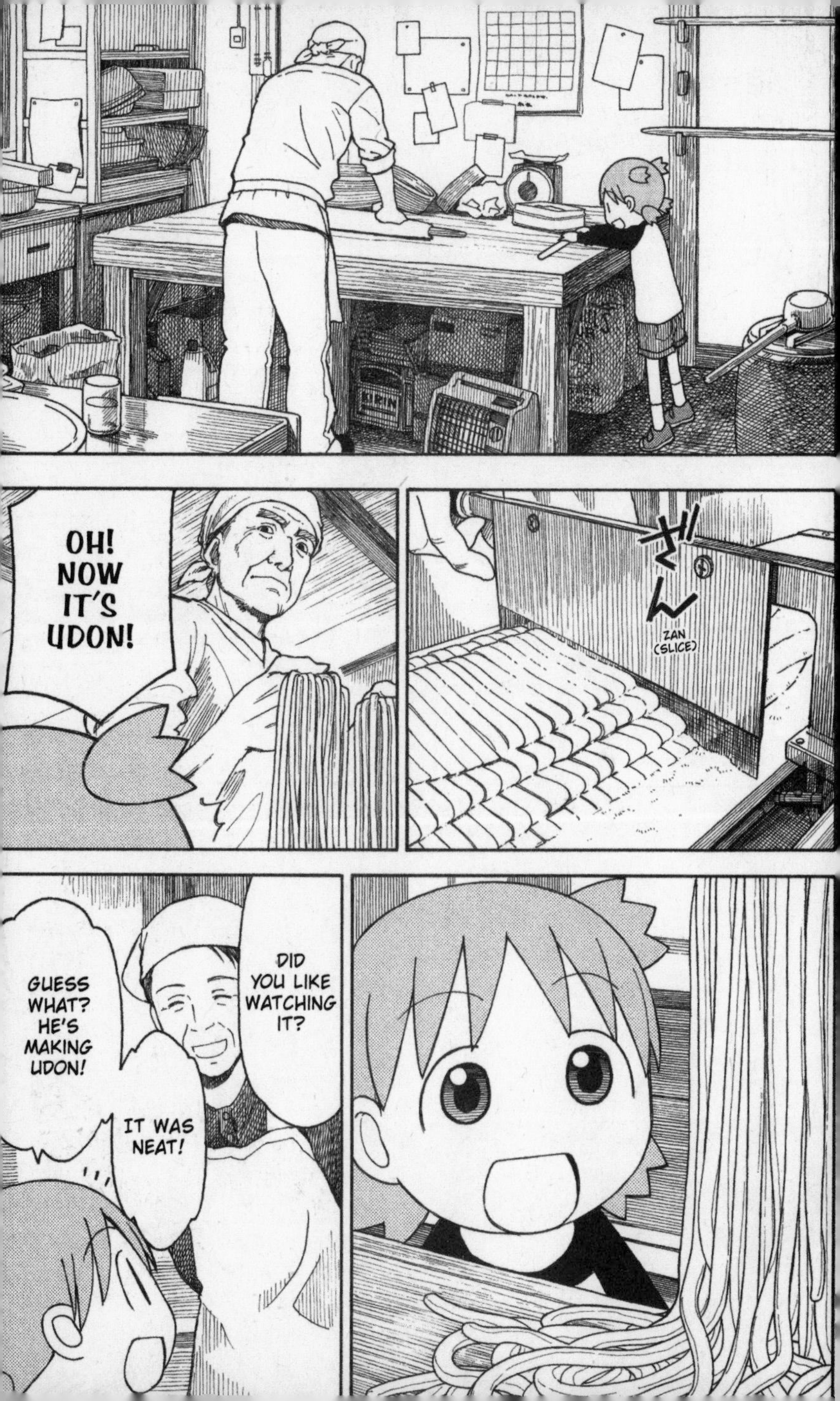
ZAN (SLICE)
OH! NOW IT'S UDON!
DID YOU LIKE WATCHING IT?
GUESS WHAT? HE'S MAKING UDON!
IT WAS NEAT!

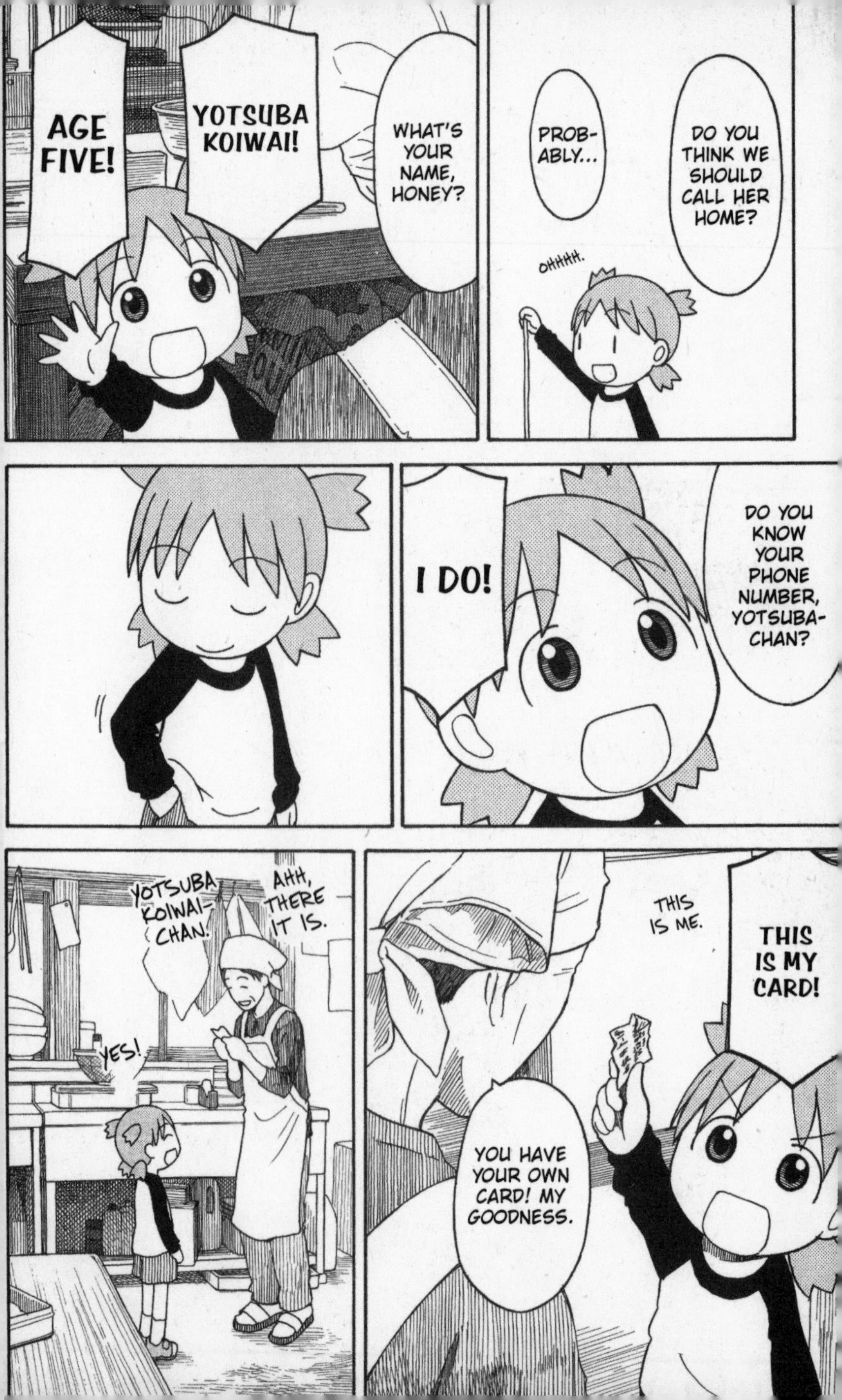
DO YOU THINK WE SHOULD CALL HER HOME?
PROB-ABLY...
OHHHH.
WHAT'S YOUR NAME, HONEY?
YOTSUBA KOIWAI!
AGE FIVE!
DO YOU KNOW YOUR PHONE NUMBER, YOTSUBA-CHAN?
I DO!
THIS IS MY CARD!
THIS IS ME.
YOU HAVE YOUR OWN CARD! MY GOODNESS.
AHH, THERE IT IS.
YOTSUBA KOIWAI-CHAN.
YES!

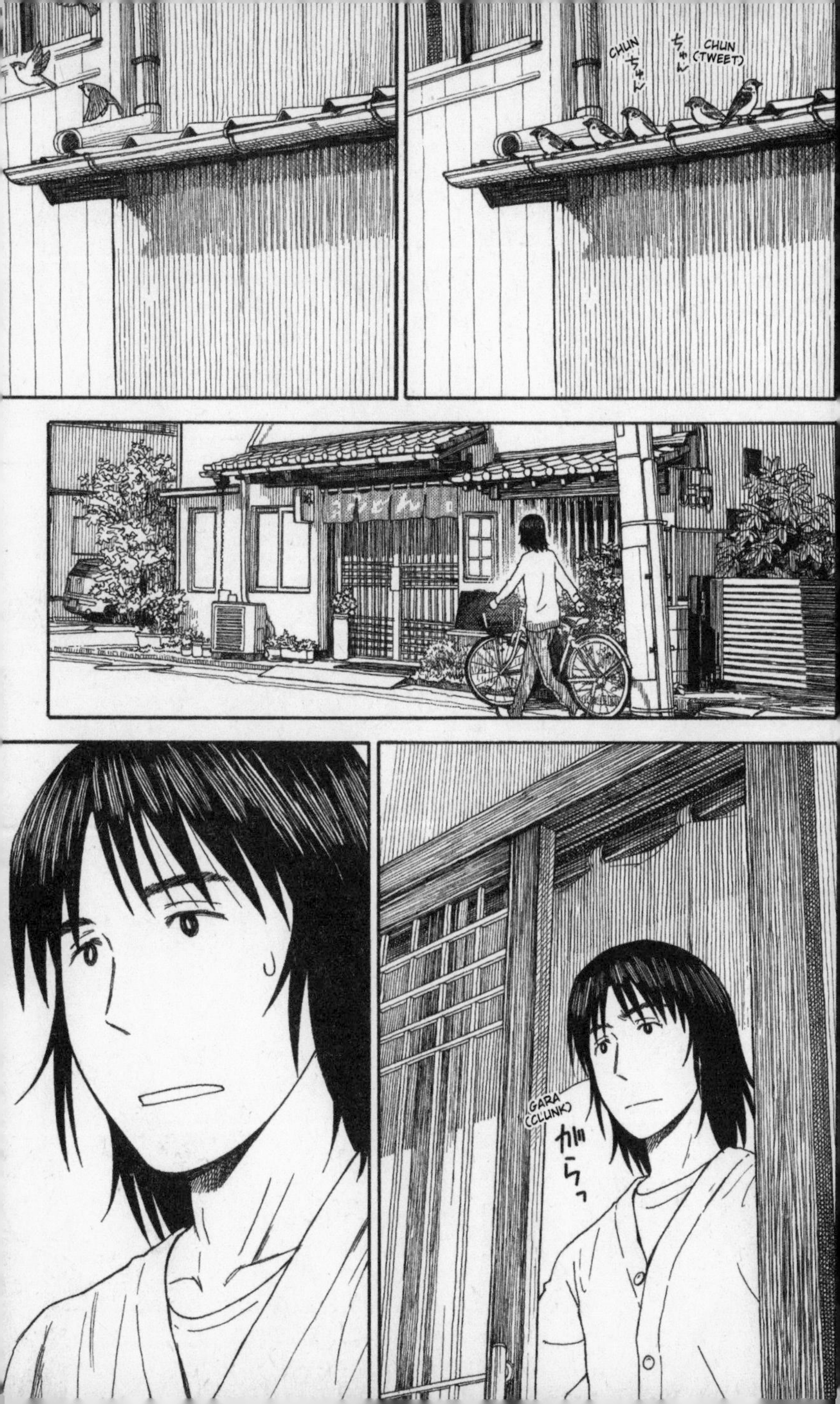
CHUN (TWEET)
ちゅん
CHUN
ちゅん
GARA (CLUNK)
がらっ

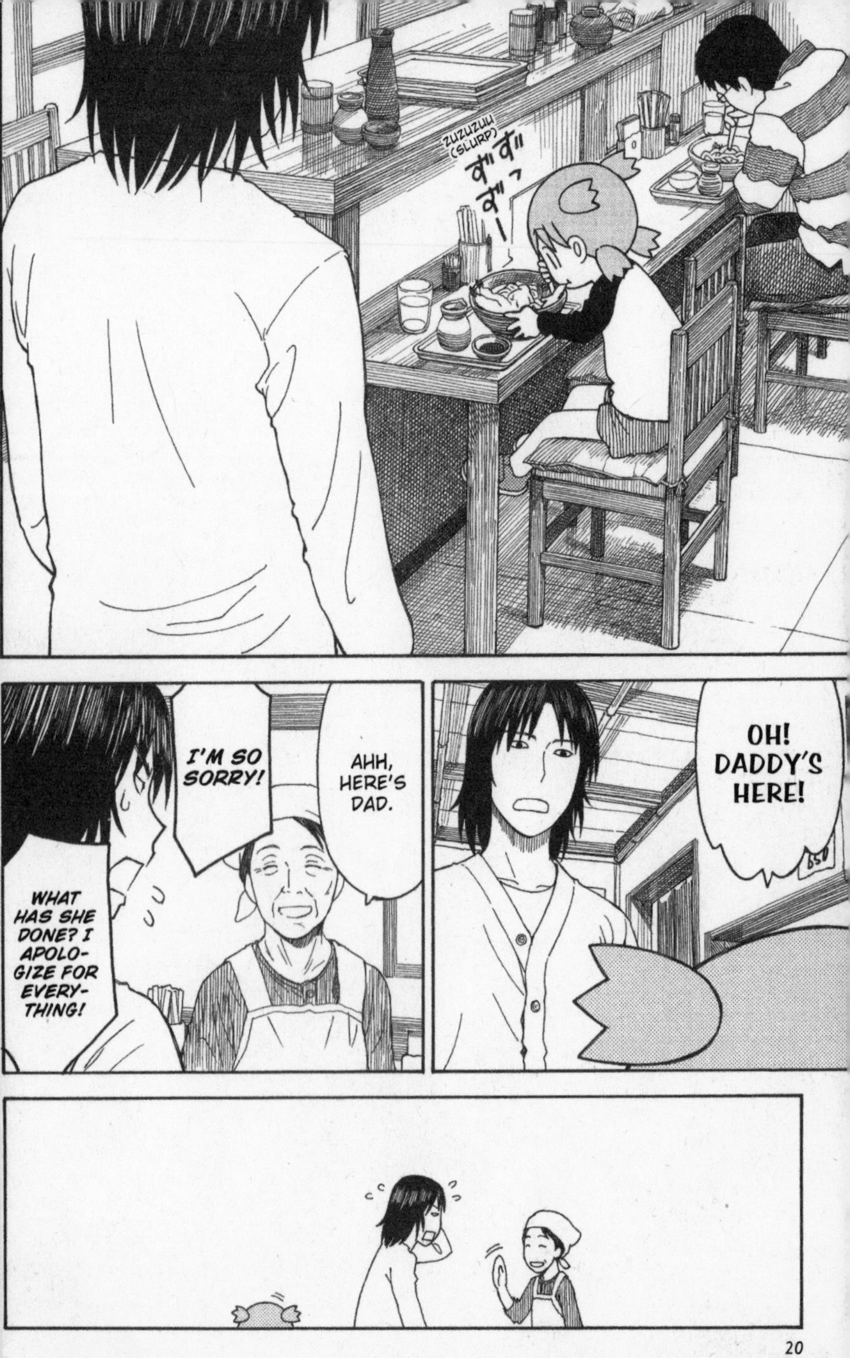

ZUZUZUU (SLURP)
ずずずー
OH! DADDY'S HERE!
AHH, HERE'S DAD.
I'M SO SORRY!
WHAT HAS SHE DONE? I APOLOGIZE FOR EVERYTHING!

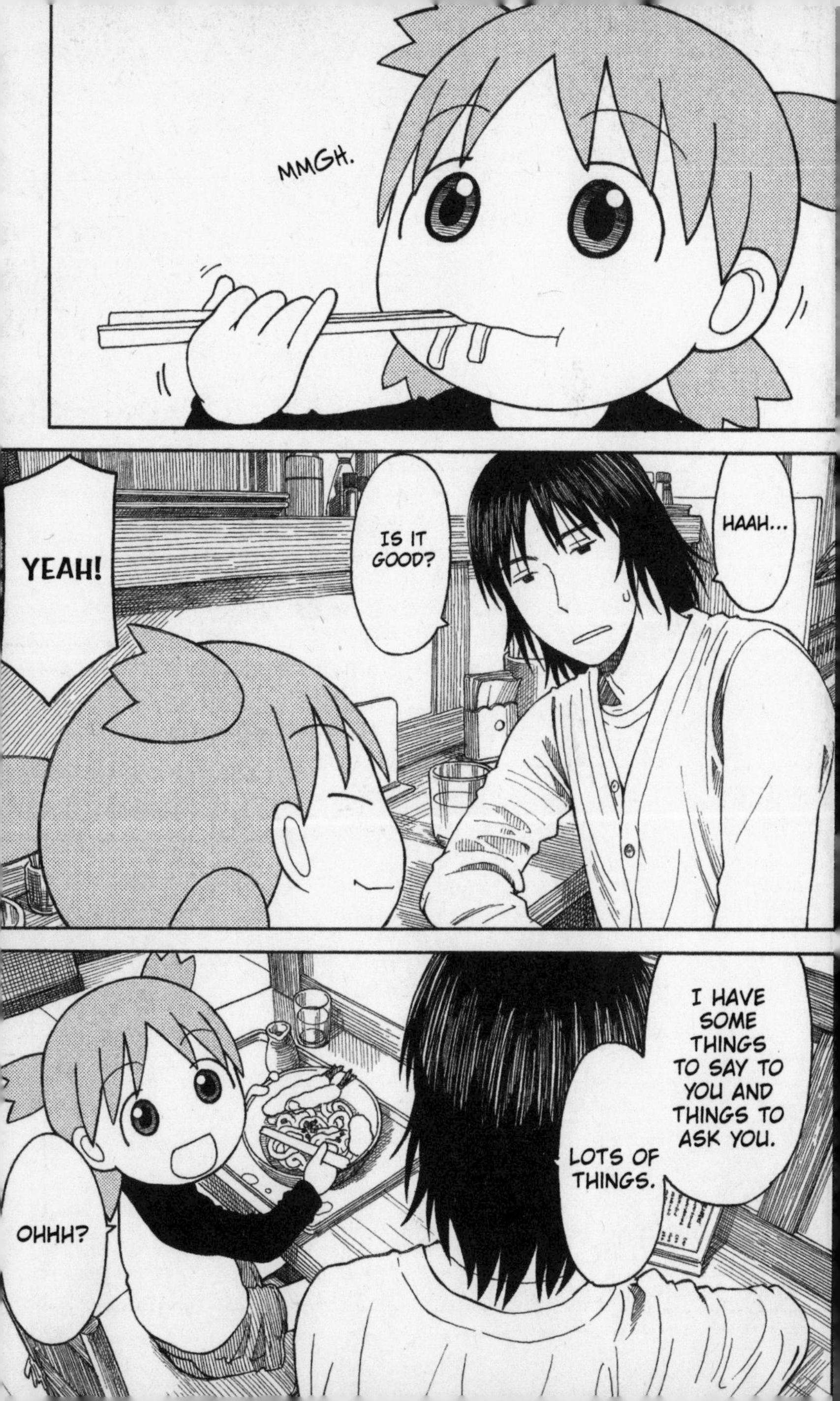
MMGH.
HAAH...
IS IT GOOD?
YEAH!
I HAVE SOME THINGS TO SAY TO YOU AND THINGS TO ASK YOU.
LOTS OF THINGS.
OHHH?

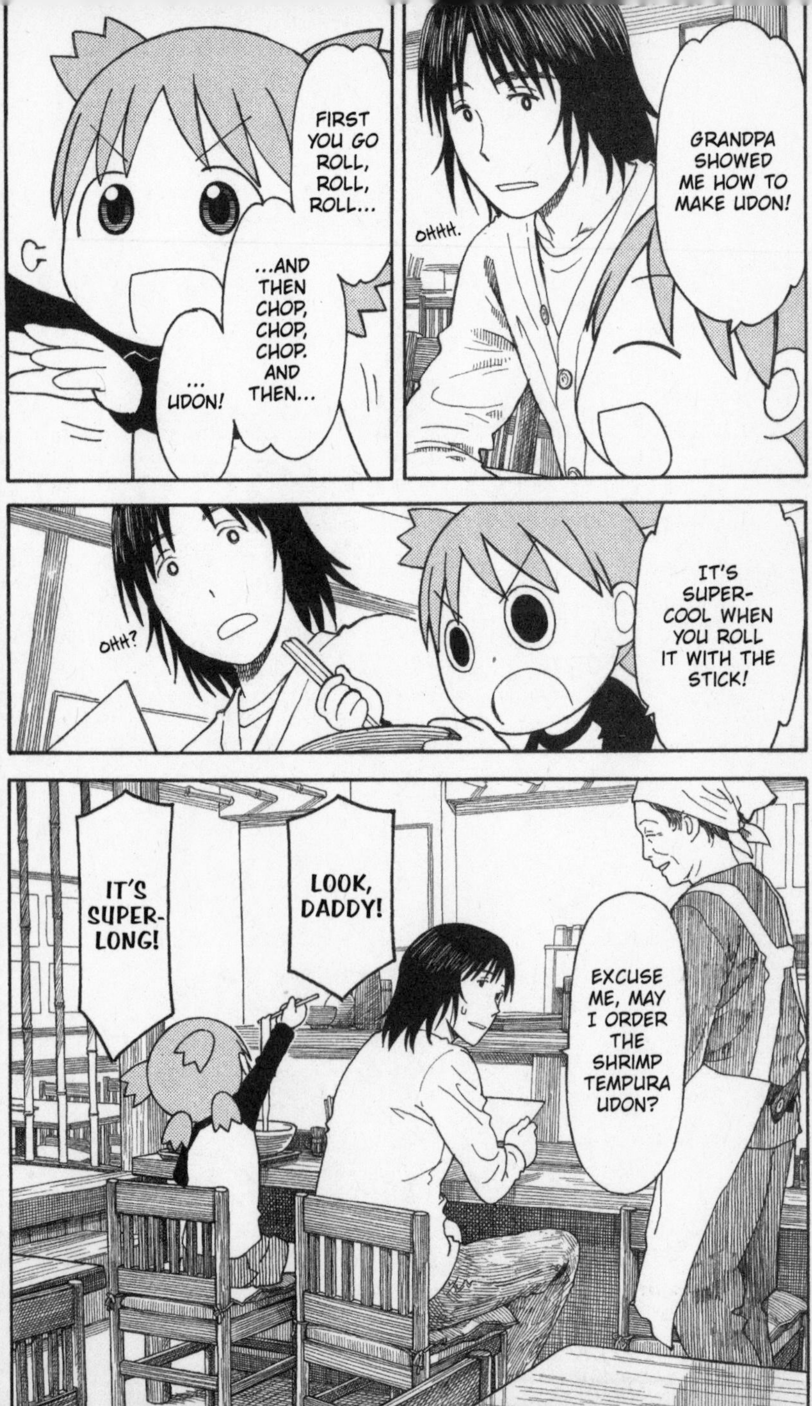
GRANDPA SHOWED ME HOW TO MAKE UDON!
OHHH.
FIRST YOU GO ROLL, ROLL, ROLL...
...AND THEN CHOP, CHOP, CHOP. AND THEN...
... UDON!
IT'S SUPER-COOL WHEN YOU ROLL IT WITH THE STICK!
OHH?
EXCUSE ME, MAY I ORDER THE SHRIMP TEMPURA UDON?
LOOK, DADDY!
IT'S SUPER-LONG!

YOTSUBA&!

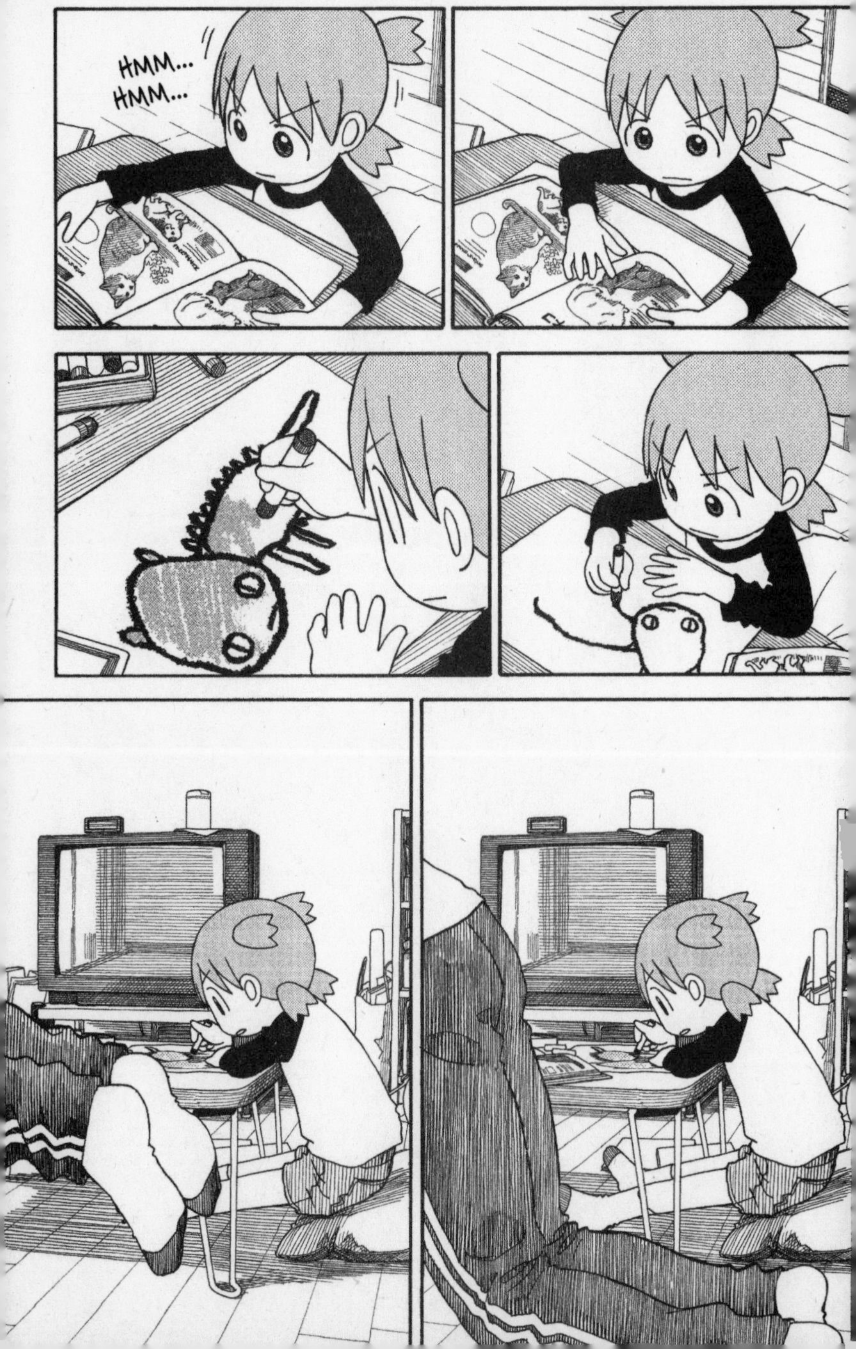
HMM...
HMM...

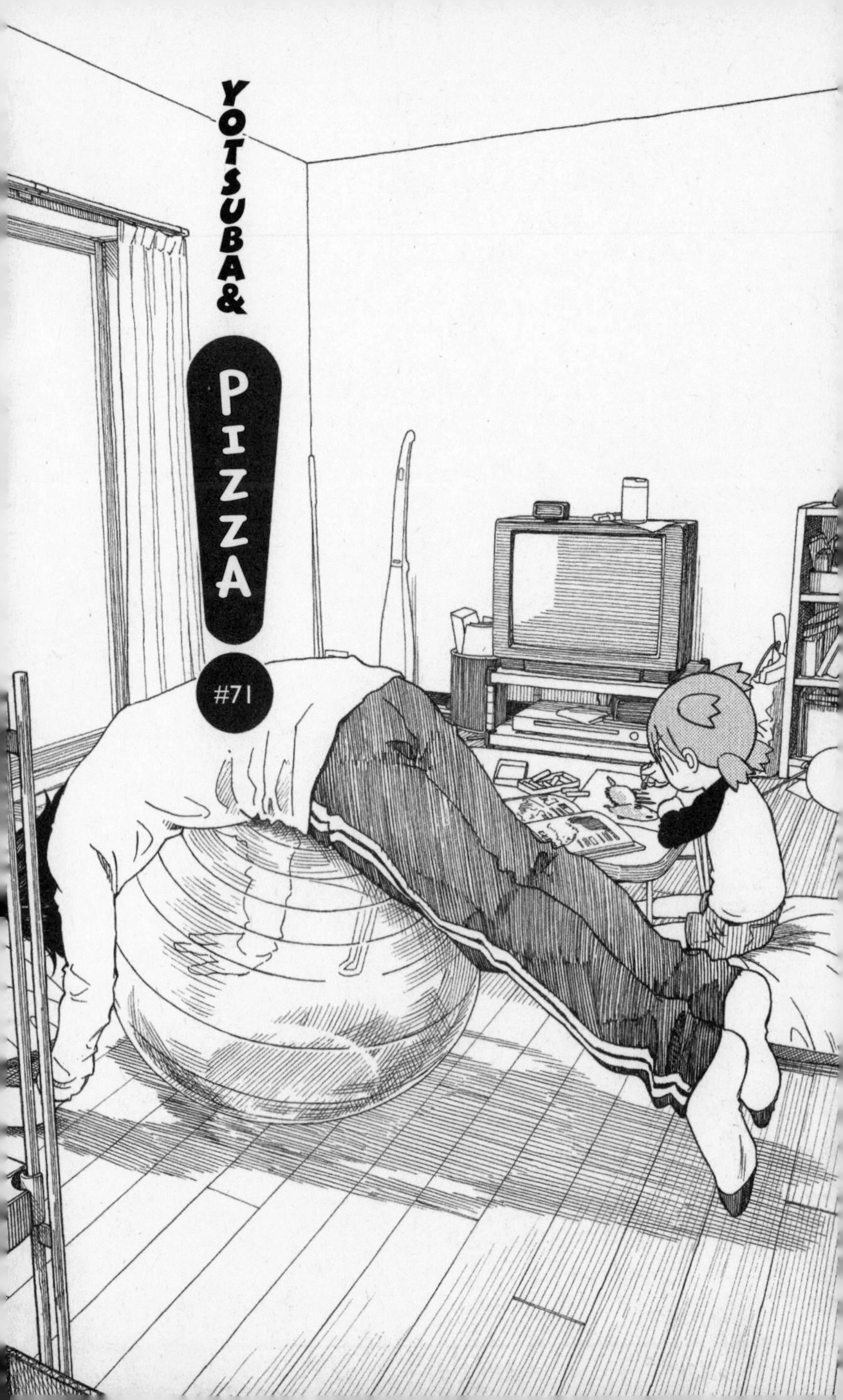
YOTSUBA&
PIZZA
#71

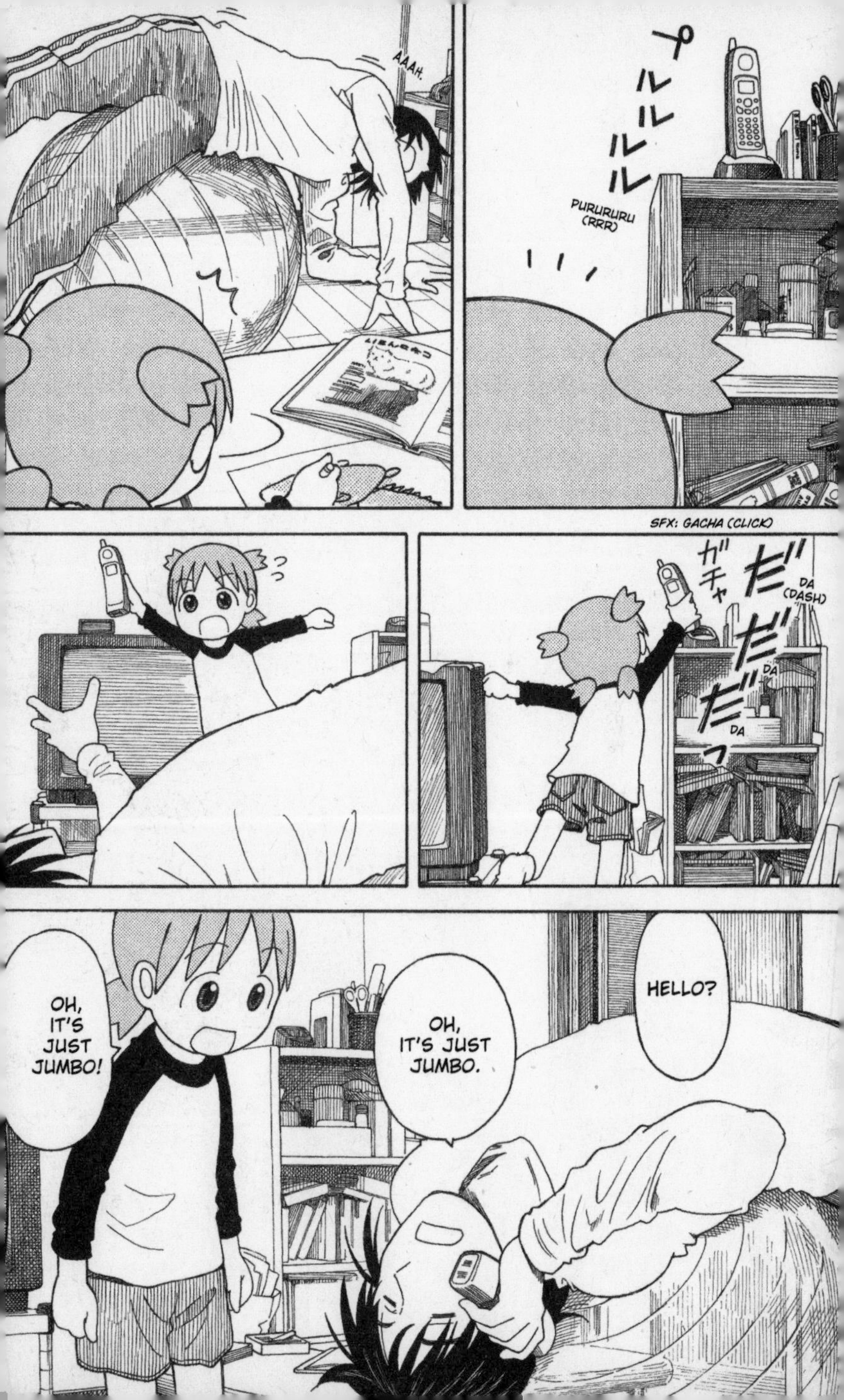

プルルルル
PURURURU
(RRR)
AAAH.
SFX: GACHA (CLICK)
ガチャ
だだだっ
DA
(DASH)
DA
DA
HELLO?
OH, IT'S JUST JUMBO.
OH, IT'S JUST JUMBO!

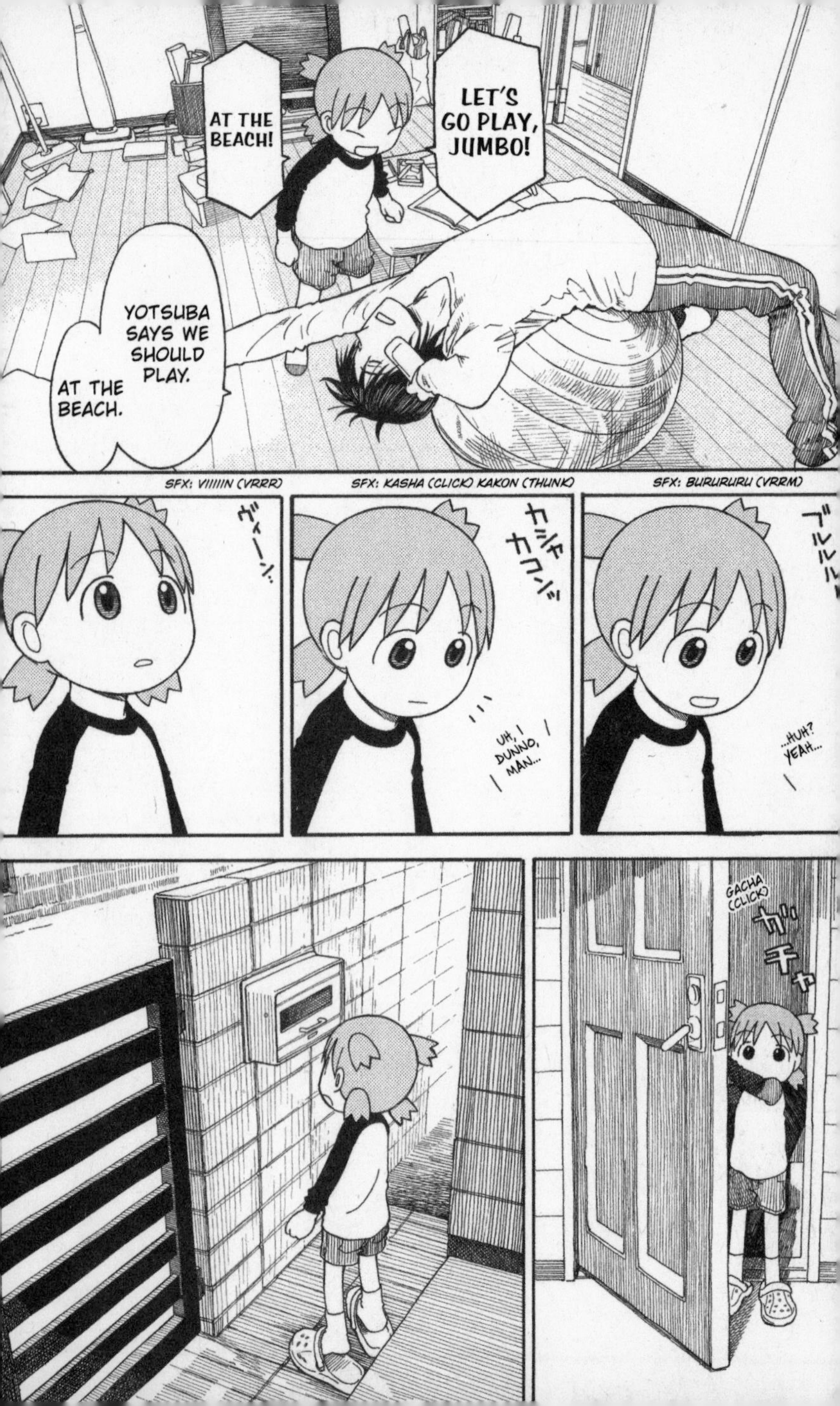
LET'S GO PLAY, JUMBO!
AT THE BEACH!
YOTSUBA SAYS WE SHOULD PLAY.
AT THE BEACH.
SFX: BURURURU (VRRM)
SFX: KASHA (CLICK) KAKON (THUNK)
SFX: VIIIIIN (VRRR)
ブルルル
...HUH? YEAH...
カシャ カコンッ
UH, I DUNNO, MAN...
ヴィーン…
GACHA (CLICK)
ガチャ

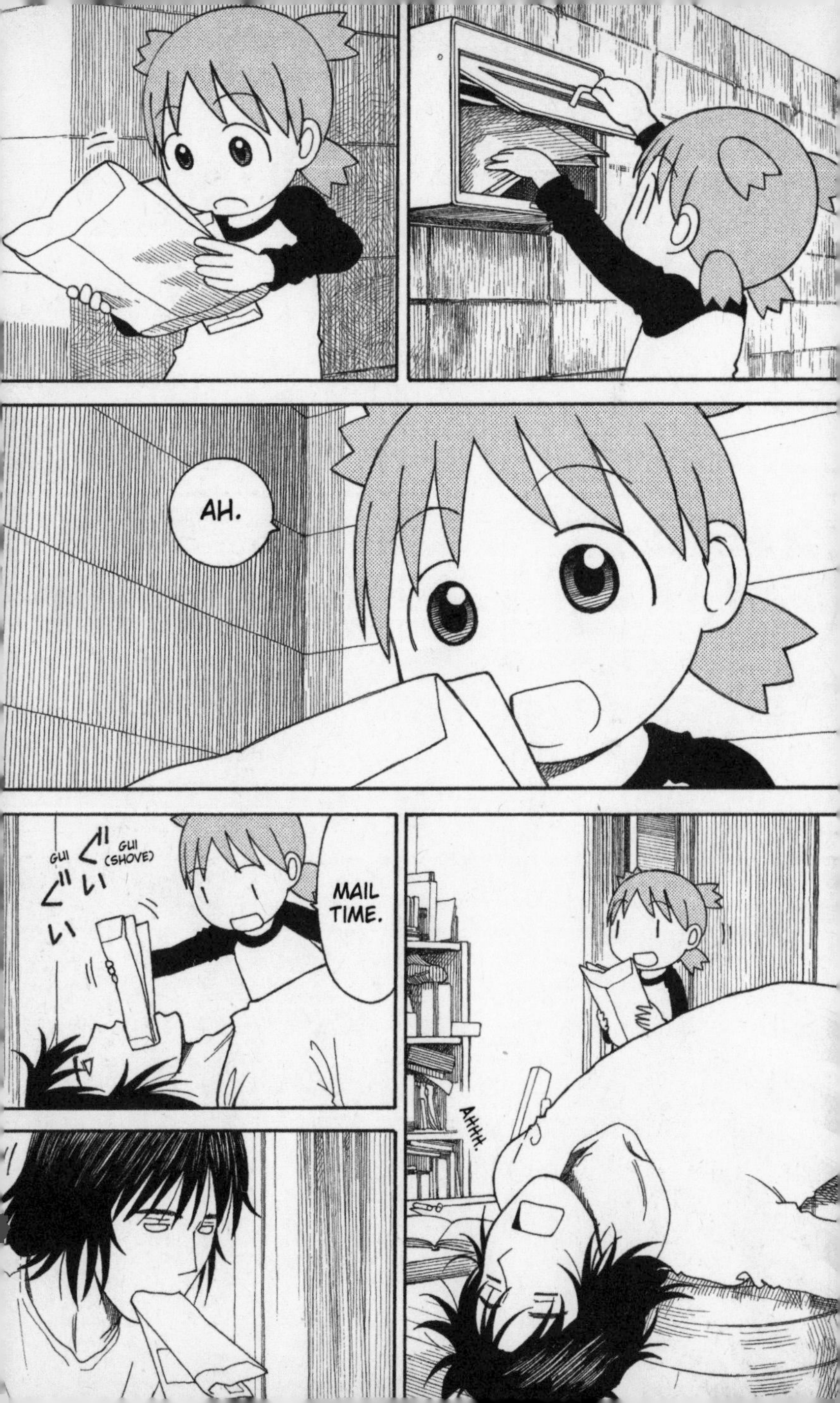
AH.
GUI
GUI (SHOVE)
ぐい
ぐい
MAIL TIME.
AHHH.

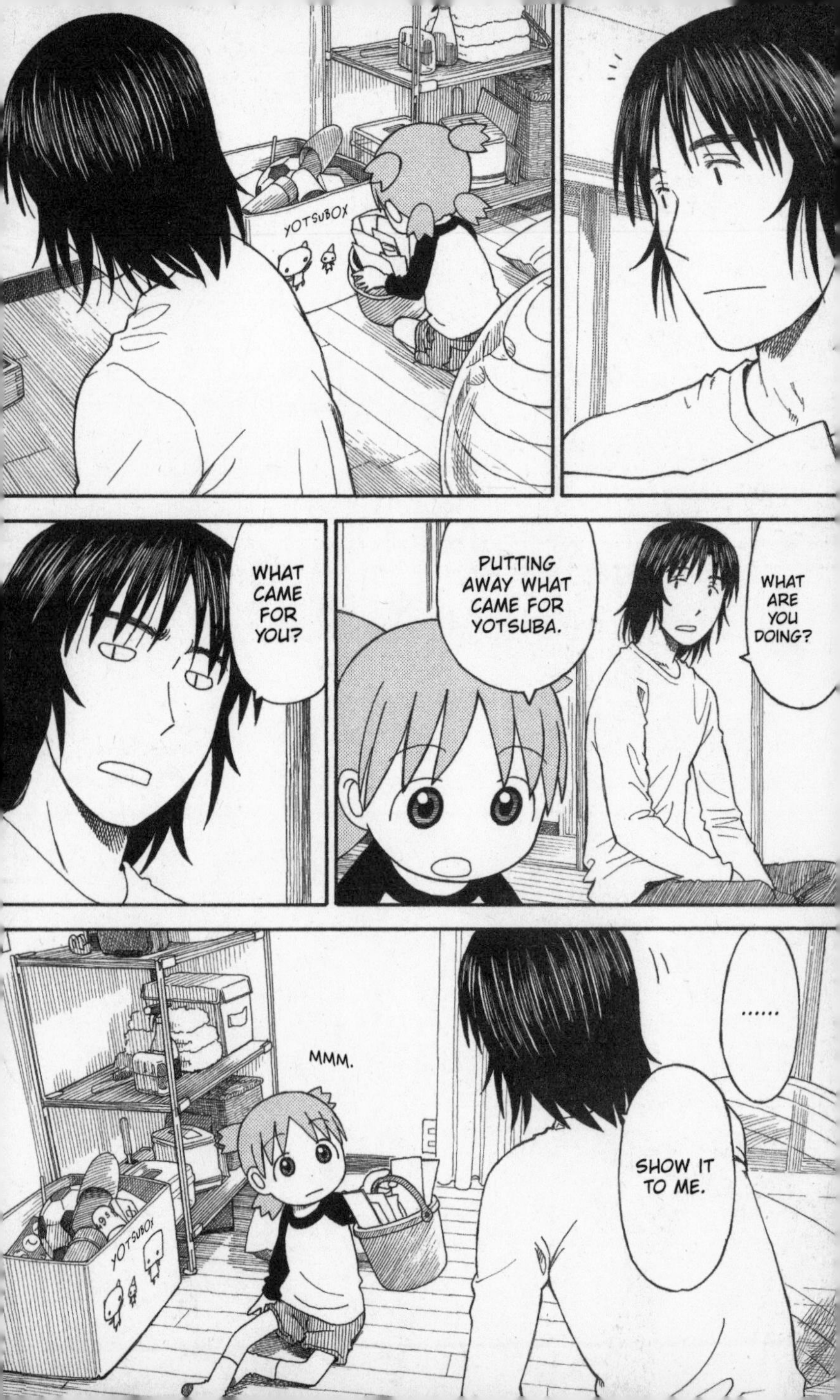
YOTSUBOX
WHAT ARE YOU DOING?
PUTTING AWAY WHAT CAME FOR YOTSUBA.
WHAT CAME FOR YOU?
......
SHOW IT TO ME.
MMM.
YOTSUBOX

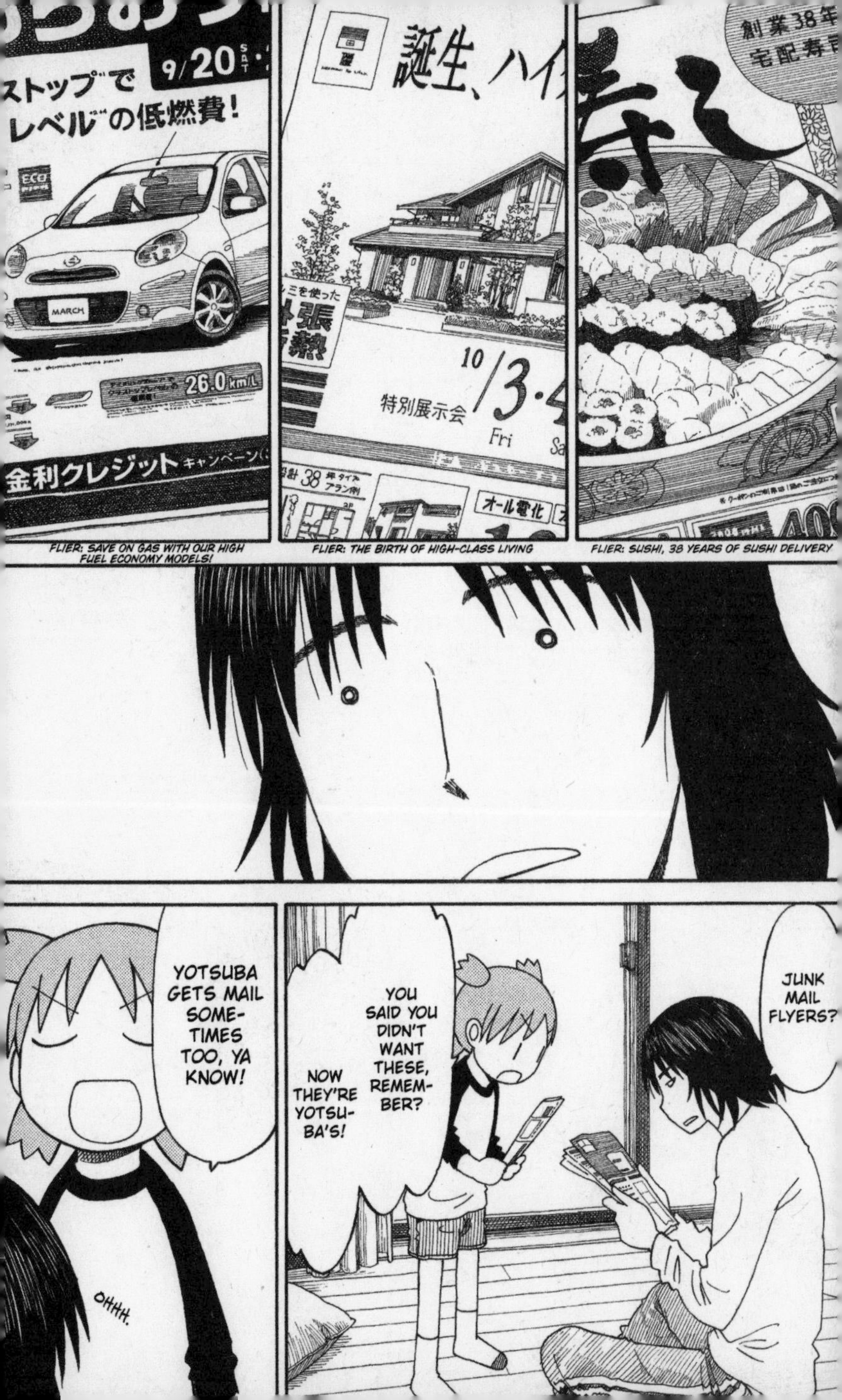
創業38年
宅配寿司
FLIER: SUSHI, 38 YEARS OF SUSHI DELIVERY
誕生、ハイ
10/3・4
特別展示会
Fri
オール電化
FLIER: THE BIRTH OF HIGH-CLASS LIVING
9/20
ストップ"で
レベル"の低燃費！
ECO
MARCH
26.0km/L
金利クレジット キャンペーン
FLIER: SAVE ON GAS WITH OUR HIGH FUEL ECONOMY MODELS!
JUNK MAIL FLYERS?
YOU SAID YOU DIDN'T WANT THESE, REMEMBER?
NOW THEY'RE YOTSUBA'S!
YOTSUBA GETS MAIL SOMETIMES TOO, YA KNOW!
OHHH.

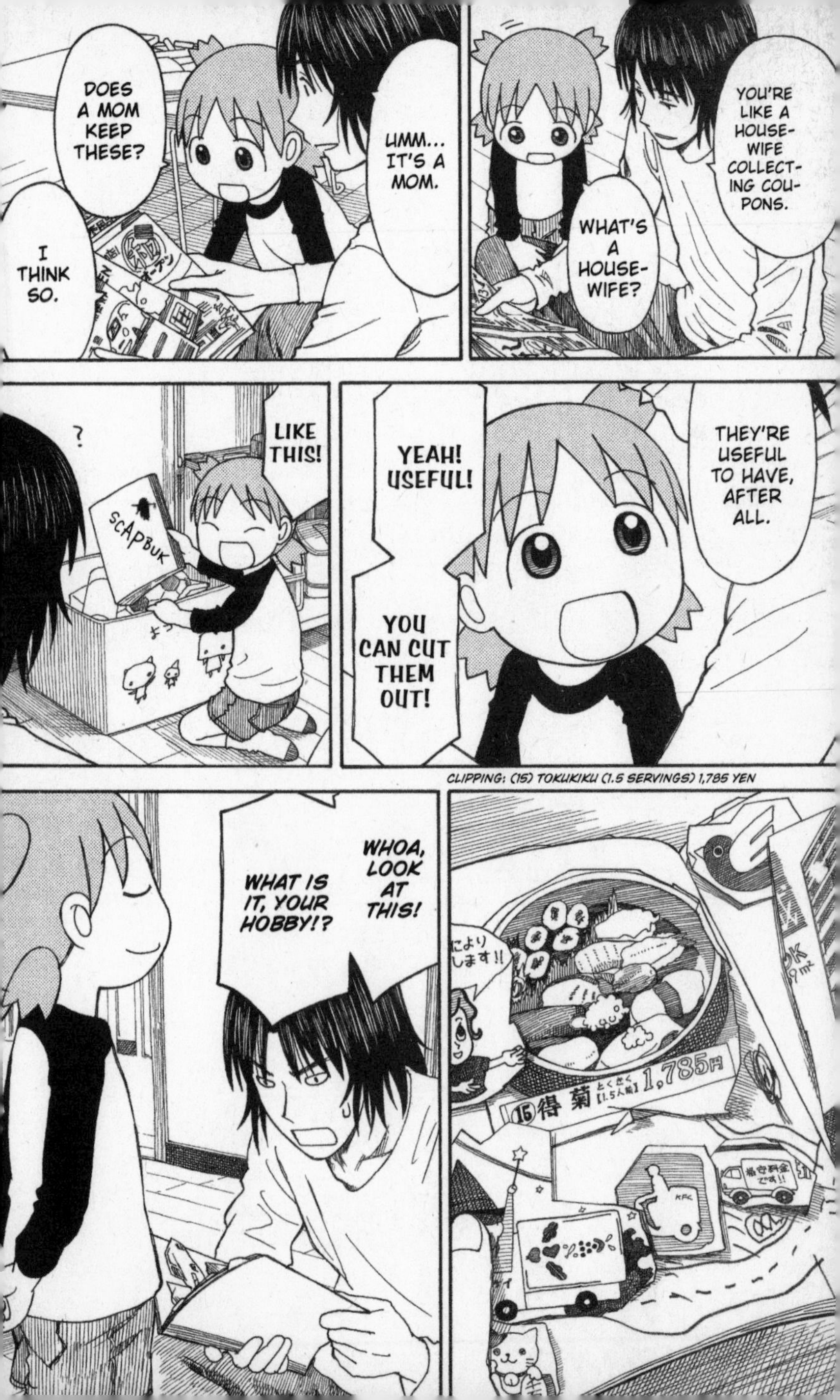
YOU'RE LIKE A HOUSE-WIFE COLLECT-ING COU-PONS.
WHAT'S A HOUSE-WIFE?
UMM... IT'S A MOM.
DOES A MOM KEEP THESE?
I THINK SO.
THEY'RE USEFUL TO HAVE, AFTER ALL.
YEAH! USEFUL!
YOU CAN CUT THEM OUT!
LIKE THIS!
?
SCAPBUK
CLIPPING: (15) TOKUKIKU (1.5 SERVINGS) 1,785 YEN
⑮ 得菊
1,785円
KFC
WHOA, LOOK AT THIS!
WHAT IS IT, YOUR HOBBY!?

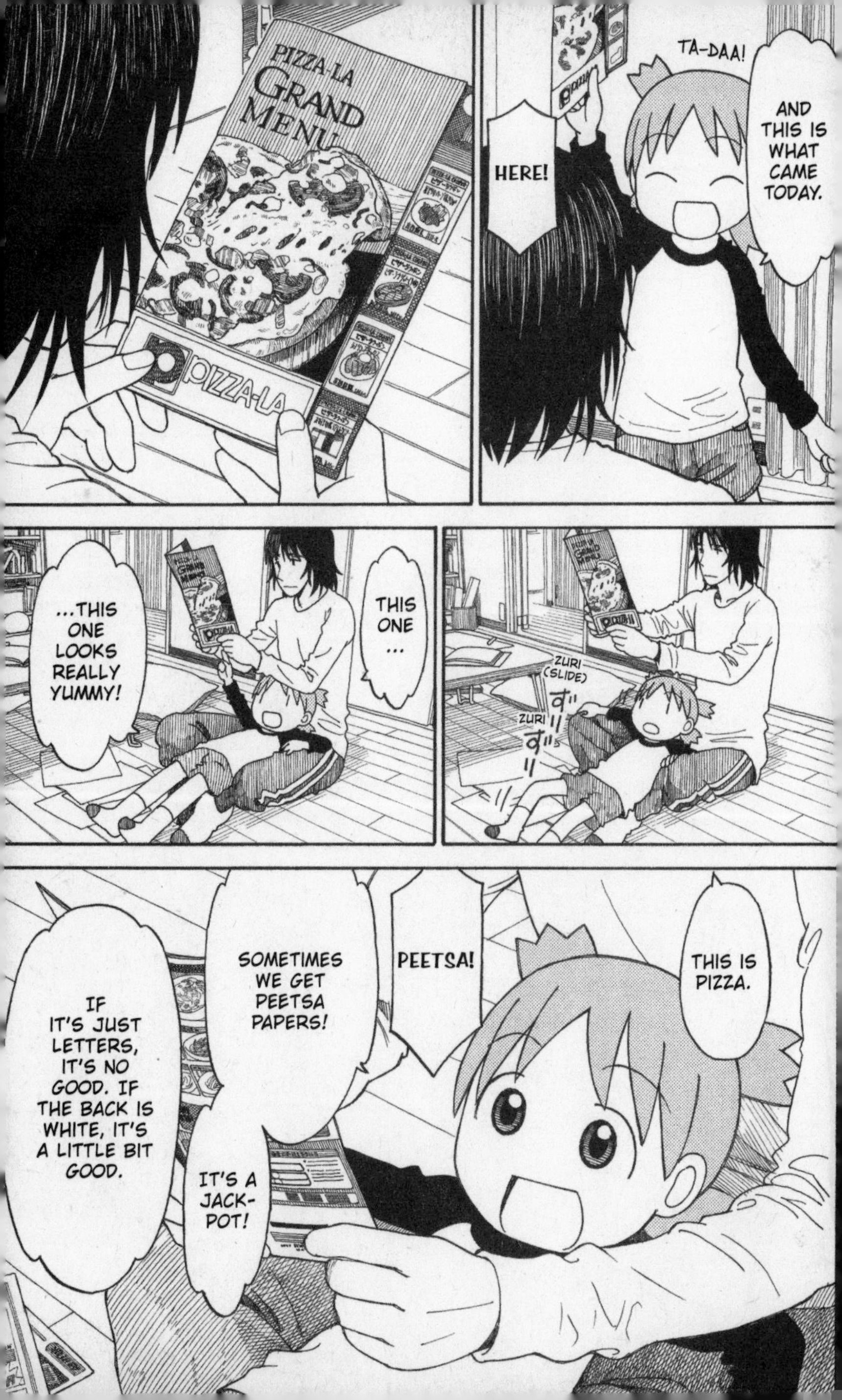
TA-DAA!
AND THIS IS WHAT CAME TODAY.
HERE!
PIZZA-LA GRAND MENU
PIZZA-LA
ZURI (SLIDE)
ZURI
ずりずり
THIS ONE ...
...THIS ONE LOOKS REALLY YUMMY!
THIS IS PIZZA.
PEETSA!
SOMETIMES WE GET PEETSA PAPERS!
IF IT'S JUST LETTERS, IT'S NO GOOD. IF THE BACK IS WHITE, IT'S A LITTLE BIT GOOD.
IT'S A JACKPOT!

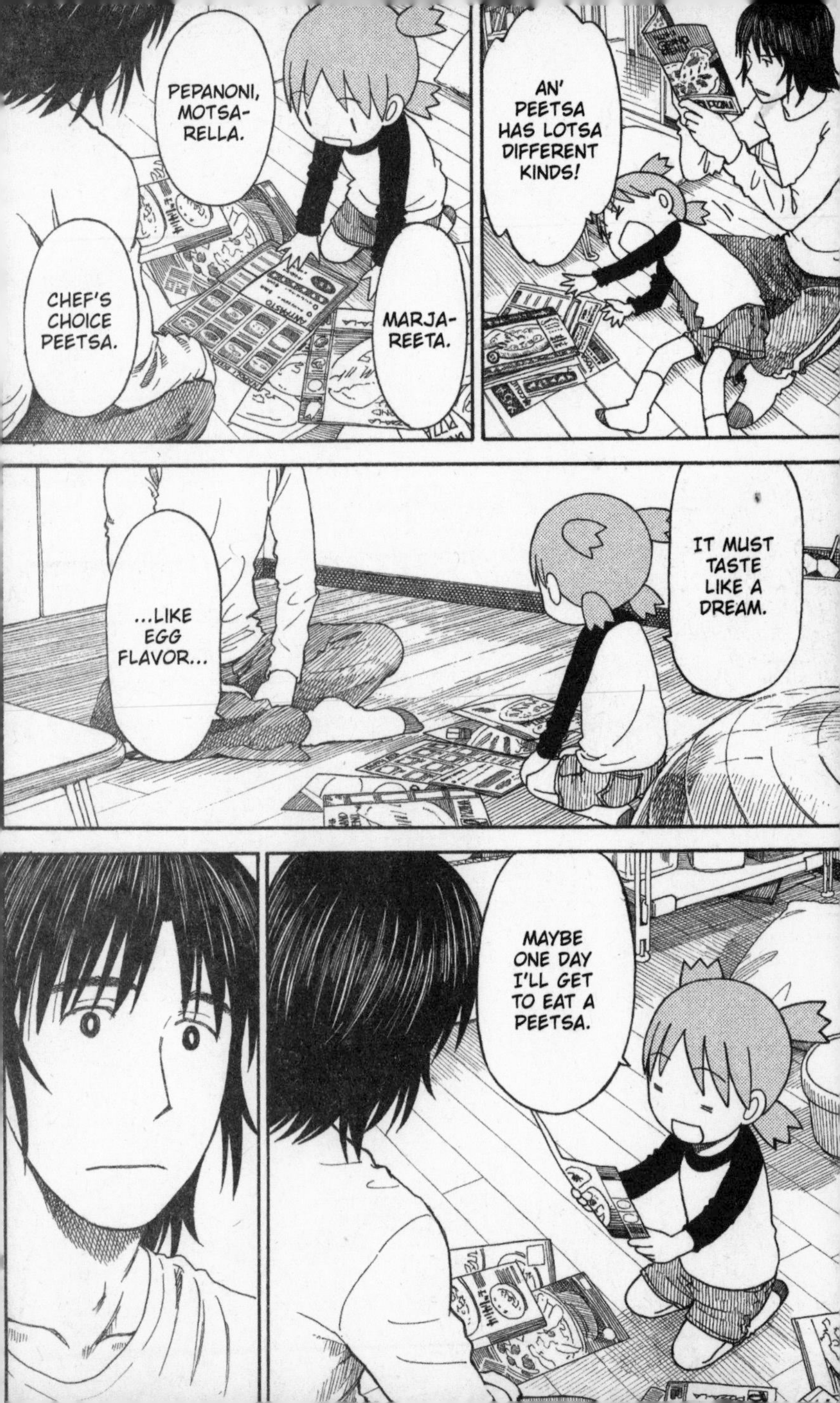
AN' PEETSA HAS LOTSA DIFFERENT KINDS!
PEPANONI, MOTSA-RELLA.
MARJA-REETA.
CHEF'S CHOICE PEETSA.
IT MUST TASTE LIKE A DREAM.
...LIKE EGG FLAVOR...
MAYBE ONE DAY I'LL GET TO EAT A PEETSA.

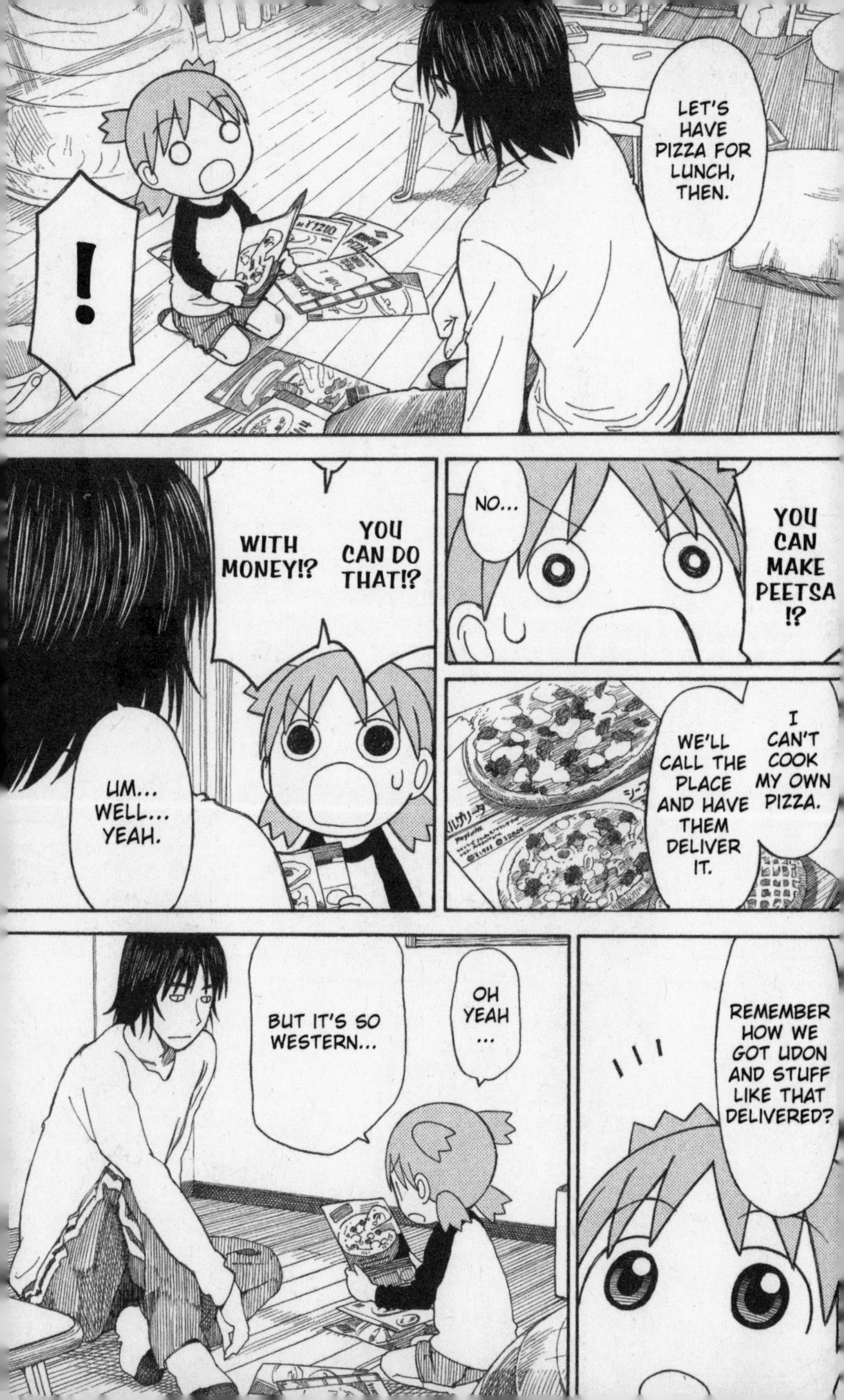
LET'S HAVE PIZZA FOR LUNCH, THEN.
!
YOU CAN MAKE PEETSA !?
NO...
I CAN'T COOK MY OWN PIZZA.
WE'LL CALL THE PLACE AND HAVE THEM DELIVER IT.
YOU CAN DO THAT!?
WITH MONEY!?
UM... WELL... YEAH.
REMEMBER HOW WE GOT UDON AND STUFF LIKE THAT DELIVERED?
OH YEAH ...
BUT IT'S SO WESTERN...

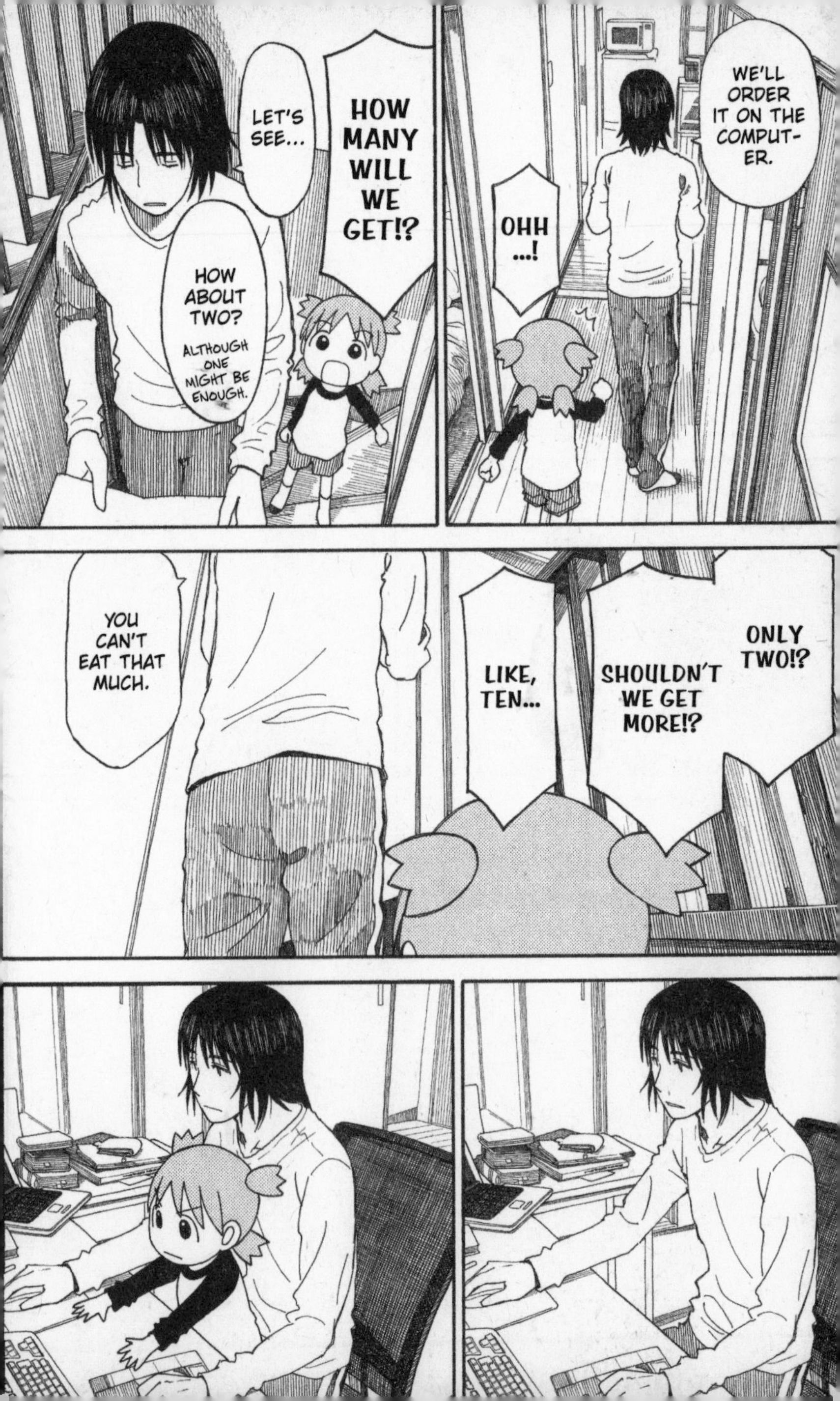
WE'LL ORDER IT ON THE COMPUTER.
OHH ...!
HOW MANY WILL WE GET!?
LET'S SEE...
HOW ABOUT TWO?
ALTHOUGH ONE MIGHT BE ENOUGH.
ONLY TWO!?
SHOULDN'T WE GET MORE!?
LIKE, TEN...
YOU CAN'T EAT THAT MUCH.

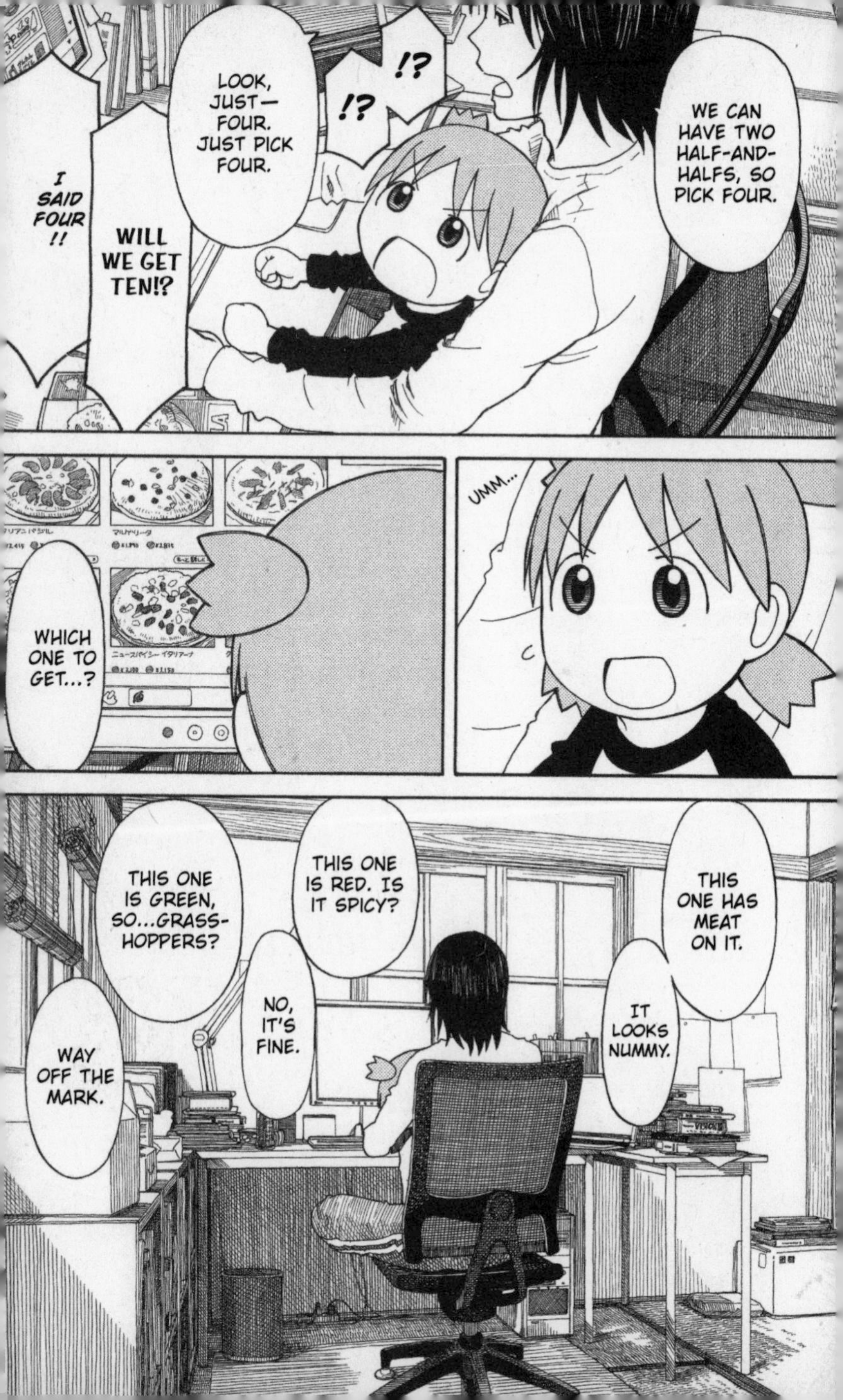
WE CAN HAVE TWO HALF-AND-HALFS, SO PICK FOUR.
!?
!?
LOOK, JUST— FOUR. JUST PICK FOUR.
WILL WE GET TEN!?
I SAID FOUR!!
UMM...
WHICH ONE TO GET...?
THIS ONE HAS MEAT ON IT.
IT LOOKS NUMMY.
THIS ONE IS RED. IS IT SPICY?
NO, IT'S FINE.
THIS ONE IS GREEN, SO...GRASS-HOPPERS?
WAY OFF THE MARK.

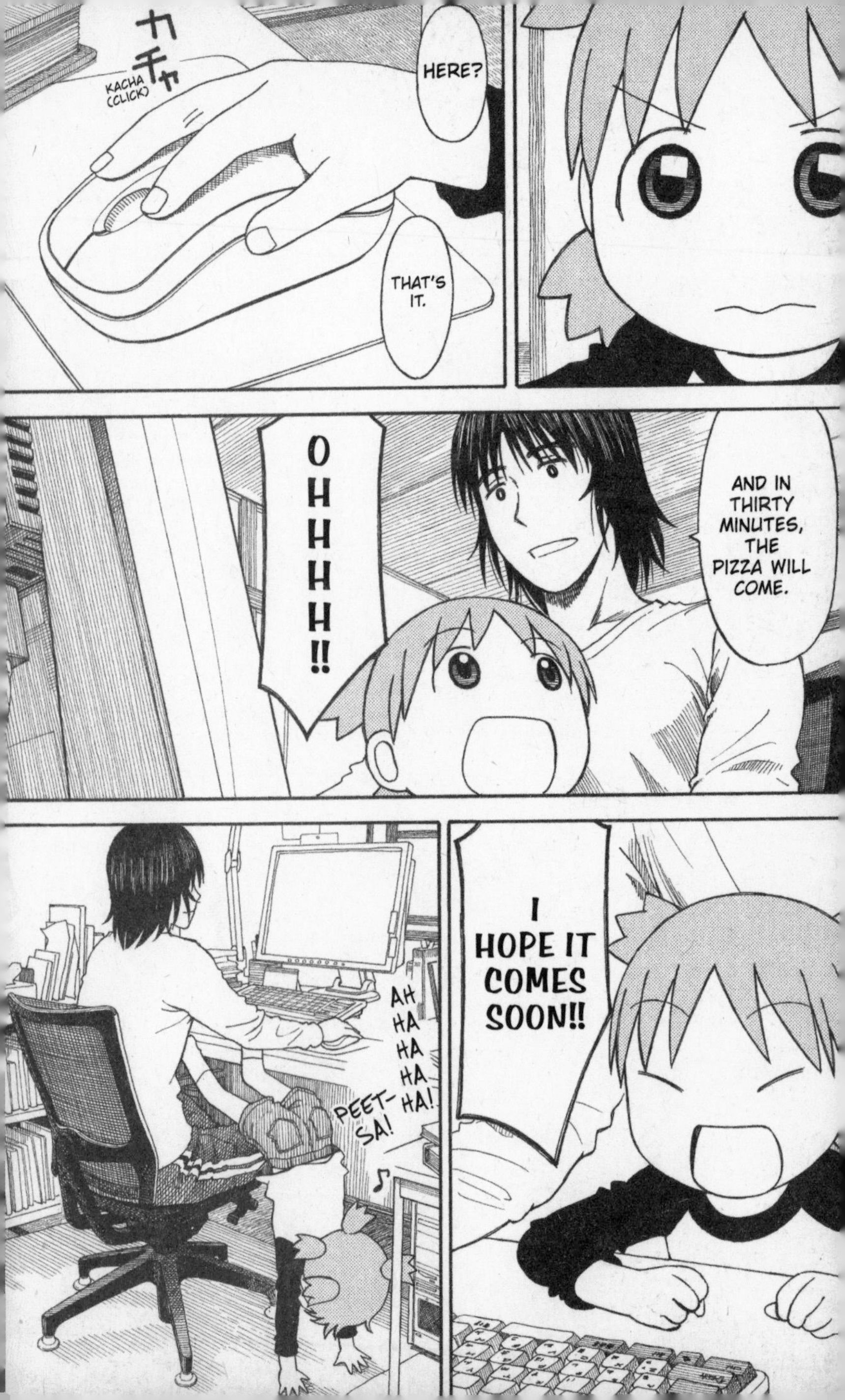
HERE?
カチャ
KACHA (CLICK)
THAT'S IT.
AND IN THIRTY MINUTES, THE PIZZA WILL COME.
OHHHHH!!
I HOPE IT COMES SOON!!
AH HA HA HA HA HA!
PEET-SA!

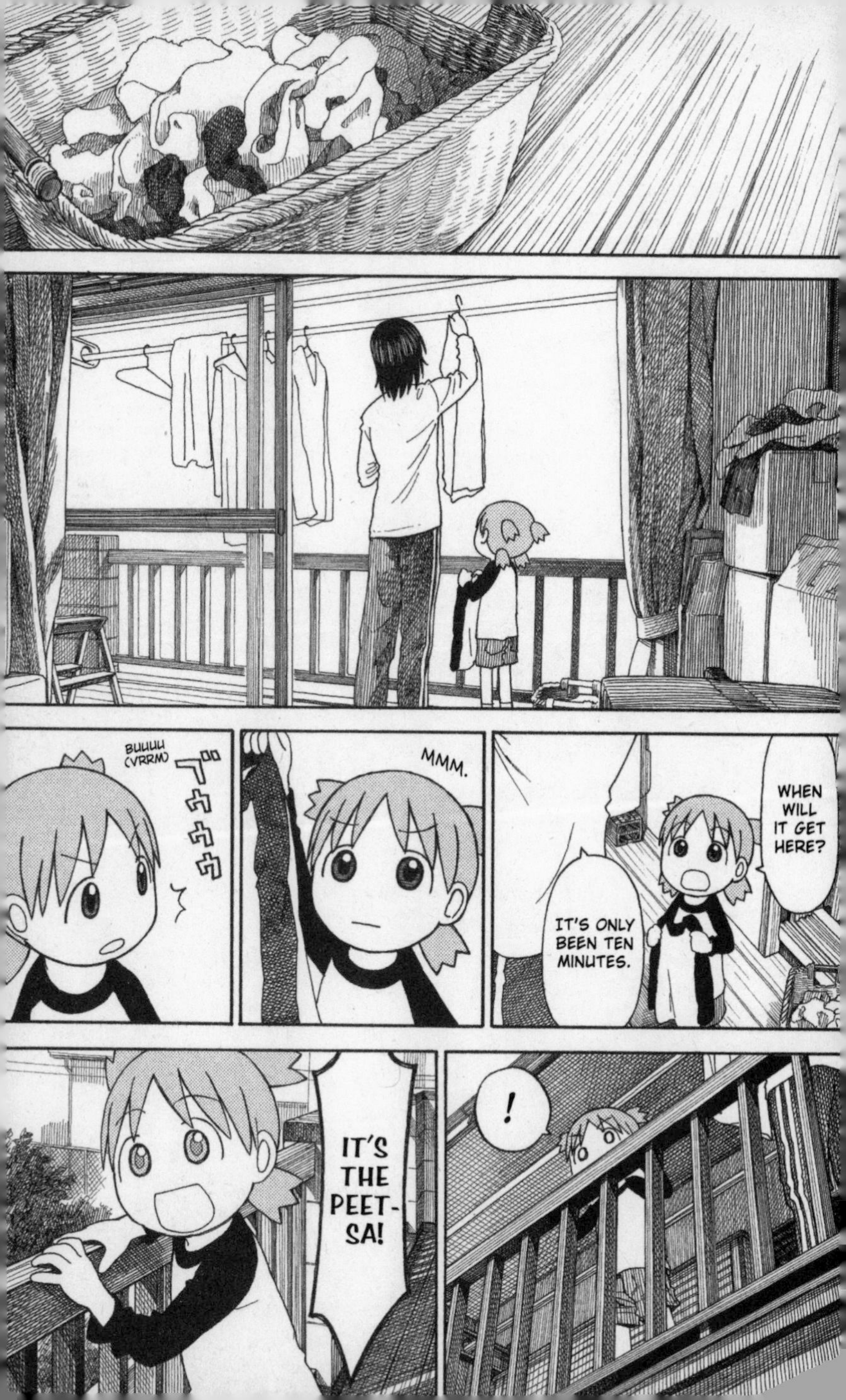
WHEN WILL IT GET HERE?
IT'S ONLY BEEN TEN MINUTES.
MMM.
BUUUU (VRRM)
!
IT'S THE PEET-SA!

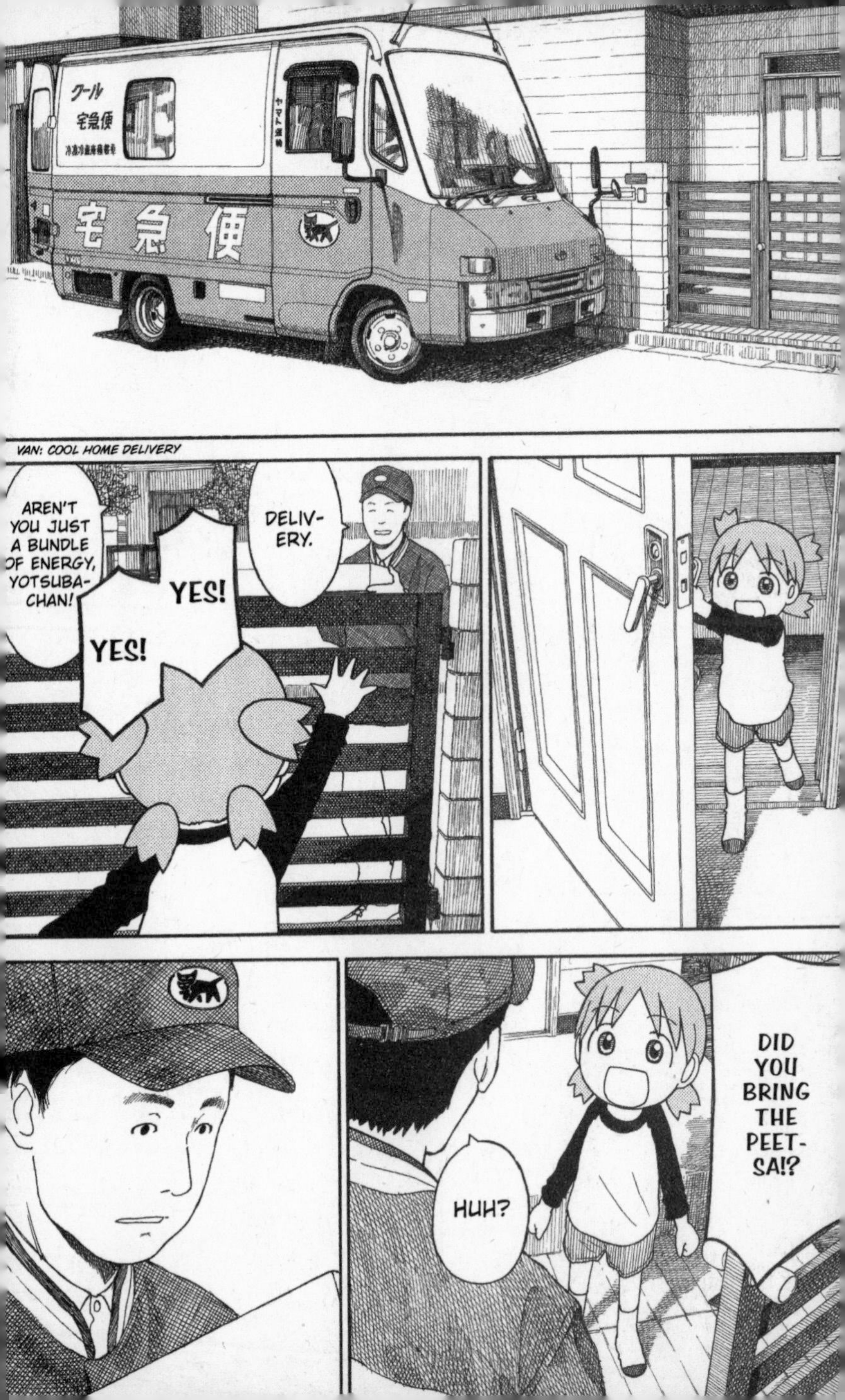
クール
宅急便
宅急便
VAN: COOL HOME DELIVERY
DELIVERY.
YES!
YES!
AREN'T YOU JUST A BUNDLE OF ENERGY, YOTSUBA-CHAN!
DID YOU BRING THE PEET-SA!?
HUH?

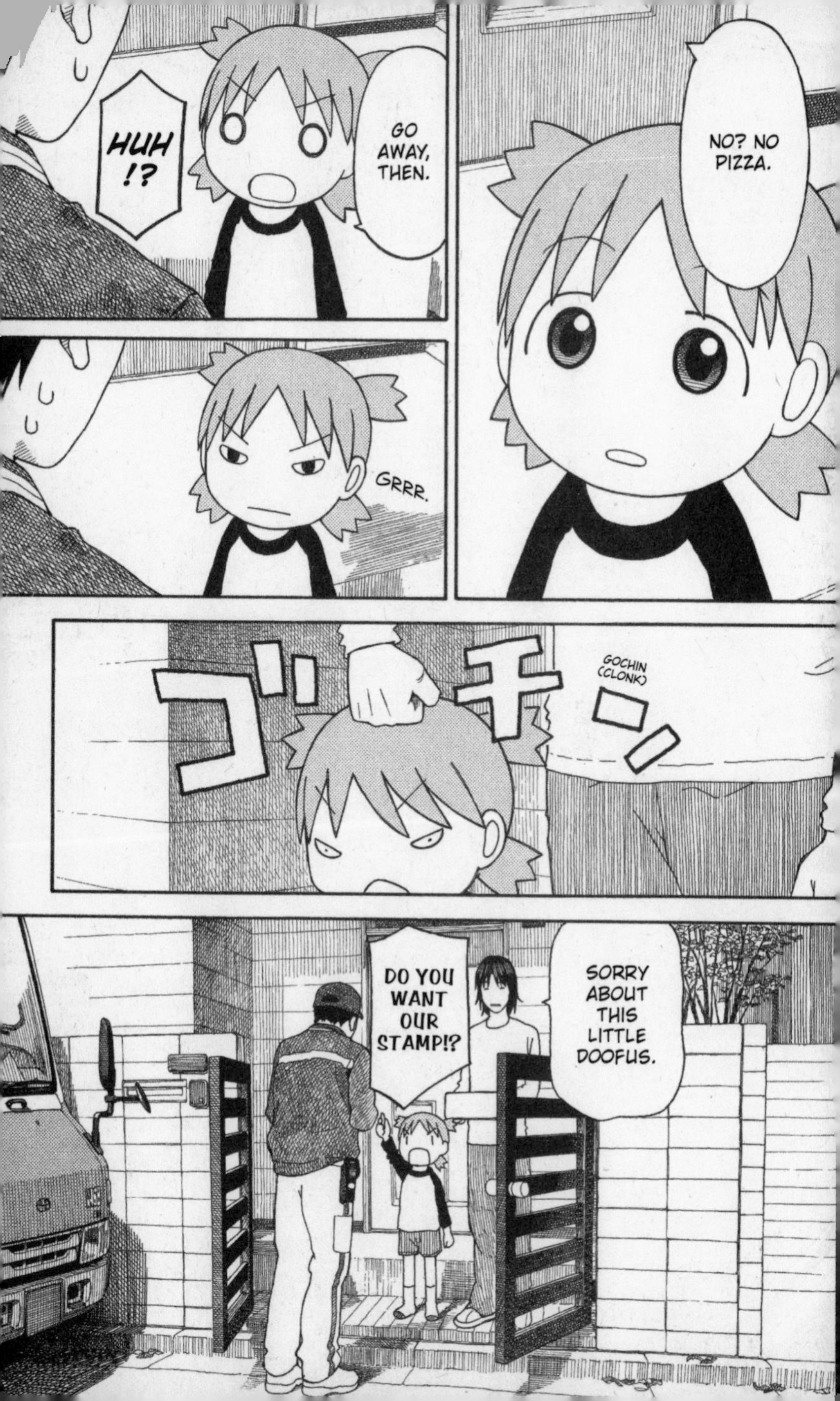
NO? NO PIZZA.
GO AWAY, THEN.
HUH !?
GRRR.
GOCHIN (CLONK)
SORRY ABOUT THIS LITTLE DOOFUS.
DO YOU WANT OUR STAMP!?

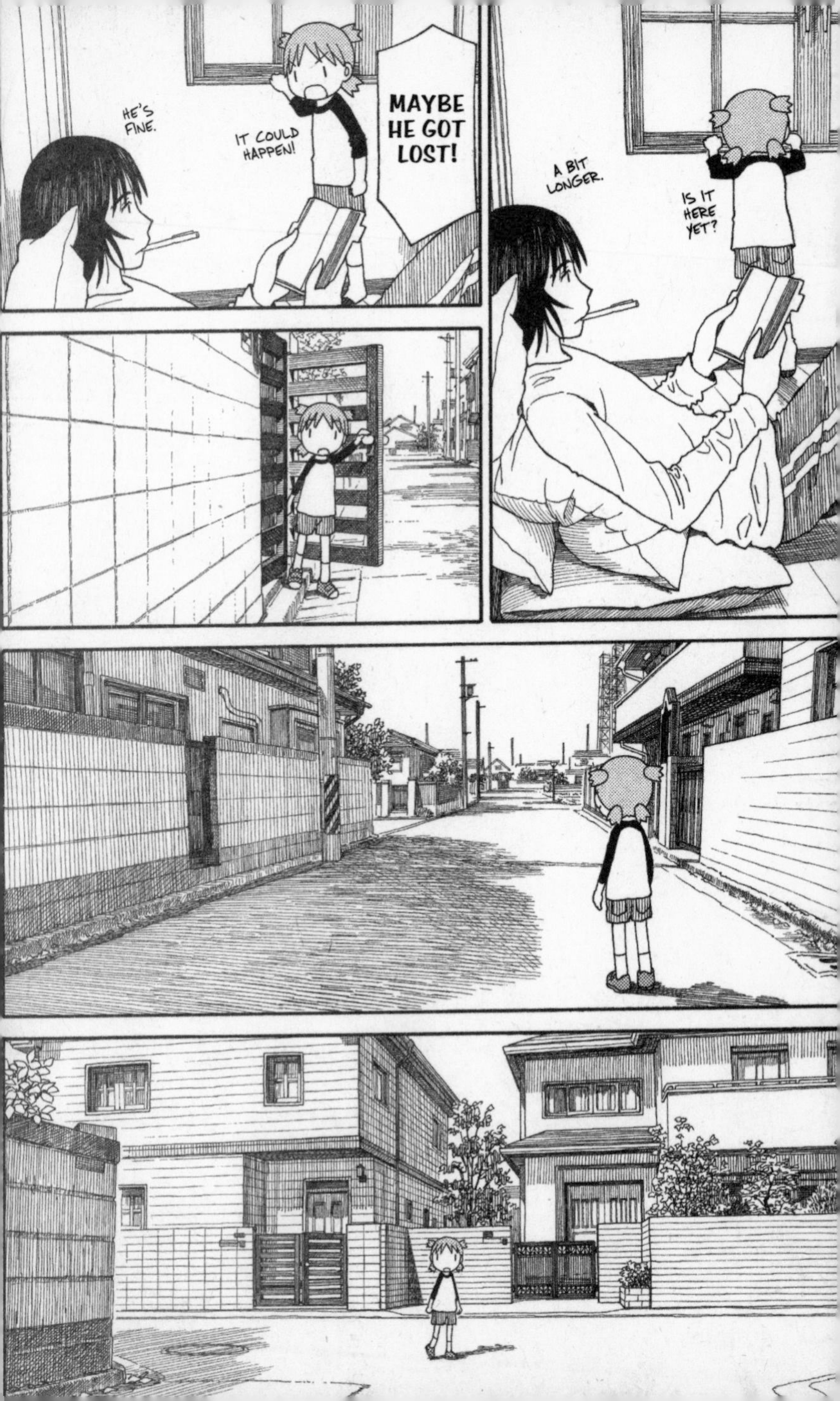
IS IT HERE YET?
A BIT LONGER.
MAYBE HE GOT LOST!
IT COULD HAPPEN!
HE'S FINE.

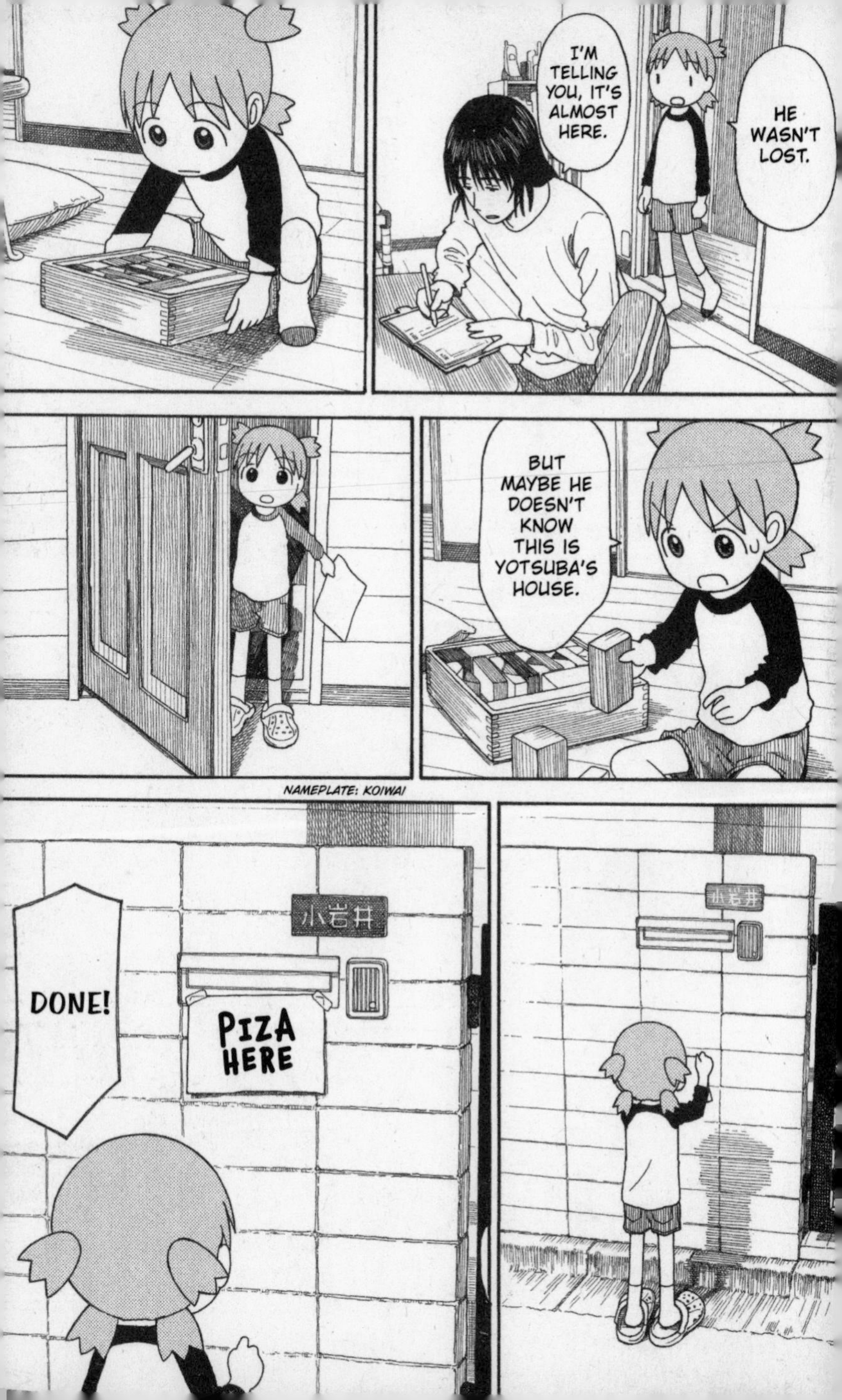
HE WASN'T LOST.
I'M TELLING YOU, IT'S ALMOST HERE.
BUT MAYBE HE DOESN'T KNOW THIS IS YOTSUBA'S HOUSE.
NAMEPLATE: KOIWAI
小岩井
DONE!
PIZA HERE

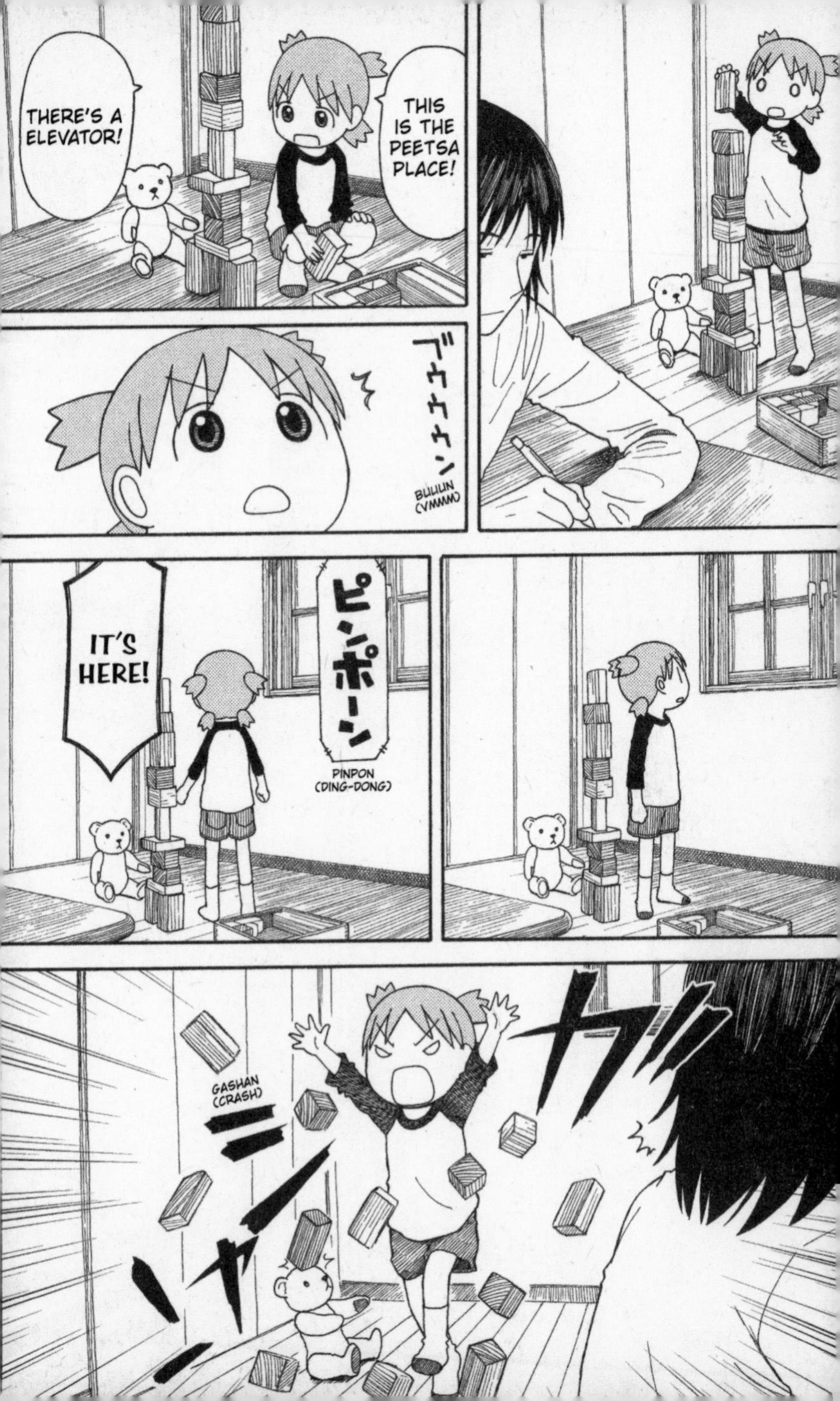
THIS IS THE PEETSA PLACE!
THERE'S A ELEVATOR!
ブウウウン
BUUUN (VMMM)
ピンポーン
PINPON (DING-DONG)
IT'S HERE!
GASHAN (CRASH)

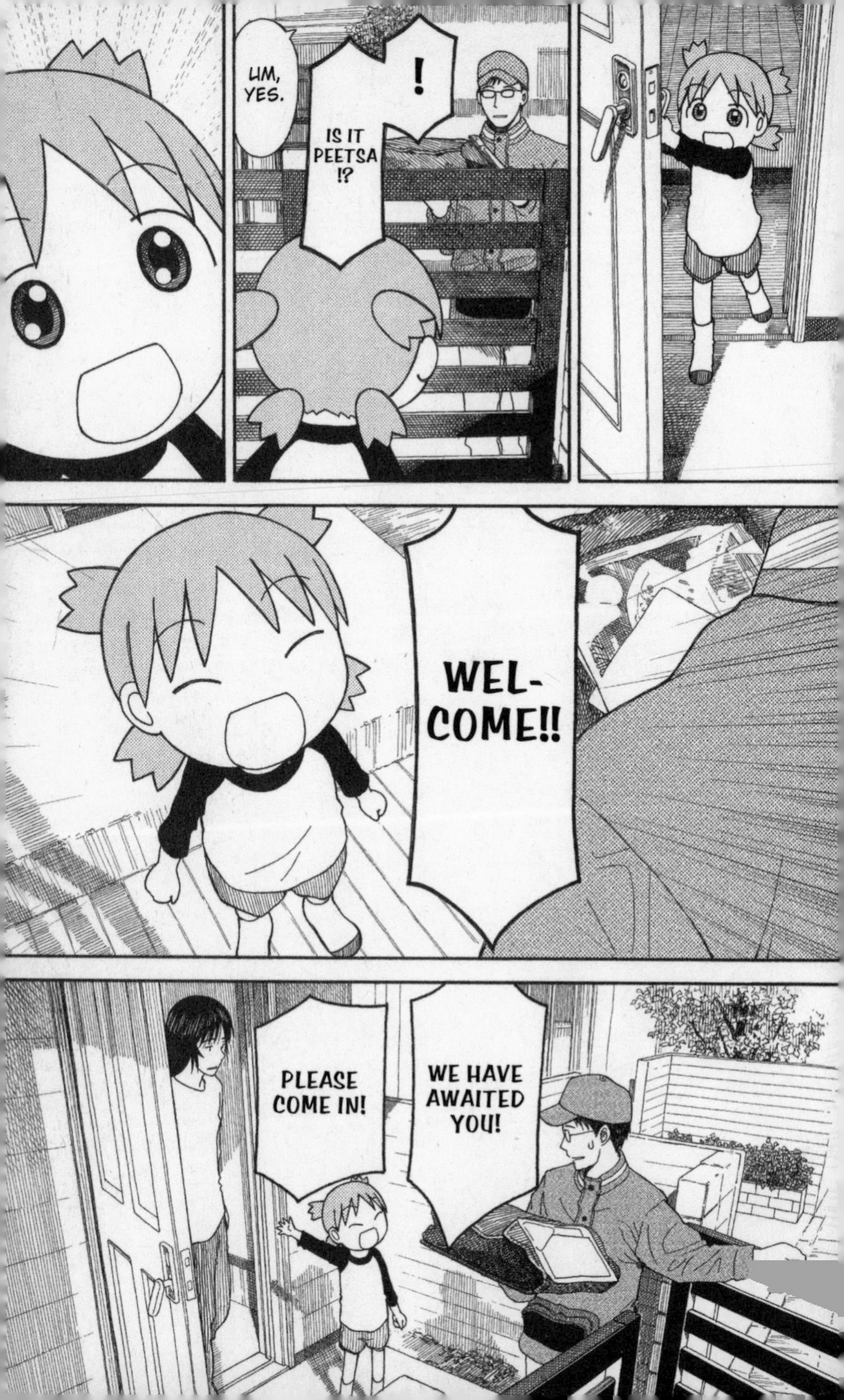
!
IS IT PEETSA !?
UM, YES.
WEL-COME!!
WE HAVE AWAITED YOU!
PLEASE COME IN!

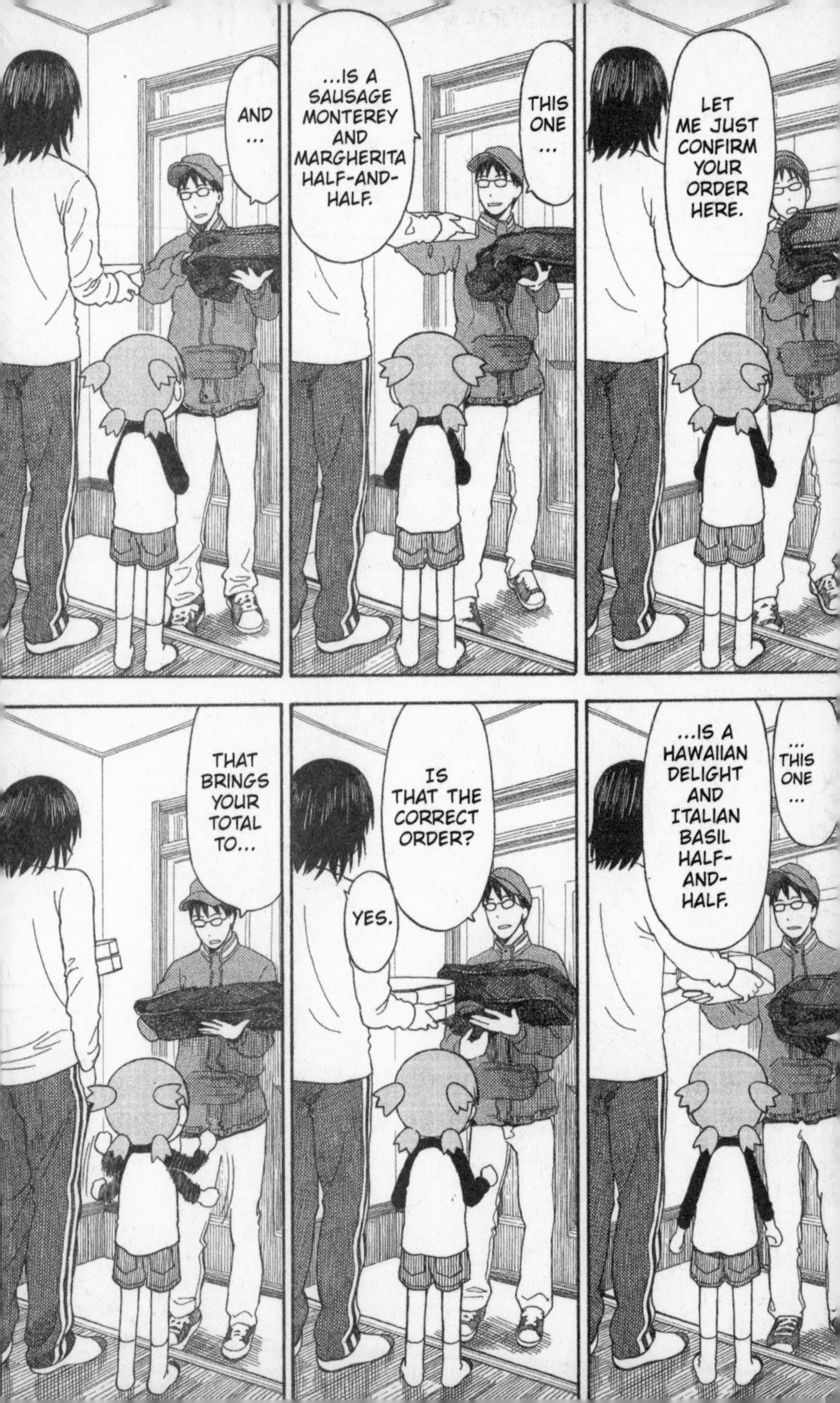
LET ME JUST CONFIRM YOUR ORDER HERE.
THIS ONE ...
...IS A SAUSAGE MONTEREY AND MARGHERITA HALF-AND-HALF.
AND ...
... THIS ONE ...
...IS A HAWAIIAN DELIGHT AND ITALIAN BASIL HALF-AND-HALF.
IS THAT THE CORRECT ORDER?
YES.
THAT BRINGS YOUR TOTAL TO...

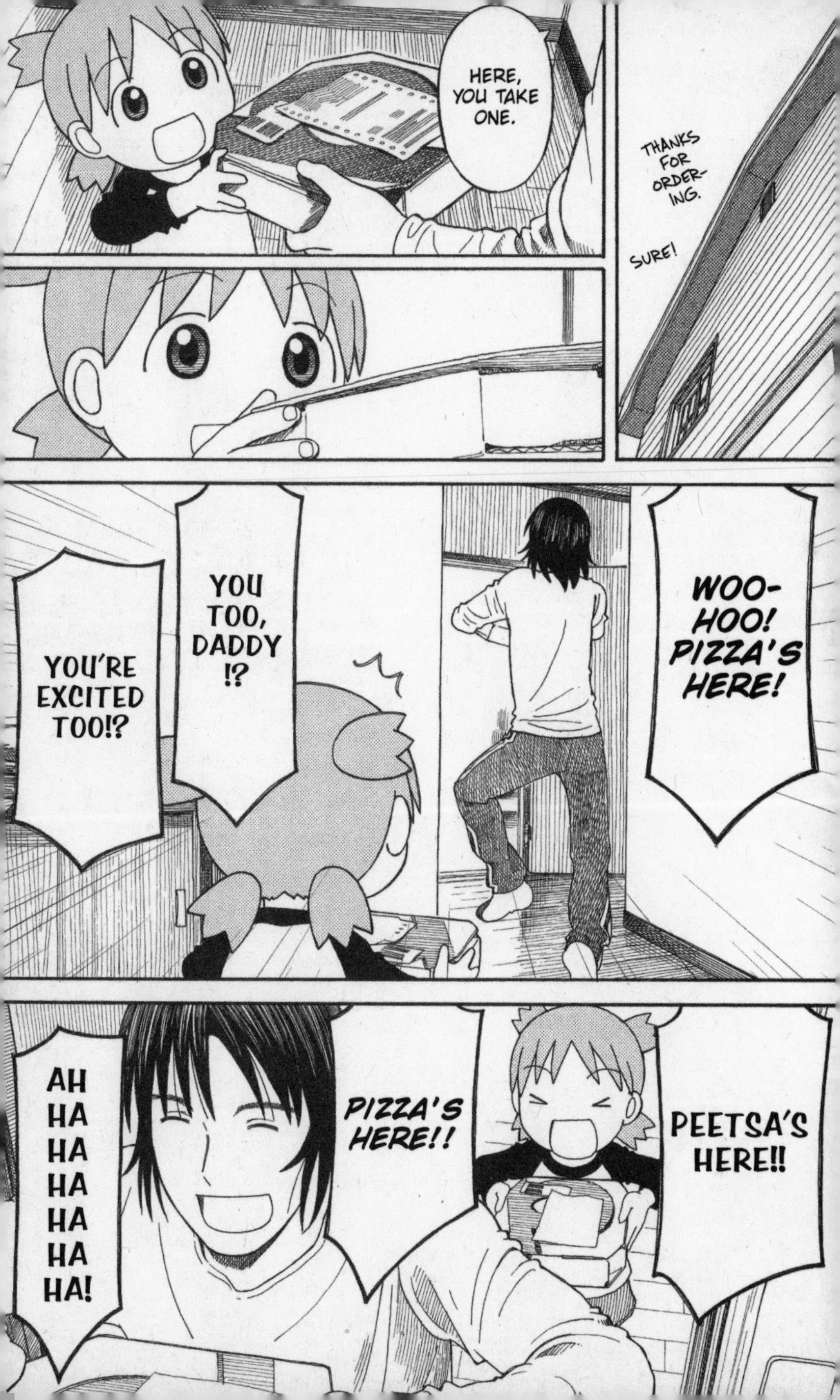
THANKS FOR ORDER-ING.
SURE!
HERE, YOU TAKE ONE.
WOO-HOO! PIZZA'S HERE!
YOU TOO, DADDY!?
YOU'RE EXCITED TOO!?
PEETSA'S HERE!!
PIZZA'S HERE!!
AH HA HA HA HA HA HA HA!

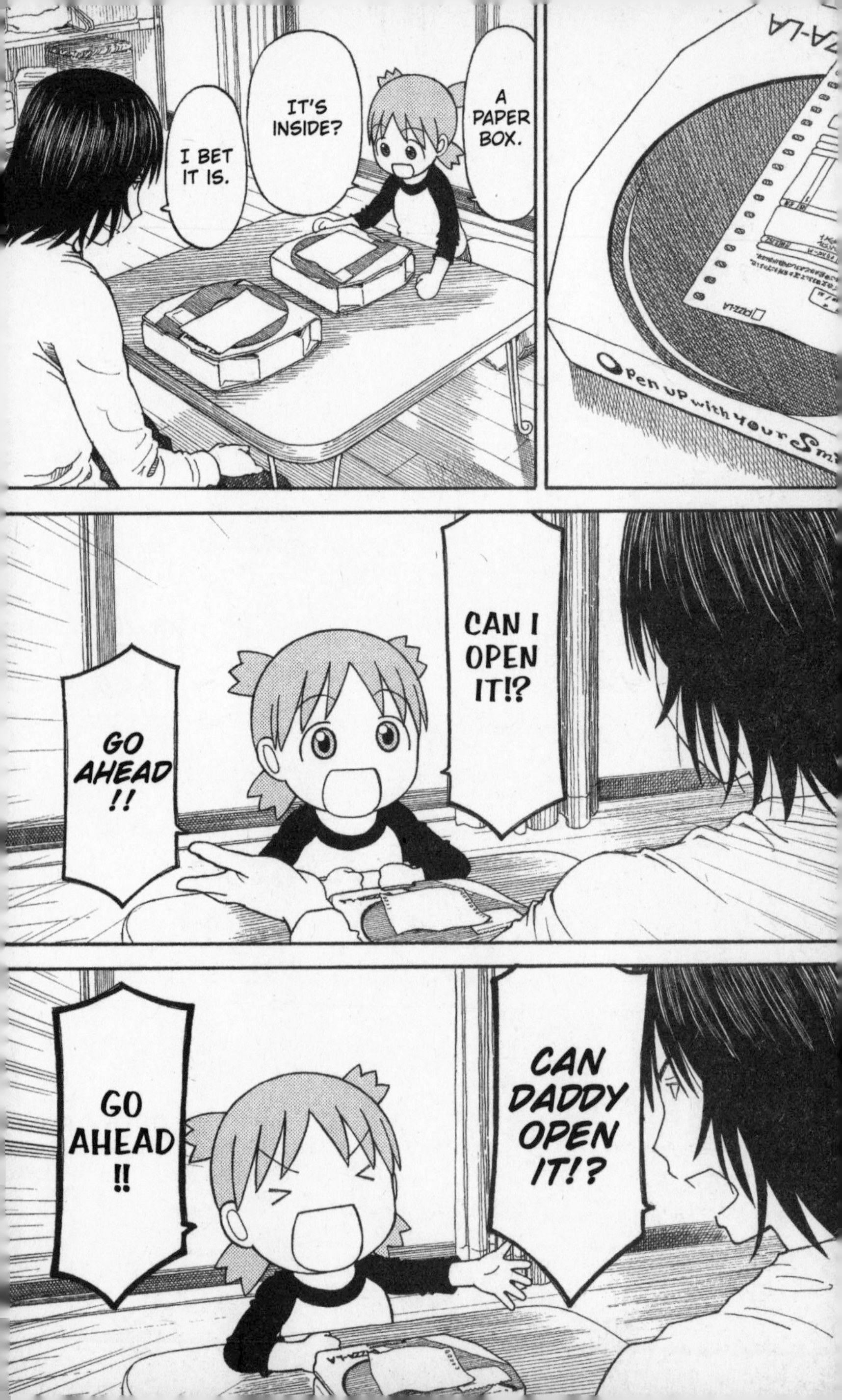

A PAPER BOX.
IT'S INSIDE?
I BET IT IS.
CAN I OPEN IT!?
GO AHEAD !!
CAN DADDY OPEN IT!?
GO AHEAD !!

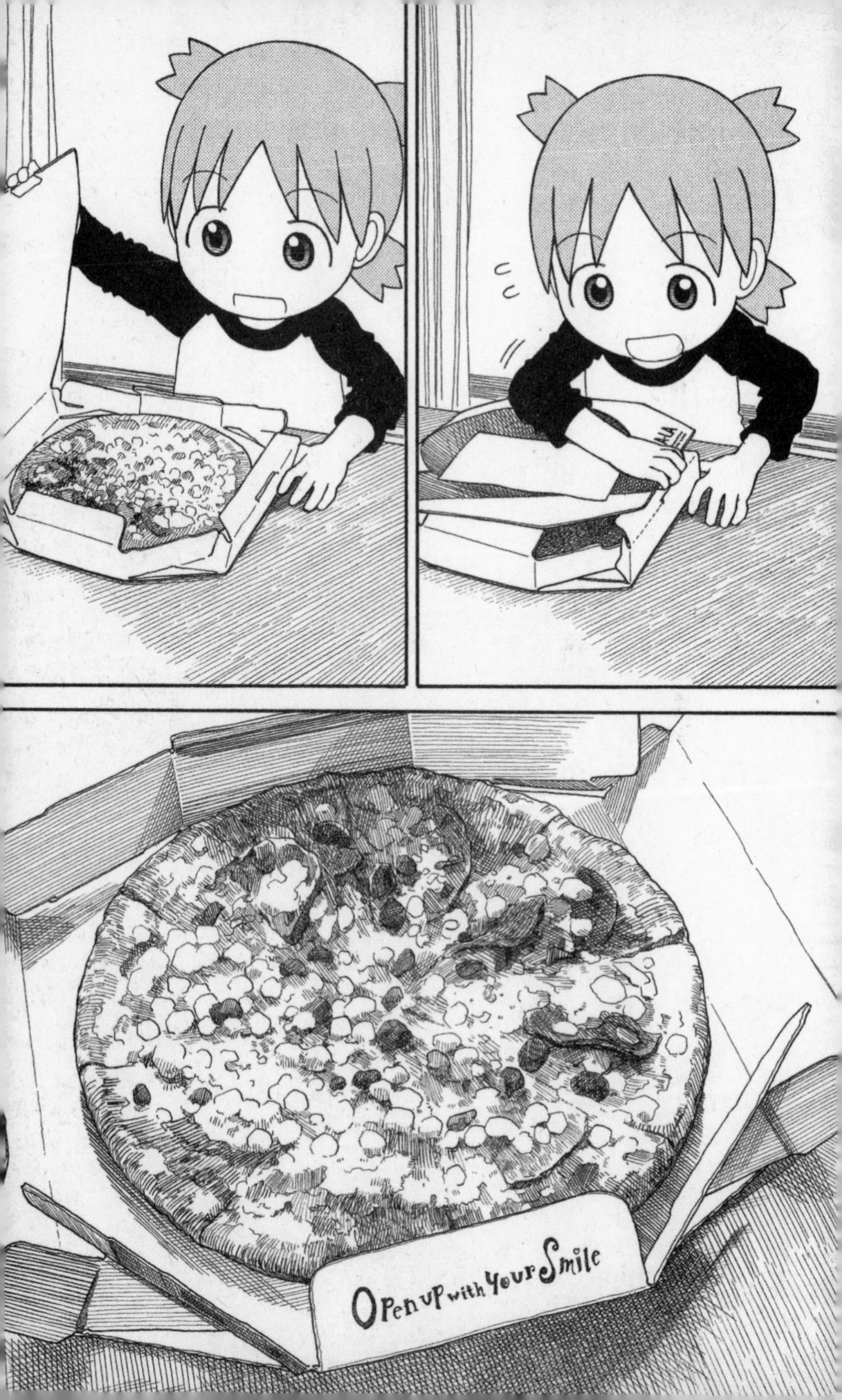
Open up with Your Smile

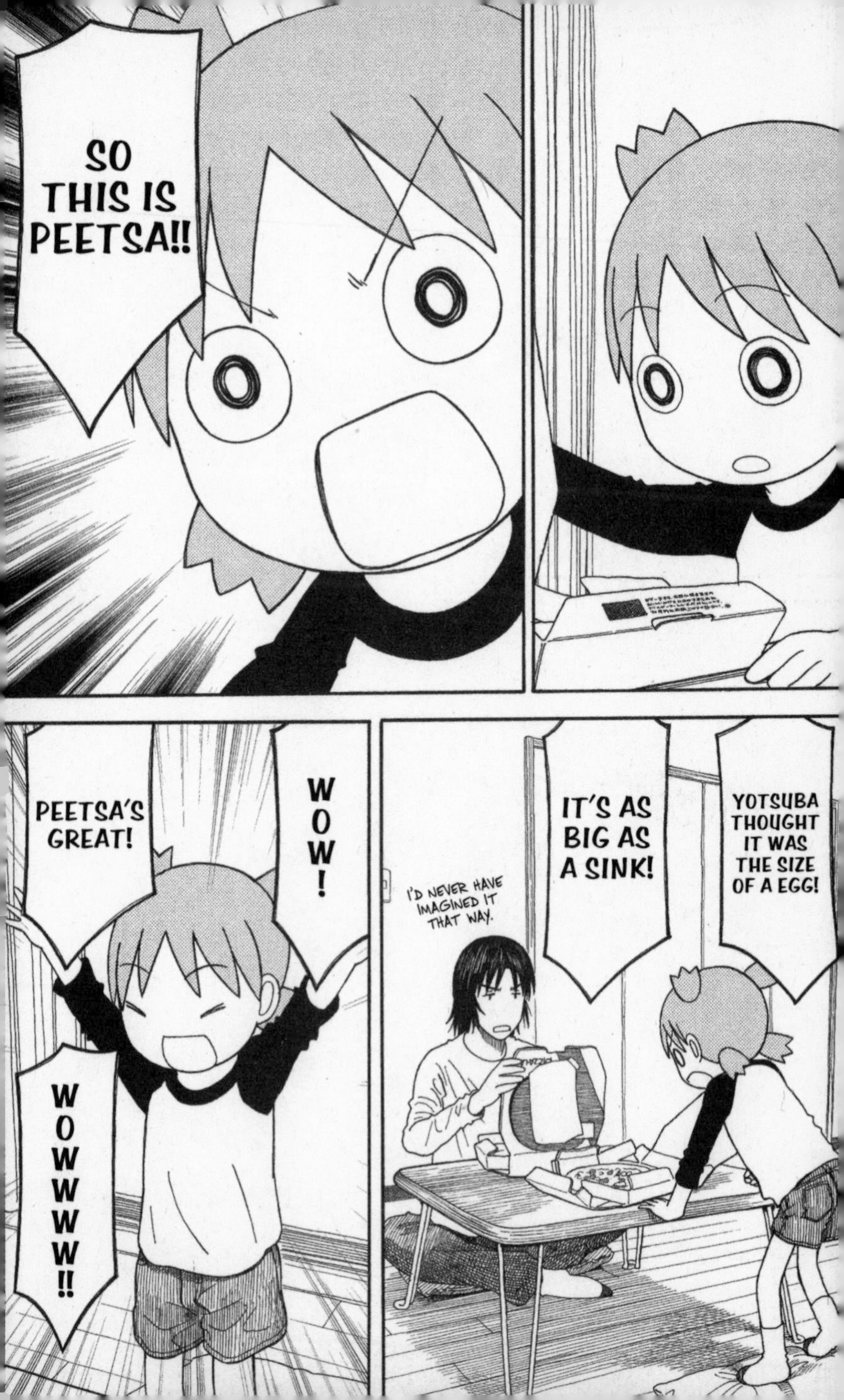
SO THIS IS PEETSA!!
YOTSUBA THOUGHT IT WAS THE SIZE OF A EGG!
IT'S AS BIG AS A SINK!
I'D NEVER HAVE IMAGINED IT THAT WAY.
WOW!
PEETSA'S GREAT!
WOWWWWW!!

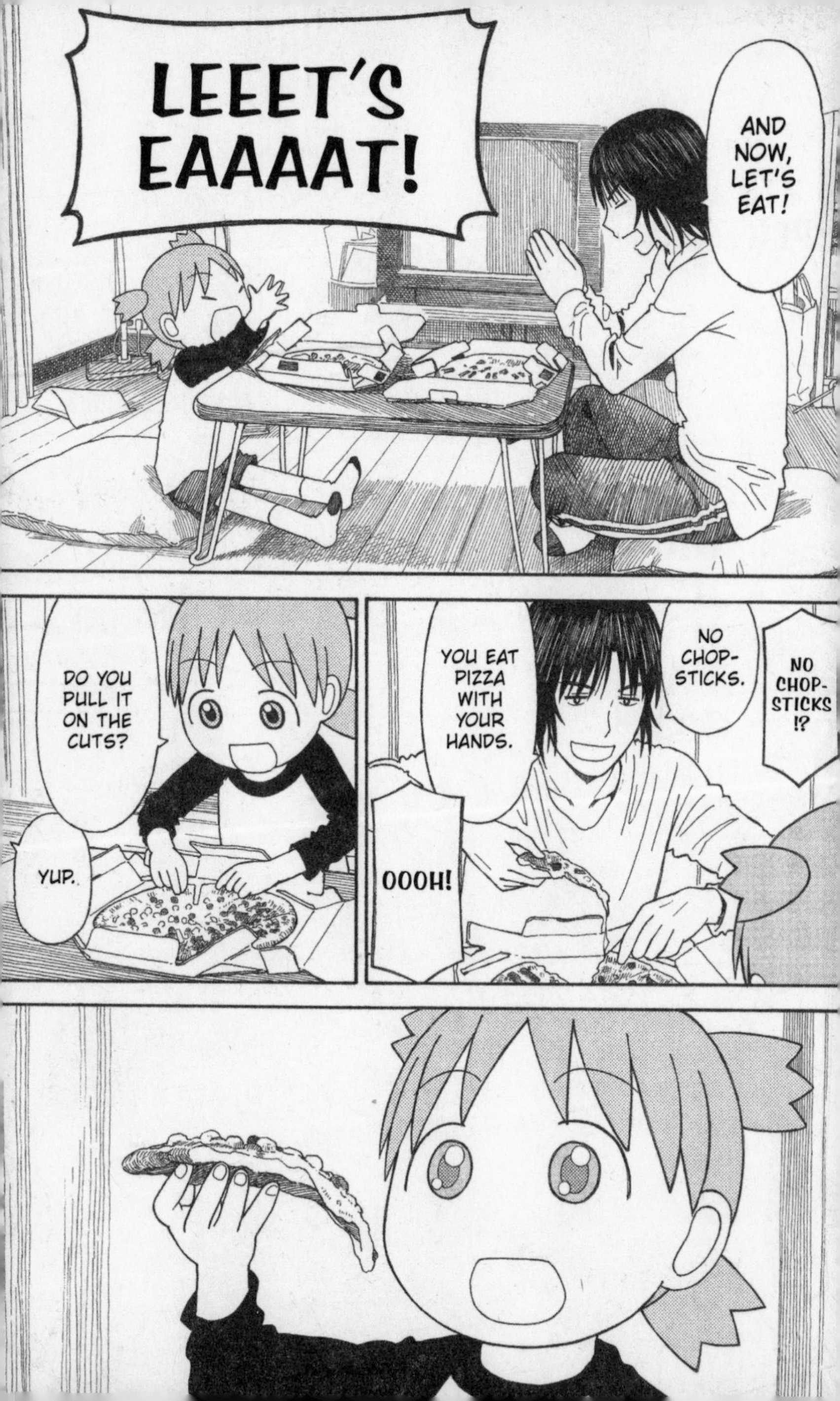
AND NOW, LET'S EAT!
LEEET'S EAAAAT!
NO CHOP-STICKS!?
NO CHOP-STICKS.
YOU EAT PIZZA WITH YOUR HANDS.
OOOH!
DO YOU PULL IT ON THE CUTS?
YUP.

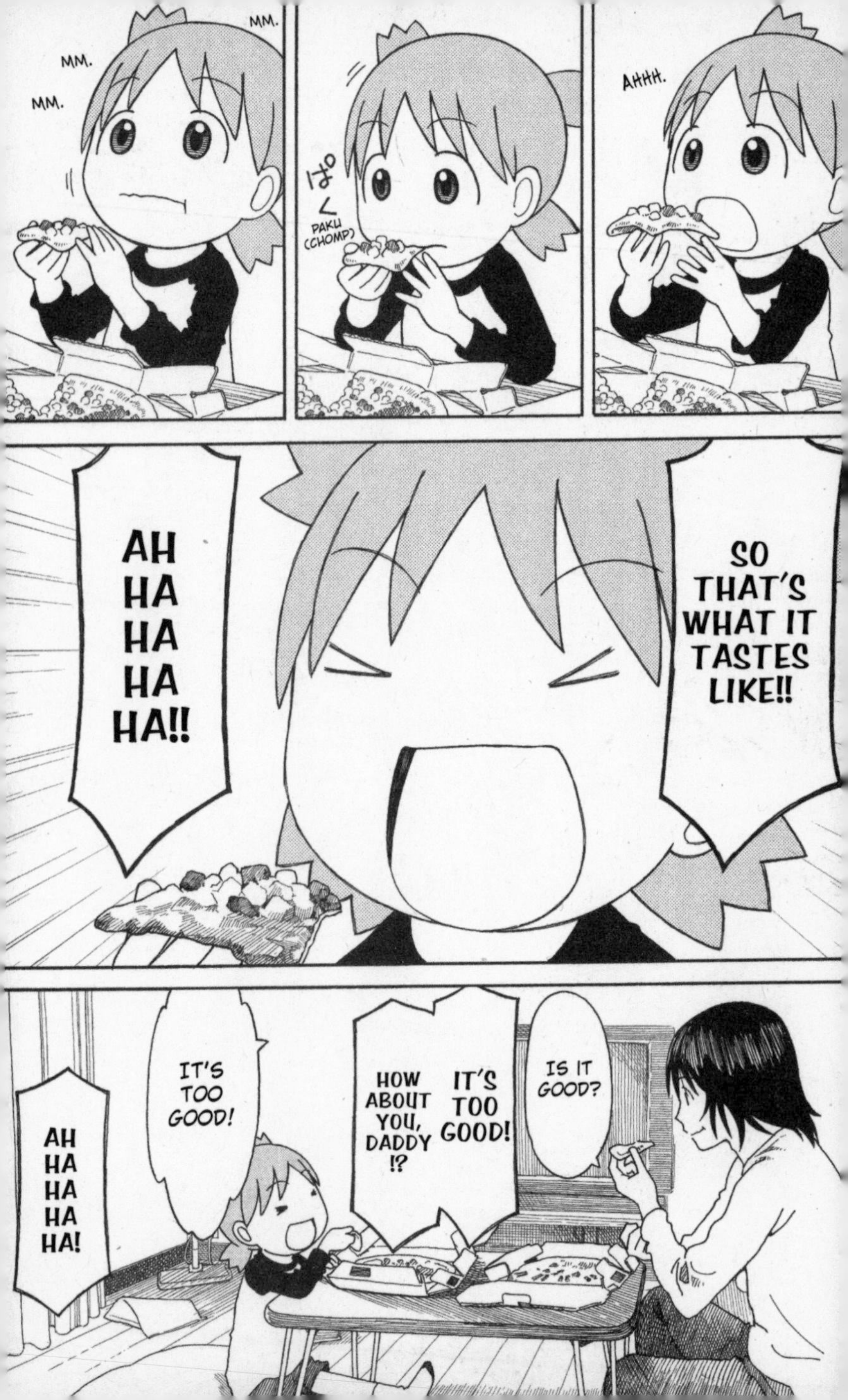
AHHH.
ぱく
PAKU (CHOMP)
MM.
MM.
MM.
SO THAT'S WHAT IT TASTES LIKE!!
AH HA HA HA HA HA!!
IS IT GOOD?
IT'S TOO GOOD!
HOW ABOUT YOU, DADDY!?
IT'S TOO GOOD!
AH HA HA HA HA HA!

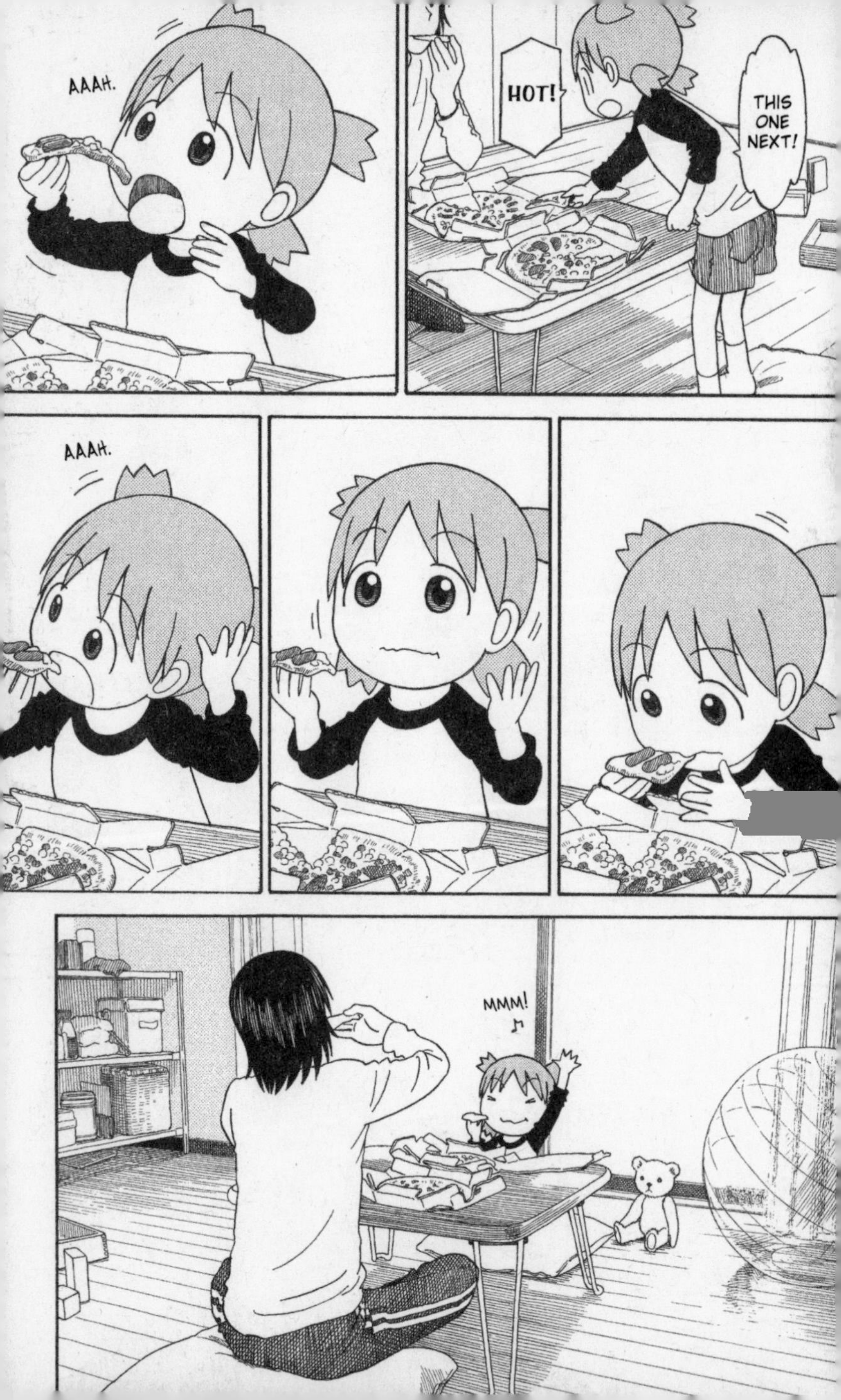
THIS ONE NEXT!
HOT!
AAAH.
AAAH.
MMM! ♪

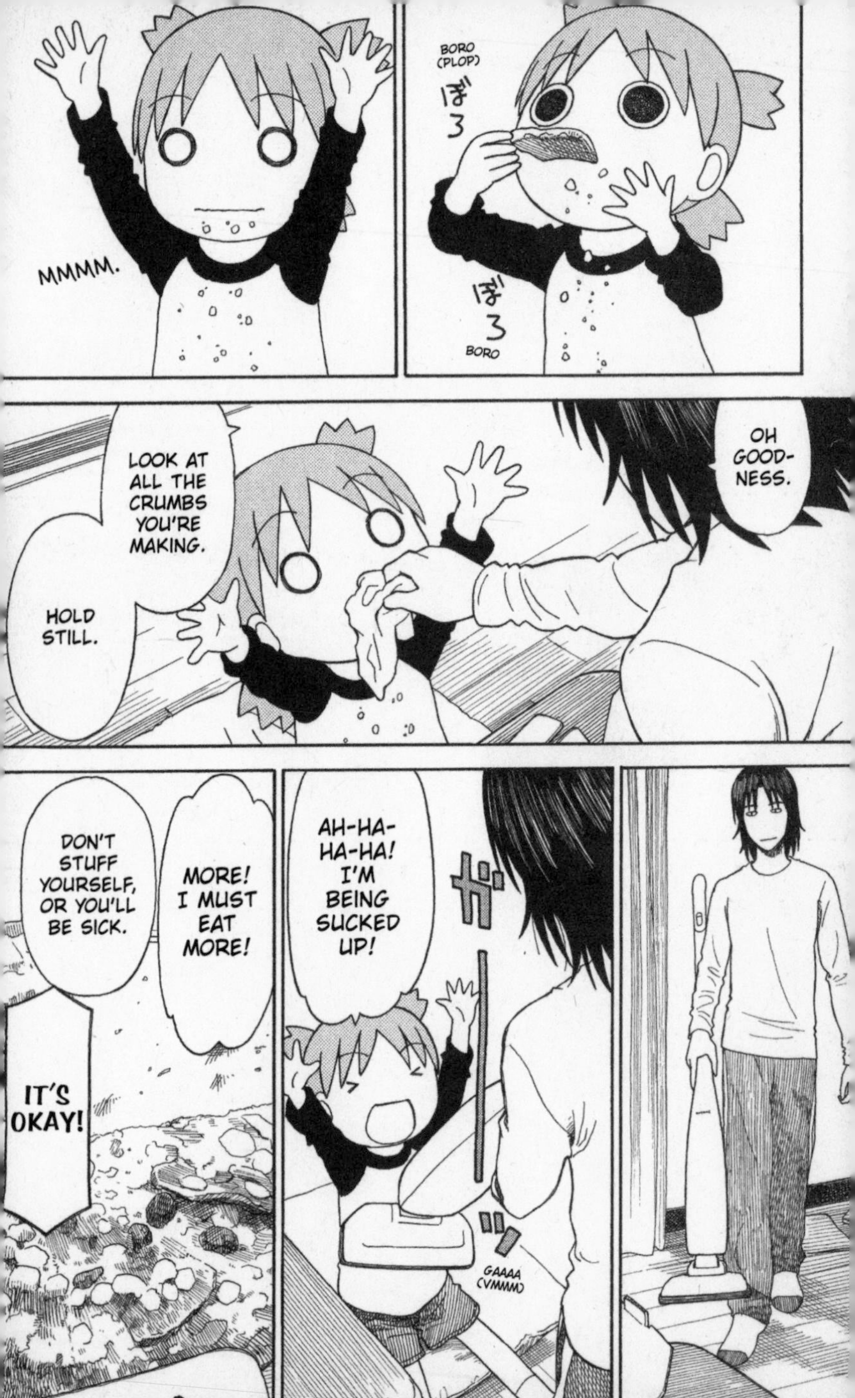
BORO (PLOP)
ぼろ
ぼろ
BORO
MMMM.
OH GOODNESS.
LOOK AT ALL THE CRUMBS YOU'RE MAKING.
HOLD STILL.
GAAAA (VMMM)
AH-HA-HA-HA! I'M BEING SUCKED UP!
MORE! I MUST EAT MORE!
DON'T STUFF YOURSELF, OR YOU'LL BE SICK.
IT'S OKAY!

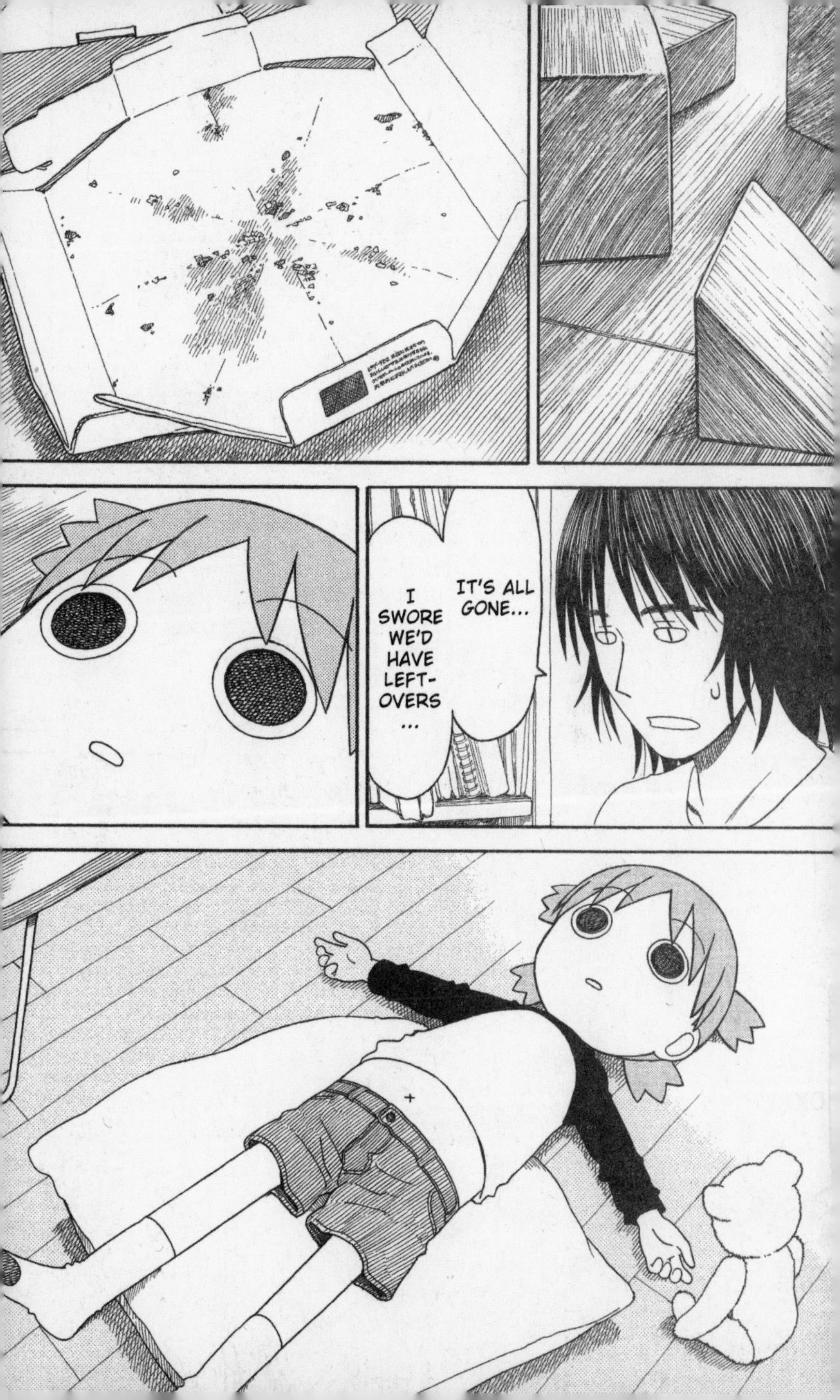

IT'S ALL GONE...
I SWORE WE'D HAVE LEFTOVERS...

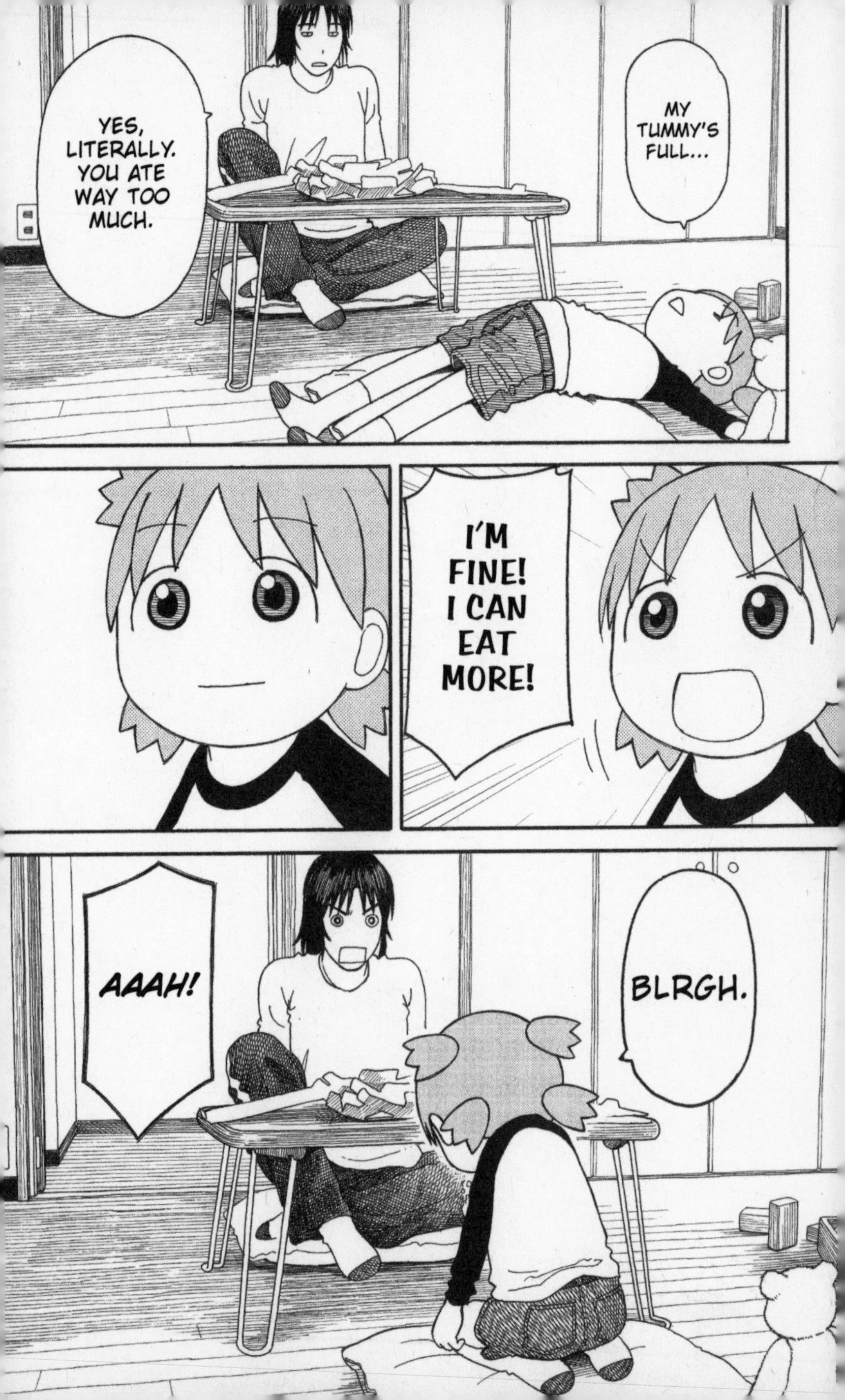
MY TUMMY'S FULL...
YES, LITERALLY. YOU ATE WAY TOO MUCH.
I'M FINE! I CAN EAT MORE!
BLRGH.
AAAH!

YOTSUBA&!

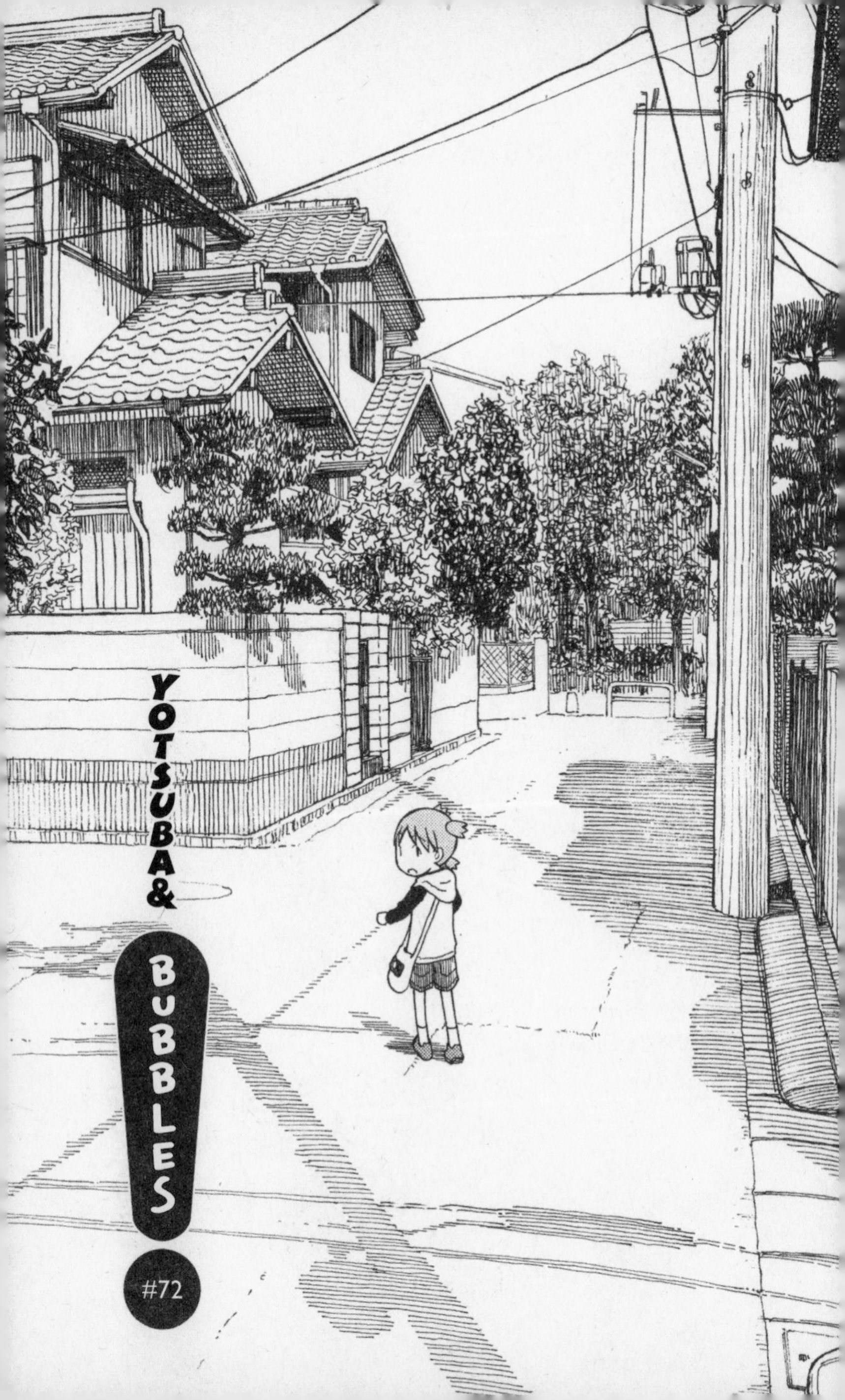
YOTSUBA&
BUBBLES
#72

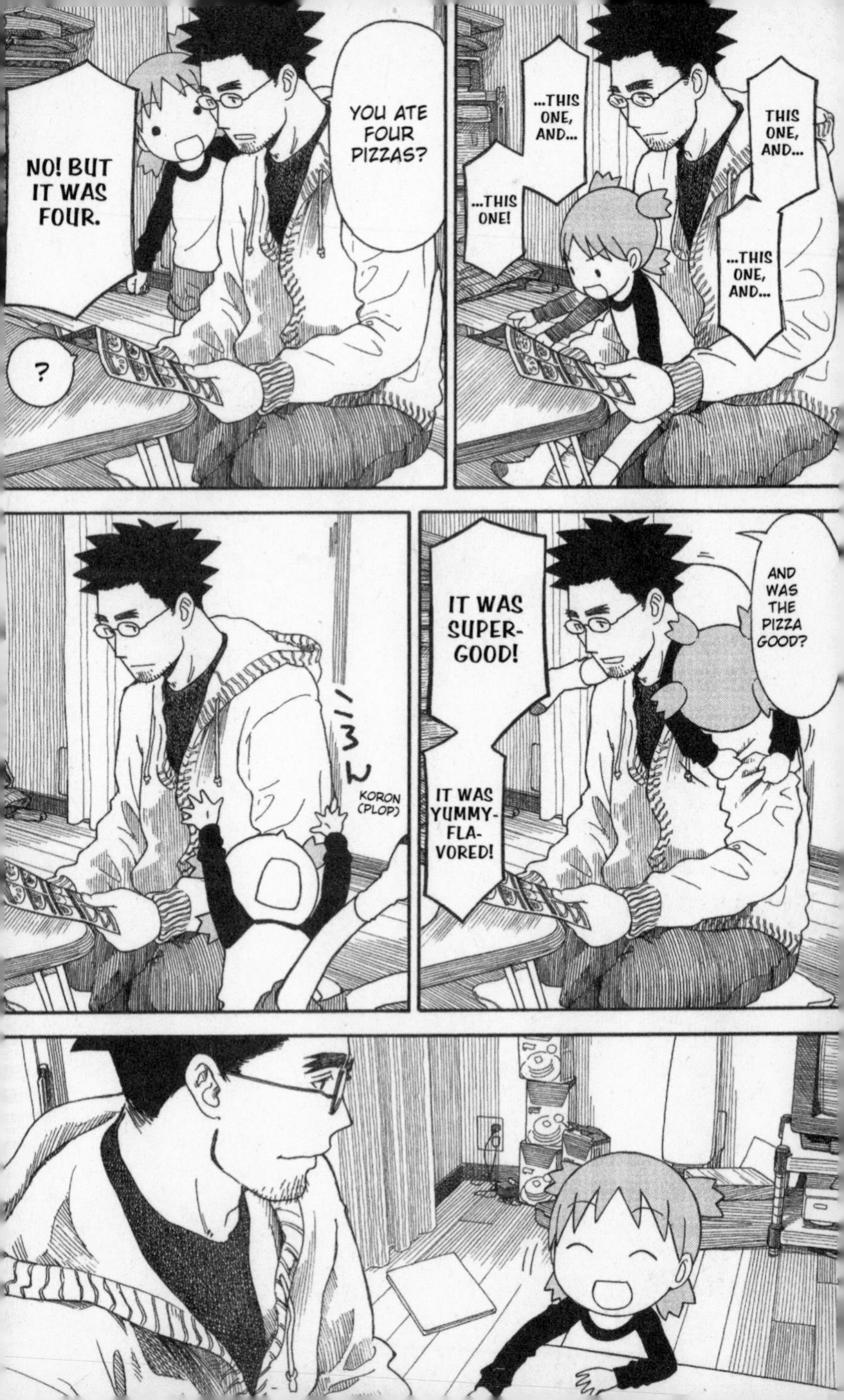
THIS ONE, AND...
...THIS ONE, AND...
...THIS ONE, AND...
...THIS ONE!
YOU ATE FOUR PIZZAS?
NO! BUT IT WAS FOUR.
?
AND WAS THE PIZZA GOOD?
IT WAS SUPER-GOOD!
IT WAS YUMMY-FLAVORED!
KORON (PLOP)

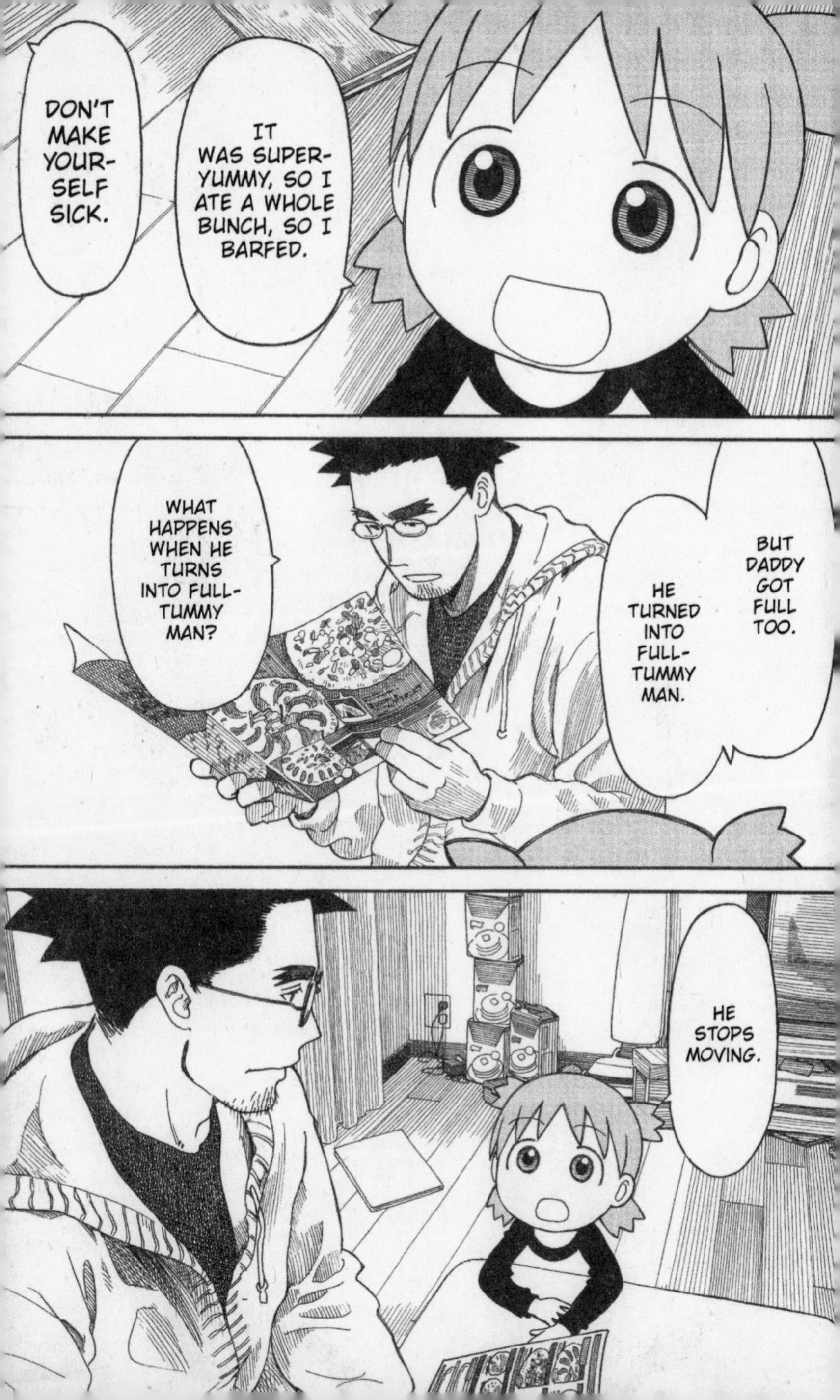
IT WAS SUPER-YUMMY, SO I ATE A WHOLE BUNCH, SO I BARFED.
DON'T MAKE YOUR-SELF SICK.
BUT DADDY GOT FULL TOO.
HE TURNED INTO FULL-TUMMY MAN.
WHAT HAPPENS WHEN HE TURNS INTO FULL-TUMMY MAN?
HE STOPS MOVING.

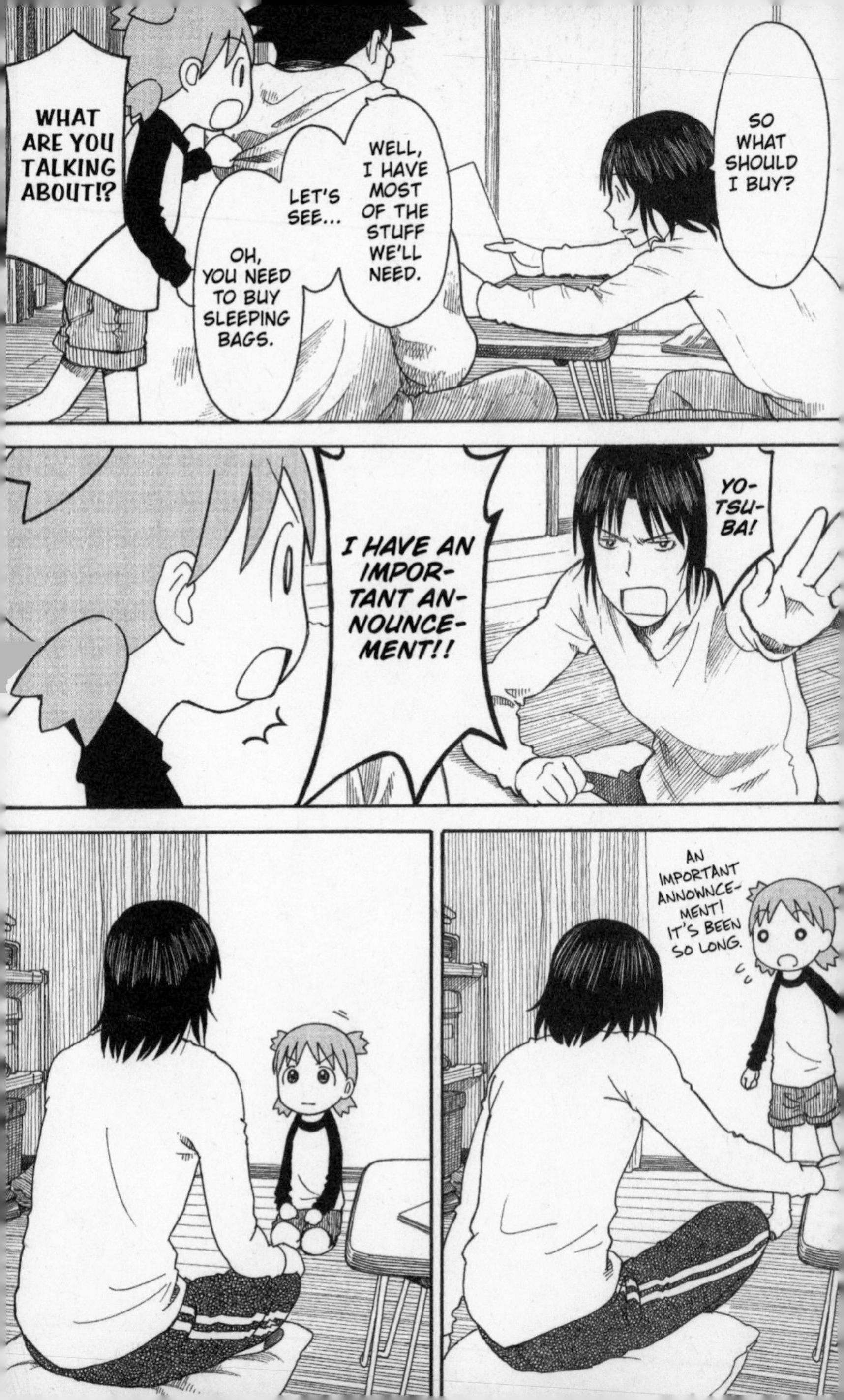
SO WHAT SHOULD I BUY?
WELL, I HAVE MOST OF THE STUFF WE'LL NEED.
LET'S SEE...
OH, YOU NEED TO BUY SLEEPING BAGS.
WHAT ARE YOU TALKING ABOUT!?
YO-TSU-BA!
I HAVE AN IMPOR-TANT AN-NOUNCE-MENT!!
AN IMPORTANT ANNOWNCE-MENT! IT'S BEEN SO LONG.

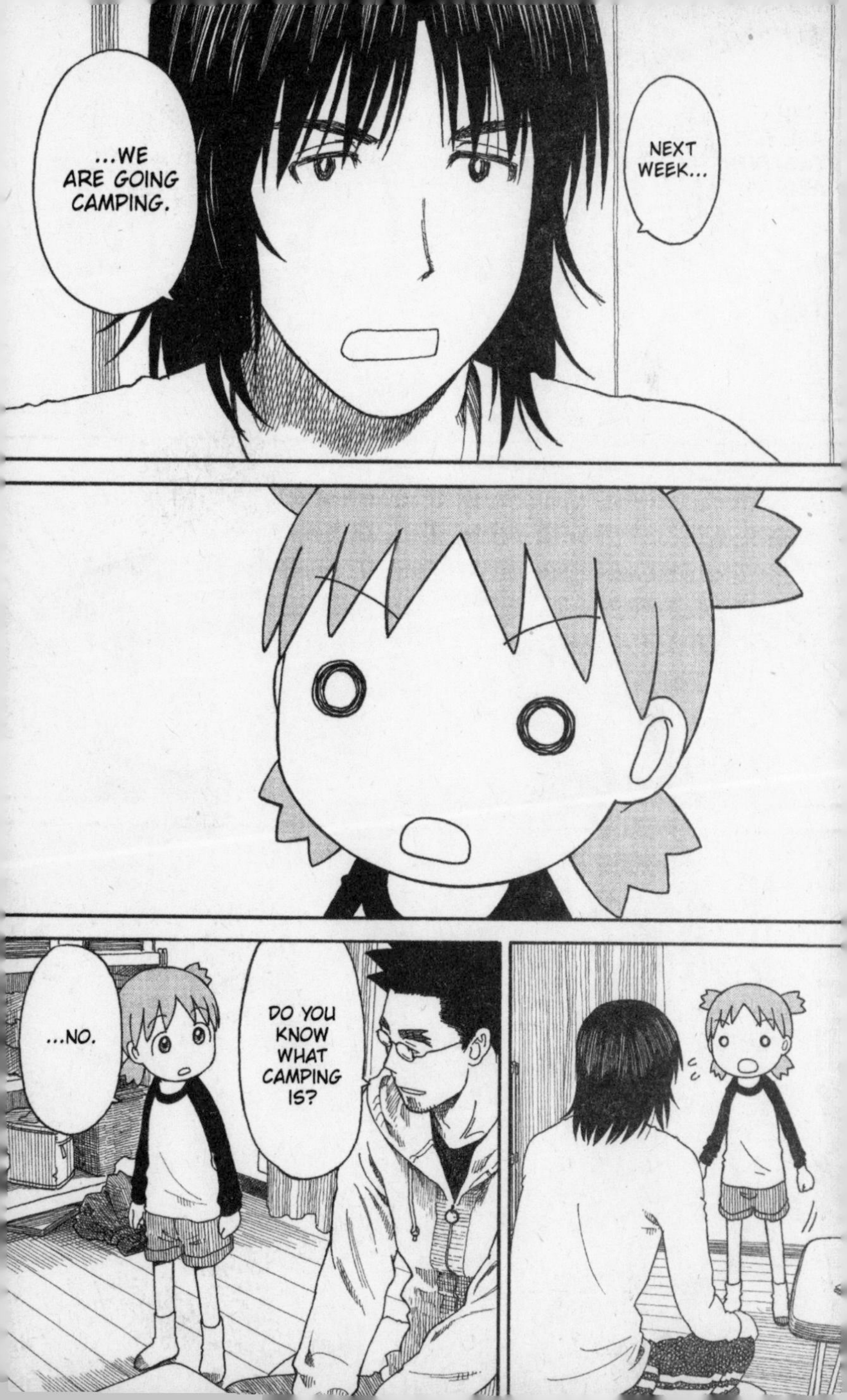
NEXT WEEK...
...WE ARE GOING CAMPING.
DO YOU KNOW WHAT CAMPING IS?
...NO.

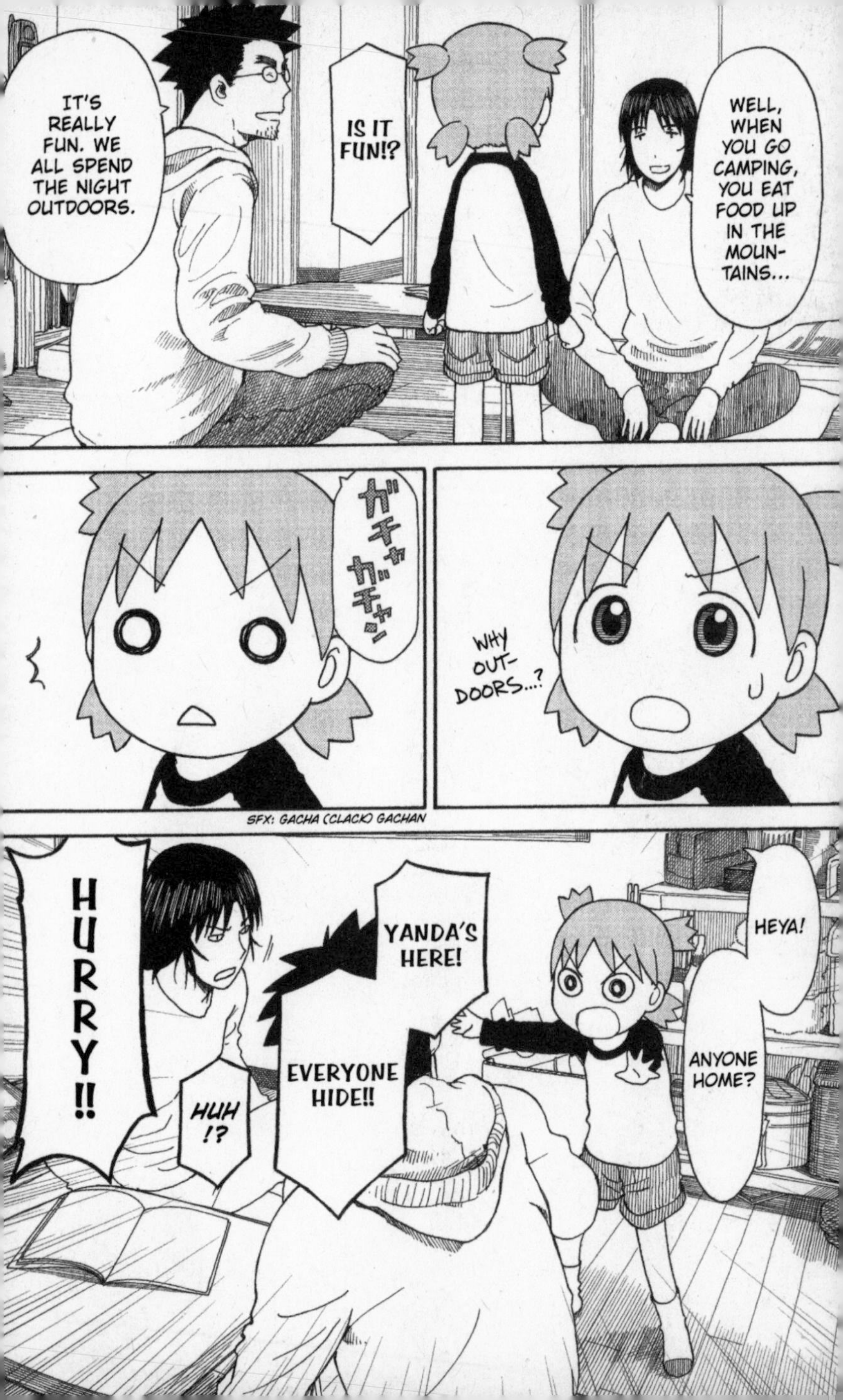
WELL, WHEN YOU GO CAMPING, YOU EAT FOOD UP IN THE MOUNTAINS...
IS IT FUN!?
IT'S REALLY FUN. WE ALL SPEND THE NIGHT OUTDOORS.
WHY OUT-DOORS...?
ガチャガチャン
SFX: GACHA (CLACK) GACHAN
HEYA!
ANYONE HOME?
YANDA'S HERE!
EVERYONE HIDE!!
HUH!?
HURRY!!

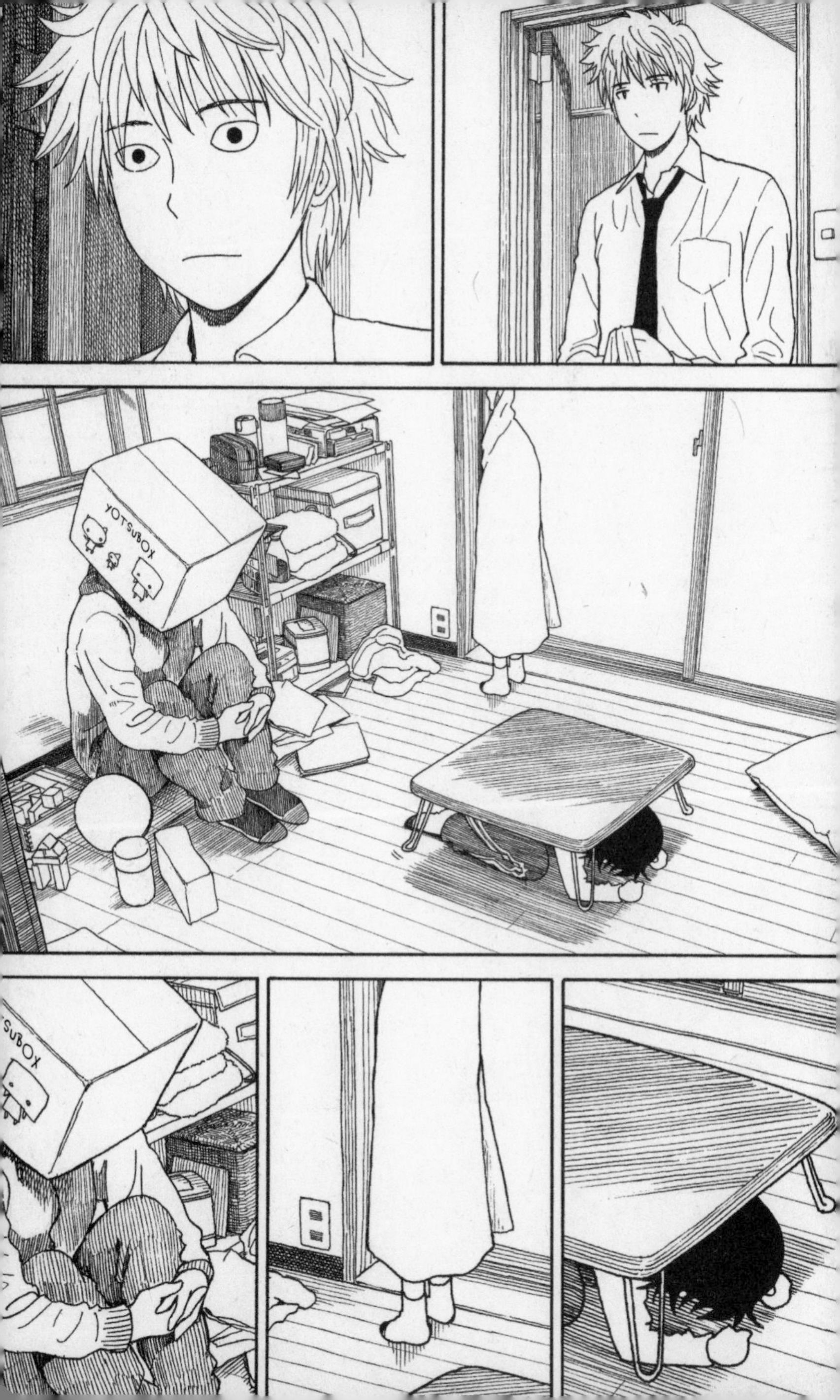
YOTSUBOX

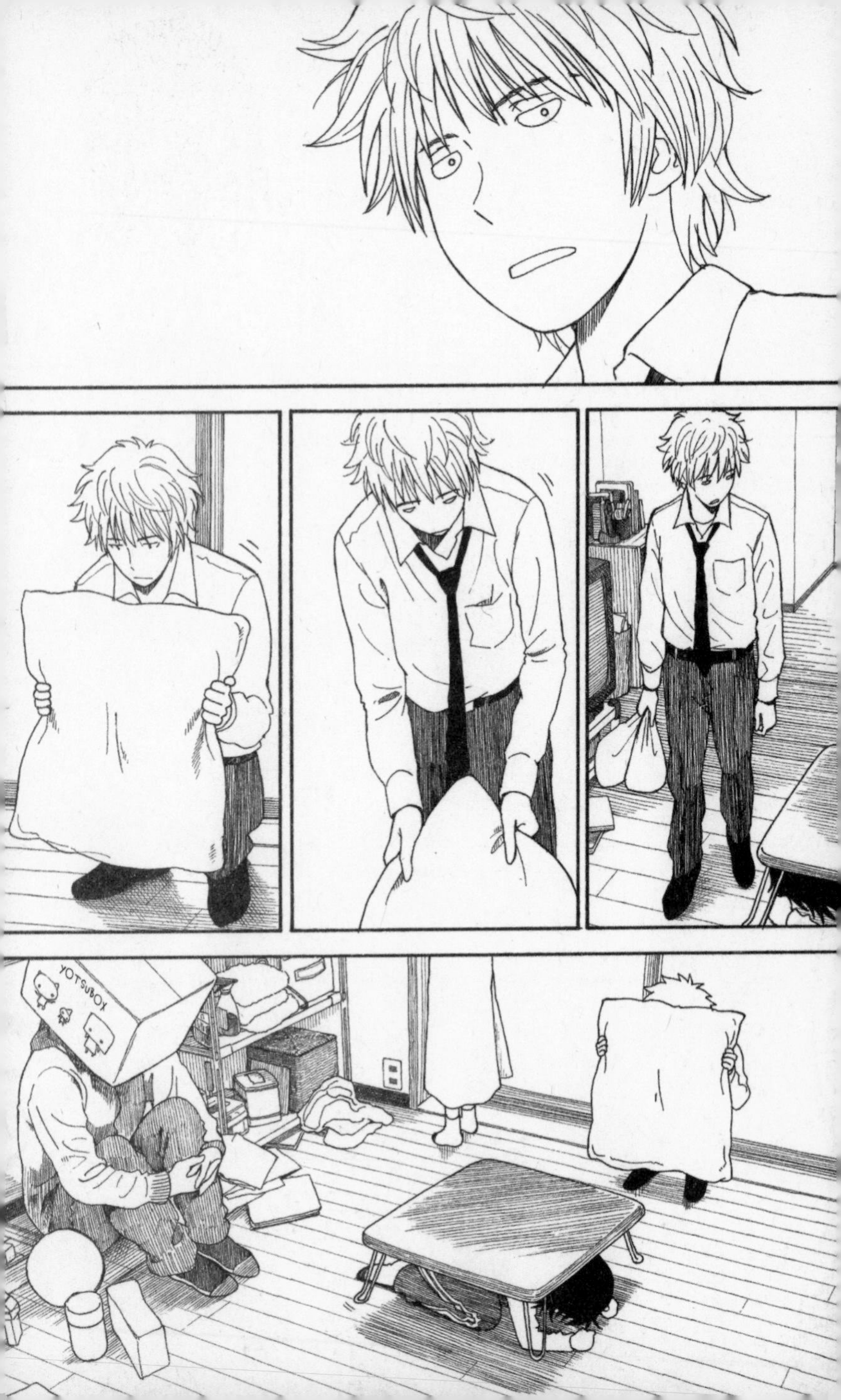
YOTSUBOX

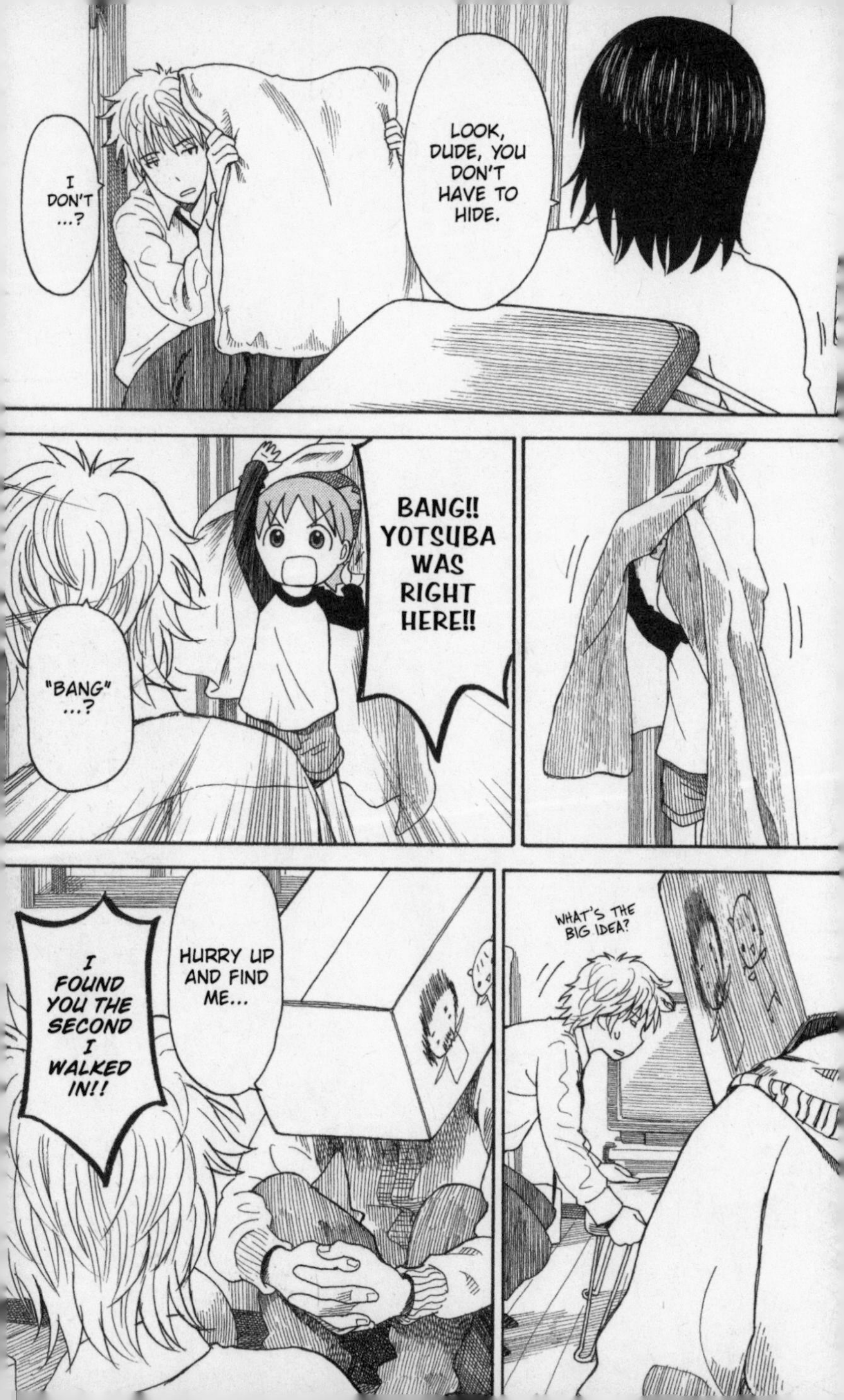
LOOK, DUDE, YOU DON'T HAVE TO HIDE.
I DON'T ...?
BANG!! YOTSUBA WAS RIGHT HERE!!
"BANG" ...?
HURRY UP AND FIND ME...
I FOUND YOU THE SECOND I WALKED IN!!
WHAT'S THE BIG IDEA?

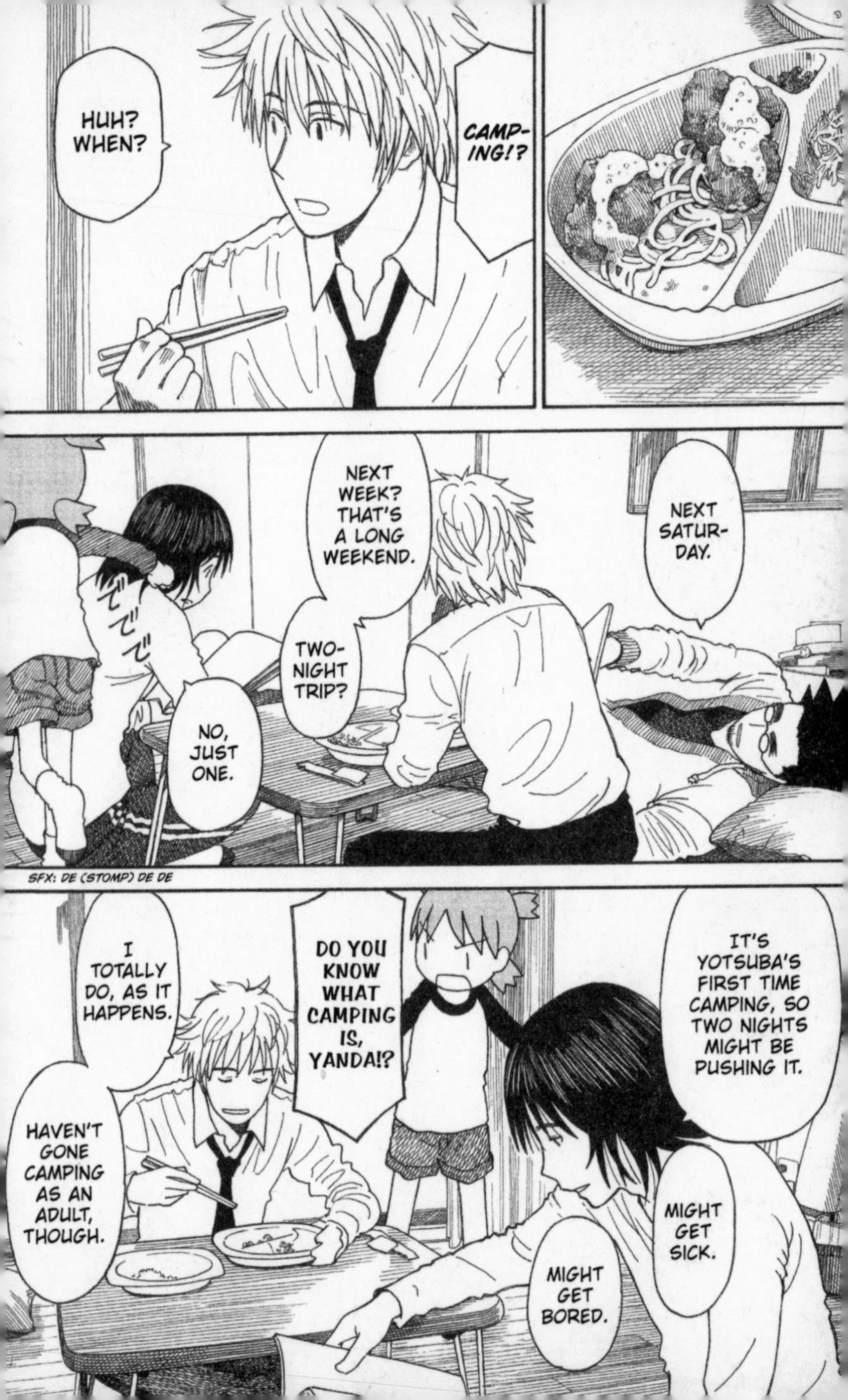
CAMP-ING!?
HUH? WHEN?
NEXT SATUR-DAY.
NEXT WEEK? THAT'S A LONG WEEKEND.
TWO-NIGHT TRIP?
NO, JUST ONE.
ででで
SFX: DE (STOMP) DE DE
IT'S YOTSUBA'S FIRST TIME CAMPING, SO TWO NIGHTS MIGHT BE PUSHING IT.
DO YOU KNOW WHAT CAMPING IS, YANDA!?
I TOTALLY DO, AS IT HAPPENS.
HAVEN'T GONE CAMPING AS AN ADULT, THOUGH.
MIGHT GET SICK.
MIGHT GET BORED.

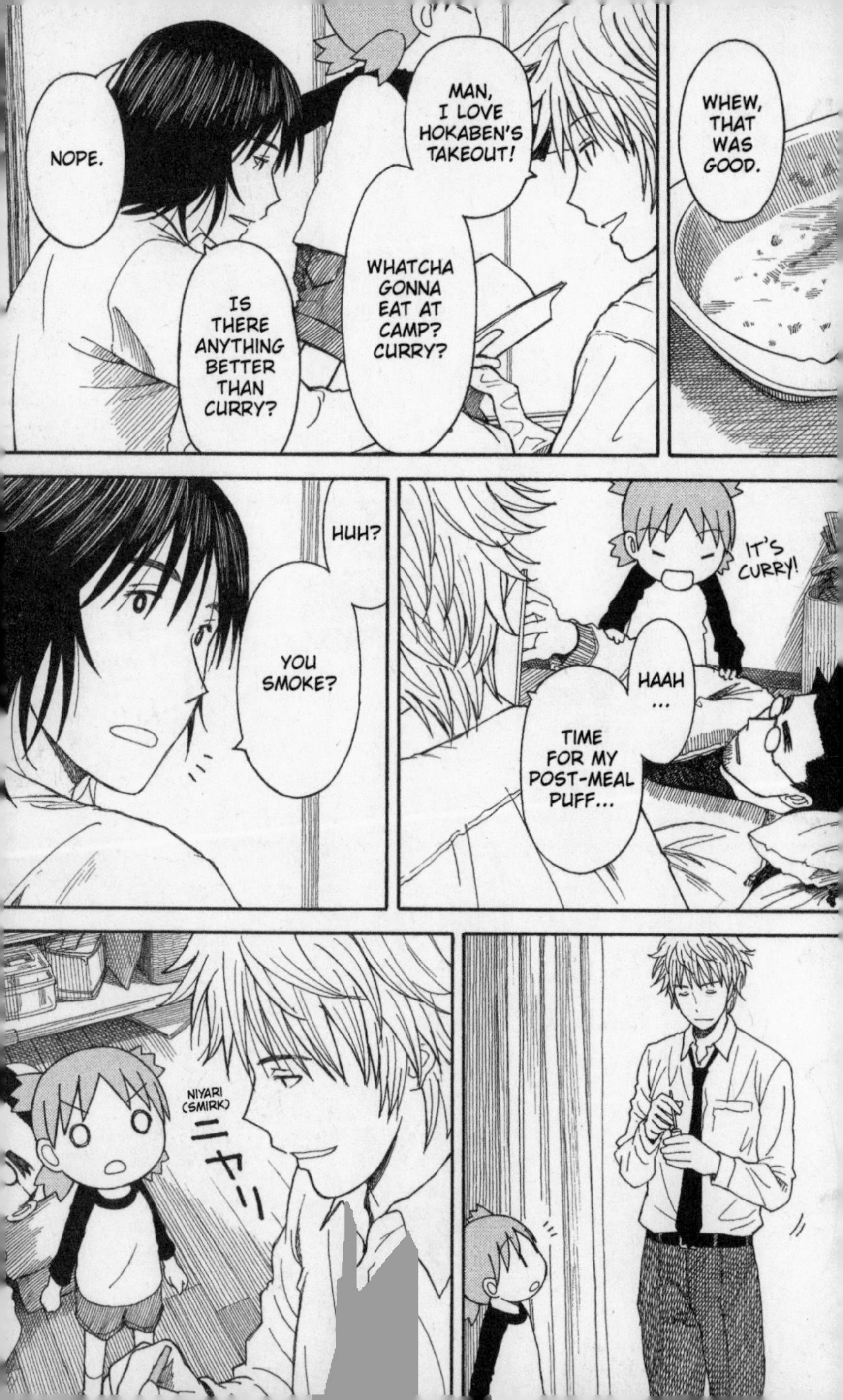
WHEW, THAT WAS GOOD.
MAN, I LOVE HOKABEN'S TAKEOUT!
WHATCHA GONNA EAT AT CAMP? CURRY?
IS THERE ANYTHING BETTER THAN CURRY?
NOPE.
IT'S CURRY!
HAAH...
TIME FOR MY POST-MEAL PUFF...
HUH?
YOU SMOKE?
NIYARI (SMIRK)
ニヤリ

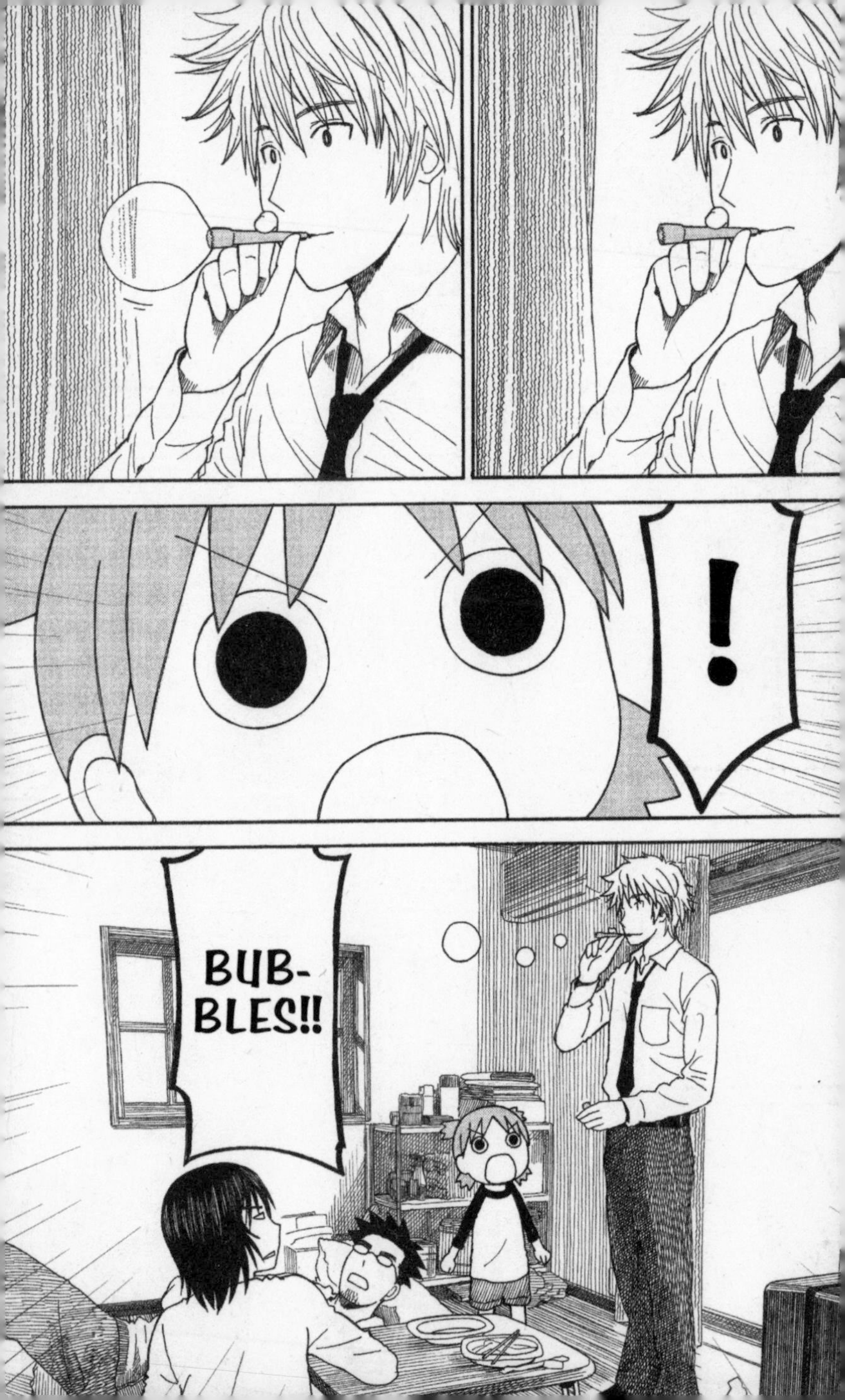
!
BUB-
BLES!!

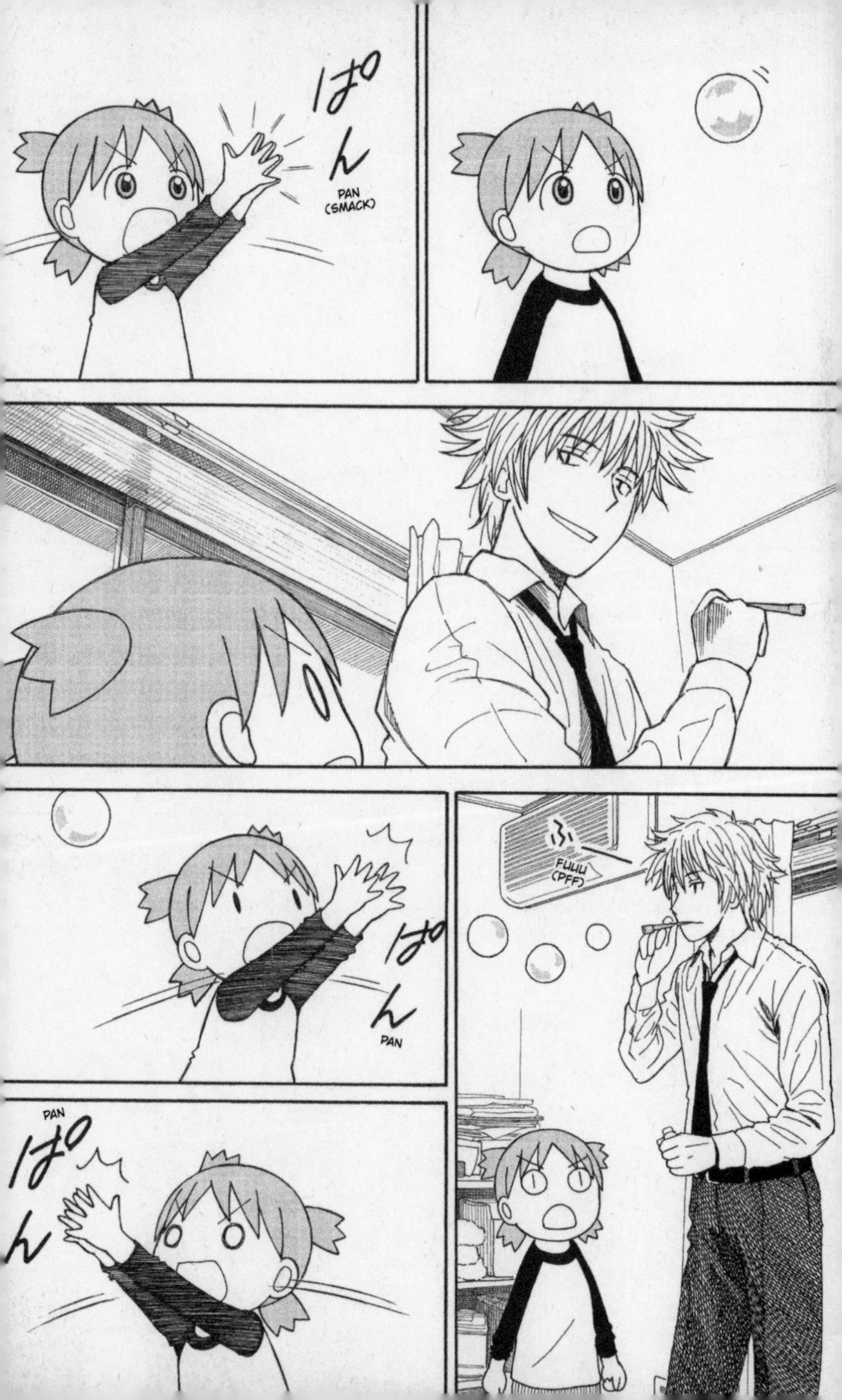

ぱん
PAN (SMACK)
ふ
FUUU (PFFF)
ぱん
PAN
ぱん
PAN

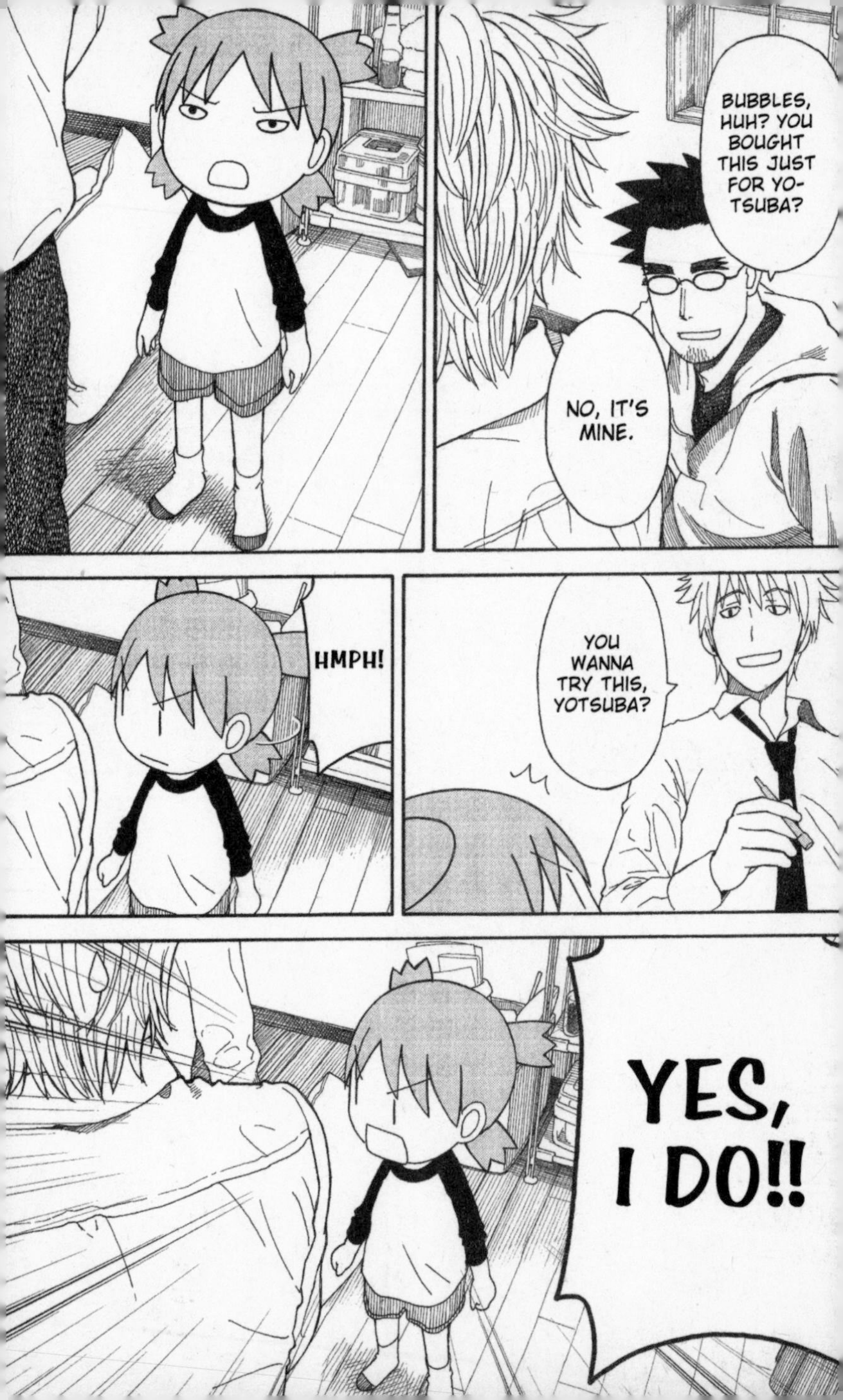
BUBBLES, HUH? YOU BOUGHT THIS JUST FOR YO-TSUBA?
NO, IT'S MINE.
YOU WANNA TRY THIS, YOTSUBA?
HMPH!
YES, I DO!!

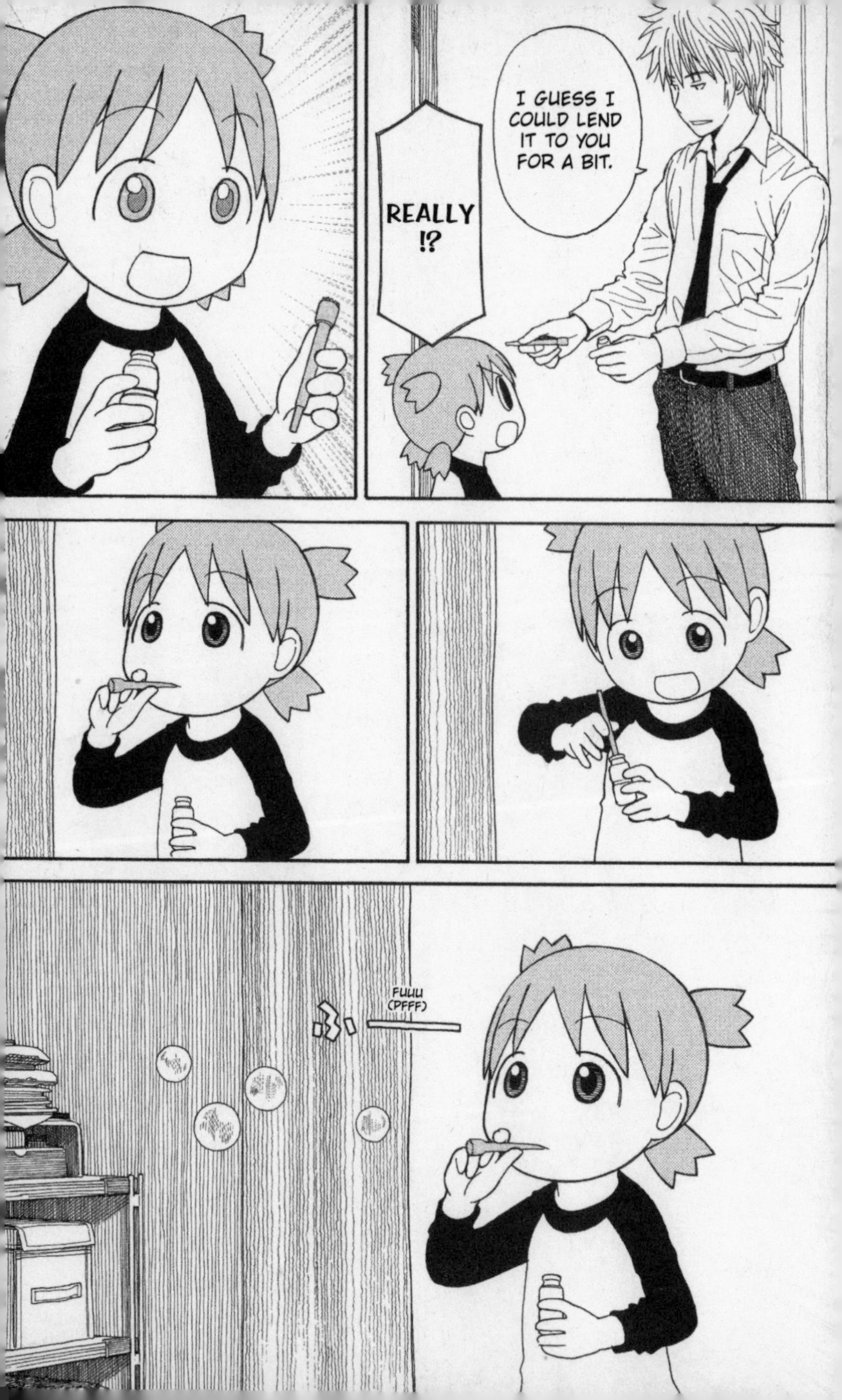
I GUESS I COULD LEND IT TO YOU FOR A BIT.
REALLY!?
FUUU
(PFFF)

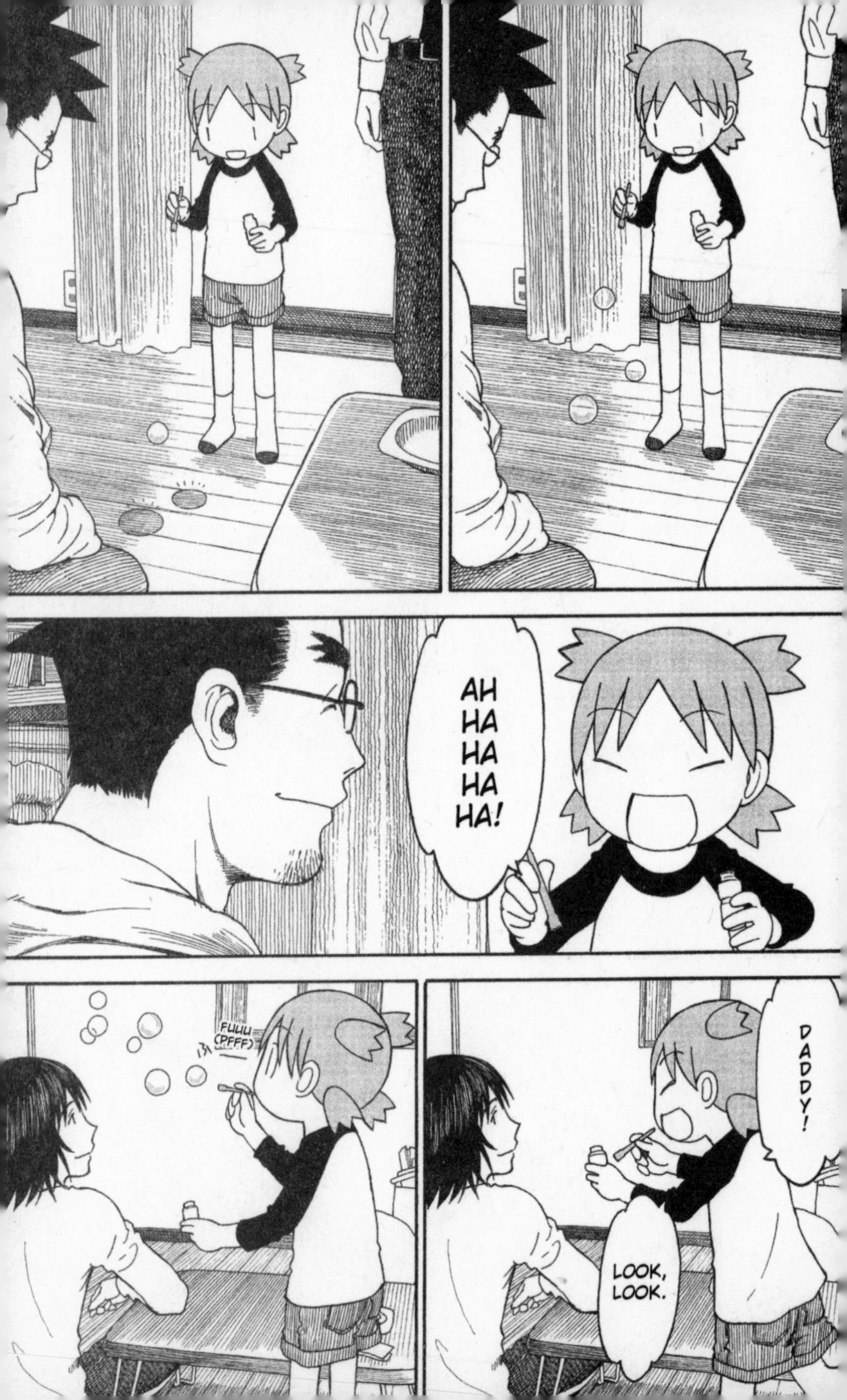
AH HA HA HA HA!
DADDY!
LOOK, LOOK.
FUUU (PFFF)

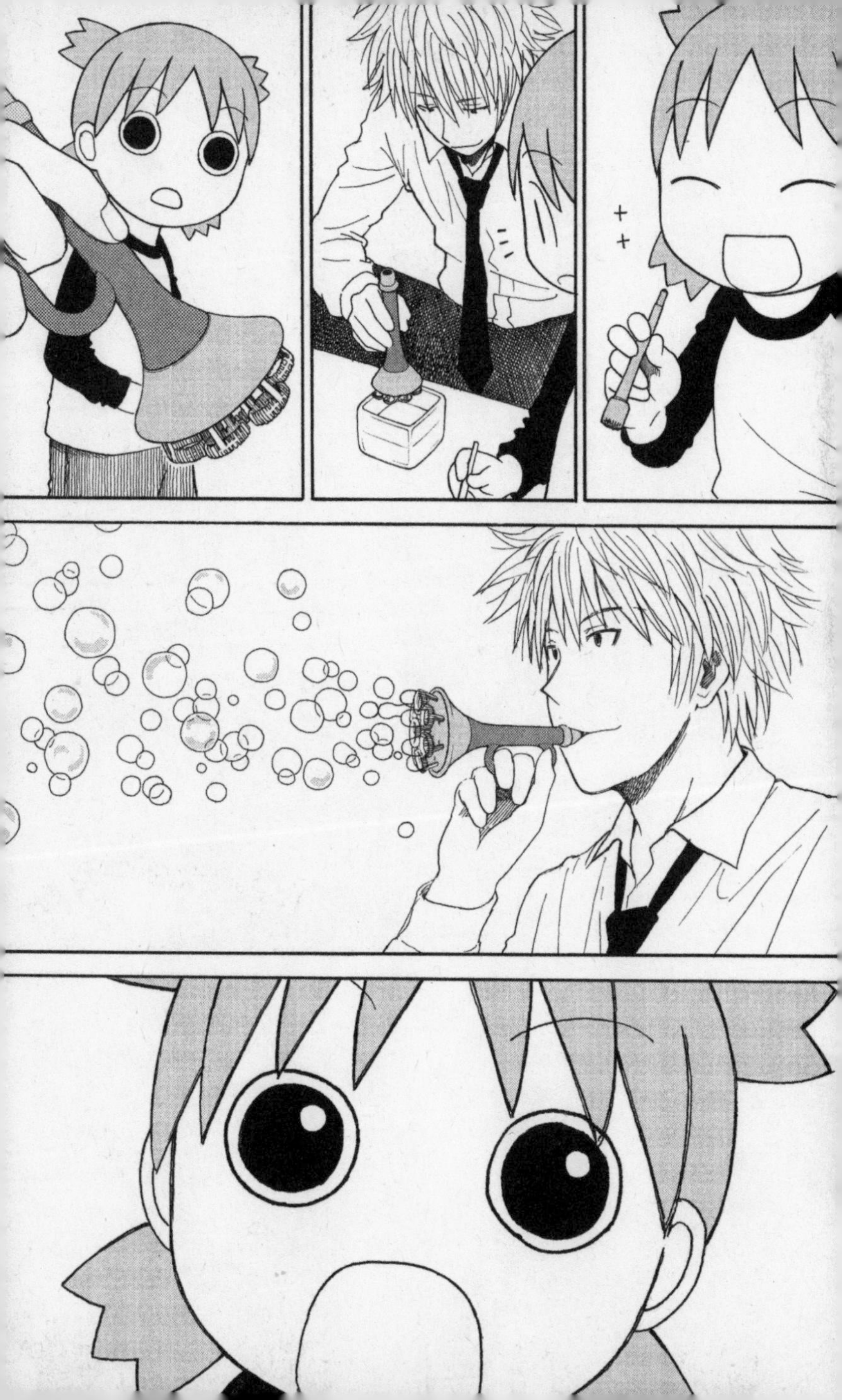

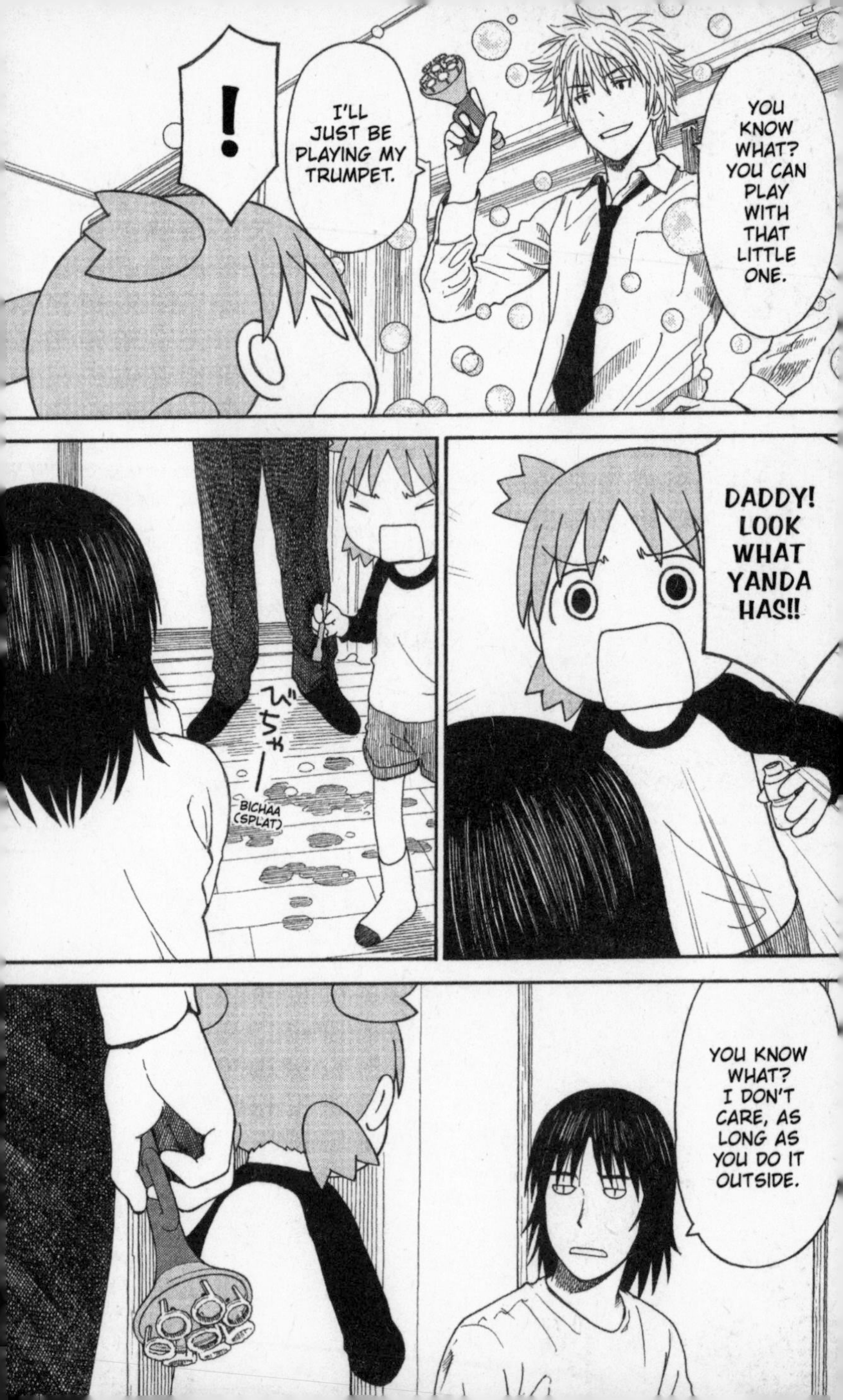
YOU KNOW WHAT? YOU CAN PLAY WITH THAT LITTLE ONE.
I'LL JUST BE PLAYING MY TRUMPET.
!
DADDY! LOOK WHAT YANDA HAS!!
びちゃー
BICHAA (SPLAT)
YOU KNOW WHAT? I DON'T CARE, AS LONG AS YOU DO IT OUTSIDE.

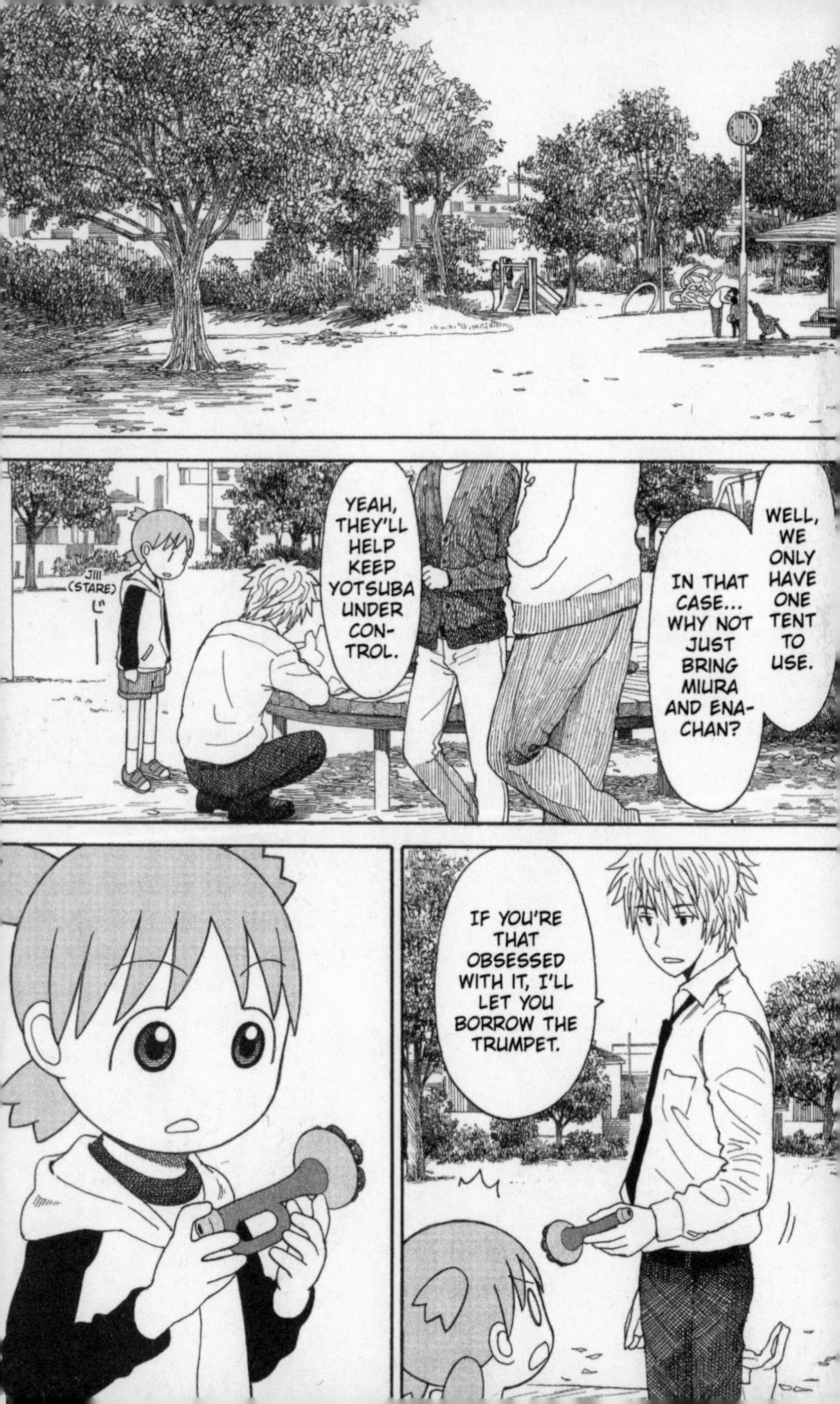

WELL, WE ONLY HAVE ONE TENT TO USE.
IN THAT CASE... WHY NOT JUST BRING MIURA AND ENA-CHAN?
YEAH, THEY'LL HELP KEEP YOTSUBA UNDER CON-TROL.
JIII (STARE)
じー
IF YOU'RE THAT OBSESSED WITH IT, I'LL LET YOU BORROW THE TRUMPET.

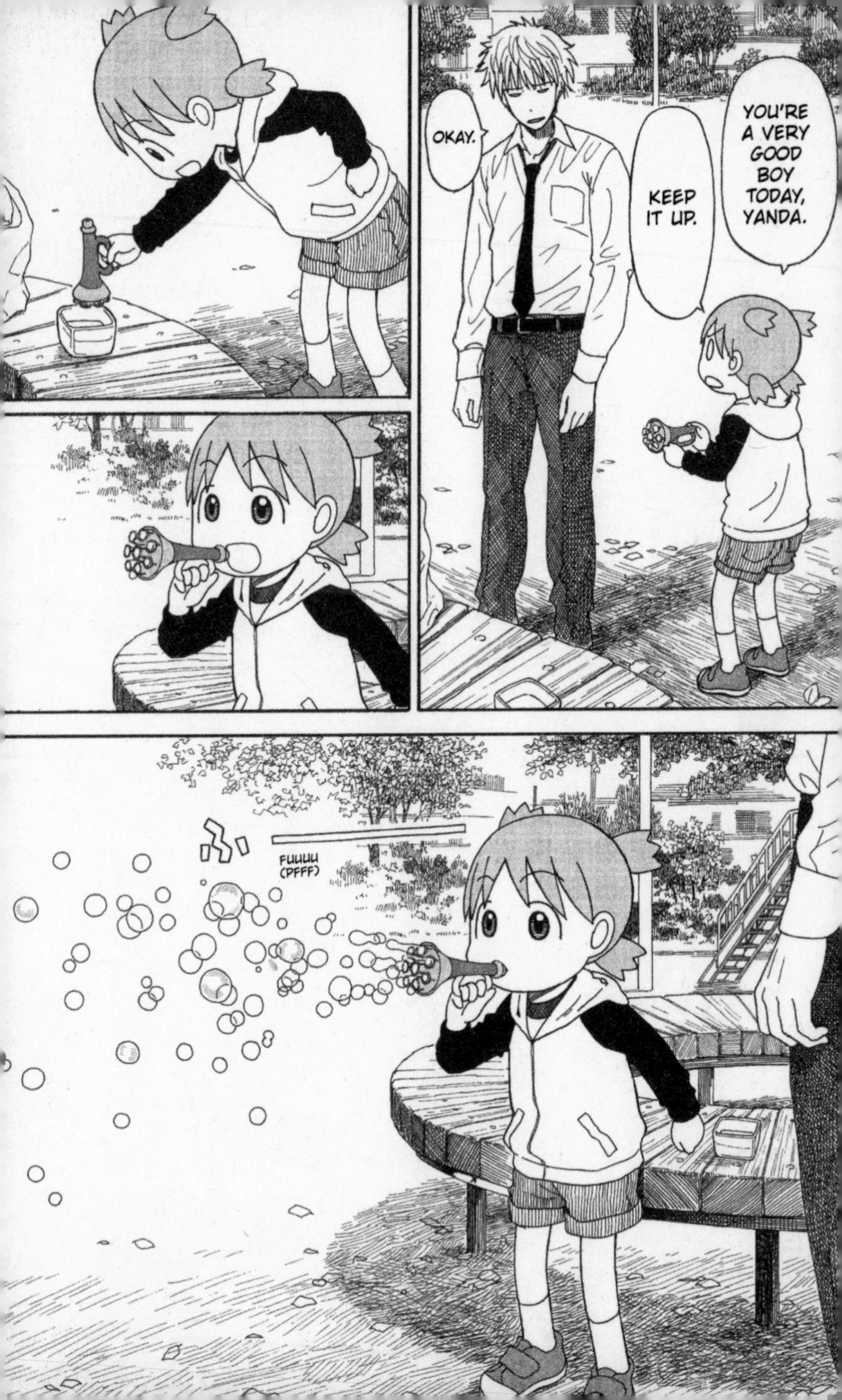
YOU'RE A VERY GOOD BOY TODAY, YANDA.
KEEP IT UP.
OKAY.
FUUUU (PFFF)

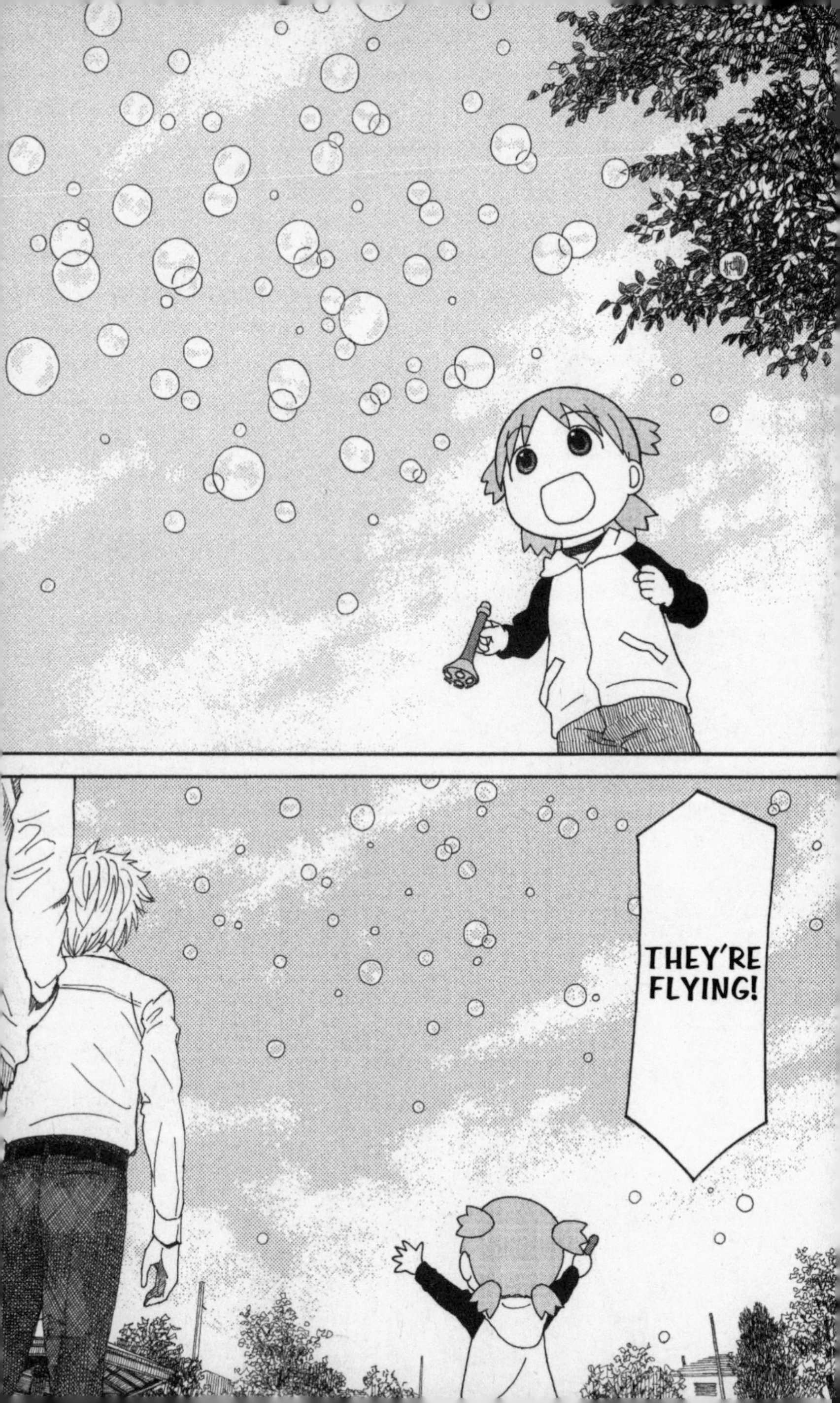
THEY'RE FLYING!

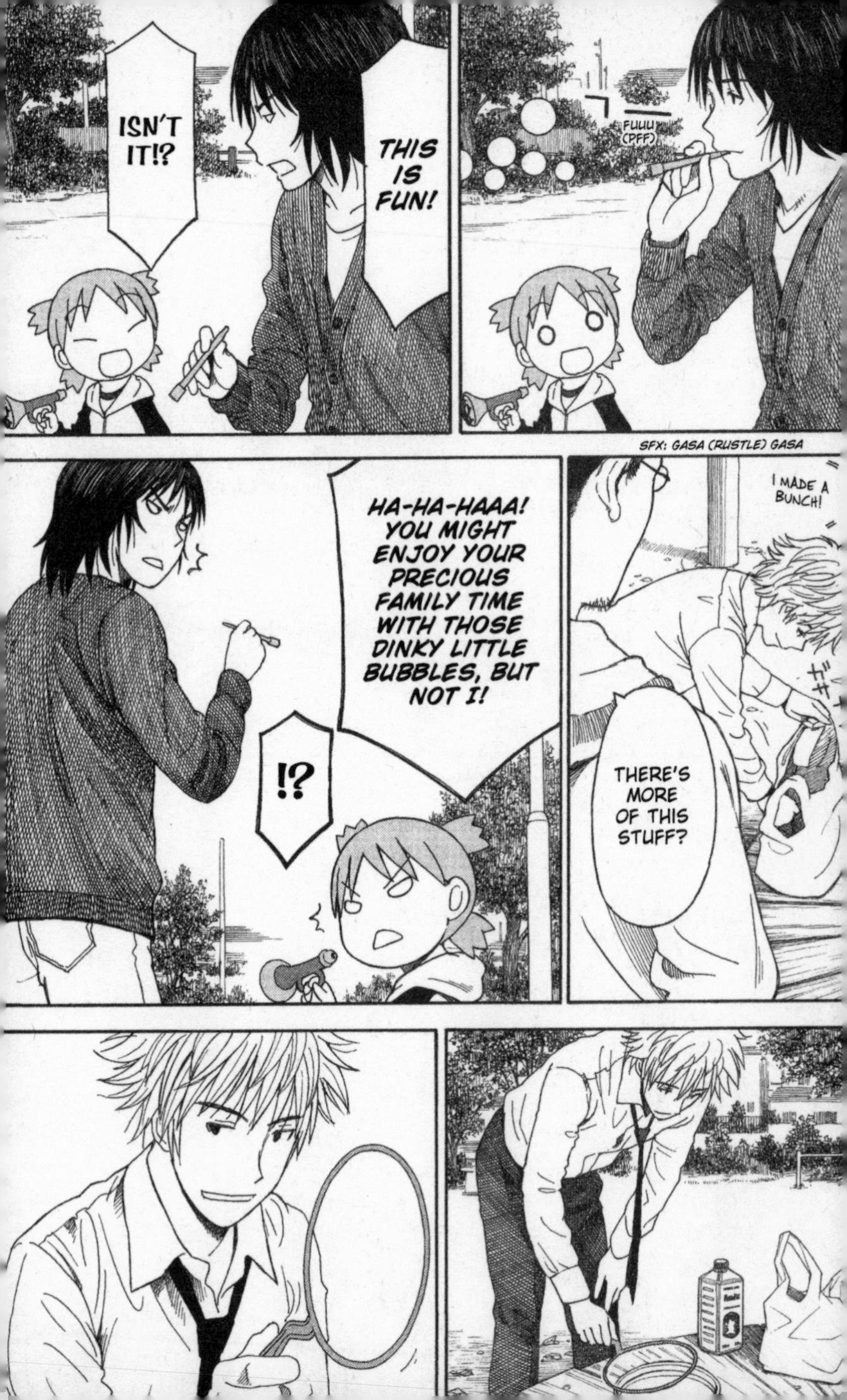
FUUU (PFFF)
THIS IS FUN!
ISN'T IT!?
SFX: GASA (RUSTLE) GASA
I MADE A BUNCH!
THERE'S MORE OF THIS STUFF?
HA-HA-HAAA! YOU MIGHT ENJOY YOUR PRECIOUS FAMILY TIME WITH THOSE DINKY LITTLE BUBBLES, BUT NOT I!
!?

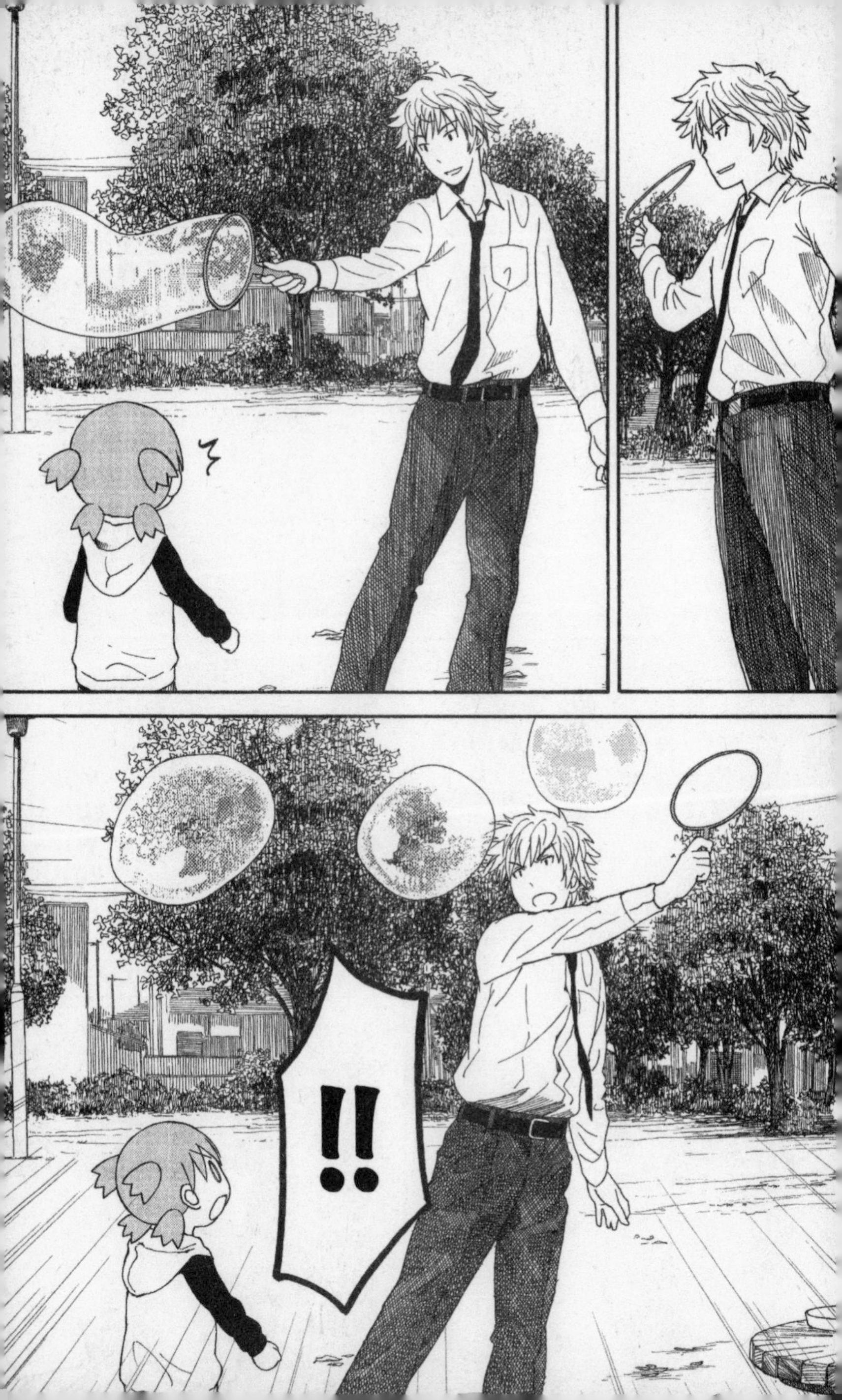
!!

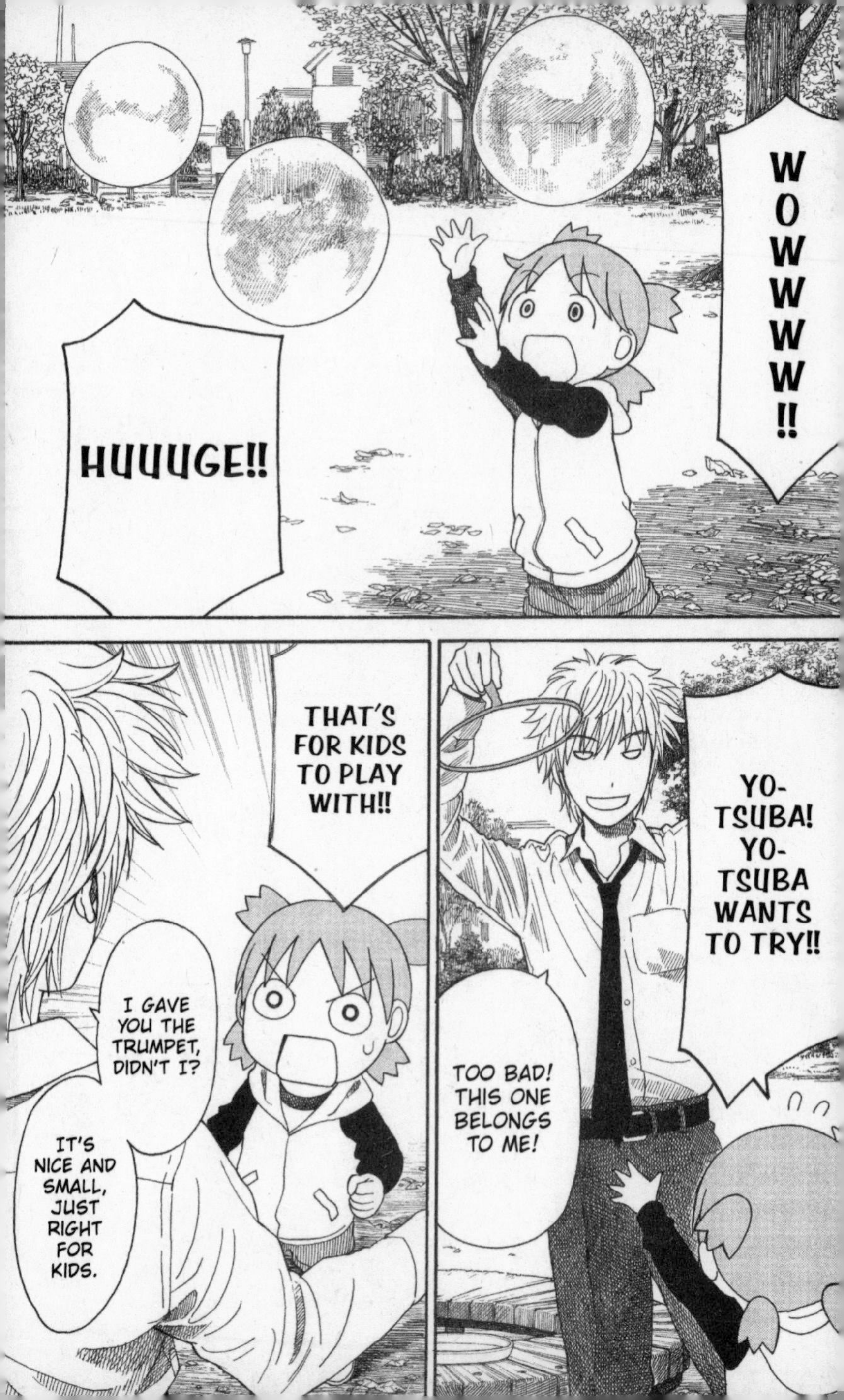
WOWWWWW!!
HUUUGE!!
YO-TSUBA! YO-TSUBA WANTS TO TRY!!
TOO BAD! THIS ONE BELONGS TO ME!
THAT'S FOR KIDS TO PLAY WITH!!
I GAVE YOU THE TRUMPET, DIDN'T I?
IT'S NICE AND SMALL, JUST RIGHT FOR KIDS.

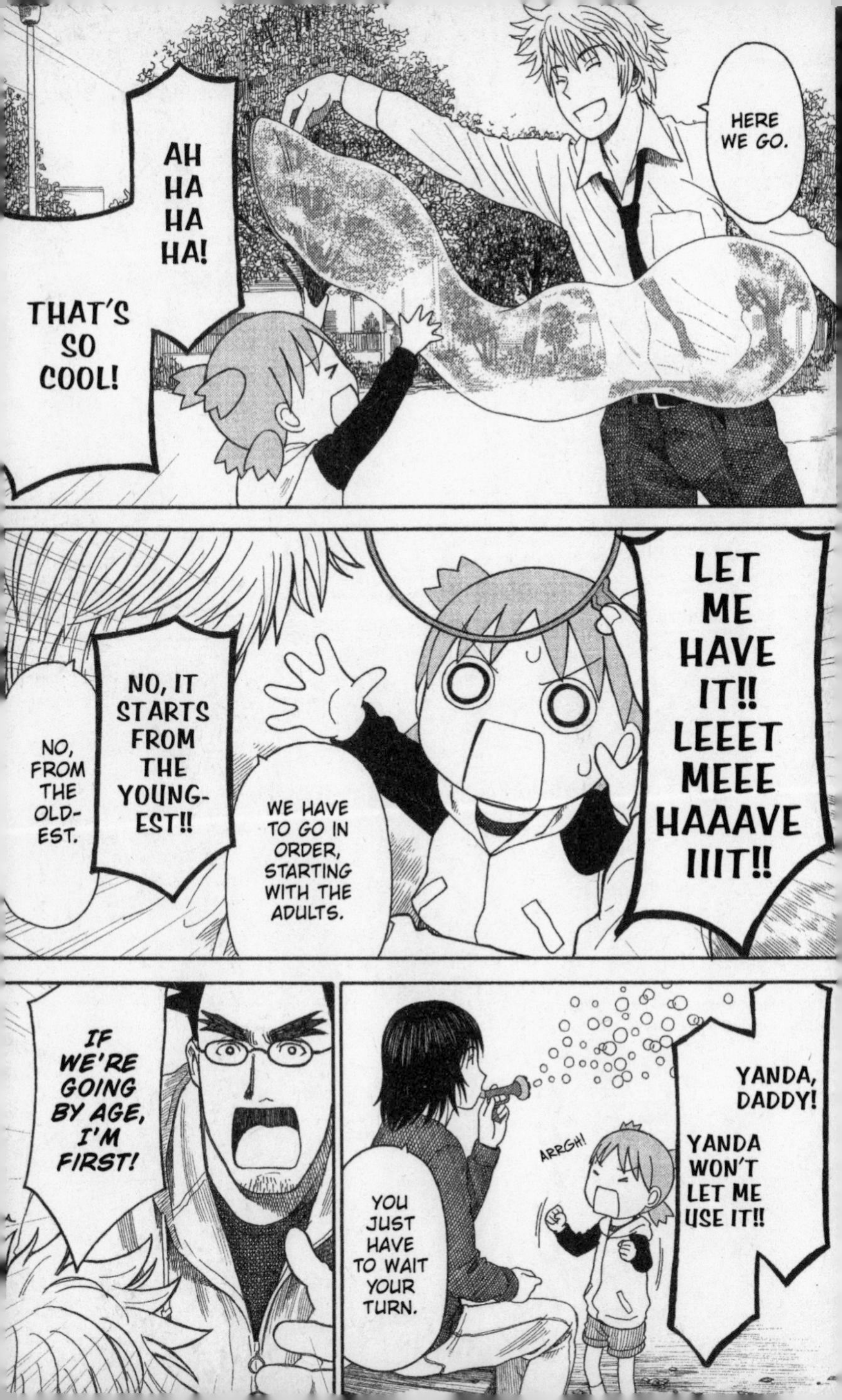
HERE WE GO.
AH HA HA HA!
THAT'S SO COOL!
LET ME HAVE IT!! LEEET MEEE HAAAVE IIIT!!
WE HAVE TO GO IN ORDER, STARTING WITH THE ADULTS.
NO, IT STARTS FROM THE YOUNG-EST!!
NO, FROM THE OLD-EST.
YANDA, DADDY!
YANDA WON'T LET ME USE IT!!
ARRGH!
YOU JUST HAVE TO WAIT YOUR TURN.
IF WE'RE GOING BY AGE, I'M FIRST!

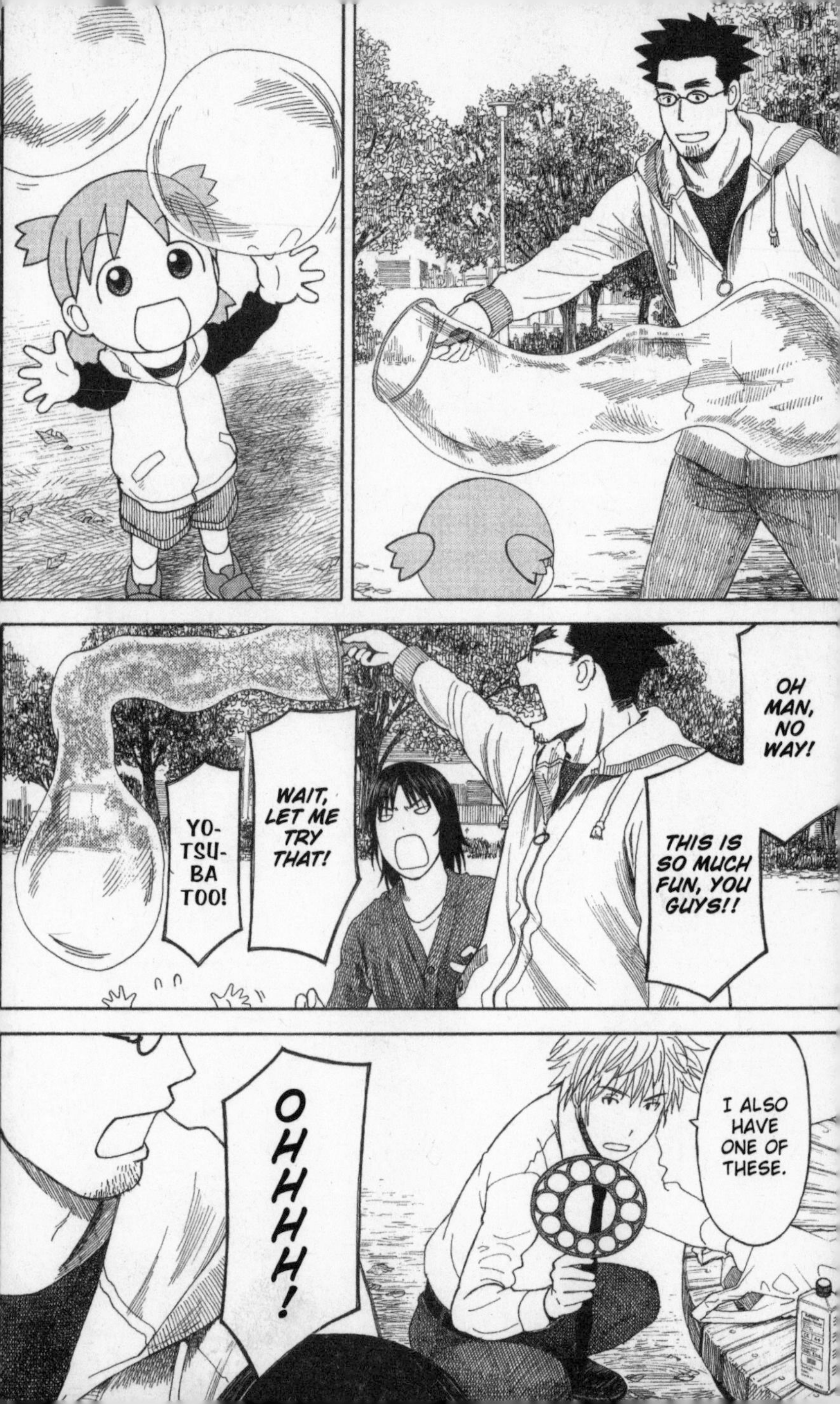
OH MAN, NO WAY!
THIS IS SO MUCH FUN, YOU GUYS!!
WAIT, LET ME TRY THAT!
YO-TSU-BA TOO!
I ALSO HAVE ONE OF THESE.
OHHHHH!

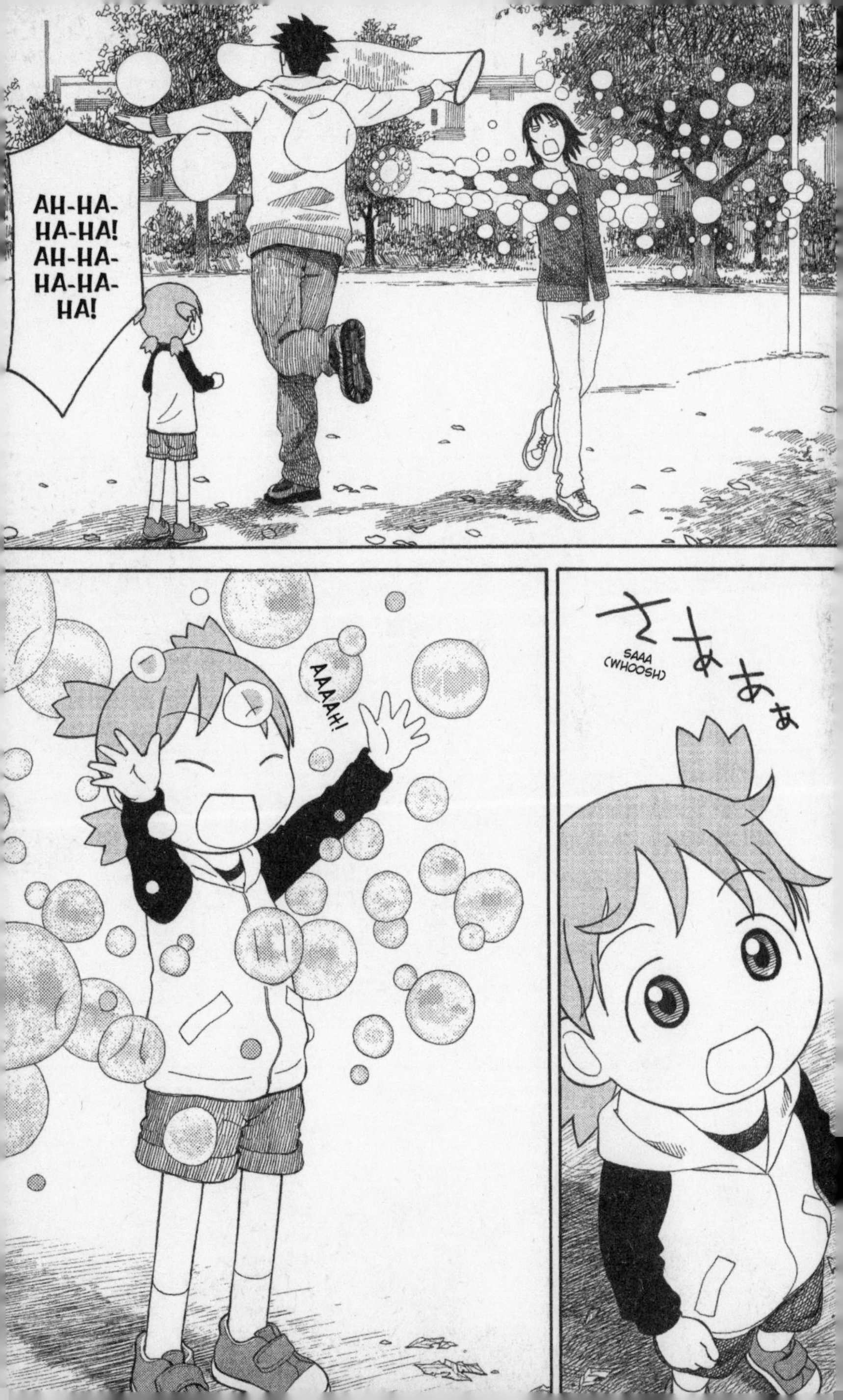
AH-HA-HA-HA! AH-HA-HA-HA-HA-HA!
さあぁぁ
SAAA (WHOOSH)
AAAAH!

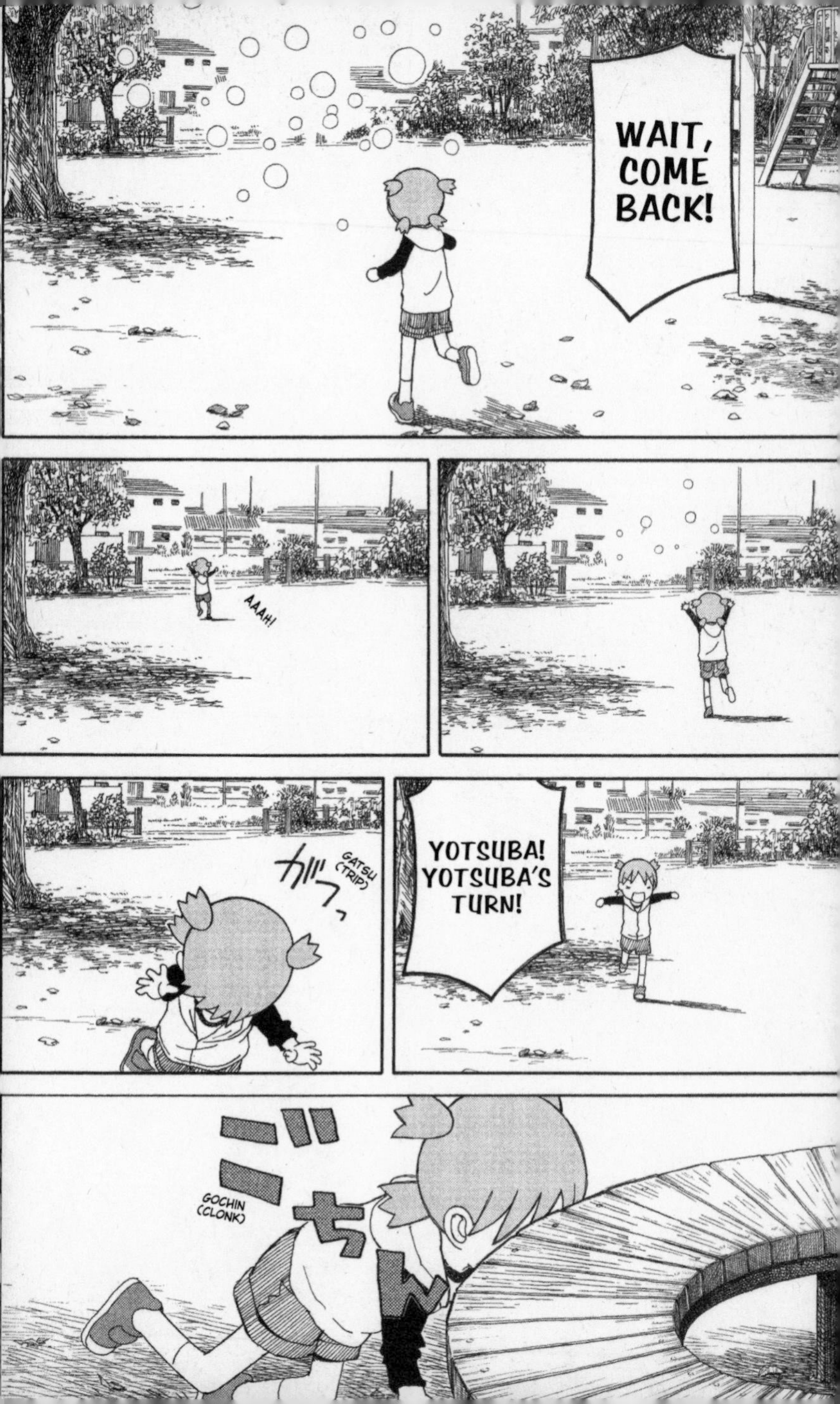
WAIT, COME BACK!
AAAH!
YOTSUBA! YOTSUBA'S TURN!
GATSU (TRIP)
GOCHIN (CLONK)

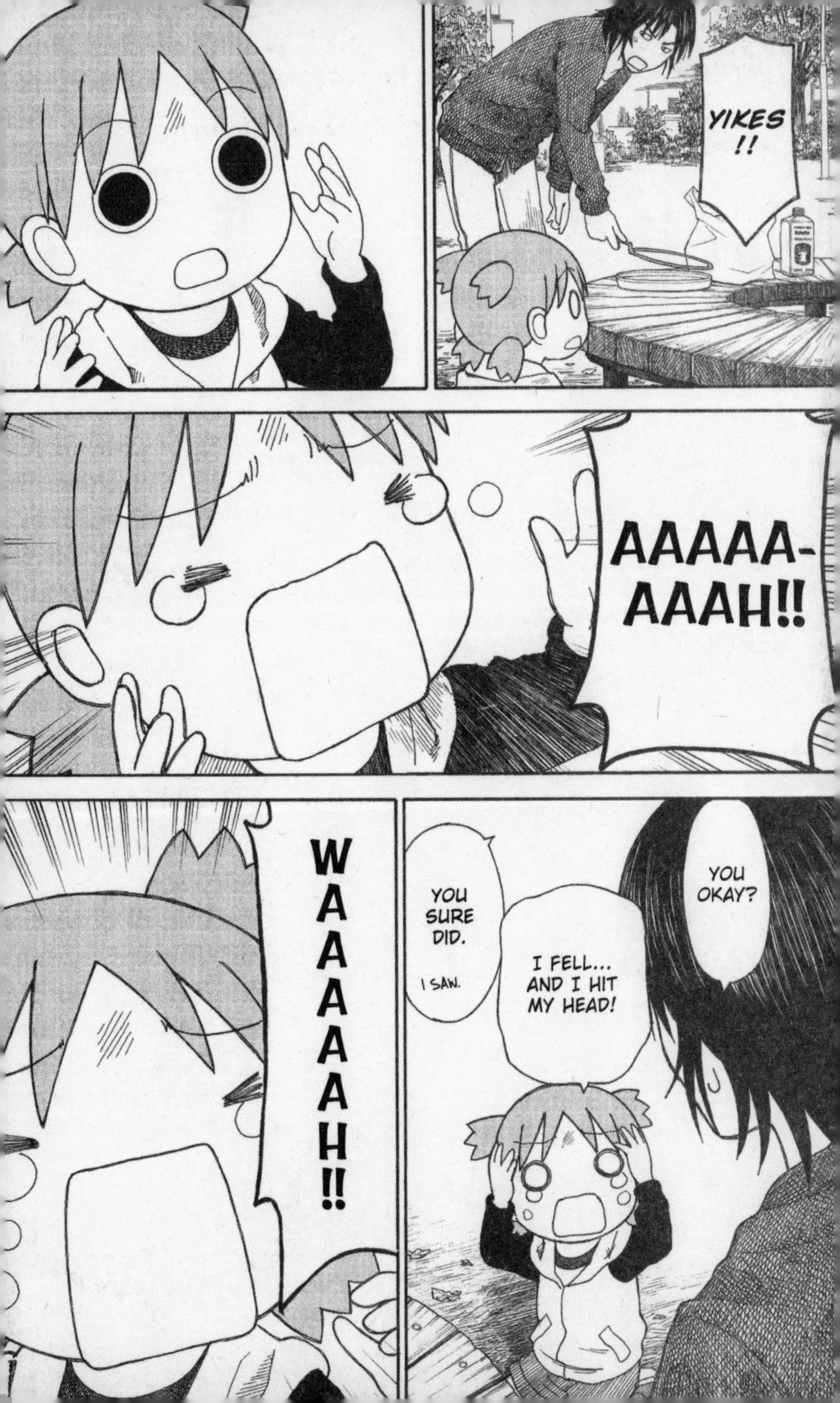
YIKES !!
AAAAA-AAAH!!
YOU OKAY?
I FELL... AND I HIT MY HEAD!
YOU SURE DID.
I SAW.
WAAAAAAAH!!

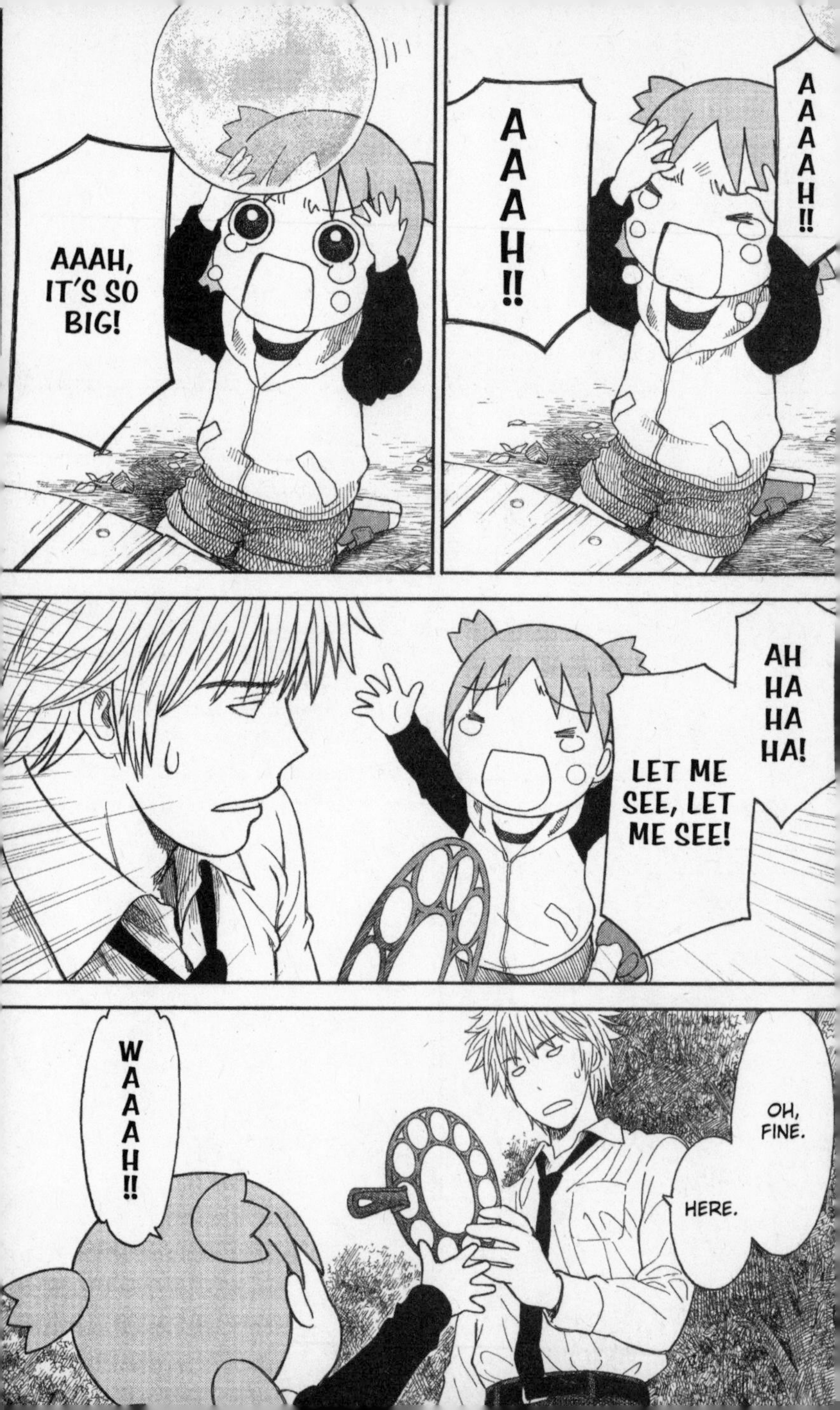
AAAAH!!
AAAH!!
AAAH, IT'S SO BIG!
AH HA HA HA!
LET ME SEE, LET ME SEE!
OH, FINE.
HERE.
WAAAAH!!

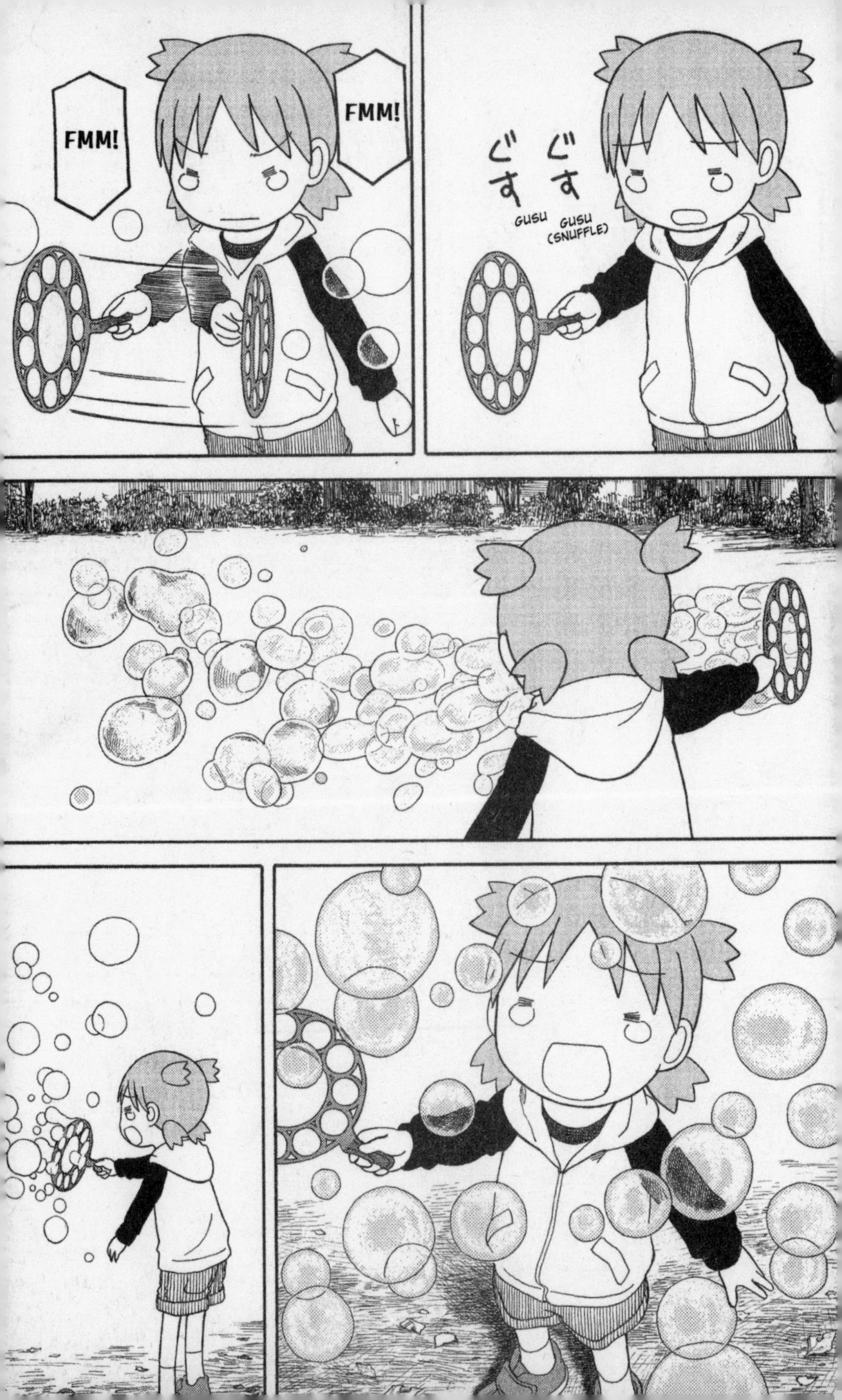

FMM!
FMM!
ぐす ぐす
GUSU GUSU (SNUFFLE)

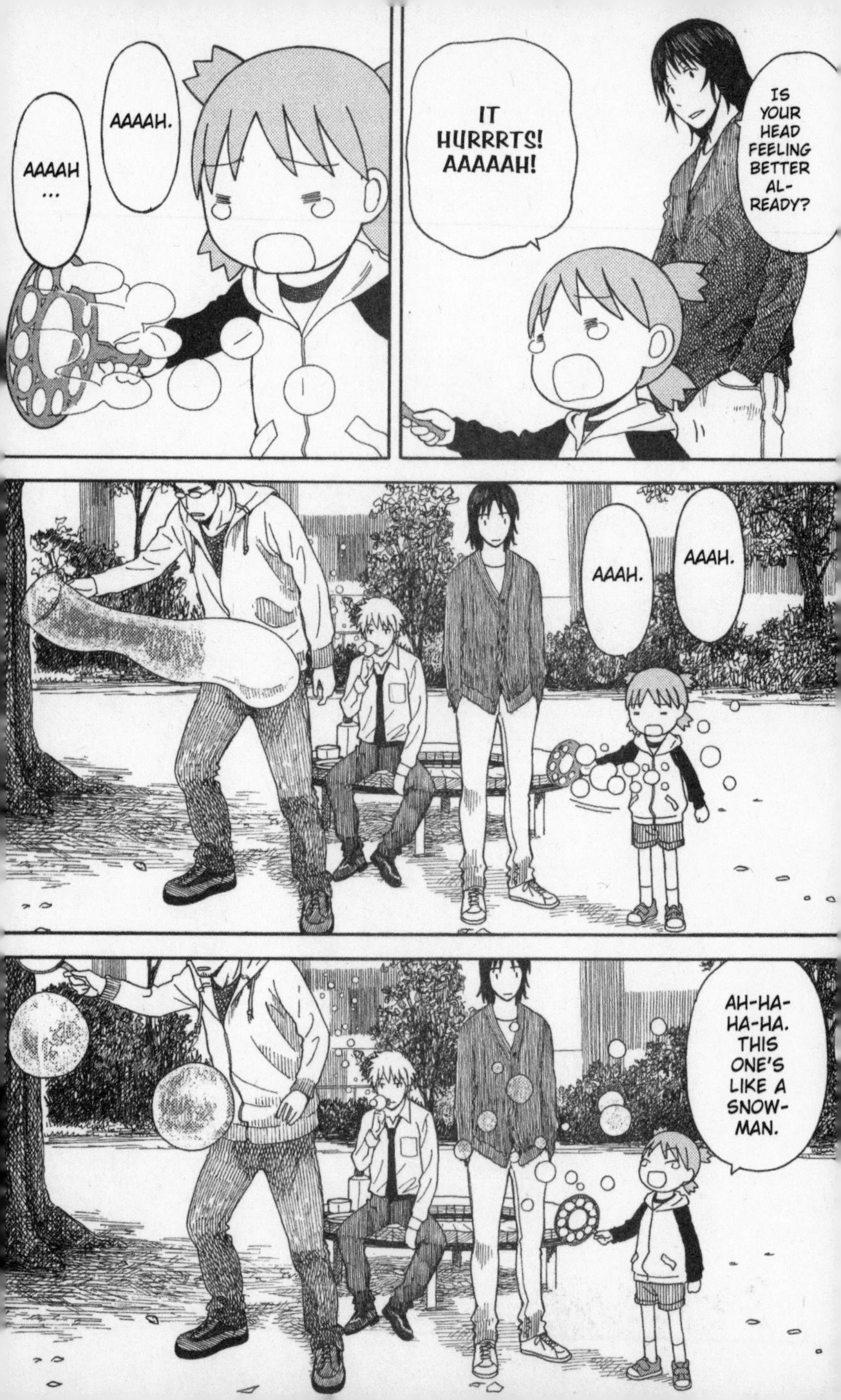
IS YOUR HEAD FEELING BETTER AL-READY?
IT HURRRTS! AAAAAH!
AAAAH.
AAAAH ...
AAAH.
AAAH.
AH-HA-HA-HA. THIS ONE'S LIKE A SNOW-MAN.

YOTSUBA&!

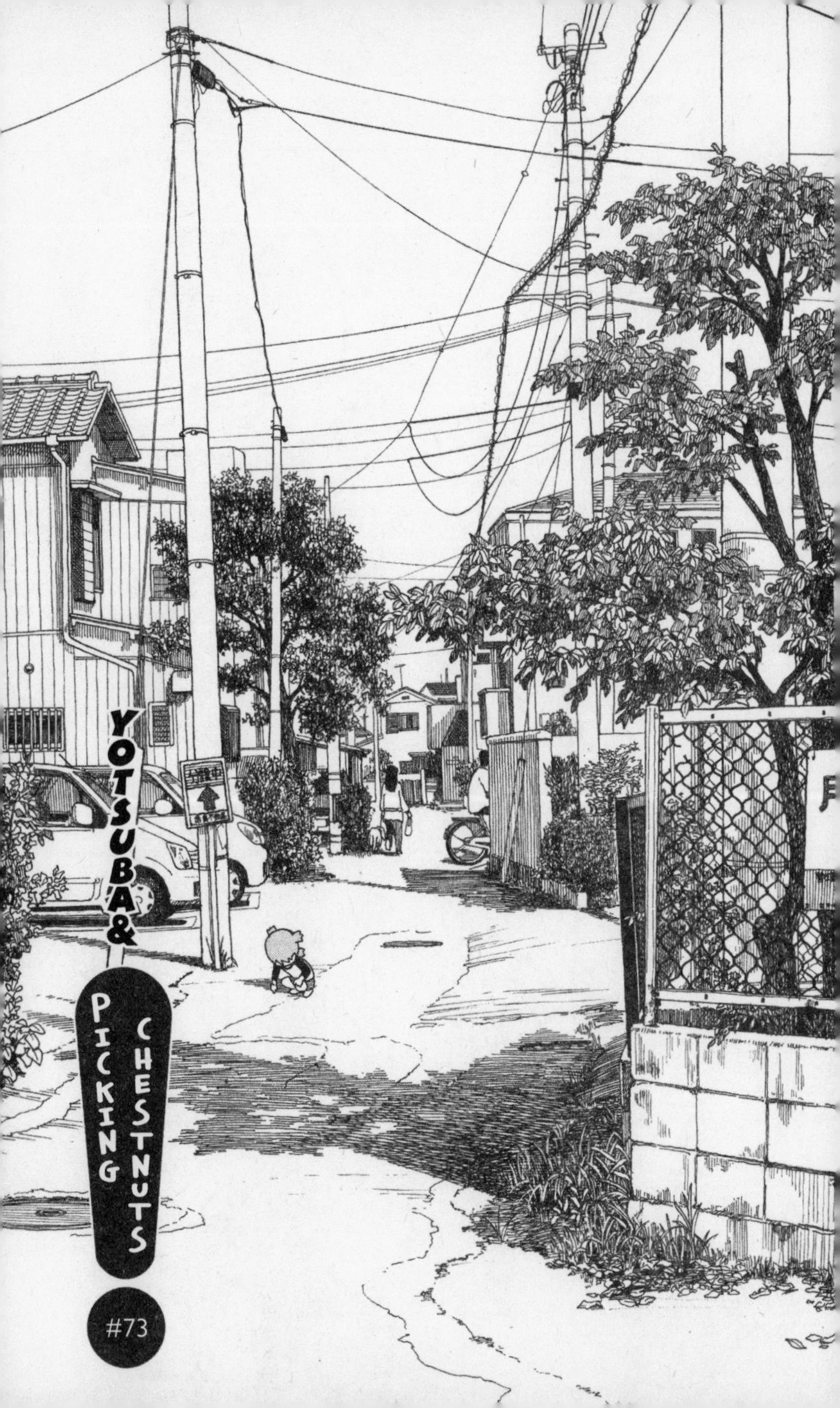
YOTSUBA&
PICKING CHESTNUTS
#73

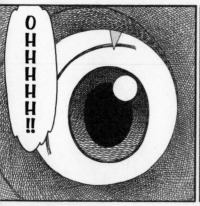

OHHHHH!!

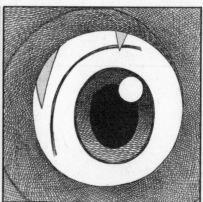

IS THIS A MAGIC TRICK!?

UMM... KIND OF.

I KNOW.

THERE'S A HOLE IN MY HAND!

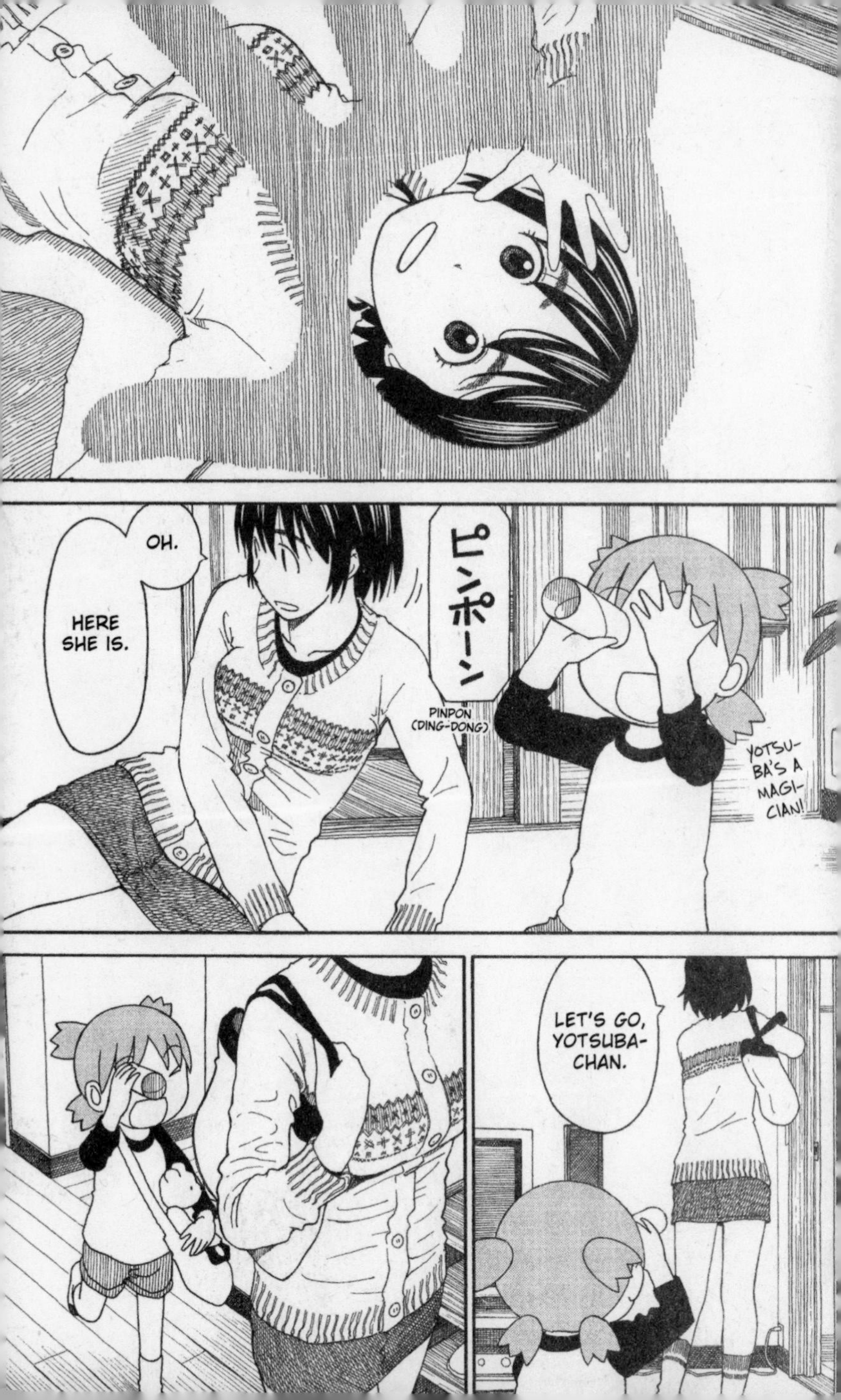
OH.
HERE SHE IS.
ピンポーン
PINPON (DING-DONG)
YOTSUBA'S A MAGICIAN!
LET'S GO, YOTSUBA-CHAN.

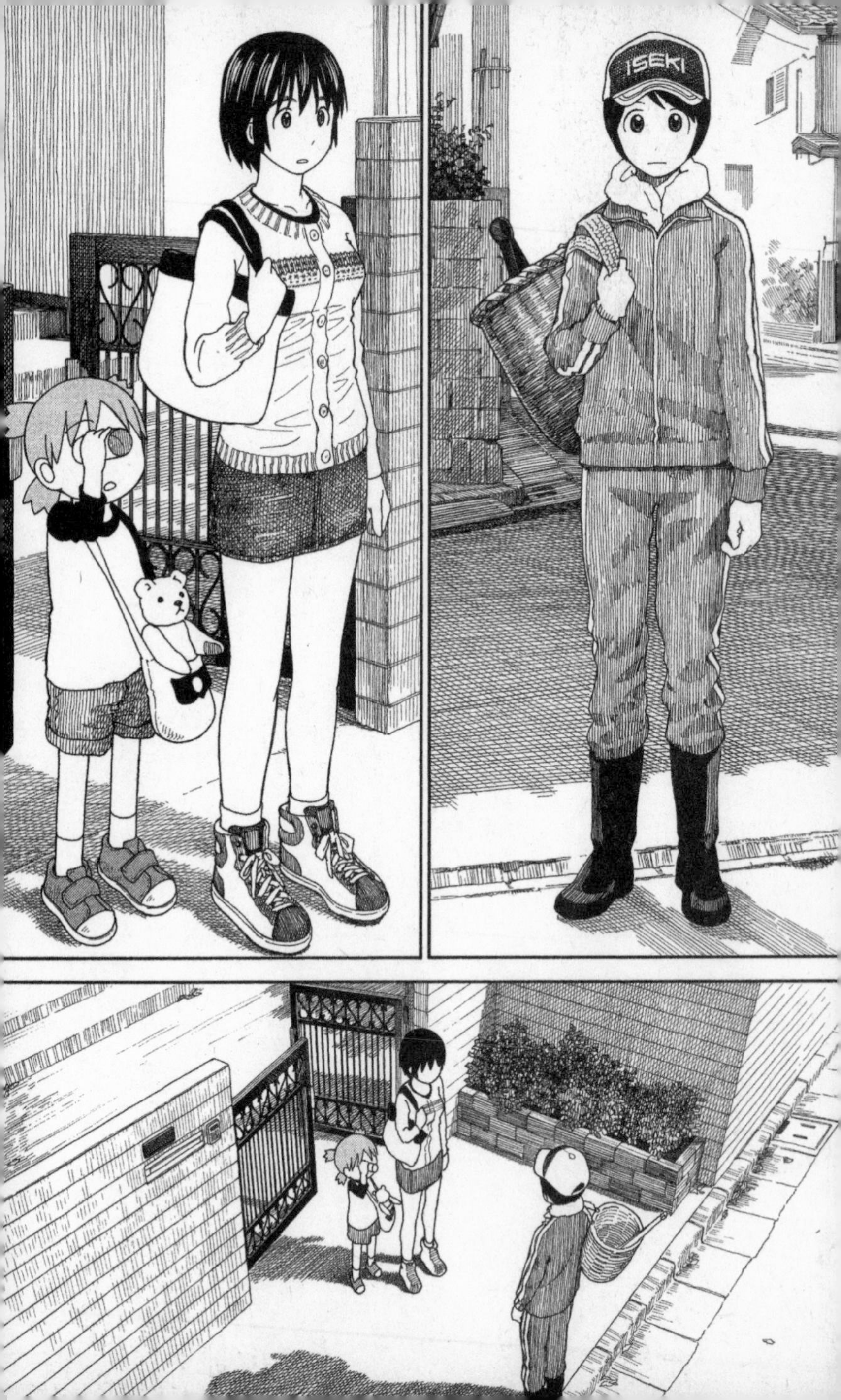
ISEKI

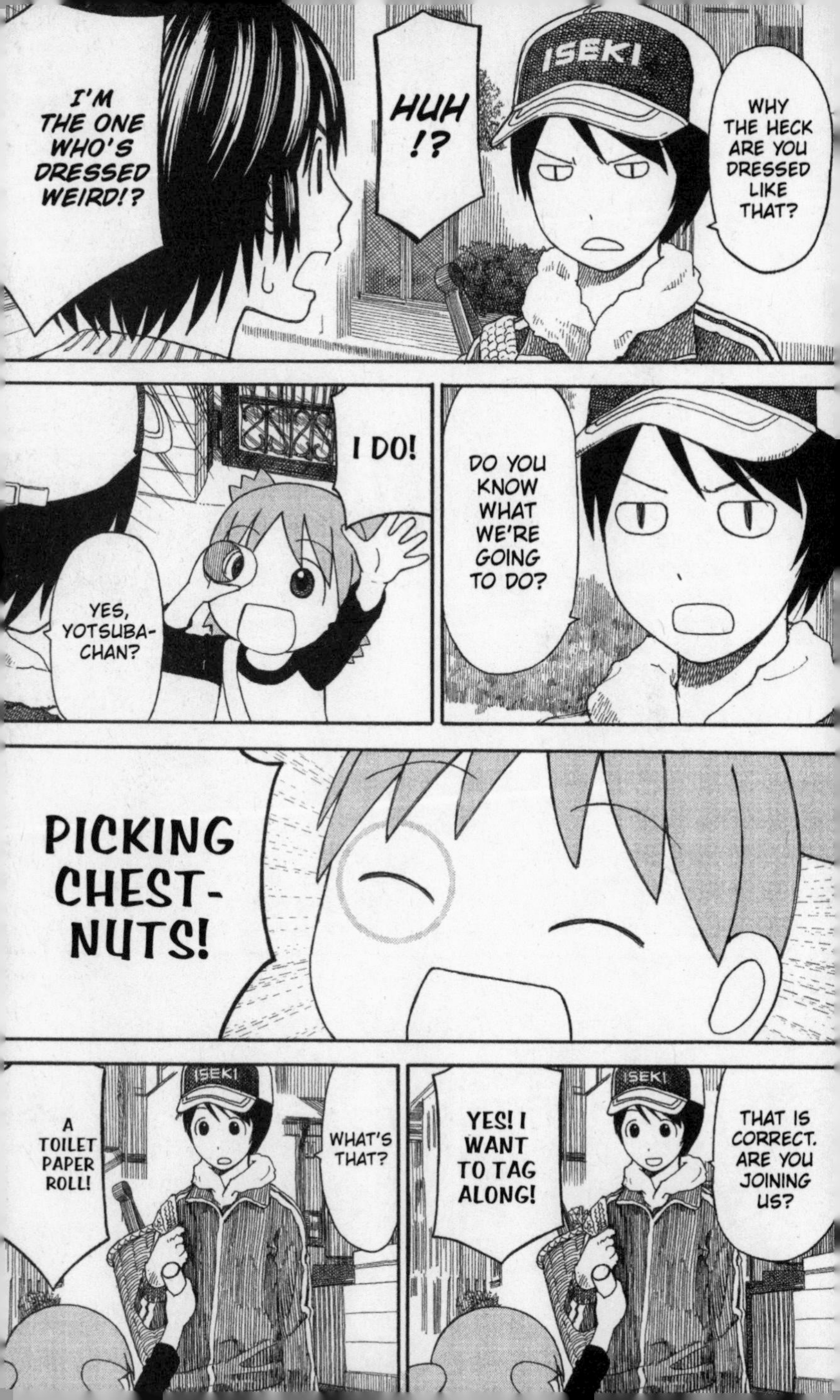
WHY THE HECK ARE YOU DRESSED LIKE THAT?
HUH!?
I'M THE ONE WHO'S DRESSED WEIRD!?
DO YOU KNOW WHAT WE'RE GOING TO DO?
I DO!
YES, YOTSUBA-CHAN?
PICKING CHEST-NUTS!
THAT IS CORRECT. ARE YOU JOINING US?
YES! I WANT TO TAG ALONG!
WHAT'S THAT?
A TOILET PAPER ROLL!

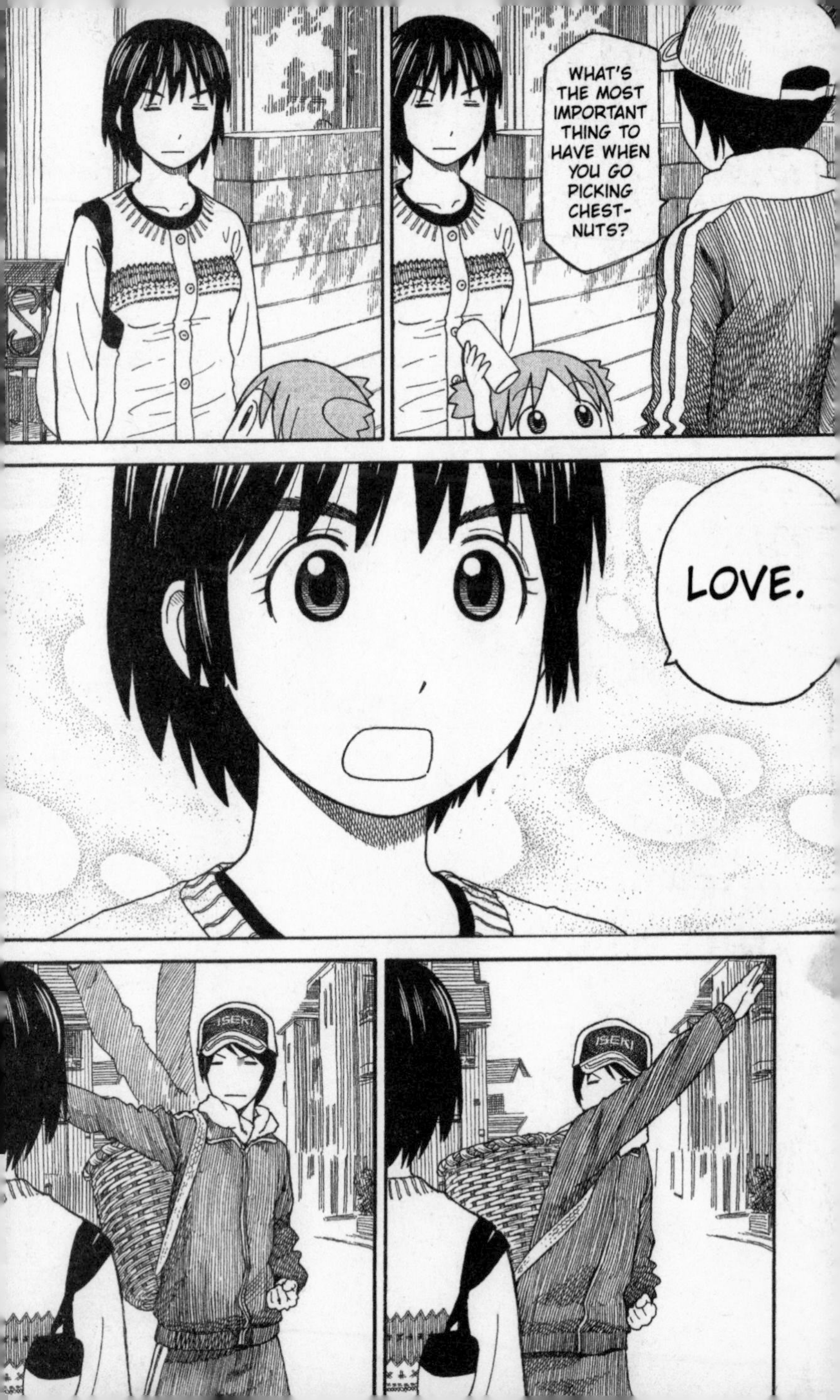
WHAT'S THE MOST IMPORTANT THING TO HAVE WHEN YOU GO PICKING CHEST-NUTS?
LOVE.

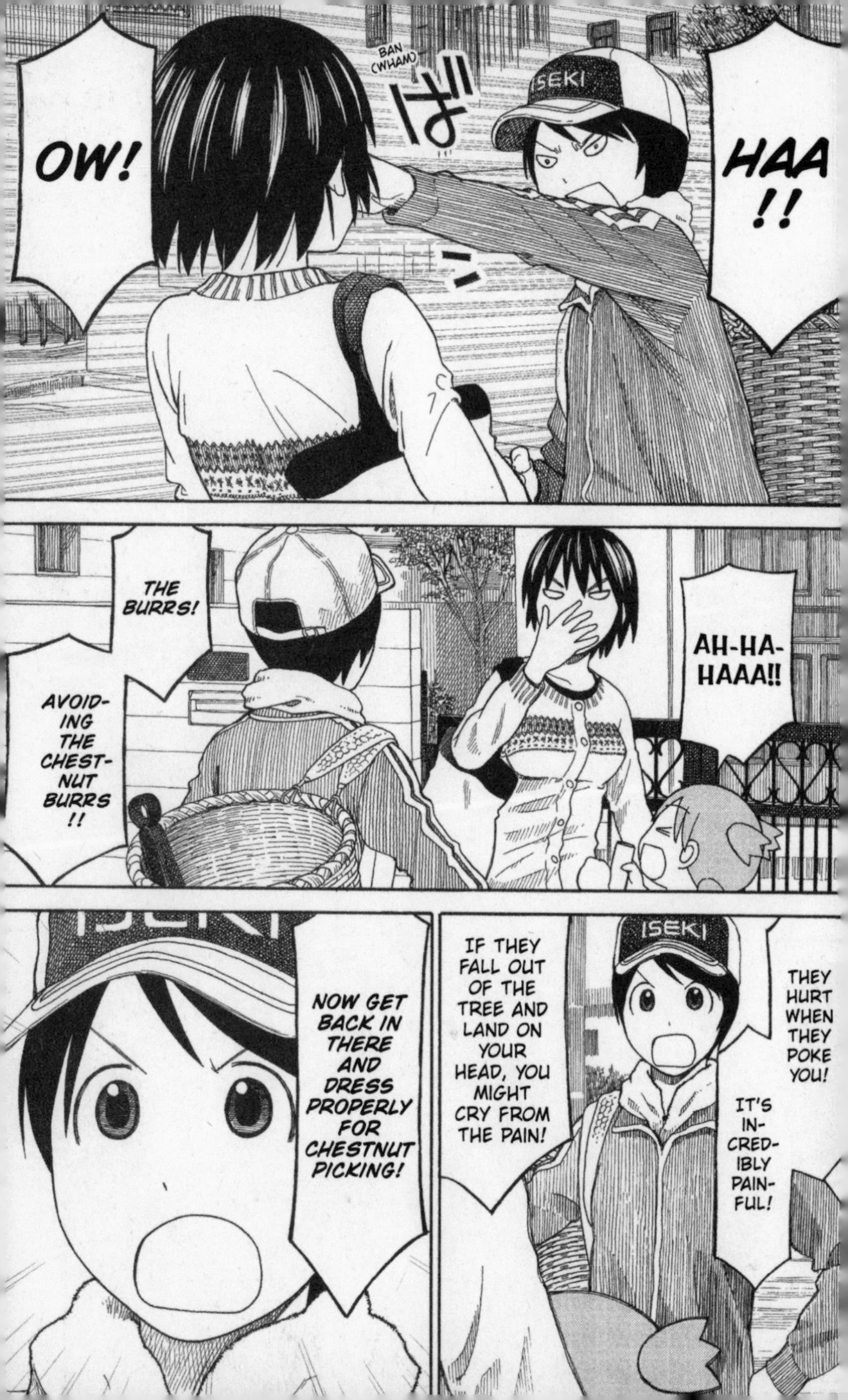

HAA!!
BAN (WHAM)
OW!
AH-HA-HAAA!!
THE BURRS!
AVOIDING THE CHESTNUT BURRS!!
THEY HURT WHEN THEY POKE YOU!
IT'S INCREDIBLY PAINFUL!
IF THEY FALL OUT OF THE TREE AND LAND ON YOUR HEAD, YOU MIGHT CRY FROM THE PAIN!
NOW GET BACK IN THERE AND DRESS PROPERLY FOR CHESTNUT PICKING!

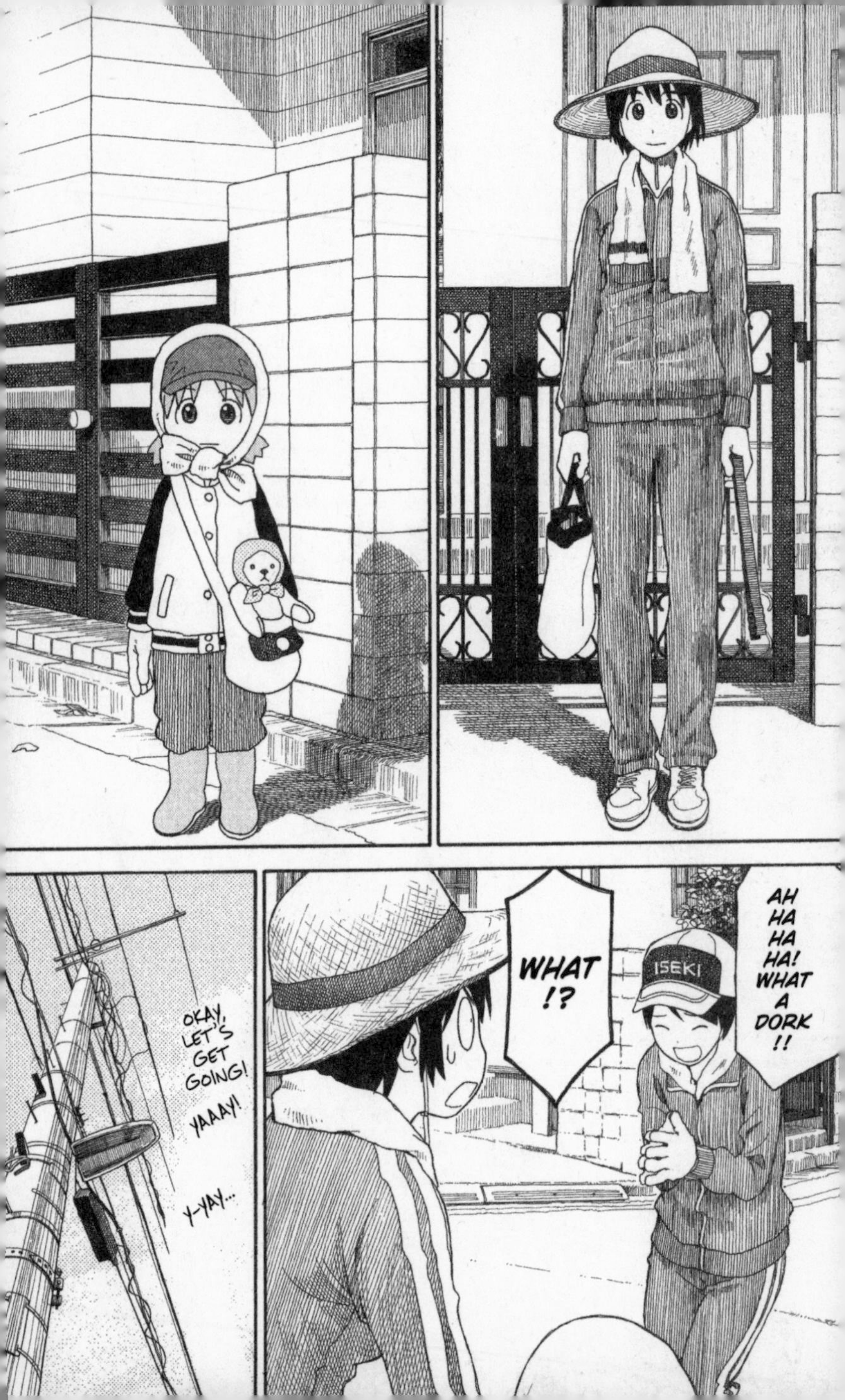
AH HA HA HA! WHAT A DORK!!
ISEKI
WHAT!?
OKAY, LET'S GET GOING!
YAAAY!
Y-YAY...

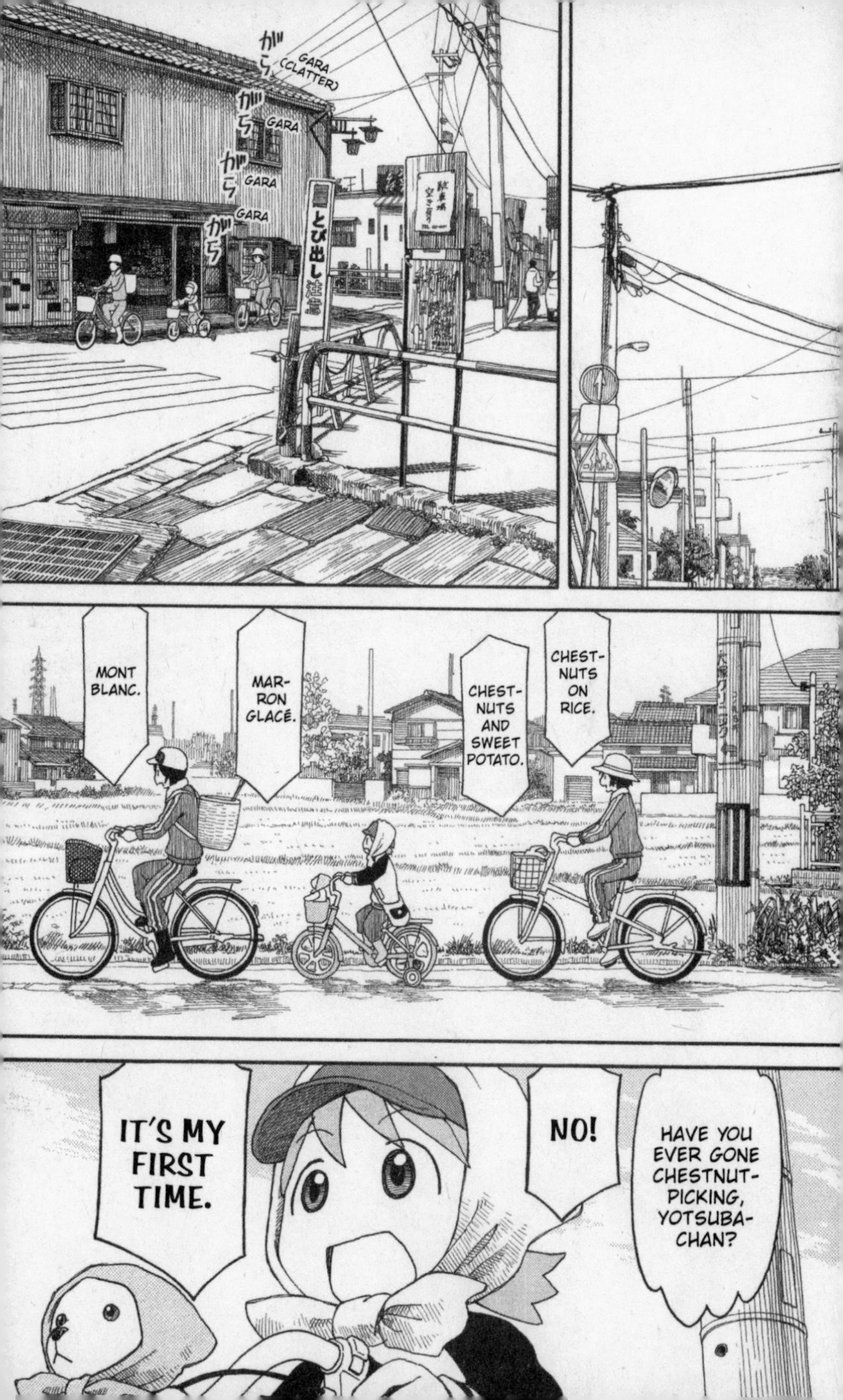
がら
GARA (CLATTER)
がら
GARA
がら
GARA
がら
GARA
とび出し注意
CHESTNUTS ON RICE.
CHESTNUTS AND SWEET POTATO.
MARRON GLACÉ.
MONT BLANC.
HAVE YOU EVER GONE CHESTNUT-PICKING, YOTSUBA-CHAN?
NO!
IT'S MY FIRST TIME.

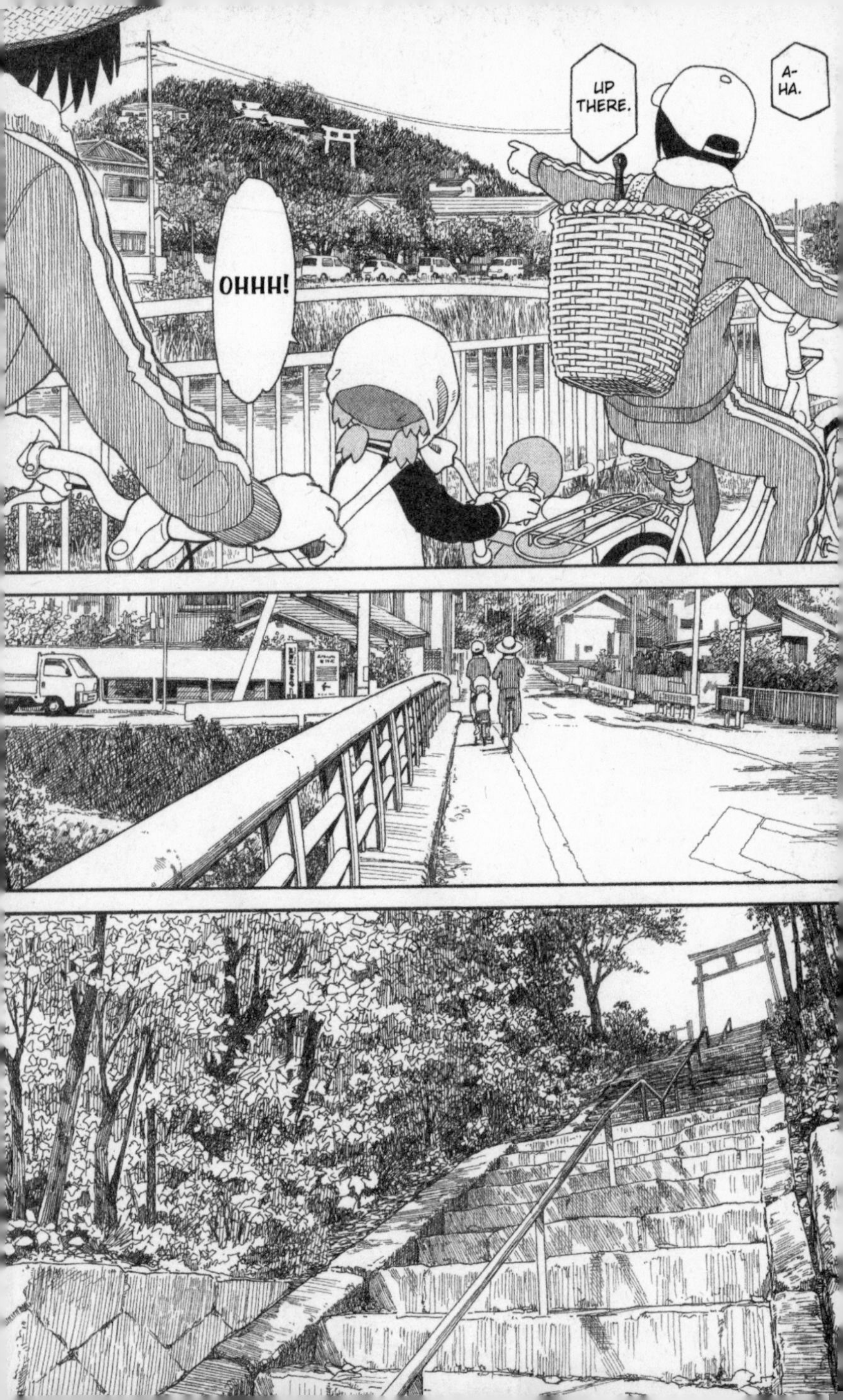
A-HA.
UP THERE.
OHHH!

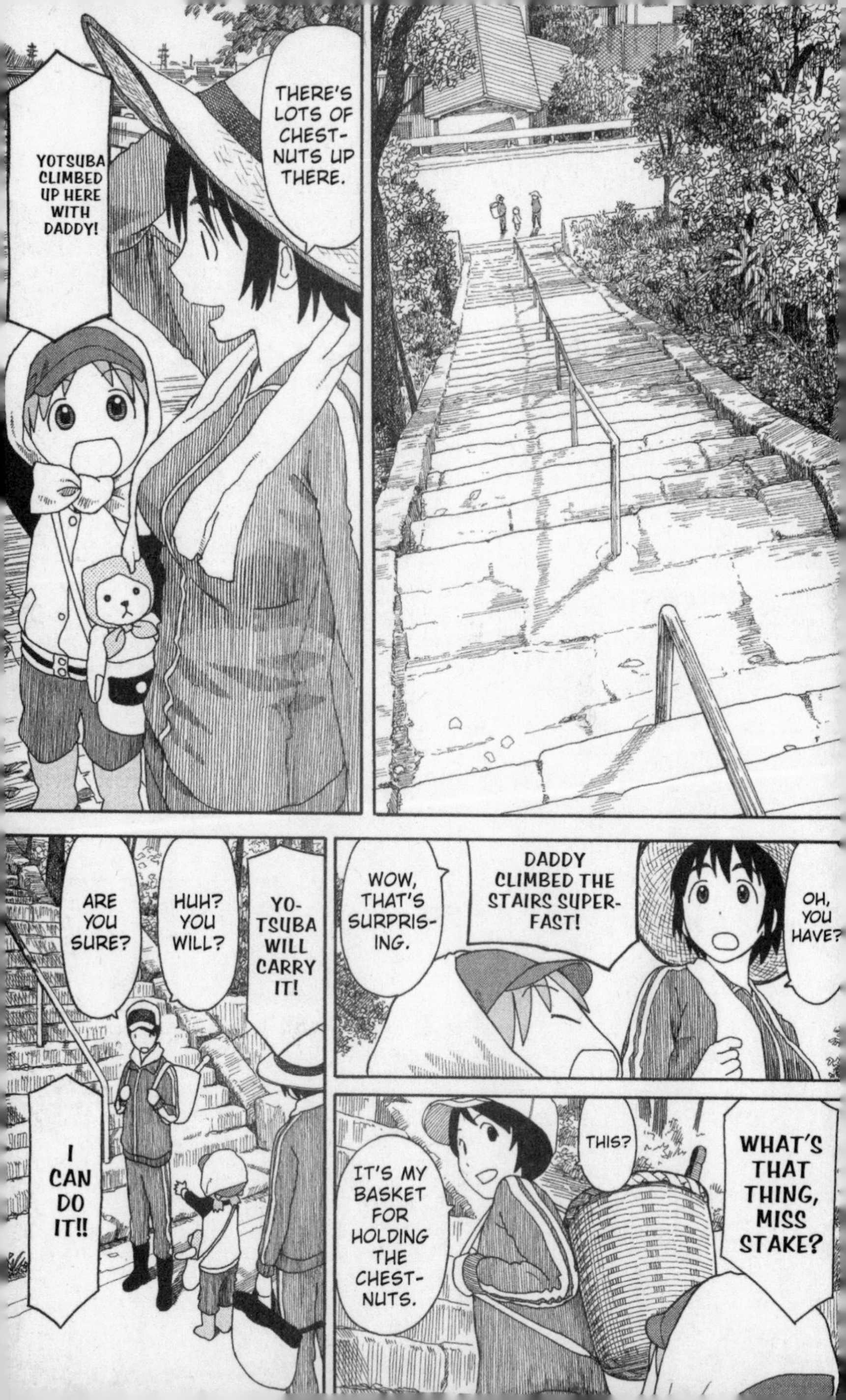
THERE'S LOTS OF CHEST-NUTS UP THERE.
YOTSUBA CLIMBED UP HERE WITH DADDY!
OH, YOU HAVE?
DADDY CLIMBED THE STAIRS SUPER-FAST!
WOW, THAT'S SURPRIS-ING.
WHAT'S THAT THING, MISS STAKE?
THIS?
IT'S MY BASKET FOR HOLDING THE CHEST-NUTS.
YO-TSUBA WILL CARRY IT!
HUH? YOU WILL?
ARE YOU SURE?
I CAN DO IT!!

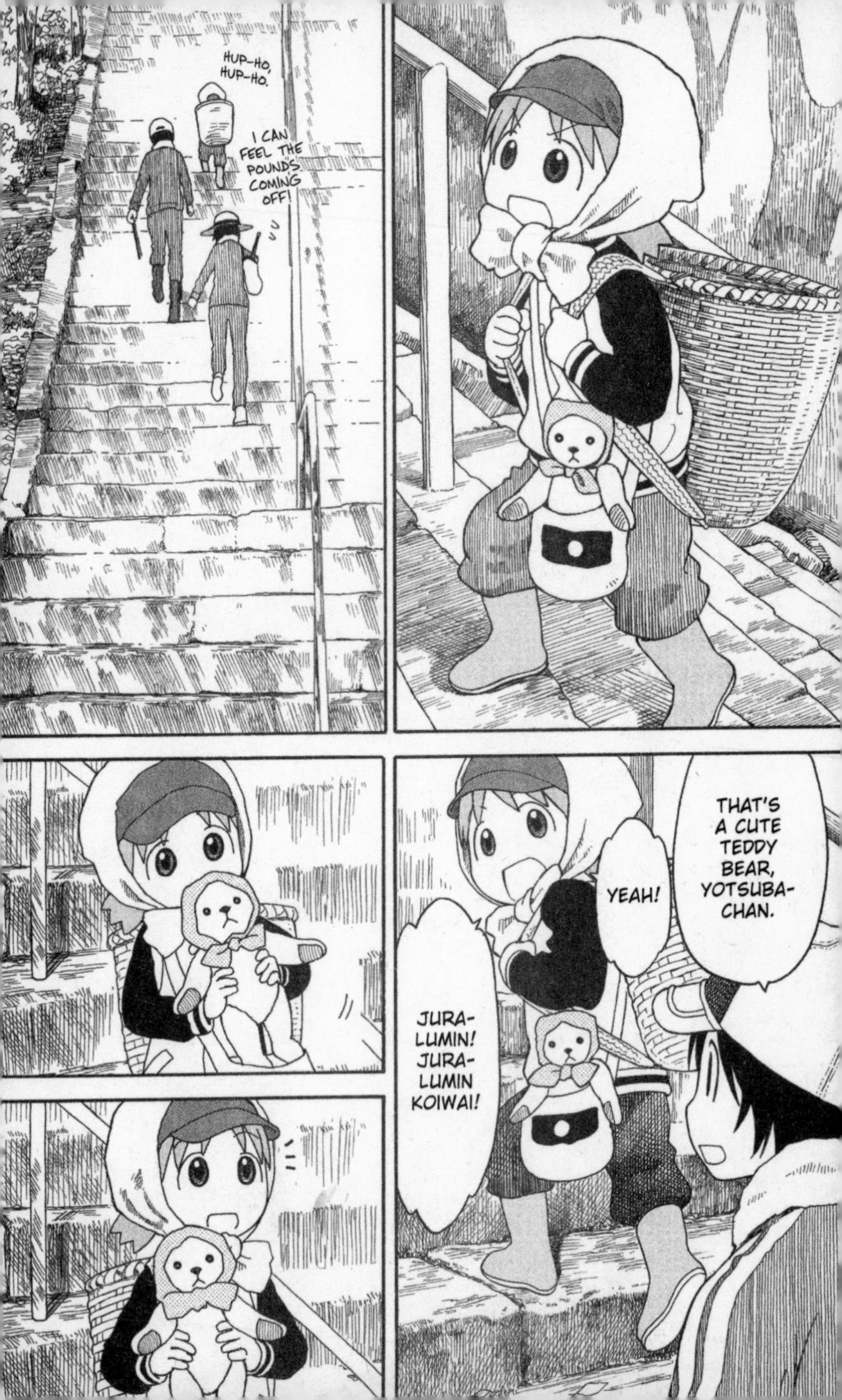

HUP-HO, HUP-HO.
I CAN FEEL THE POUNDS COMING OFF!
THAT'S A CUTE TEDDY BEAR, YOTSUBA-CHAN.
YEAH!
JURA-LUMIN! JURA-LUMIN KOIWAI!

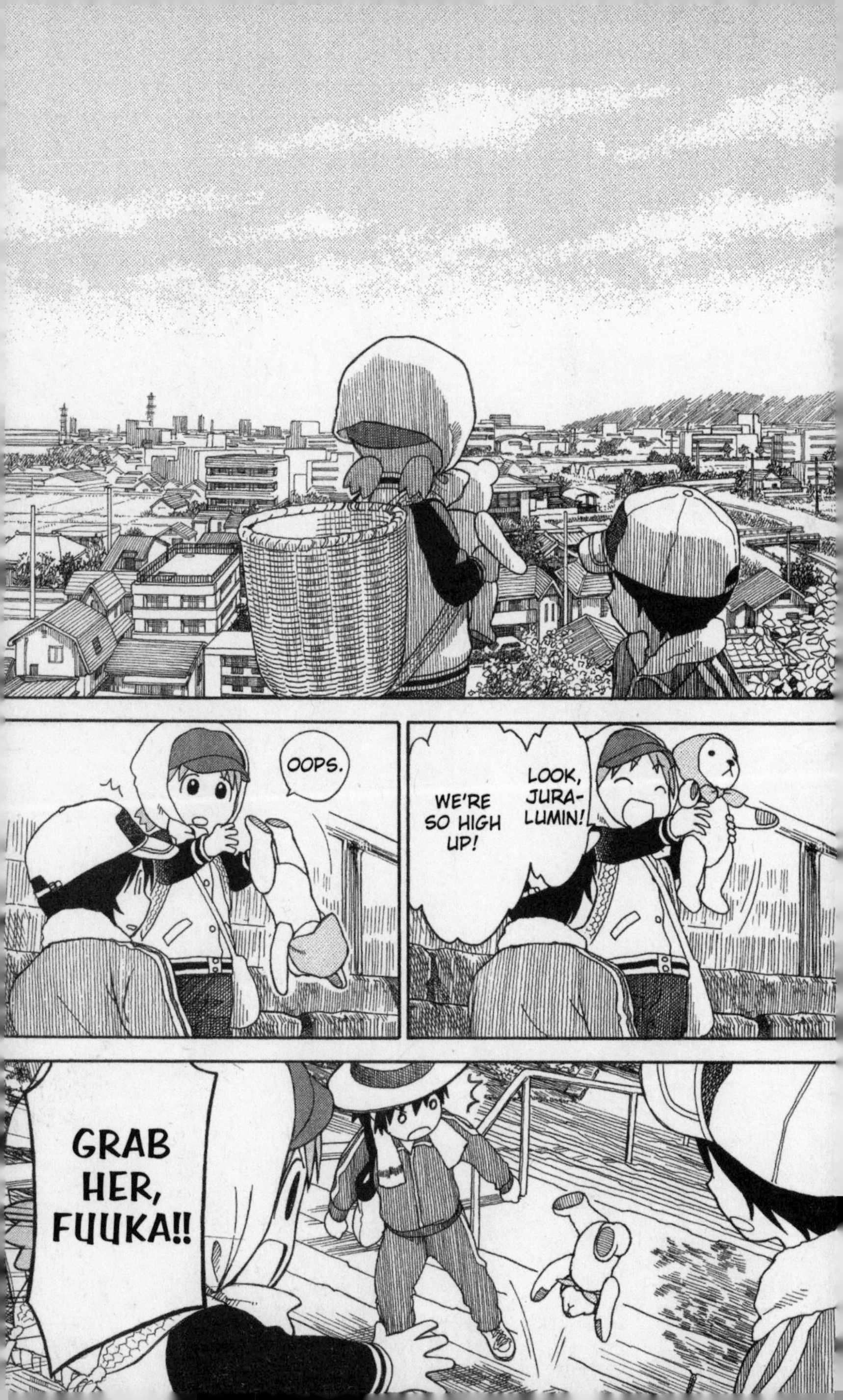
OOPS.
LOOK, JURA-LUMIN!
WE'RE SO HIGH UP!
GRAB HER, FUUKA!!

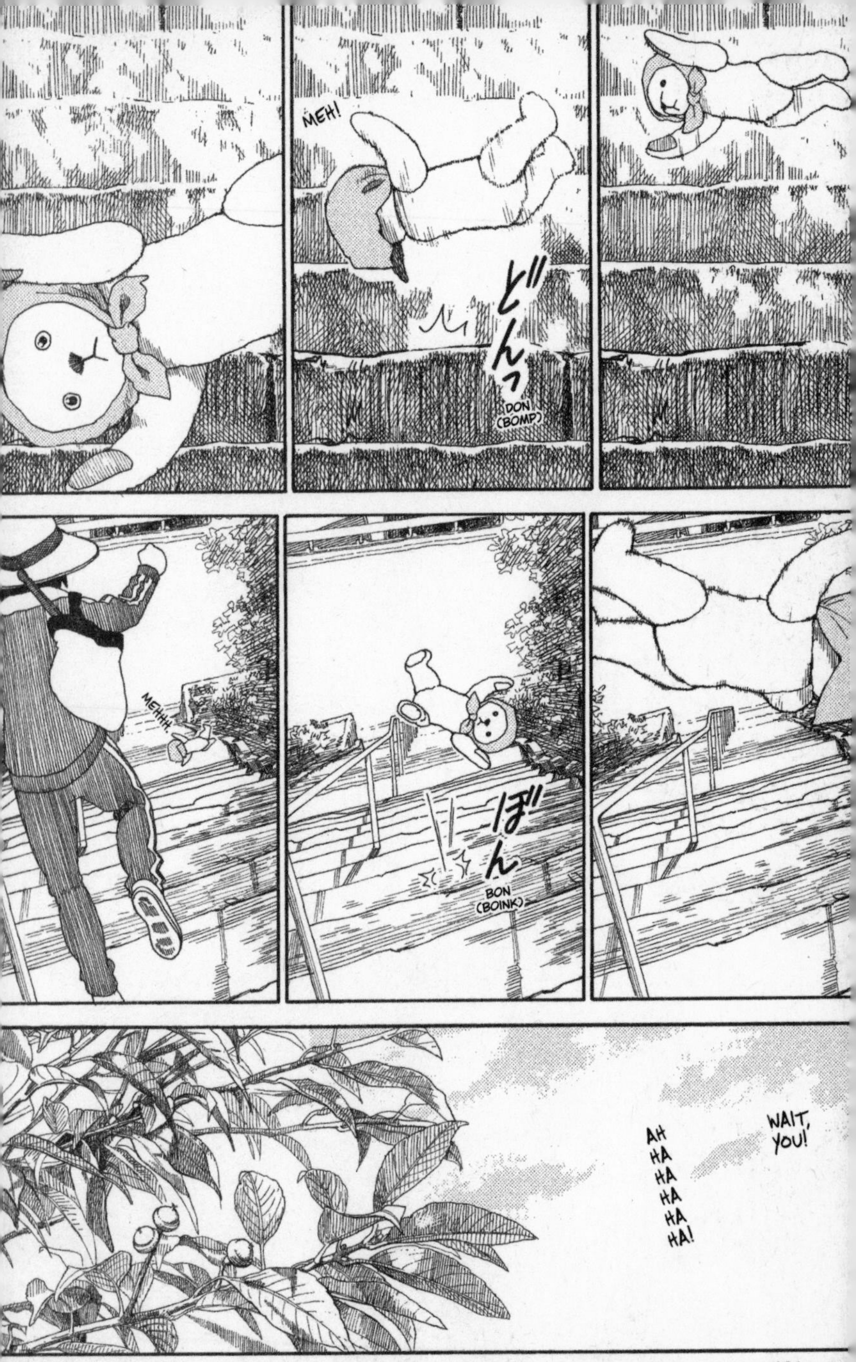

MEH!
どんっ
DON (BOMP)
MEHHH.
ぼん
BON (BOINK)
WAIT, YOU!
AH HA HA HA HA HA!

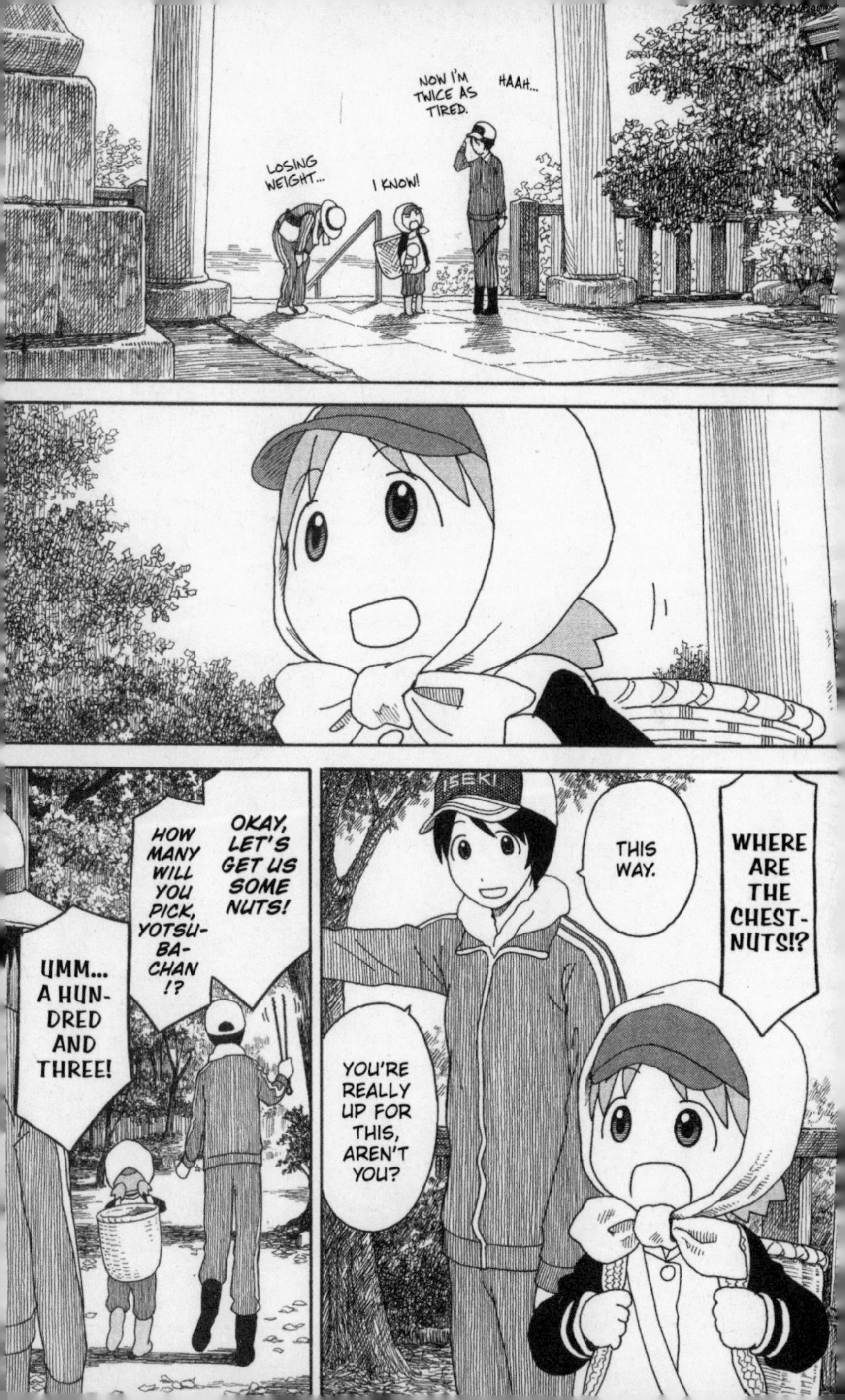
HAAH...
NOW I'M TWICE AS TIRED.
I KNOW!
LOSING WEIGHT...
WHERE ARE THE CHEST-NUTS!?
THIS WAY.
YOU'RE REALLY UP FOR THIS, AREN'T YOU?
OKAY, LET'S GET US SOME NUTS!
HOW MANY WILL YOU PICK, YOTSU-BA-CHAN!?
UMM... A HUN-DRED AND THREE!

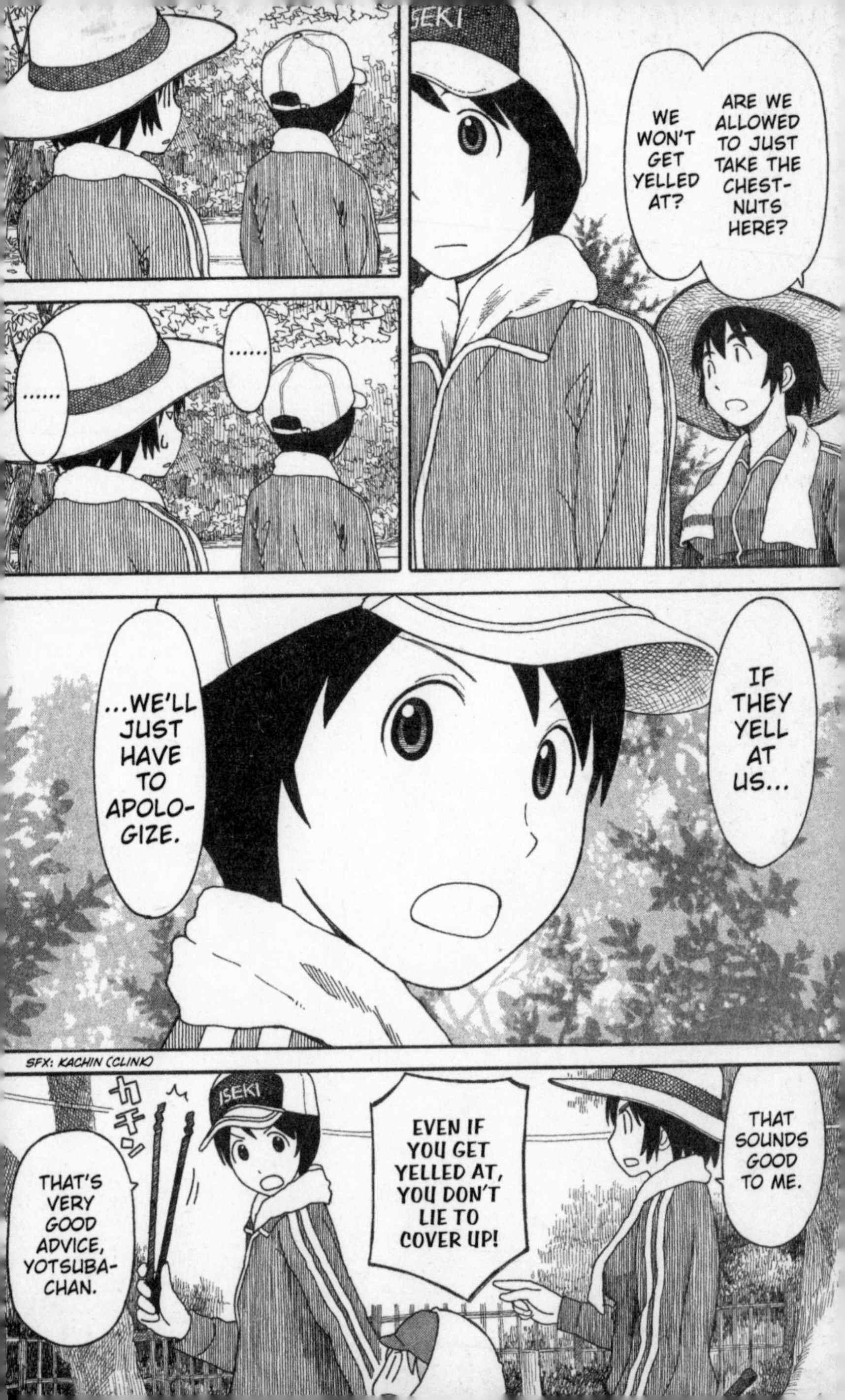
ISEKI
ARE WE ALLOWED TO JUST TAKE THE CHEST-NUTS HERE?
WE WON'T GET YELLED AT?
......
......
IF THEY YELL AT US...
...WE'LL JUST HAVE TO APOLOGIZE.
SFX: KACHIN (CLINK)
THAT SOUNDS GOOD TO ME.
EVEN IF YOU GET YELLED AT, YOU DON'T LIE TO COVER UP!
ISEKI
THAT'S VERY GOOD ADVICE, YOTSUBA-CHAN.

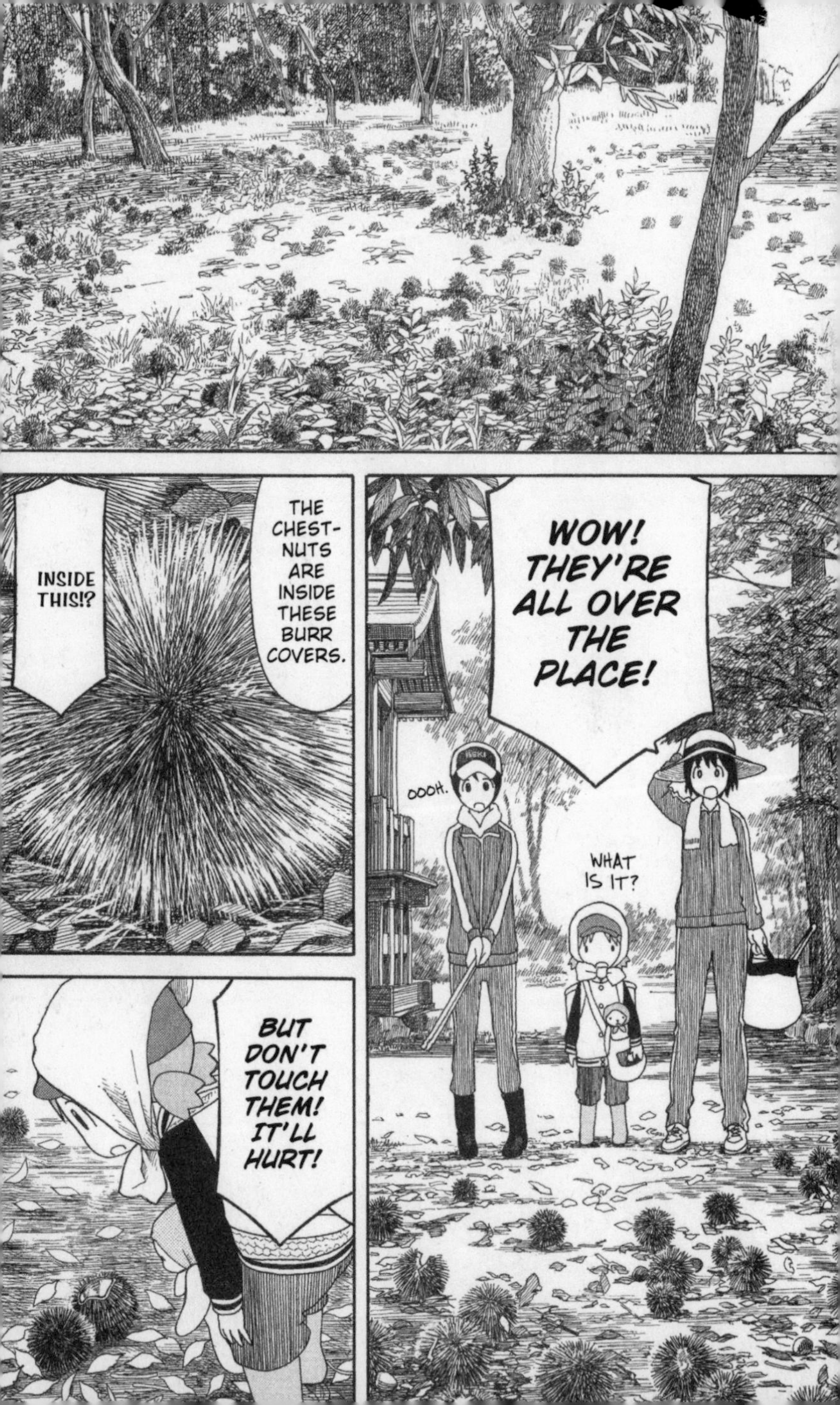
WOW! THEY'RE ALL OVER THE PLACE!
OOOH.
WHAT IS IT?
THE CHEST-NUTS ARE INSIDE THESE BURR COVERS.
INSIDE THIS!?
BUT DON'T TOUCH THEM! IT'LL HURT!

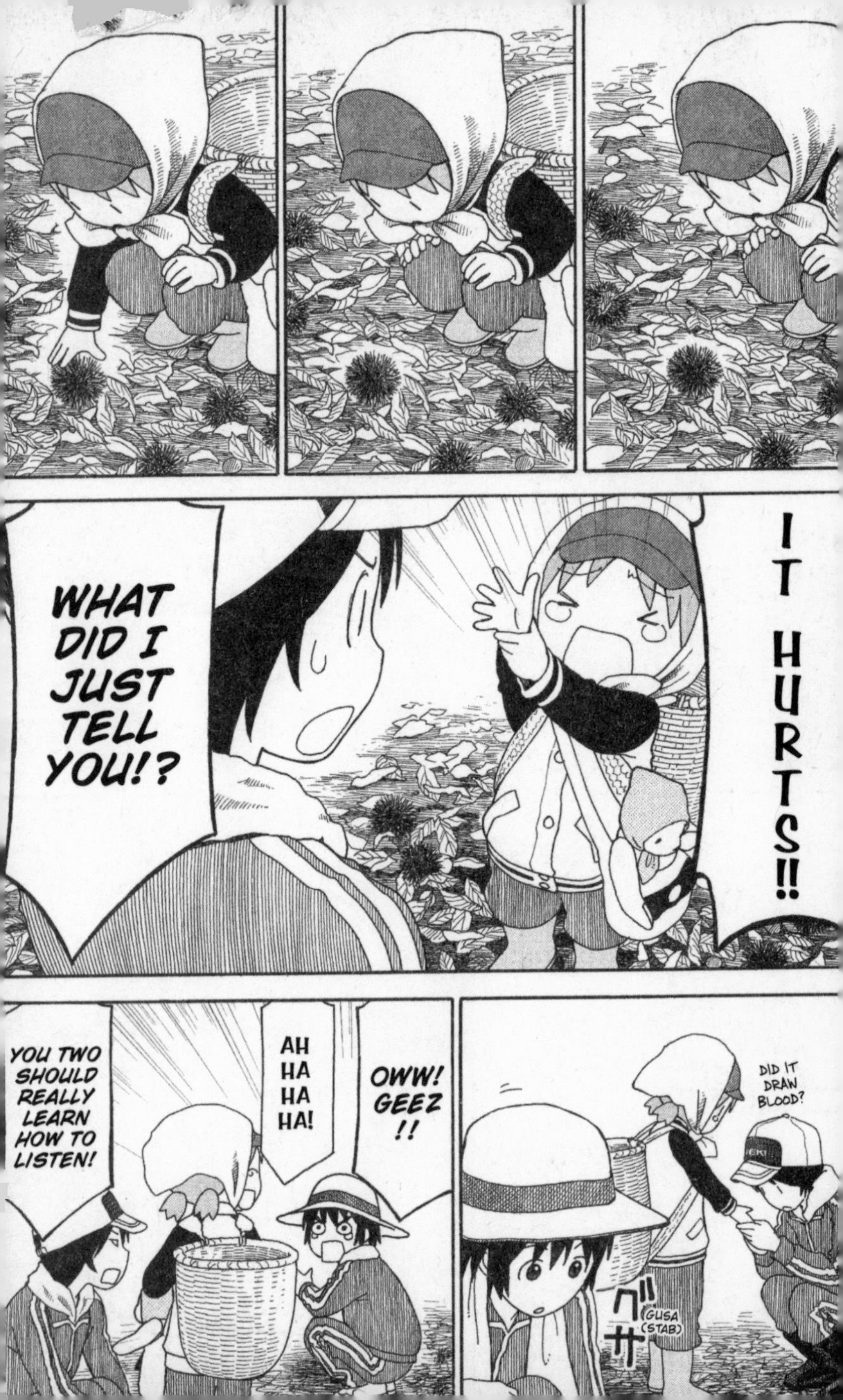
IT HURTS!!
WHAT DID I JUST TELL YOU!?
DID IT DRAW BLOOD?
グサ
GUSA (STAB)
OWW! GEEZ!!
AH HA HA HA!
YOU TWO SHOULD REALLY LEARN HOW TO LISTEN!

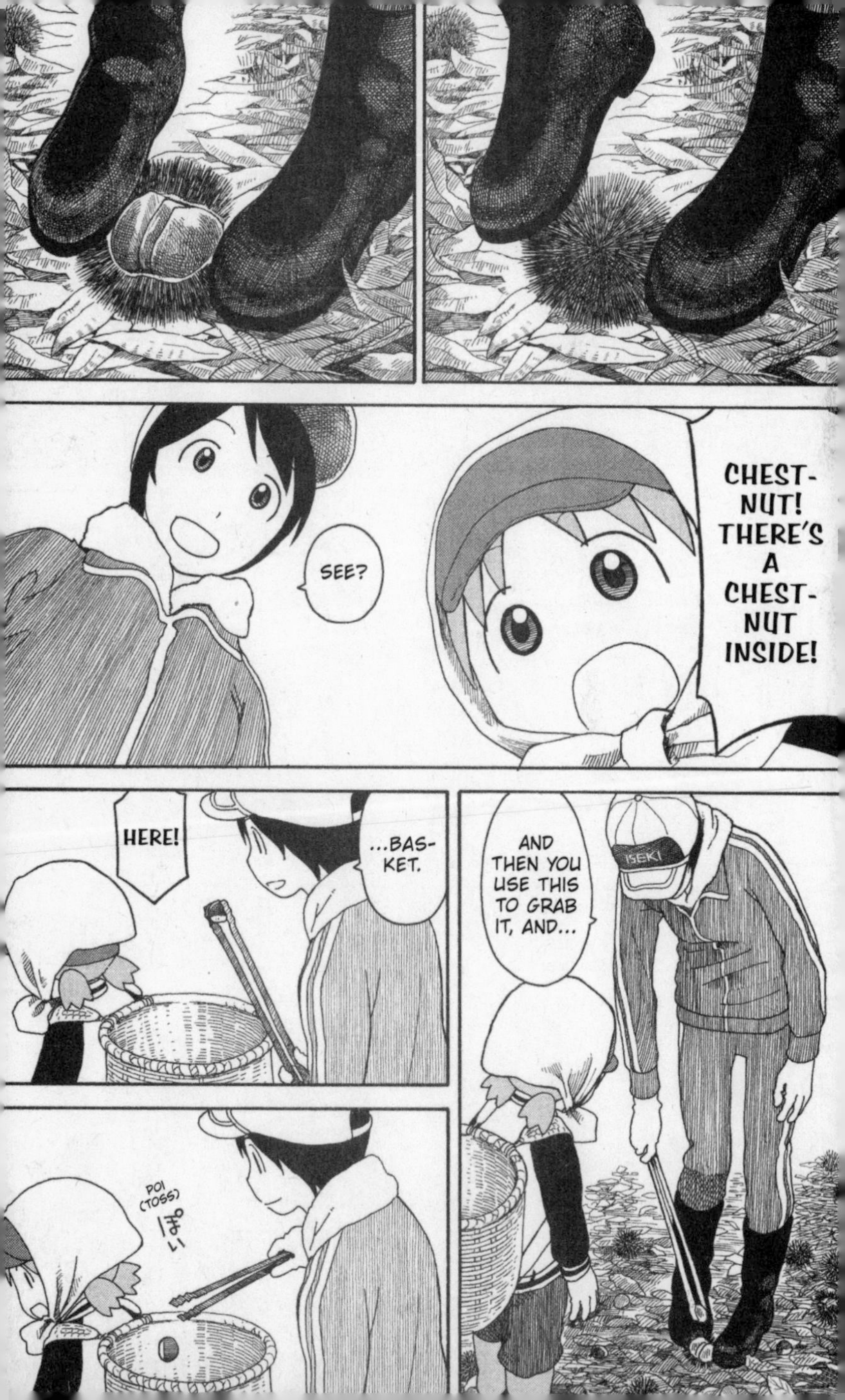
CHEST-NUT! THERE'S A CHEST-NUT INSIDE!
SEE?
AND THEN YOU USE THIS TO GRAB IT, AND...
ISEKI
...BAS-KET.
HERE!
ぽい
POI (TOSS)

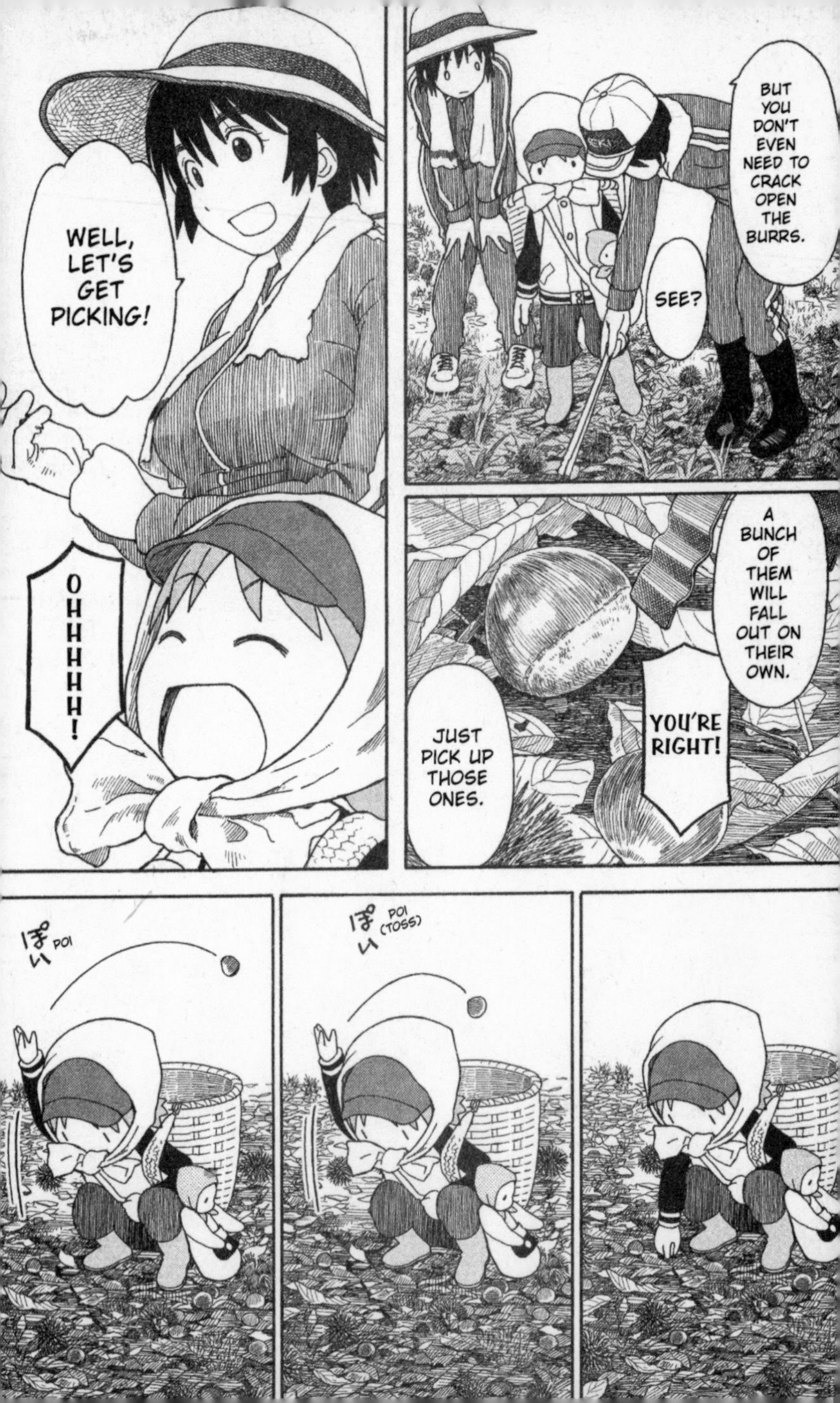

BUT YOU DON'T EVEN NEED TO CRACK OPEN THE BURRS.
SEE?
A BUNCH OF THEM WILL FALL OUT ON THEIR OWN.
JUST PICK UP THOSE ONES.
YOU'RE RIGHT!
WELL, LET'S GET PICKING!
OHHHHHH!
ぽい POI (TOSS)
ぽい POI

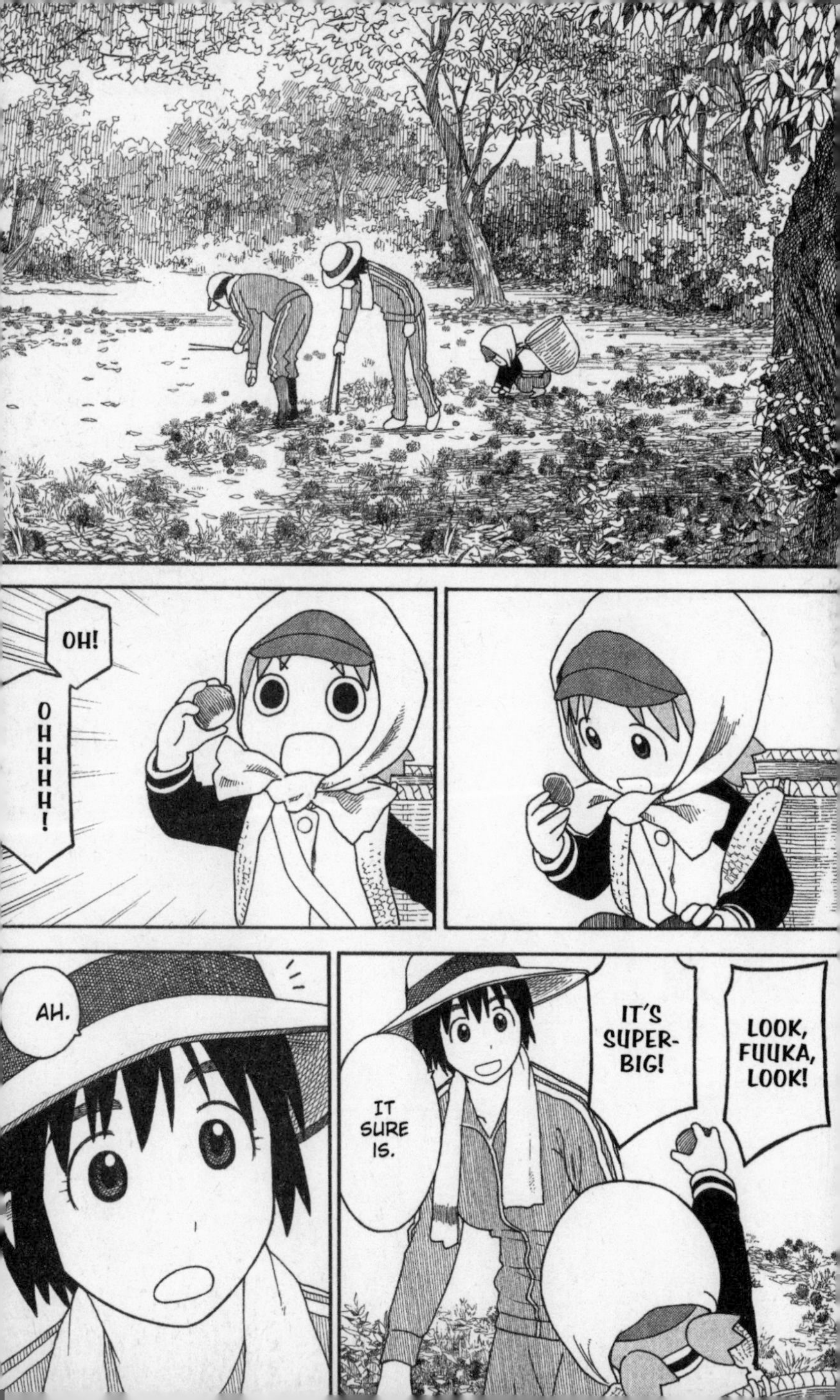
OH!
OHHHHH!
LOOK, FUUKA, LOOK!
IT'S SUPER-BIG!
IT SURE IS.
AH.

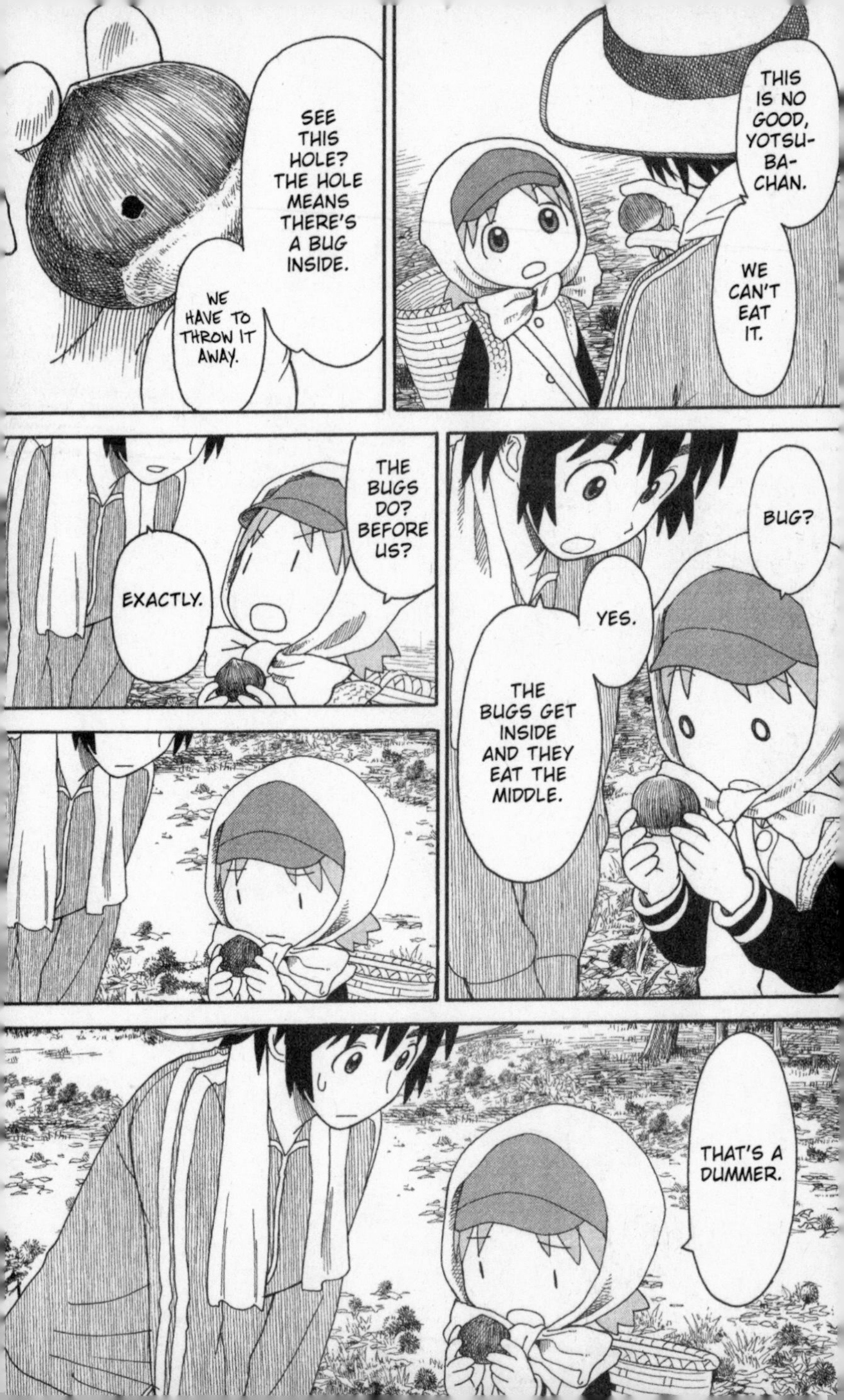
THIS IS NO GOOD, YOTSUBA-CHAN.
WE CAN'T EAT IT.
SEE THIS HOLE? THE HOLE MEANS THERE'S A BUG INSIDE.
WE HAVE TO THROW IT AWAY.
BUG?
YES.
THE BUGS GET INSIDE AND THEY EAT THE MIDDLE.
THE BUGS DO? BEFORE US?
EXACTLY.
THAT'S A DUMMER.

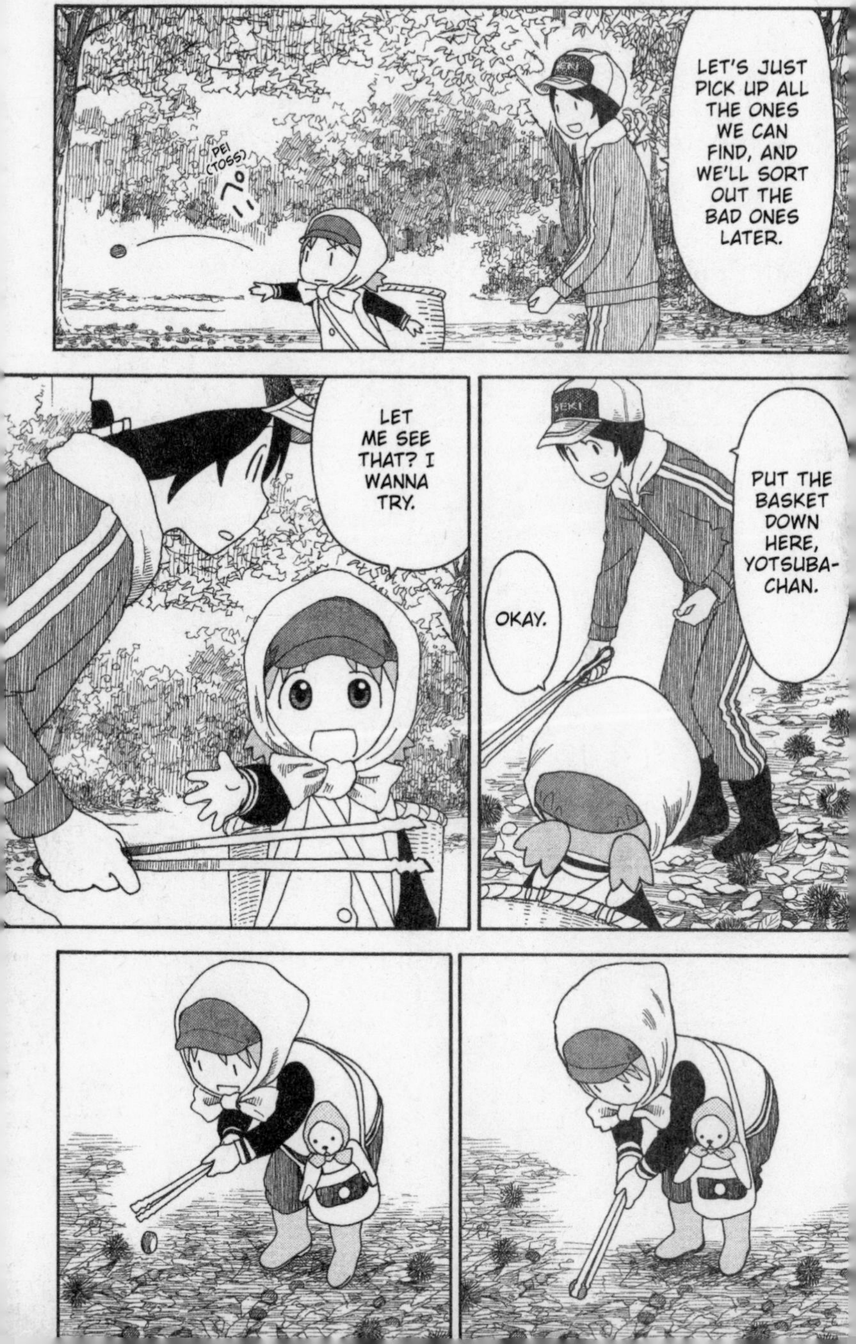
LET'S JUST PICK UP ALL THE ONES WE CAN FIND, AND WE'LL SORT OUT THE BAD ONES LATER.
PEI (TOSS)
PUT THE BASKET DOWN HERE, YOTSUBA-CHAN.
OKAY.
SEKI
LET ME SEE THAT? I WANNA TRY.

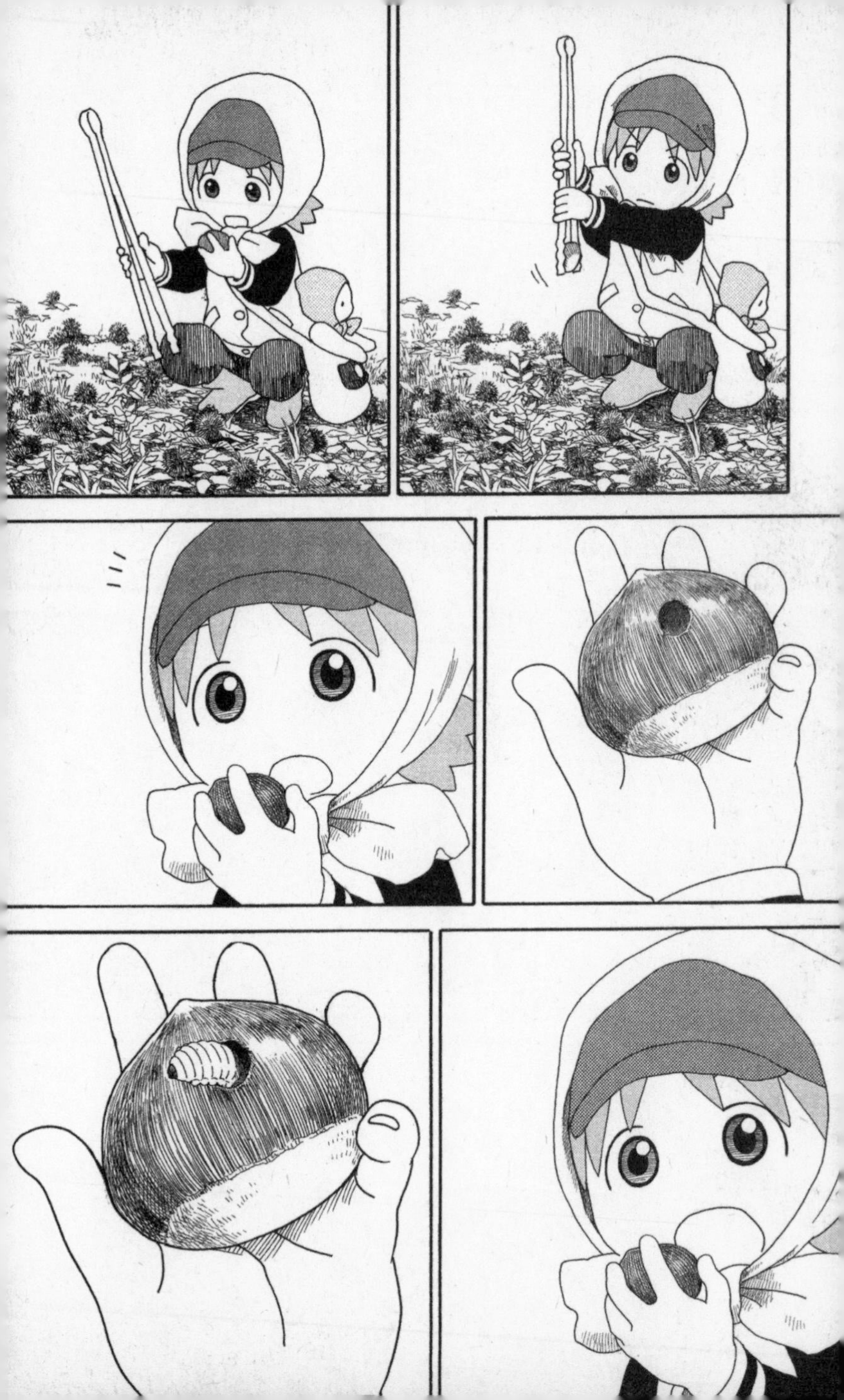

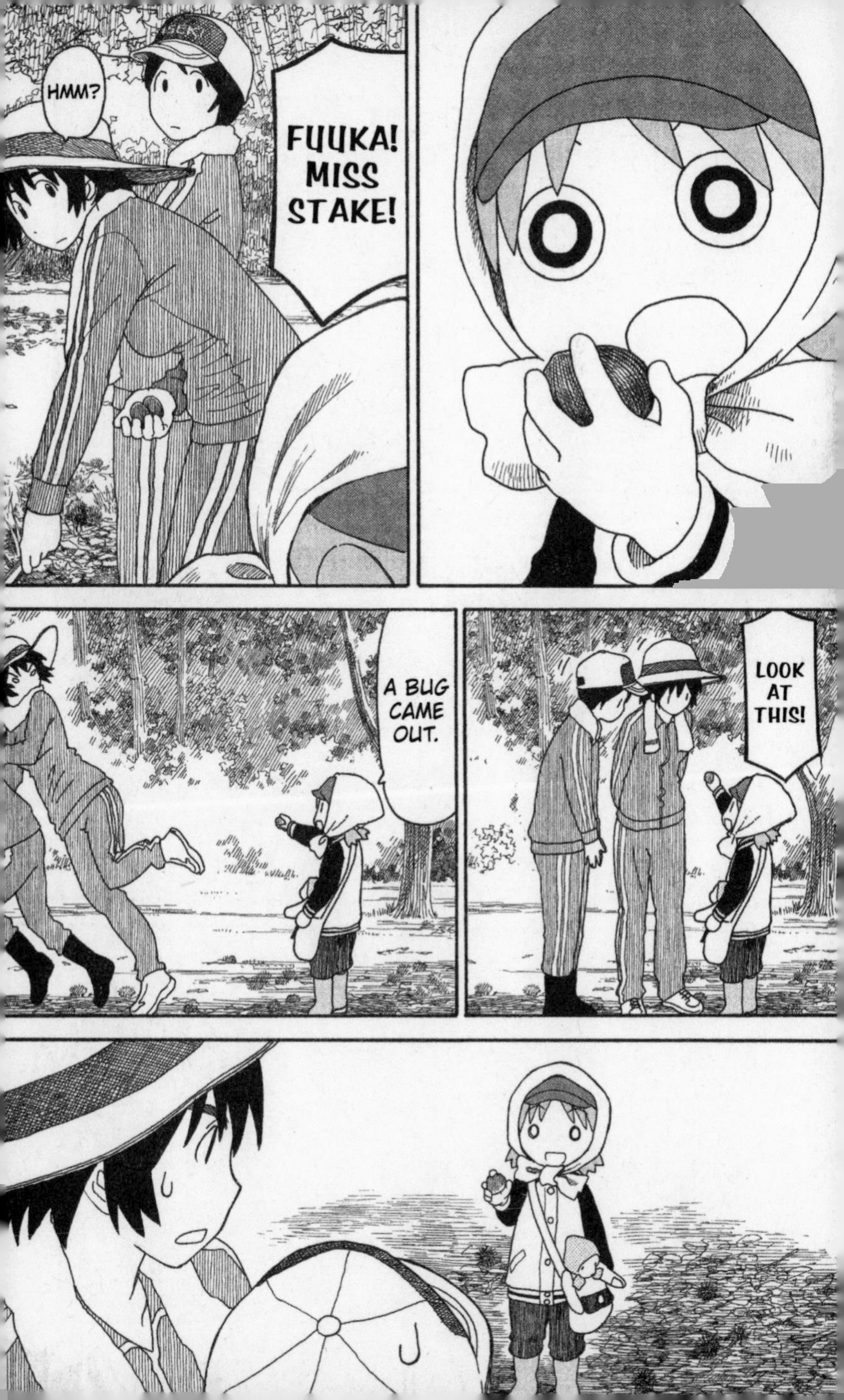
FUUKA! MISS STAKE!
HMM?
LOOK AT THIS!
A BUG CAME OUT.

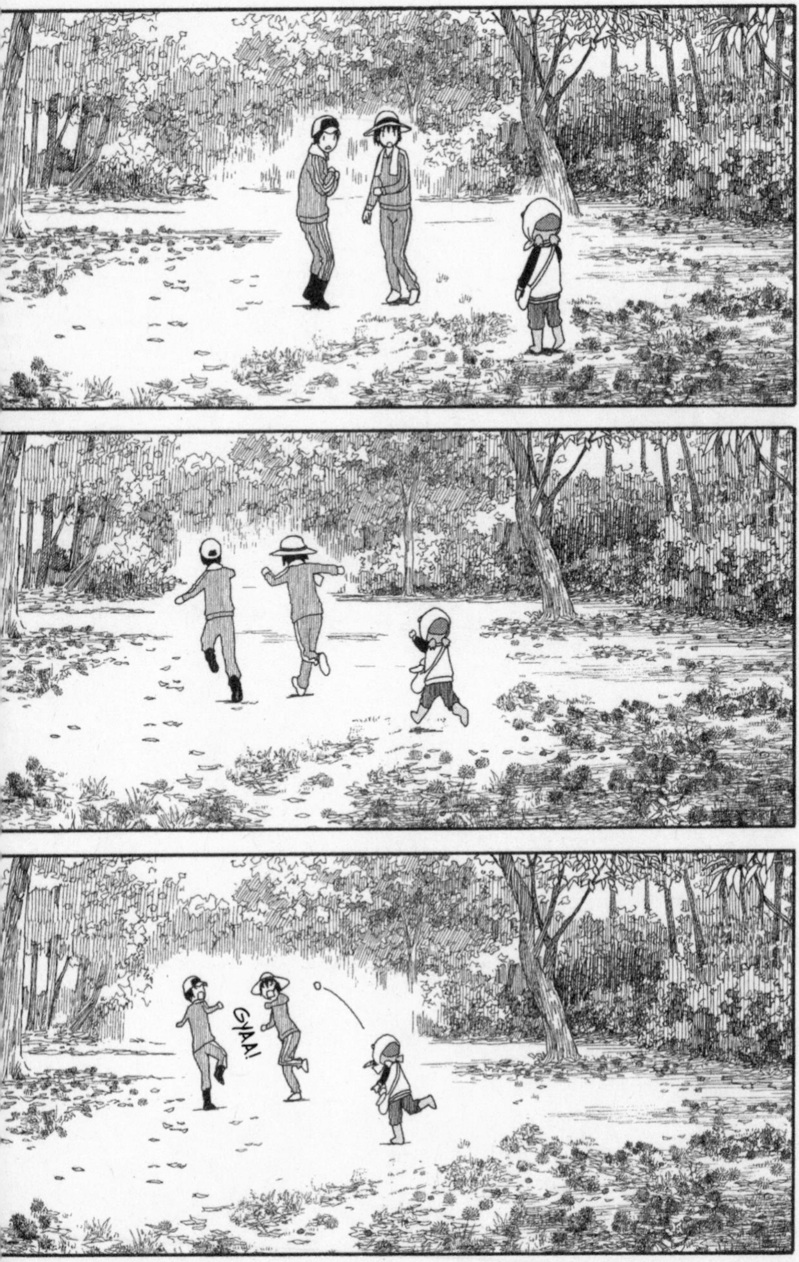
GYAA!

YOTSUBA&!

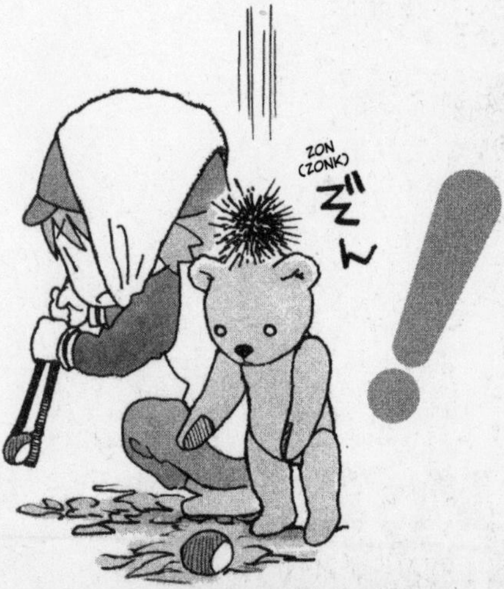
ZON
(ZONK)
ズン

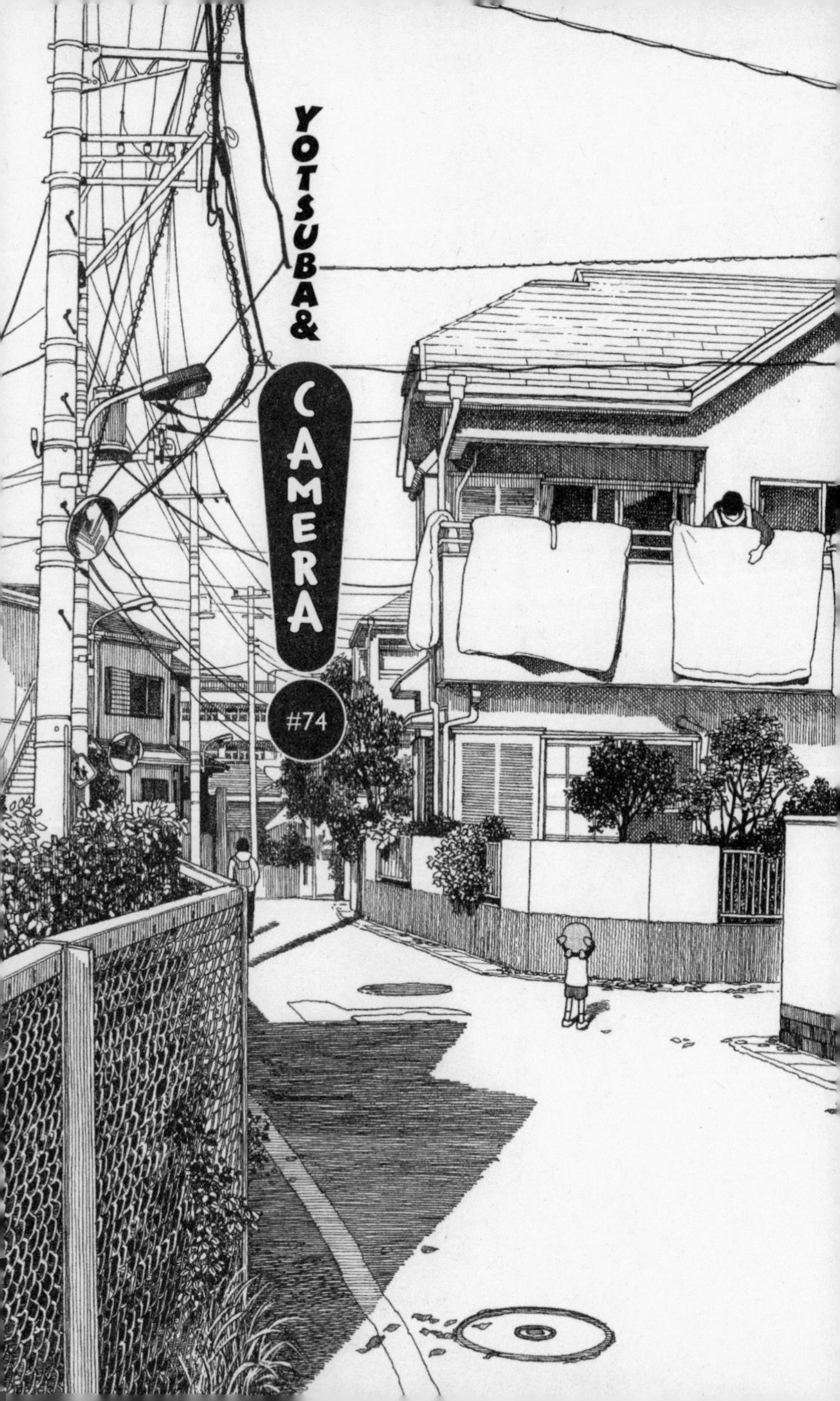
YOTSUBA&
CAMERA
#74

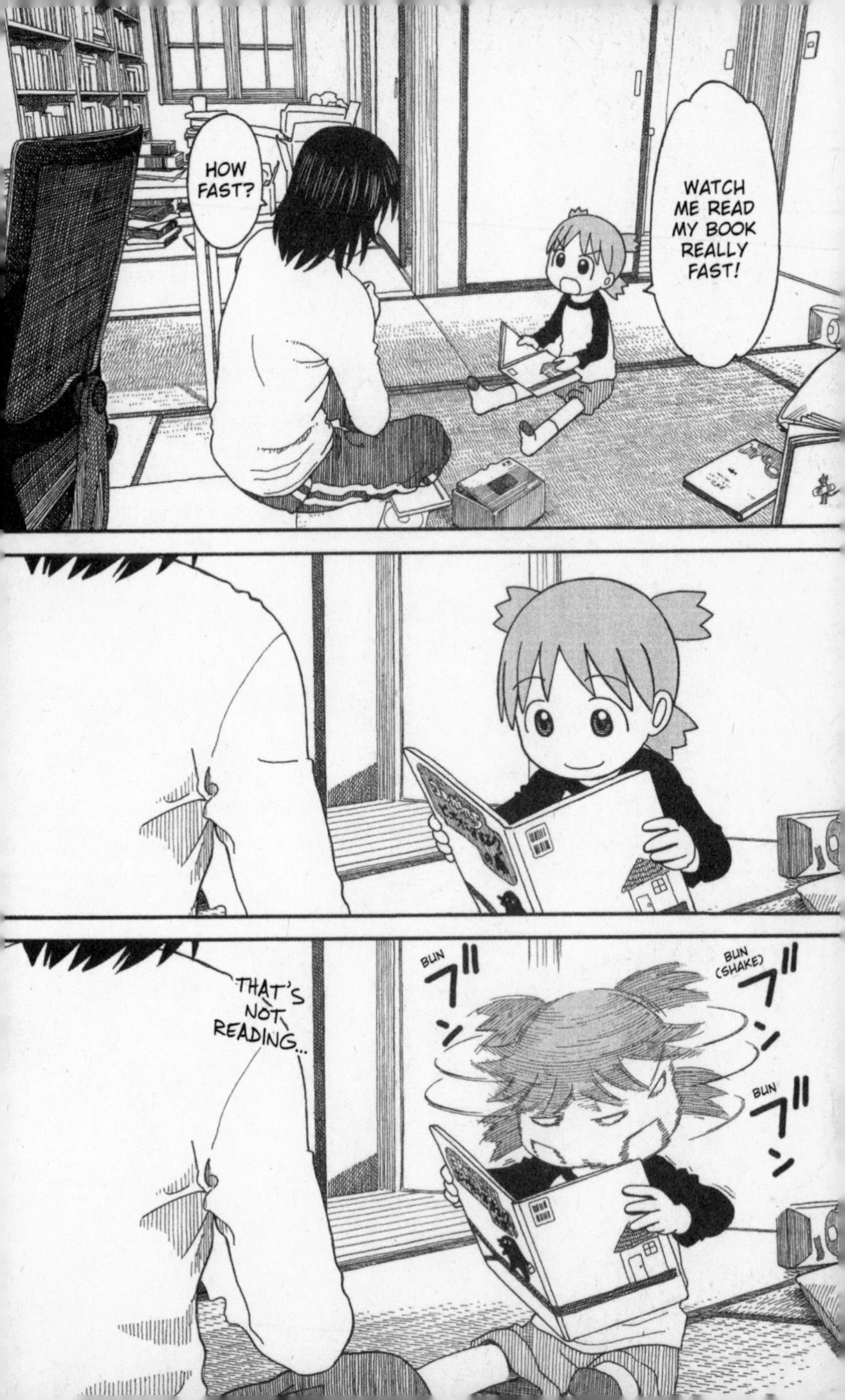
WATCH ME READ MY BOOK REALLY FAST!
HOW FAST?
BUN (SHAKE)
ブン
BUN
ブン
BUN
ブン
THAT'S NOT READING...

KASHA (CLICK)

DID YOU GET IT!?

OOOOH!!

Canon

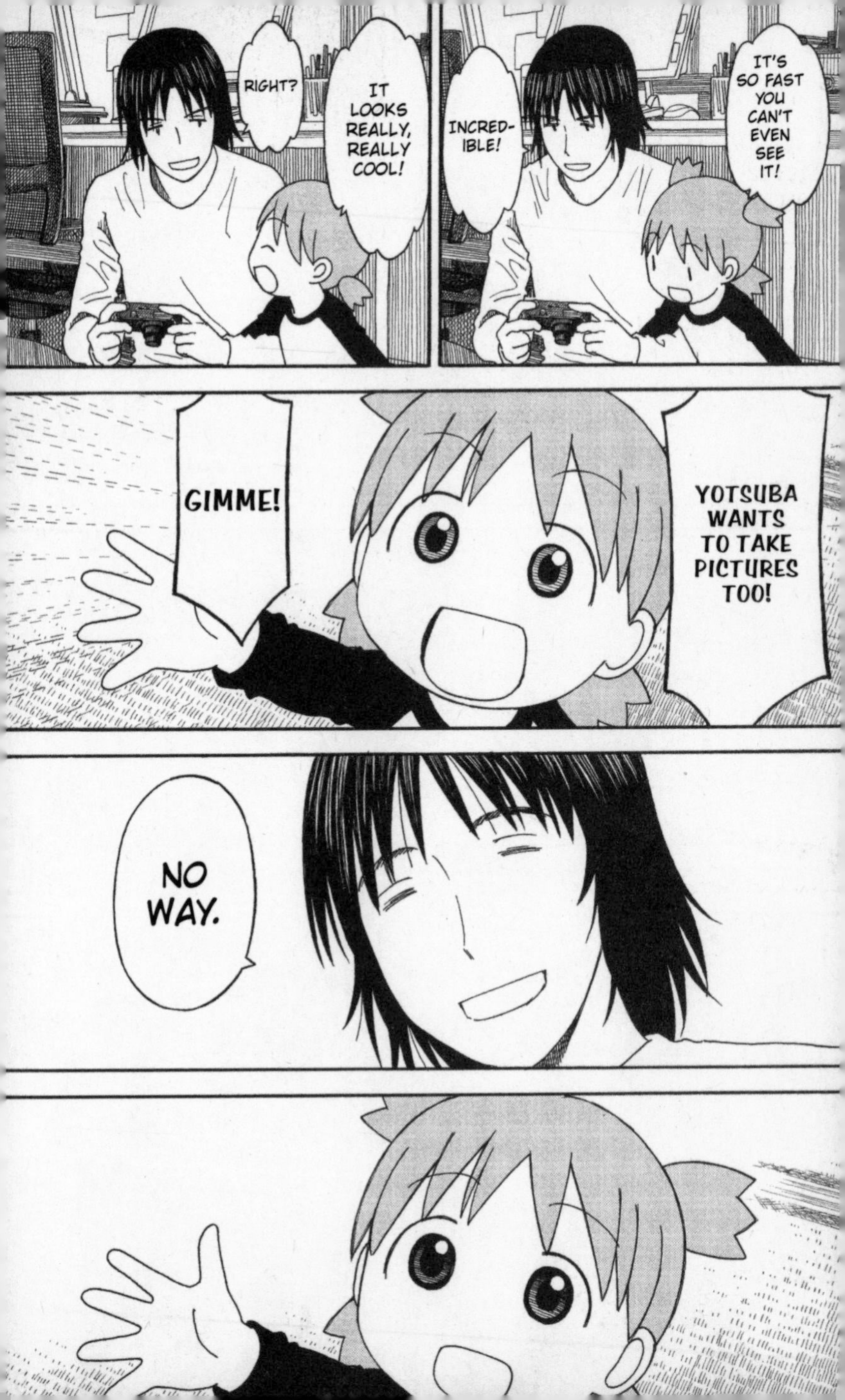
IT'S SO FAST YOU CAN'T EVEN SEE IT!
INCRED-IBLE!
IT LOOKS REALLY, REALLY COOL!
RIGHT?
YOTSUBA WANTS TO TAKE PICTURES TOO!
GIMME!
NO WAY.

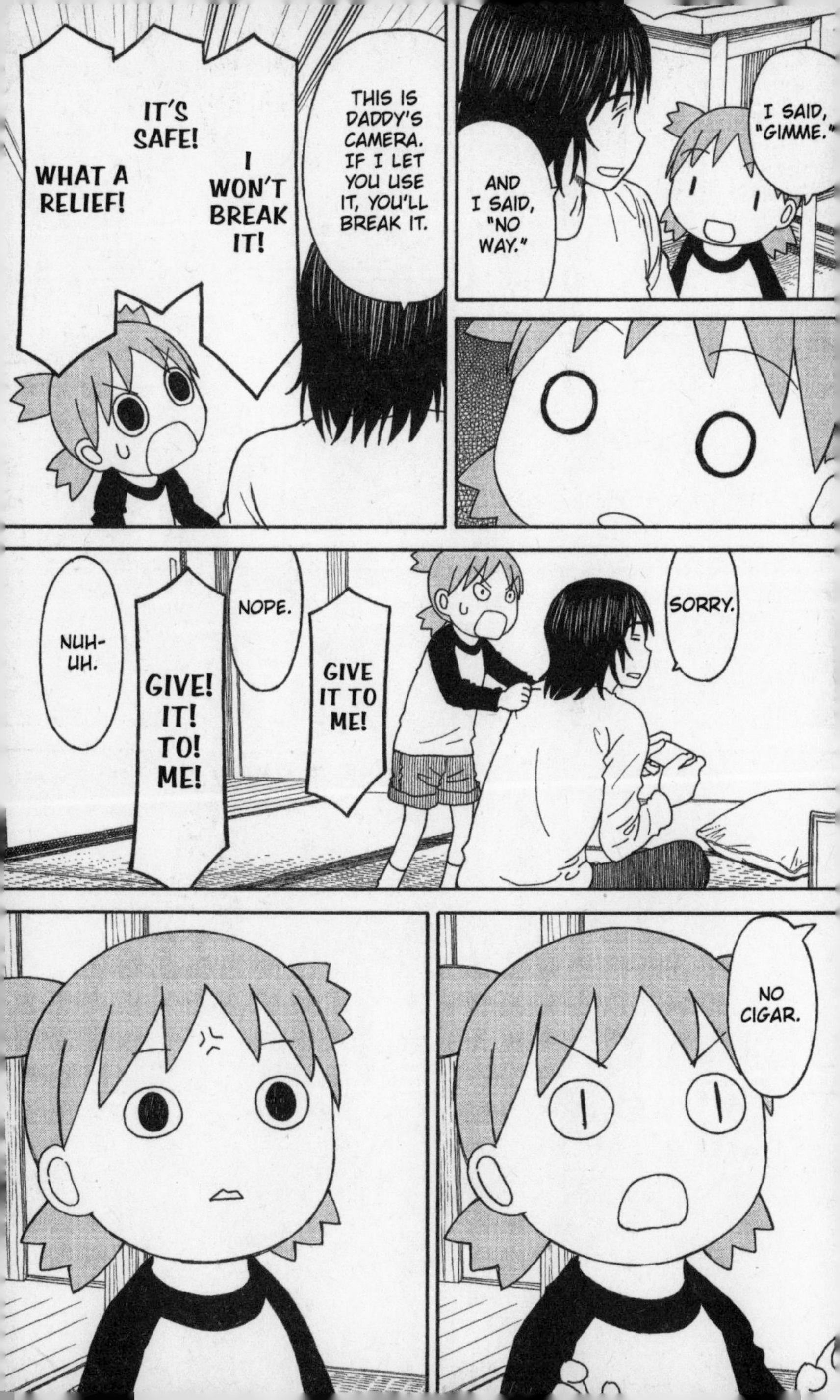
I SAID, "GIMME."
AND I SAID, "NO WAY."
THIS IS DADDY'S CAMERA. IF I LET YOU USE IT, YOU'LL BREAK IT.
I WON'T BREAK IT!
IT'S SAFE!
WHAT A RELIEF!
SORRY.
GIVE IT TO ME!
NOPE.
GIVE! IT! TO! ME!
NUH-UH.
NO CIGAR.

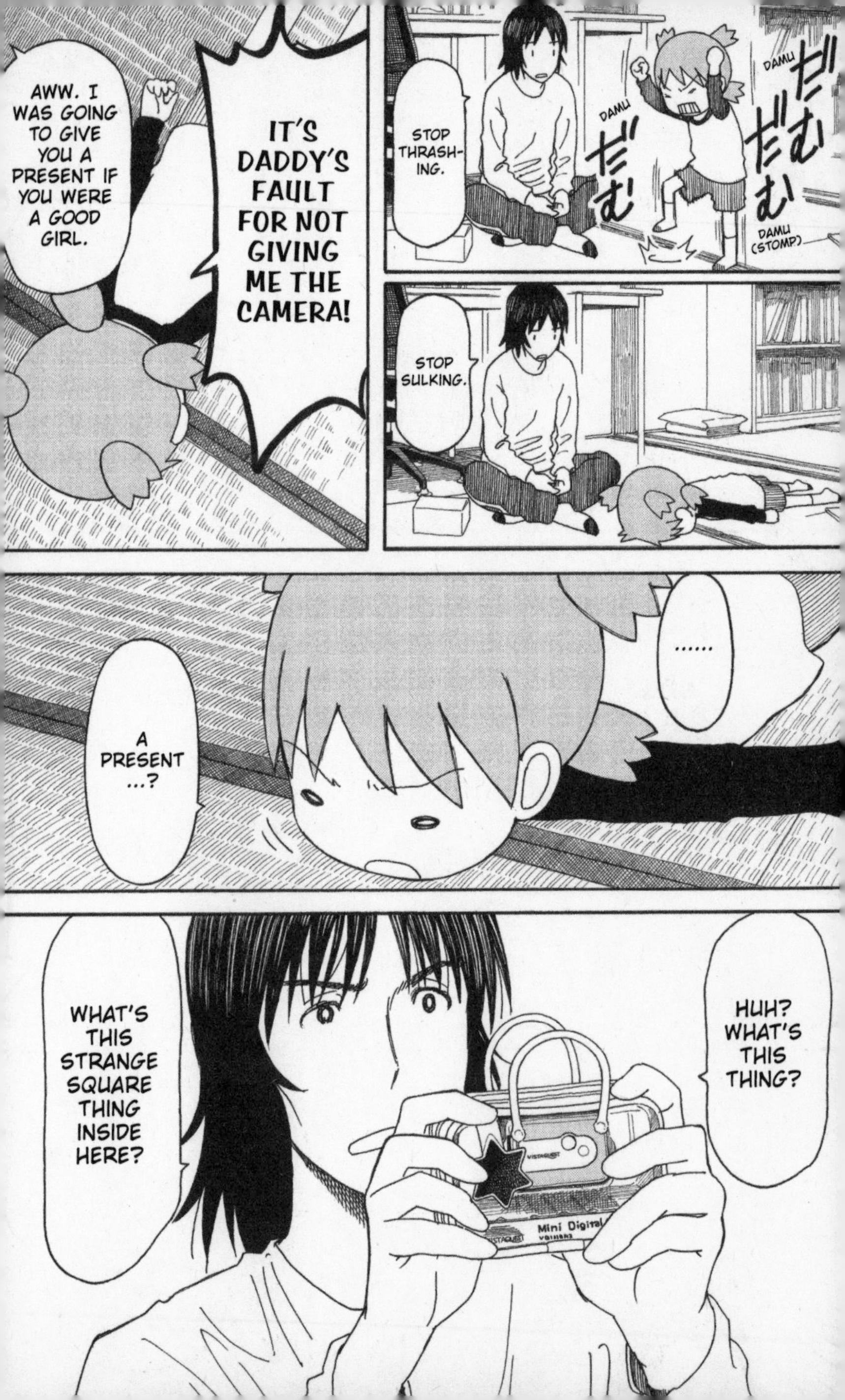
DAMU
だむ
DAMU
だむ
DAMU (STOMP)
だむ
STOP THRASH- ING.
STOP SULKING.
IT'S DADDY'S FAULT FOR NOT GIVING ME THE CAMERA!
AWW. I WAS GOING TO GIVE YOU A PRESENT IF YOU WERE A GOOD GIRL.
......
A PRESENT ...?
HUH? WHAT'S THIS THING?
WHAT'S THIS STRANGE SQUARE THING INSIDE HERE?
Mini Digital

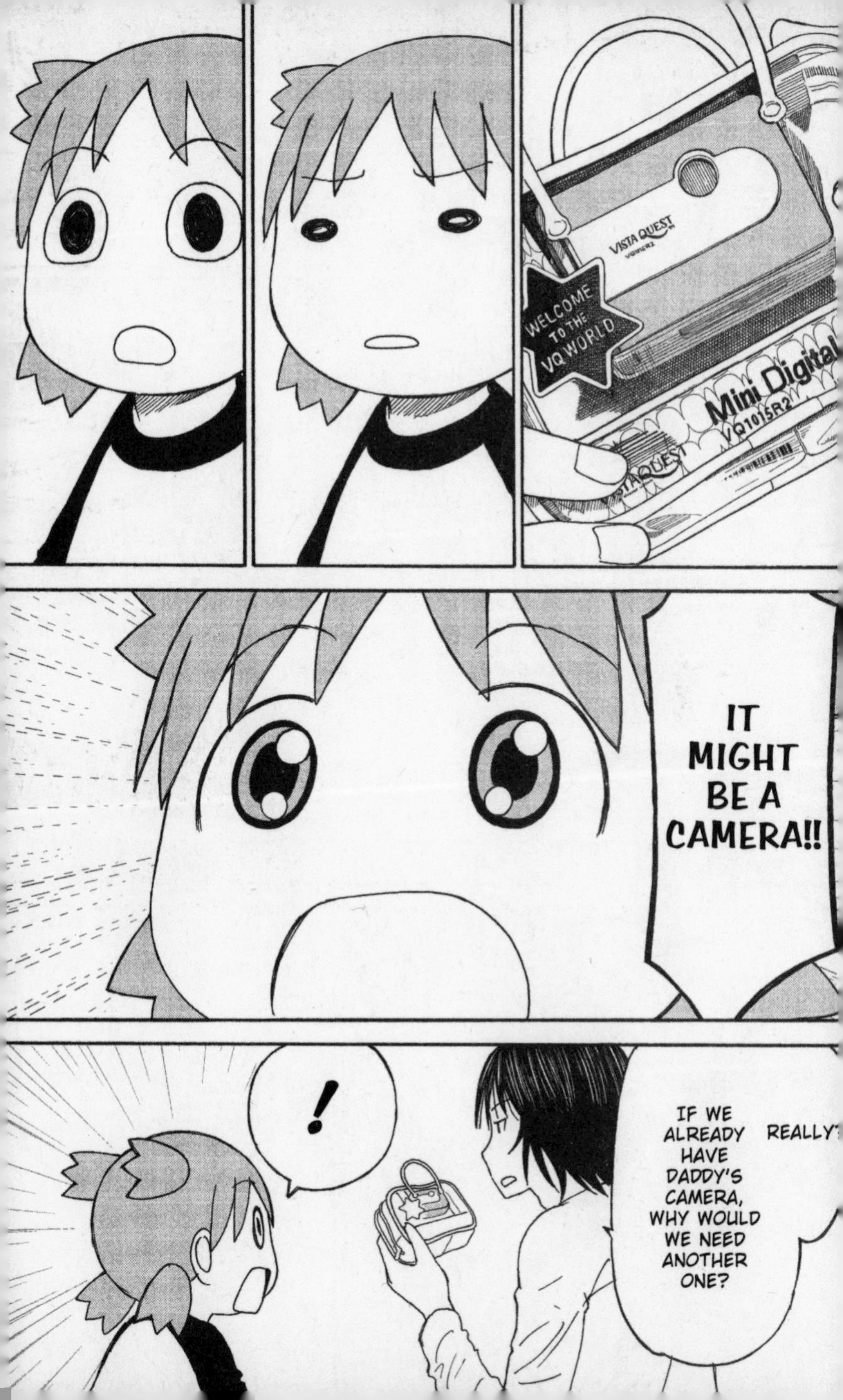
VISTA QUEST
WELCOME TO THE VQ WORLD
Mini Digital
VQ1015R2
VISTAQUEST
IT MIGHT BE A CAMERA!!
REALLY?
IF WE ALREADY HAVE DADDY'S CAMERA, WHY WOULD WE NEED ANOTHER ONE?
!

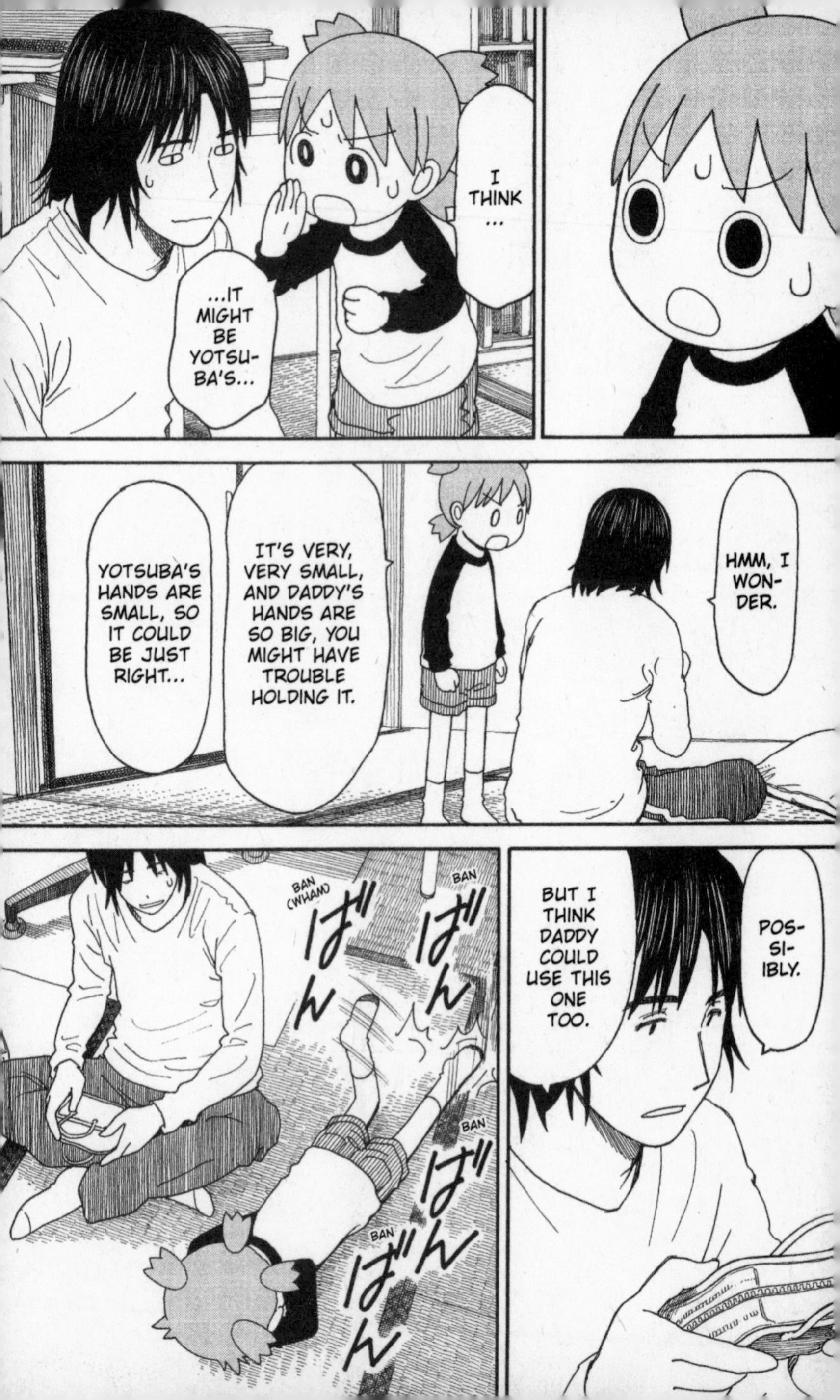
I THINK ...
...IT MIGHT BE YOTSUBA'S...
HMM, I WONDER.
IT'S VERY, VERY SMALL, AND DADDY'S HANDS ARE SO BIG, YOU MIGHT HAVE TROUBLE HOLDING IT.
YOTSUBA'S HANDS ARE SMALL, SO IT COULD BE JUST RIGHT...
POSSIBLY.
BUT I THINK DADDY COULD USE THIS ONE TOO.
ばん
BAN
ばん
BAN (WHAM)
ばん
BAN
ばん
BAN

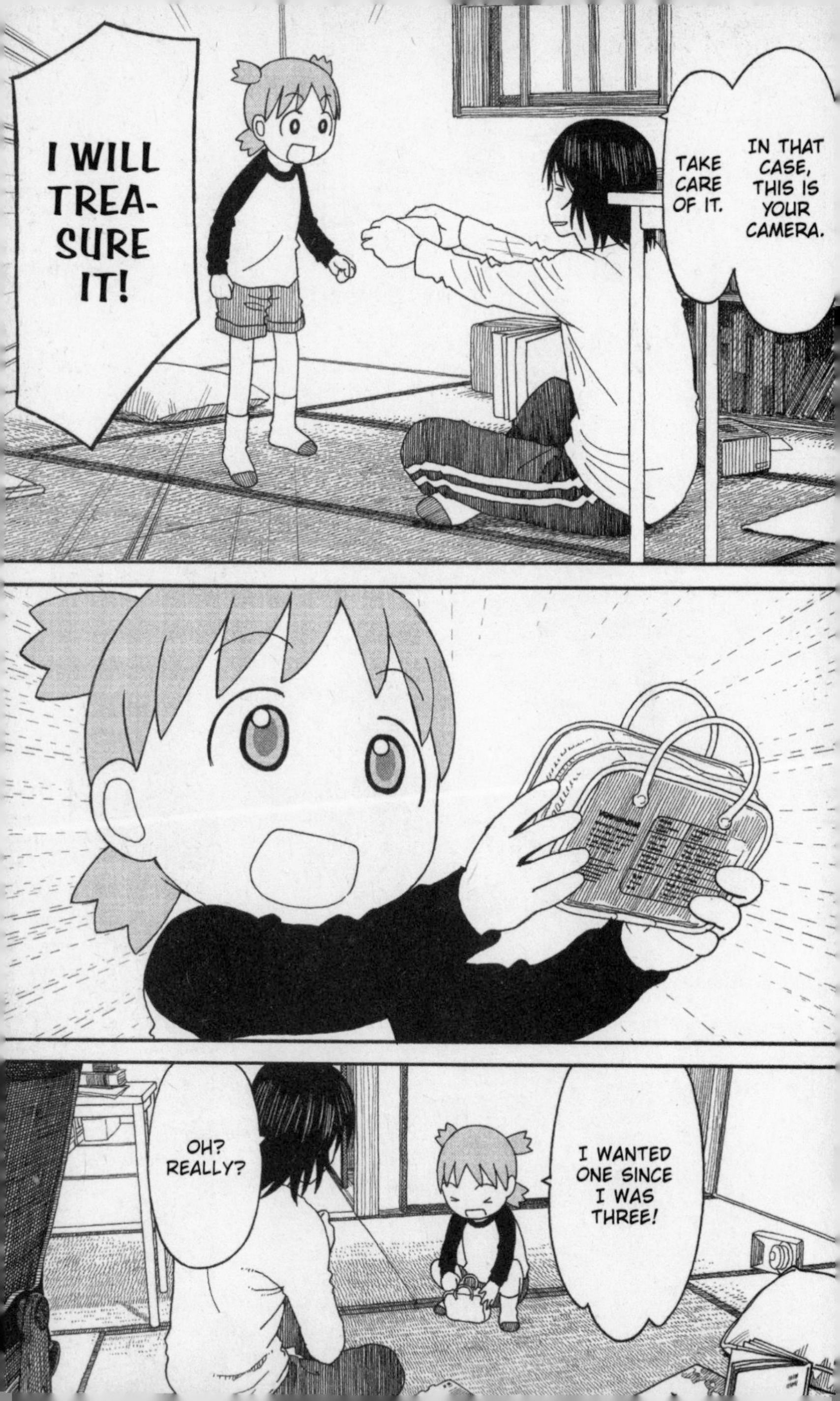
IN THAT CASE, THIS IS YOUR CAMERA.
TAKE CARE OF IT.
I WILL TREA-SURE IT!
I WANTED ONE SINCE I WAS THREE!
OH? REALLY?

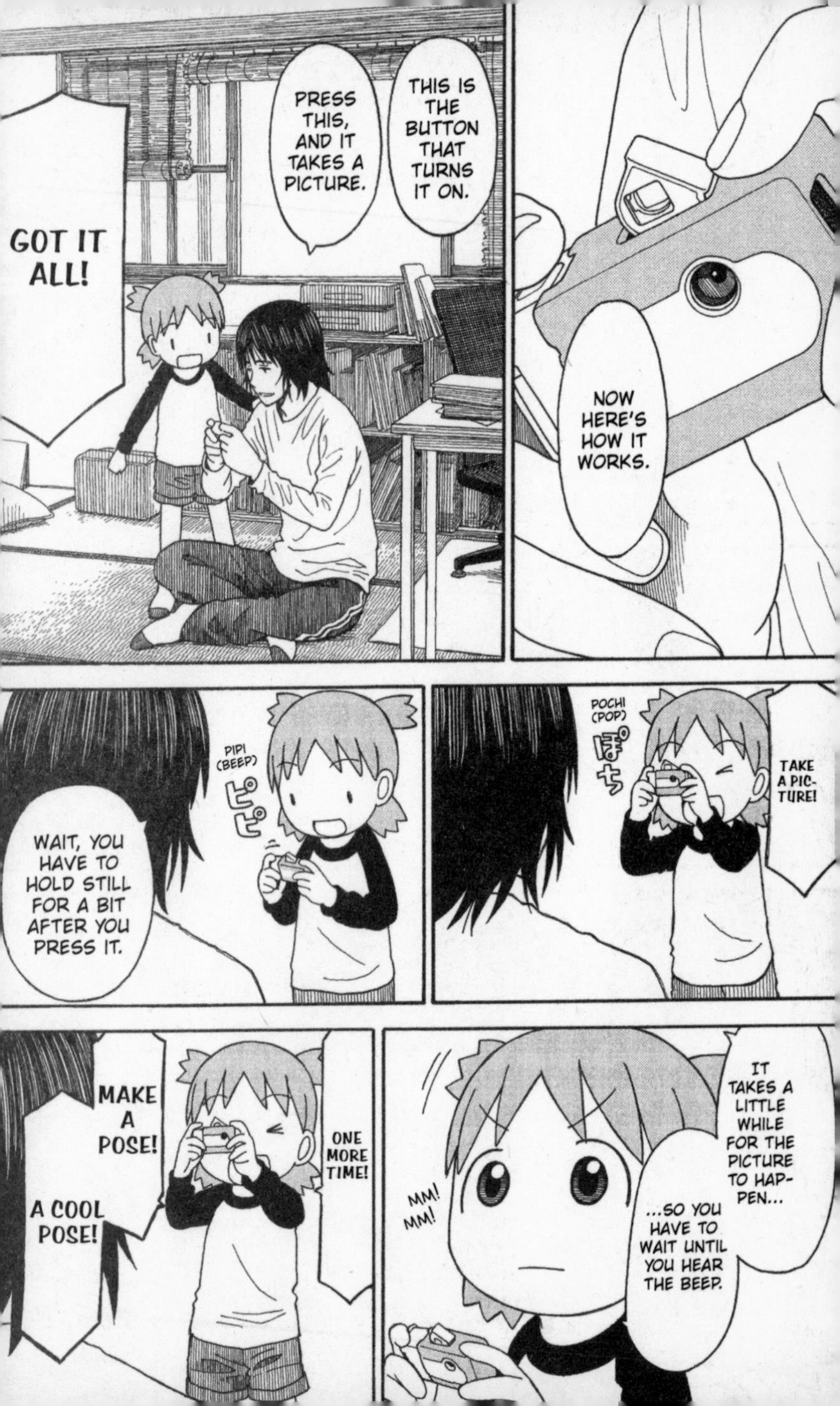
NOW HERE'S HOW IT WORKS.
THIS IS THE BUTTON THAT TURNS IT ON.
PRESS THIS, AND IT TAKES A PICTURE.
GOT IT ALL!
TAKE A PIC-TURE!
POCHI (POP)
ぽち
PIPI (BEEP)
ピピ
WAIT, YOU HAVE TO HOLD STILL FOR A BIT AFTER YOU PRESS IT.
IT TAKES A LITTLE WHILE FOR THE PICTURE TO HAP-PEN...
...SO YOU HAVE TO WAIT UNTIL YOU HEAR THE BEEP.
MM! MM!
ONE MORE TIME!
MAKE A POSE!
A COOL POSE!

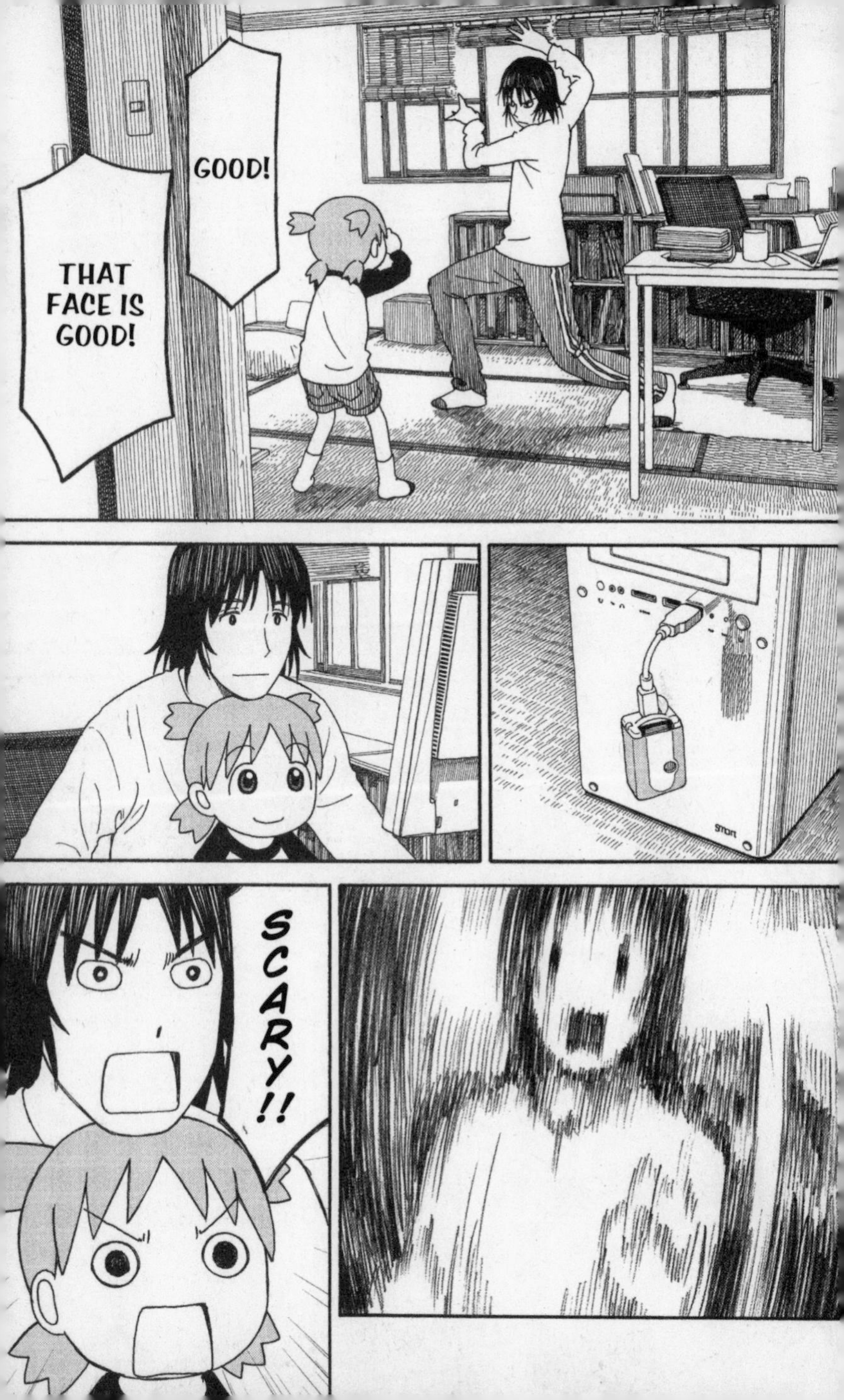
GOOD!
THAT FACE IS GOOD!
SCARY!!

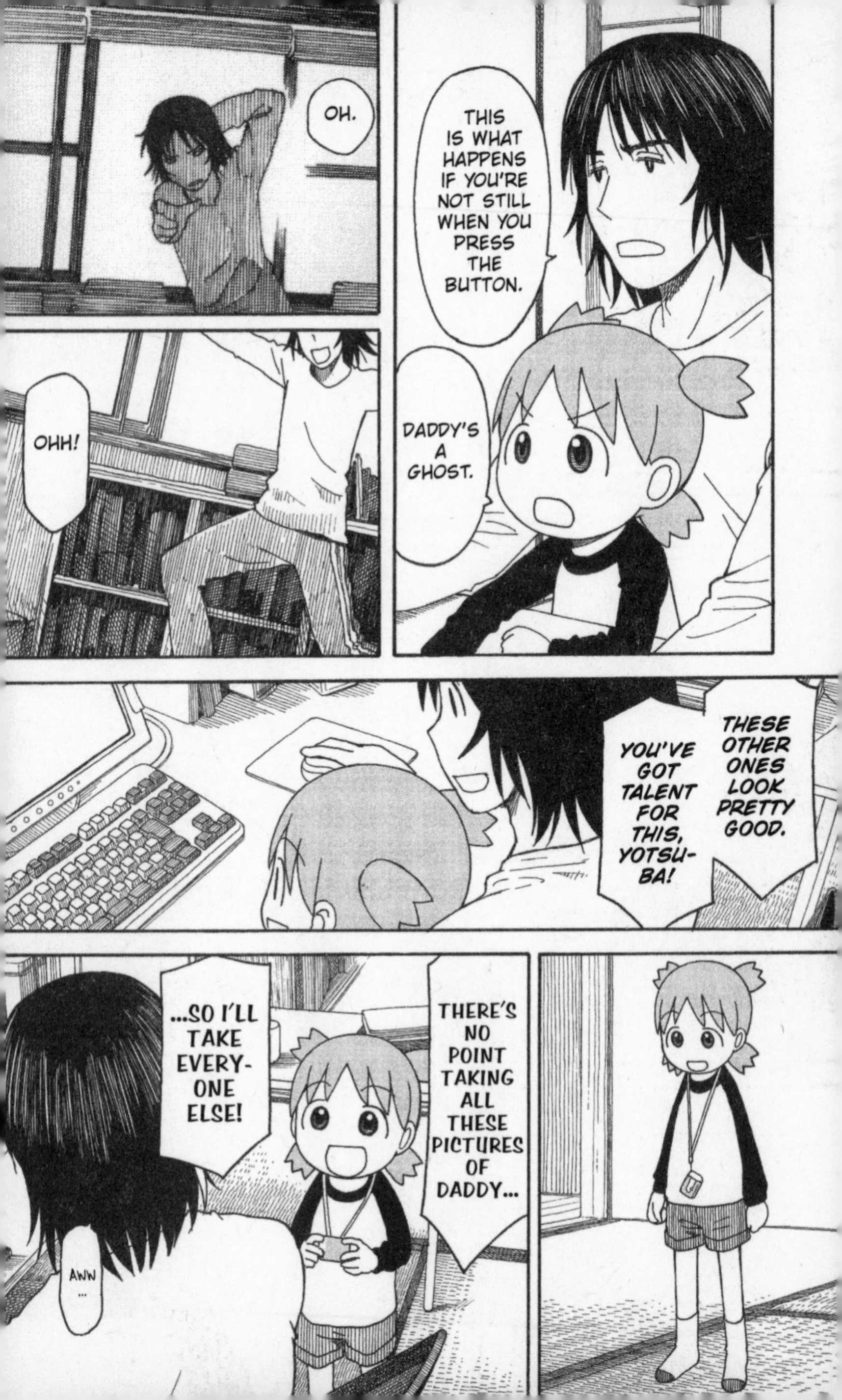
THIS IS WHAT HAPPENS IF YOU'RE NOT STILL WHEN YOU PRESS THE BUTTON.
DADDY'S A GHOST.
OH.
OHH!
THESE OTHER ONES LOOK PRETTY GOOD.
YOU'VE GOT TALENT FOR THIS, YOTSUBA!
THERE'S NO POINT TAKING ALL THESE PICTURES OF DADDY...
...SO I'LL TAKE EVERYONE ELSE!
AWW...

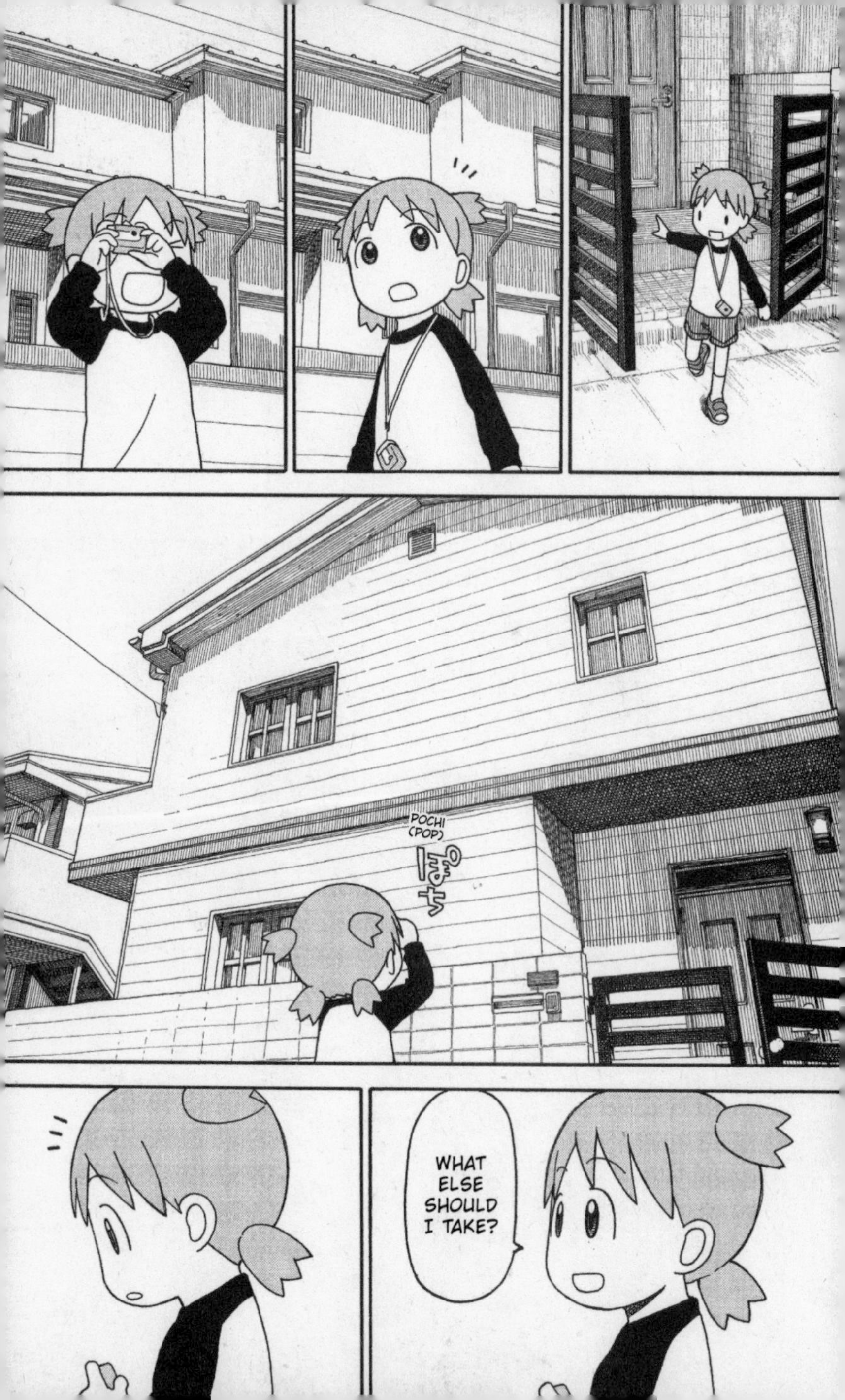
POCHI
(POP)
ぽち
WHAT ELSE SHOULD I TAKE?

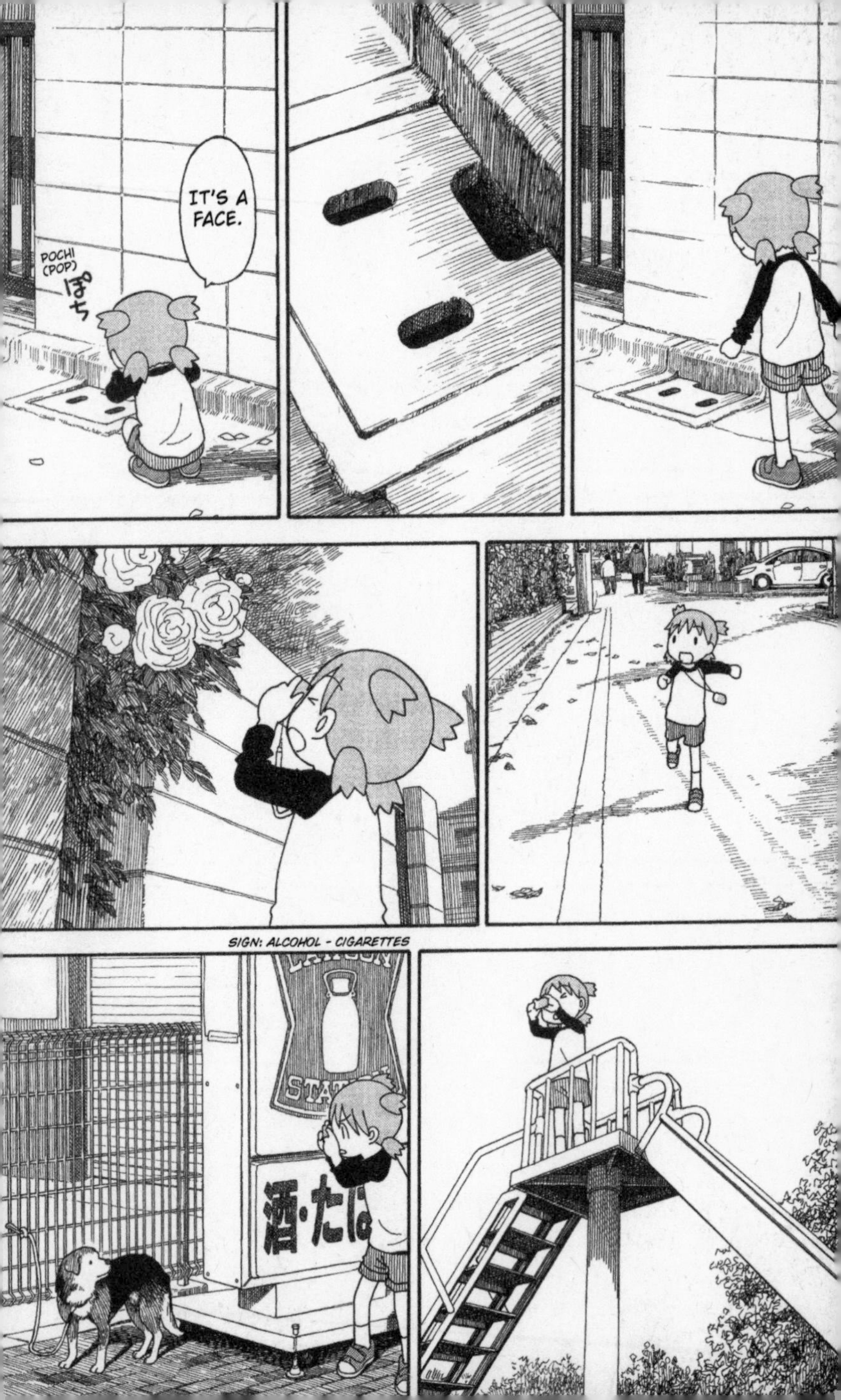
IT'S A FACE.
POCHI (POP)
ぽち
SIGN: ALCOHOL - CIGARETTES
酒・たば

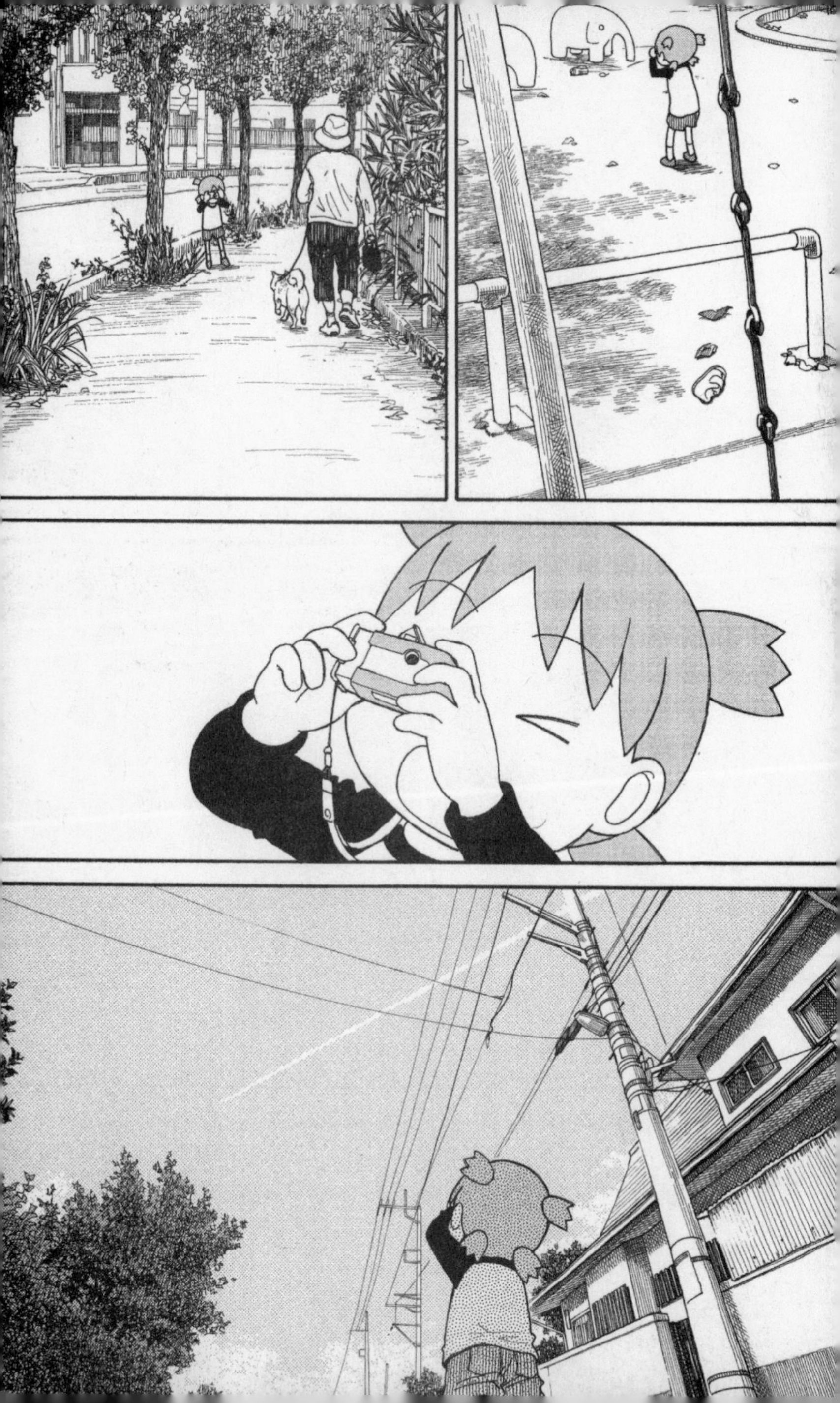

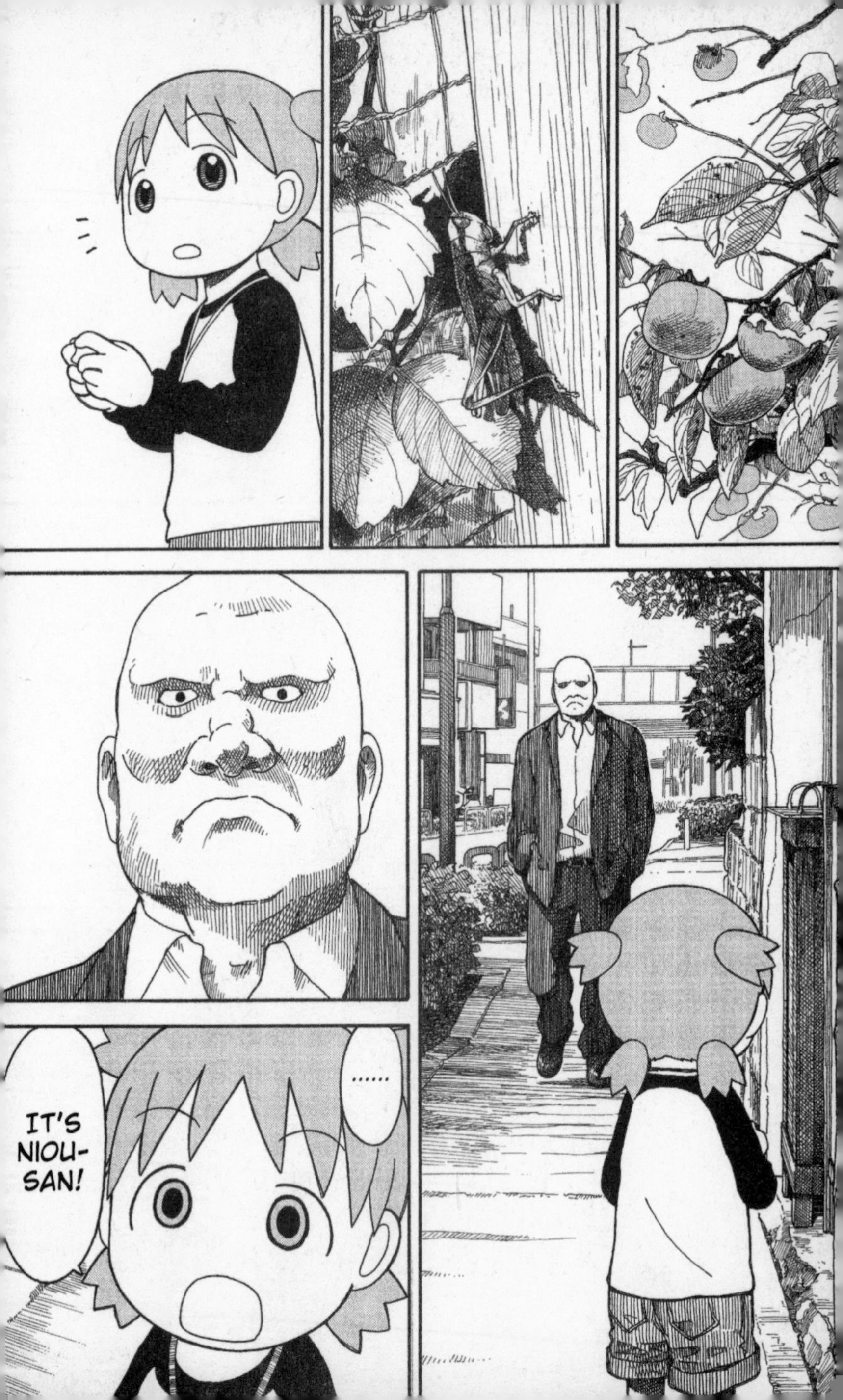
IT'S NIOU-SAN!
......

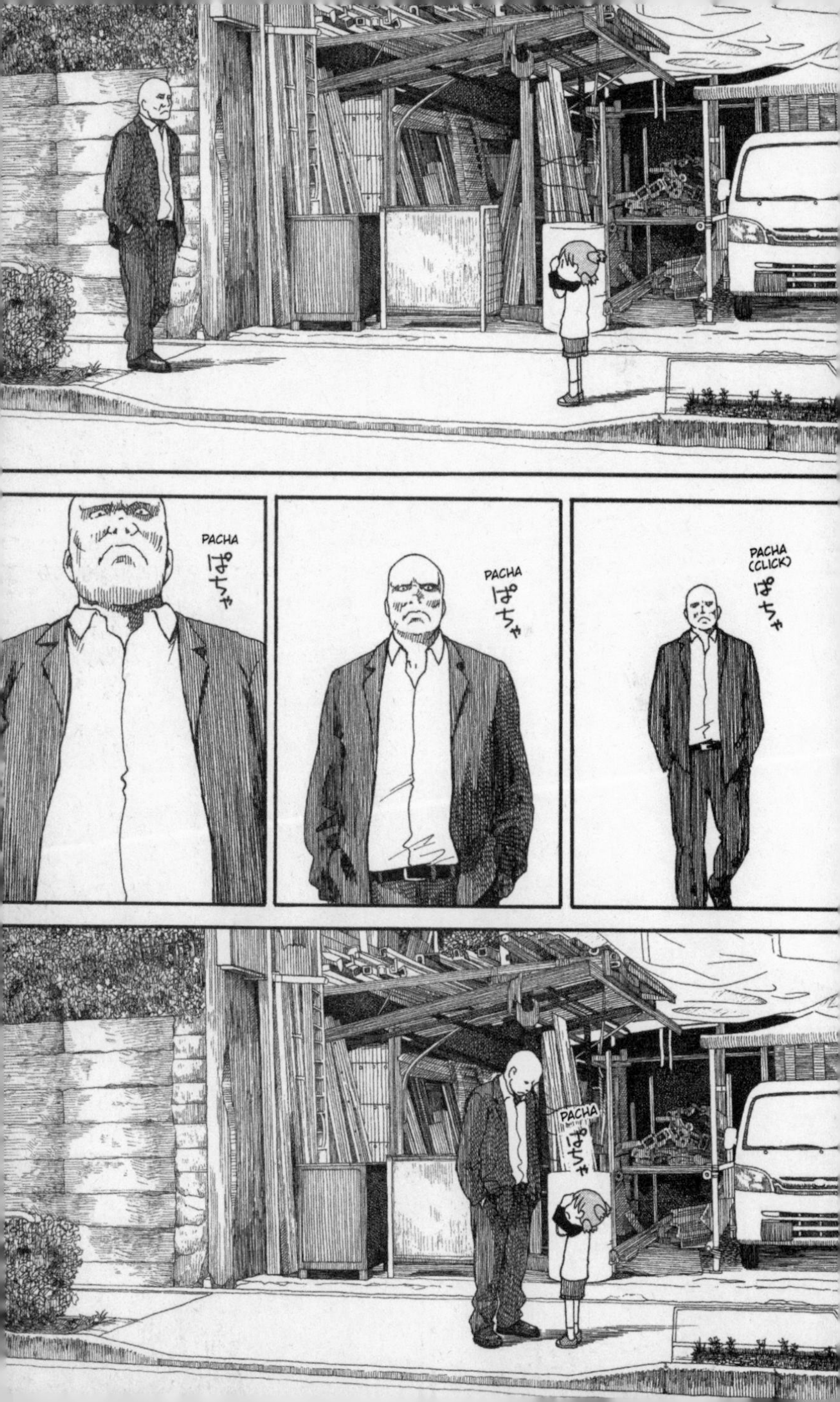
PACHA
(CLICK)
ぱちゃ
PACHA
ぱちゃ
PACHA
ぱちゃ
PACHA
ぱちゃ

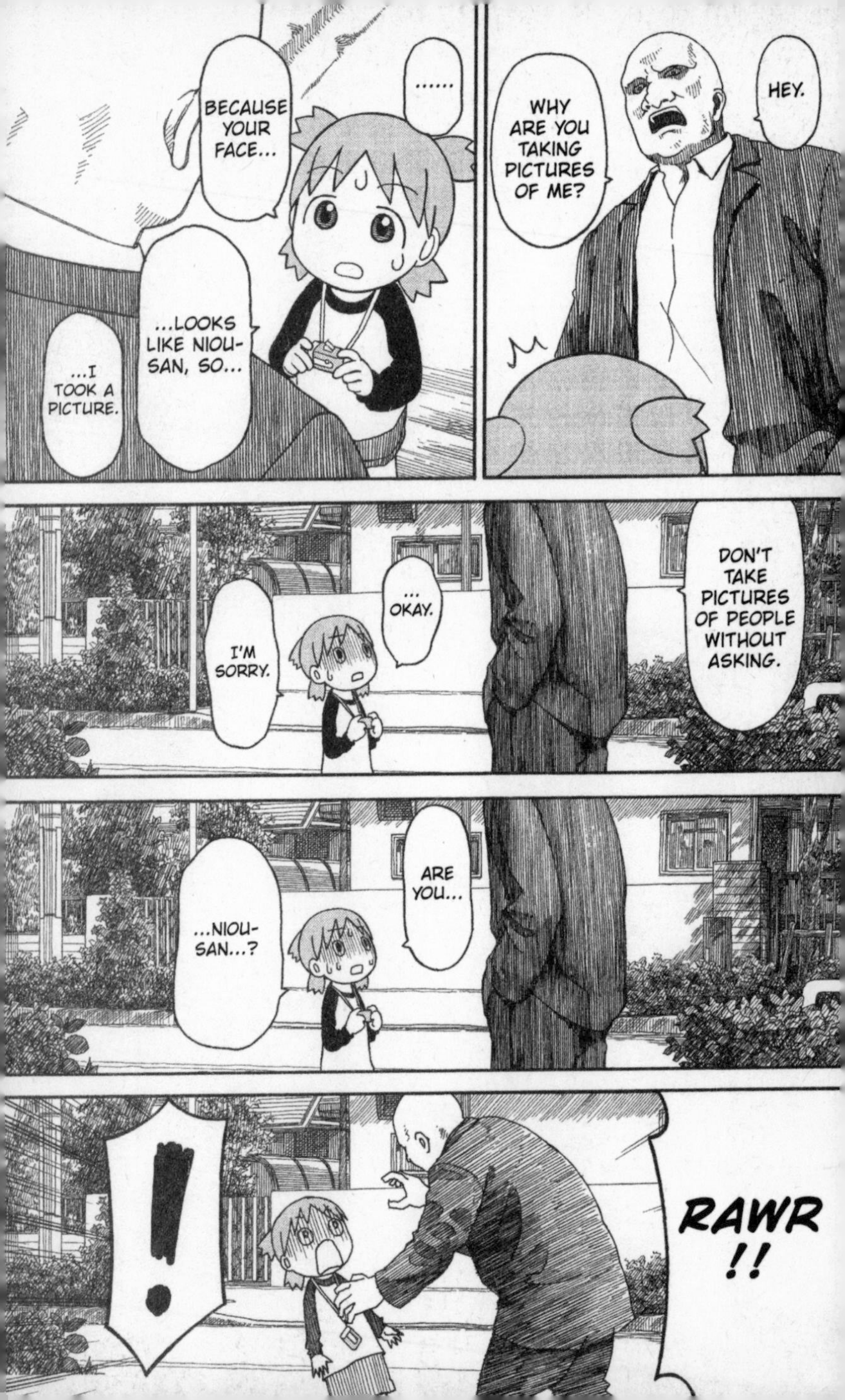
HEY.
WHY ARE YOU TAKING PICTURES OF ME?
......
BECAUSE YOUR FACE...
...LOOKS LIKE NIOU-SAN, SO...
...I TOOK A PICTURE.
DON'T TAKE PICTURES OF PEOPLE WITHOUT ASKING.
... OKAY.
I'M SORRY.
ARE YOU...
...NIOU-SAN...?
RAWR !!
!

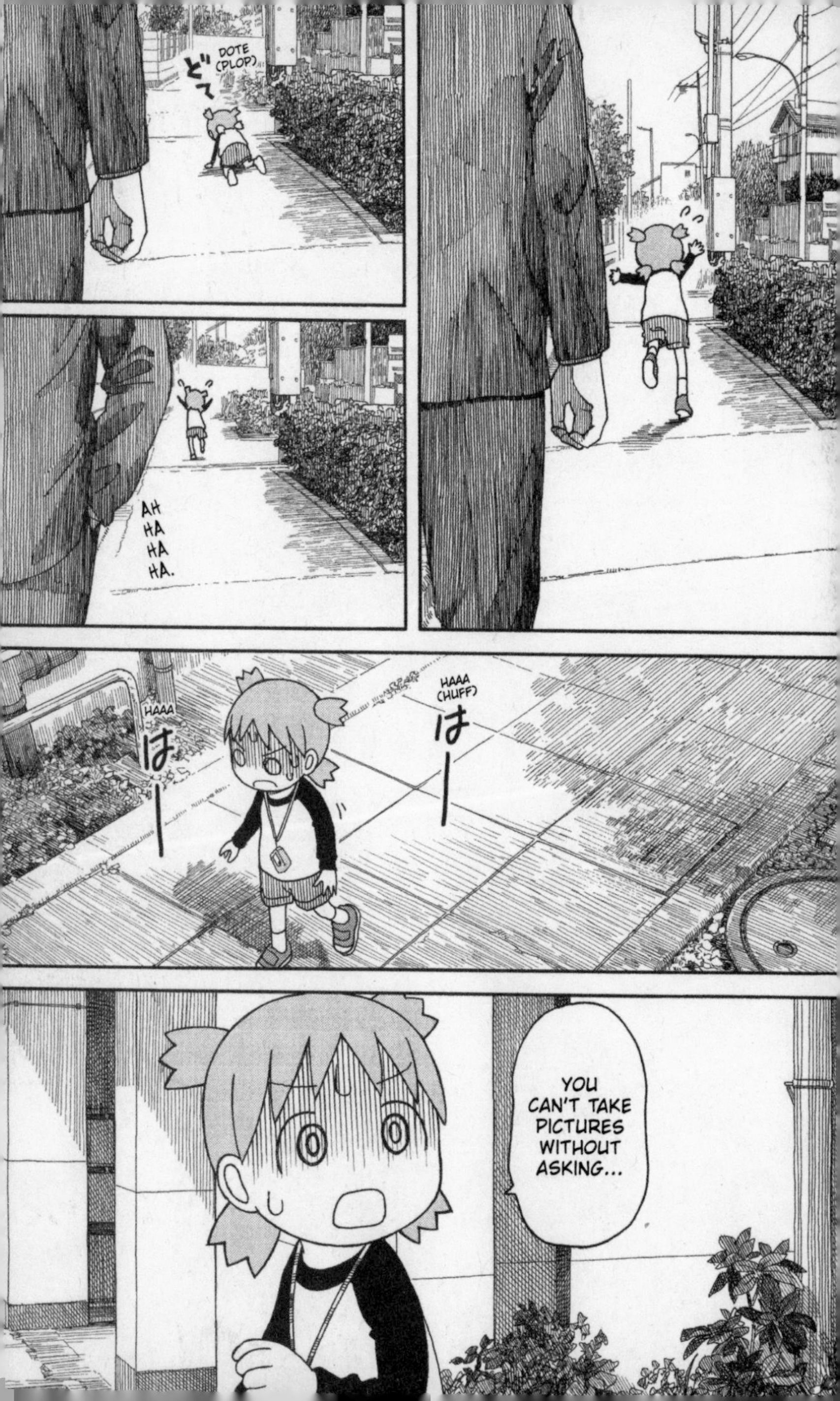
DOTE (PLOP)
どて
AH HA HA HA.
HAAA (HUFF)
は一
HAAA
は一
YOU CAN'T TAKE PICTURES WITHOUT ASKING...

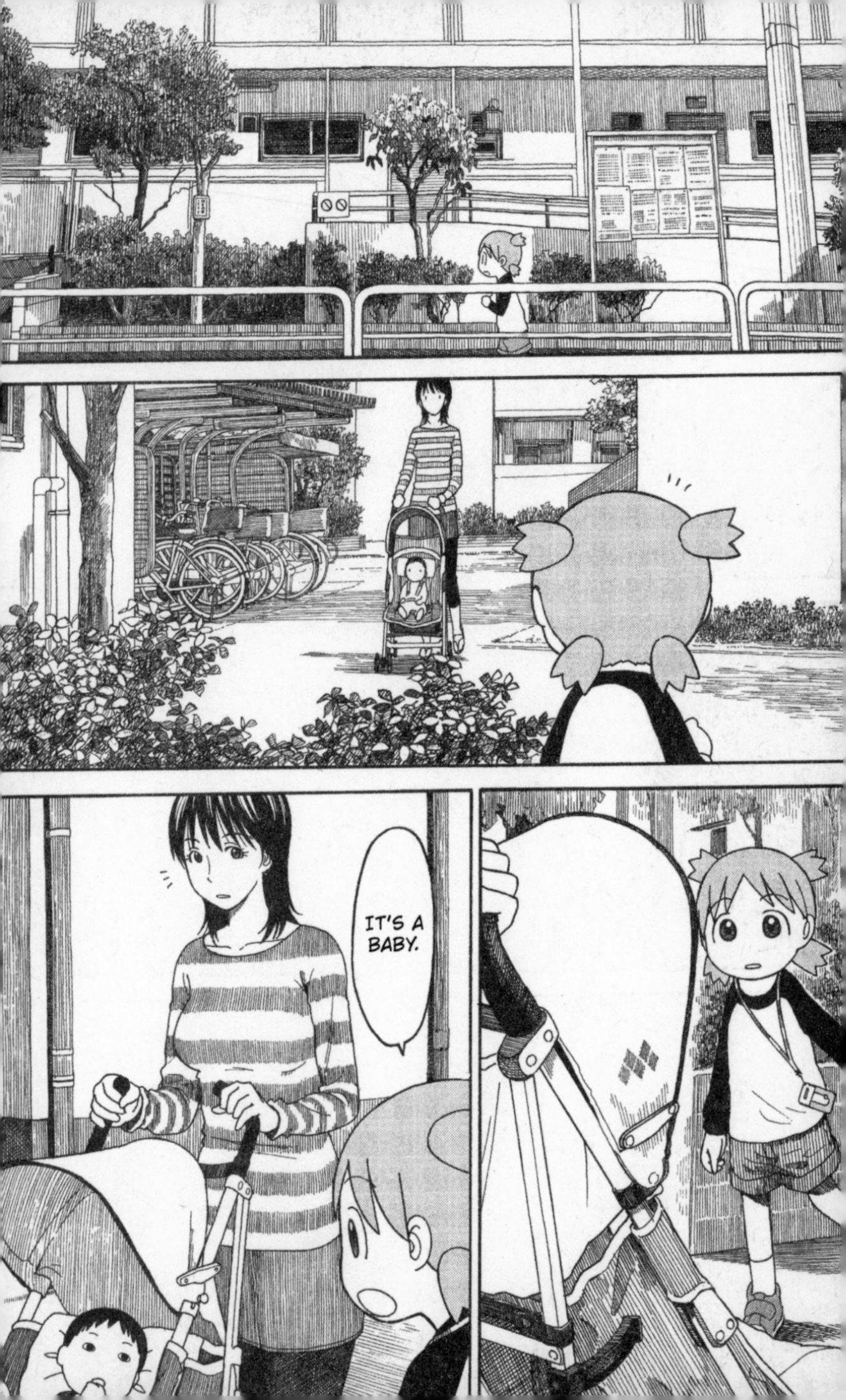
IT'S A BABY.

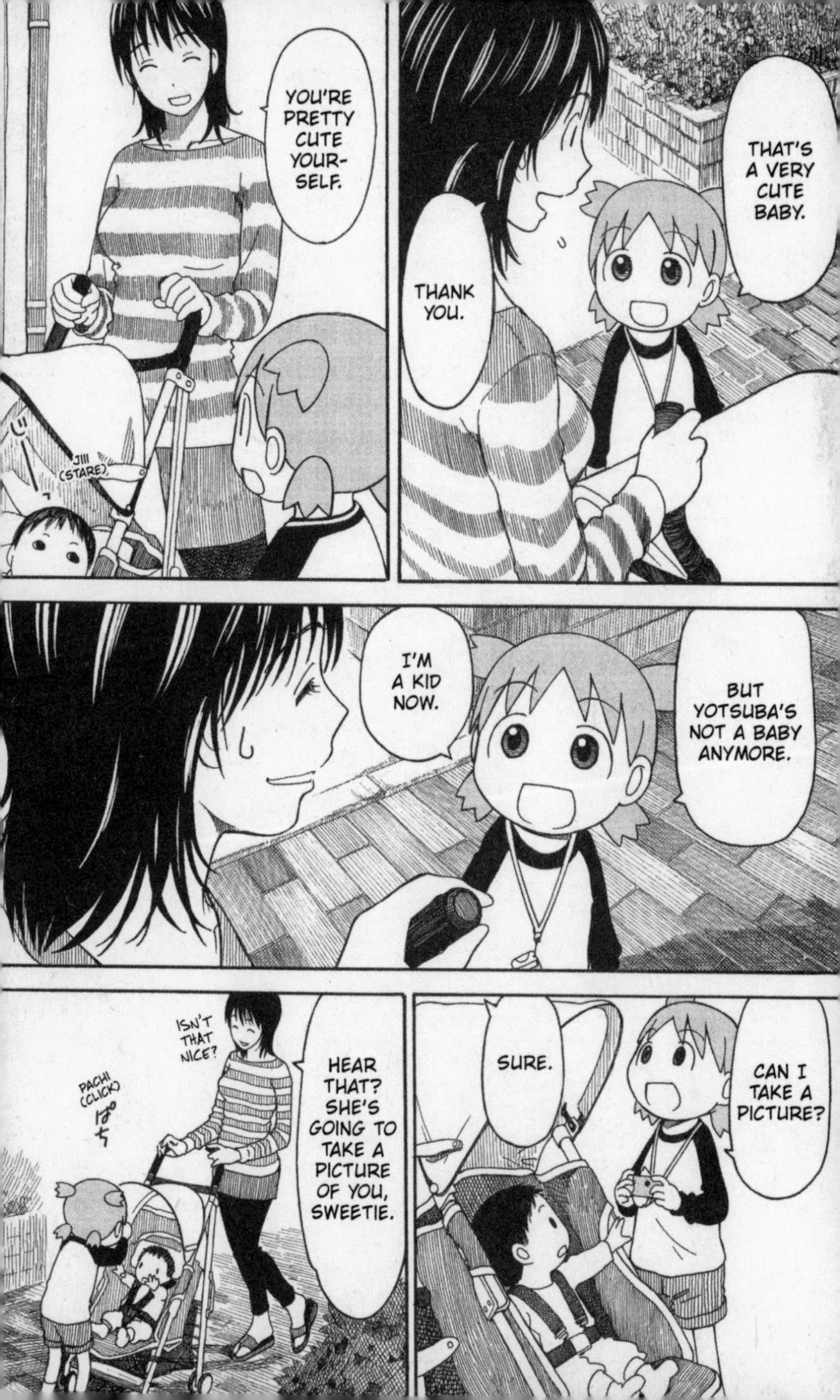
THAT'S A VERY CUTE BABY.
THANK YOU.
YOU'RE PRETTY CUTE YOUR-SELF.
JIII (STARE)
BUT YOTSUBA'S NOT A BABY ANYMORE.
I'M A KID NOW.
CAN I TAKE A PICTURE?
SURE.
HEAR THAT? SHE'S GOING TO TAKE A PICTURE OF YOU, SWEETIE.
ISN'T THAT NICE?
PACHI (CLICK)
ぱち

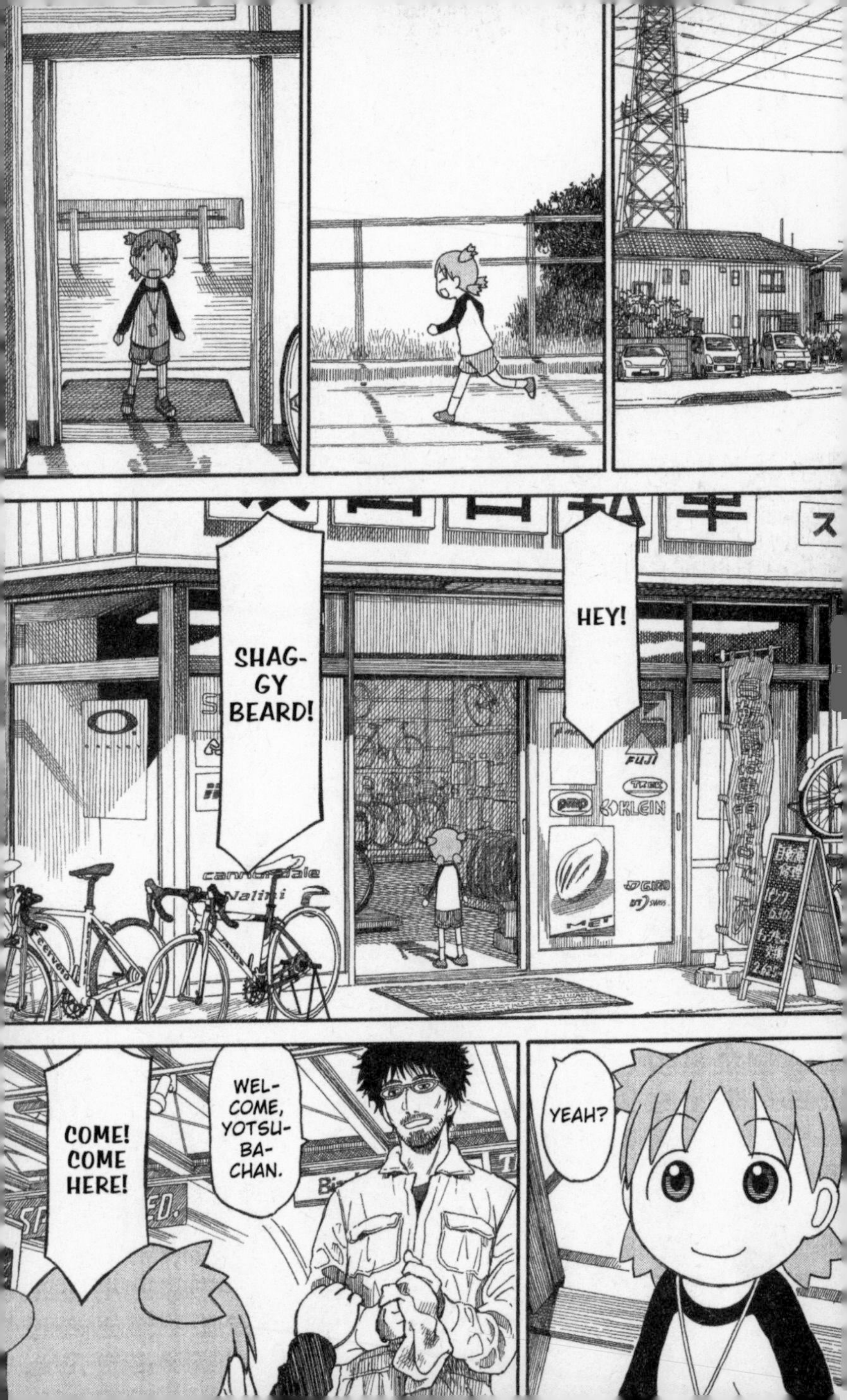

HEY!
SHAG-GY BEARD!
YEAH?
WEL-COME, YOTSU-BA-CHAN.
COME! COME HERE!

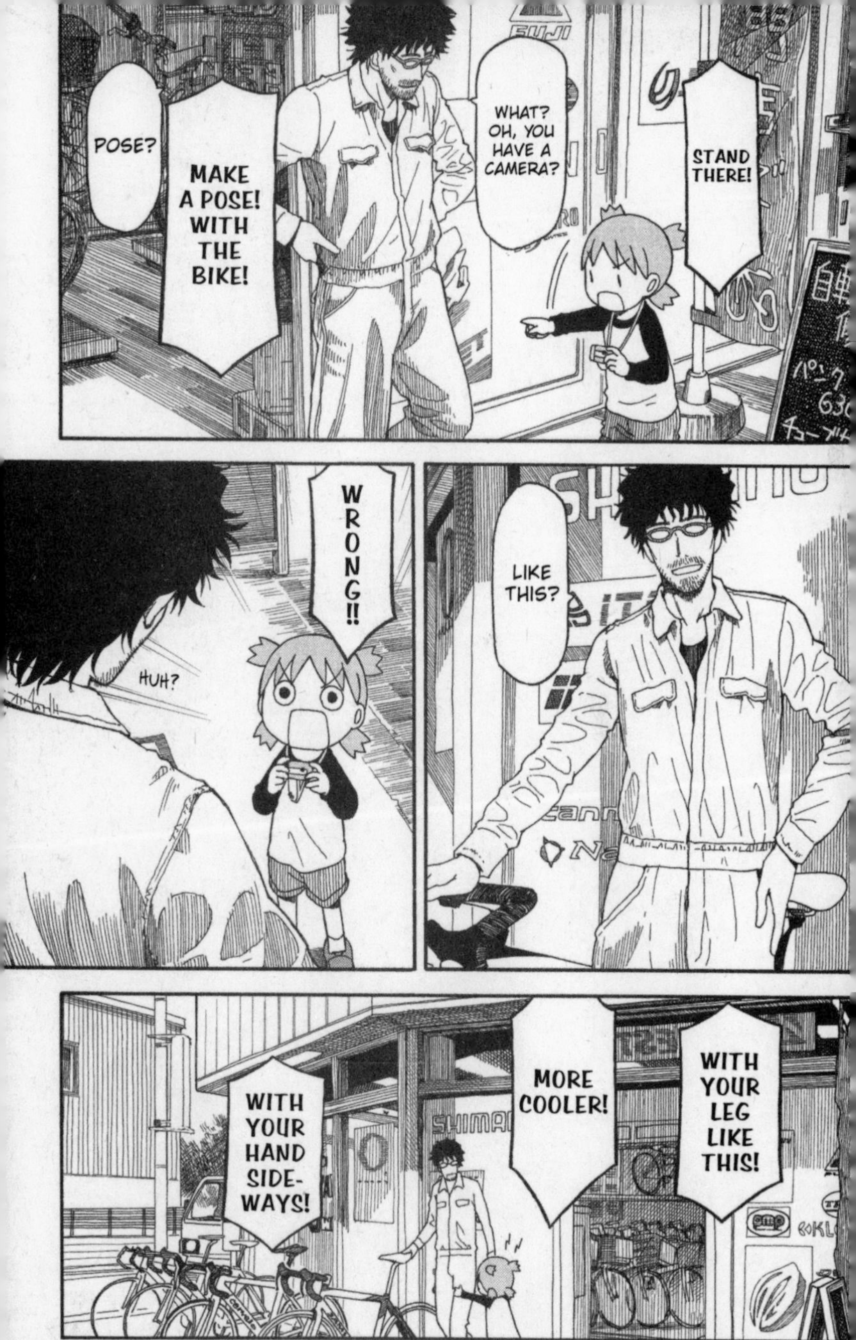
STAND THERE!
WHAT? OH, YOU HAVE A CAMERA?
MAKE A POSE! WITH THE BIKE!
POSE?
LIKE THIS?
WRONG!!
HUH?
WITH YOUR LEG LIKE THIS!
MORE COOLER!
WITH YOUR HAND SIDE-WAYS!

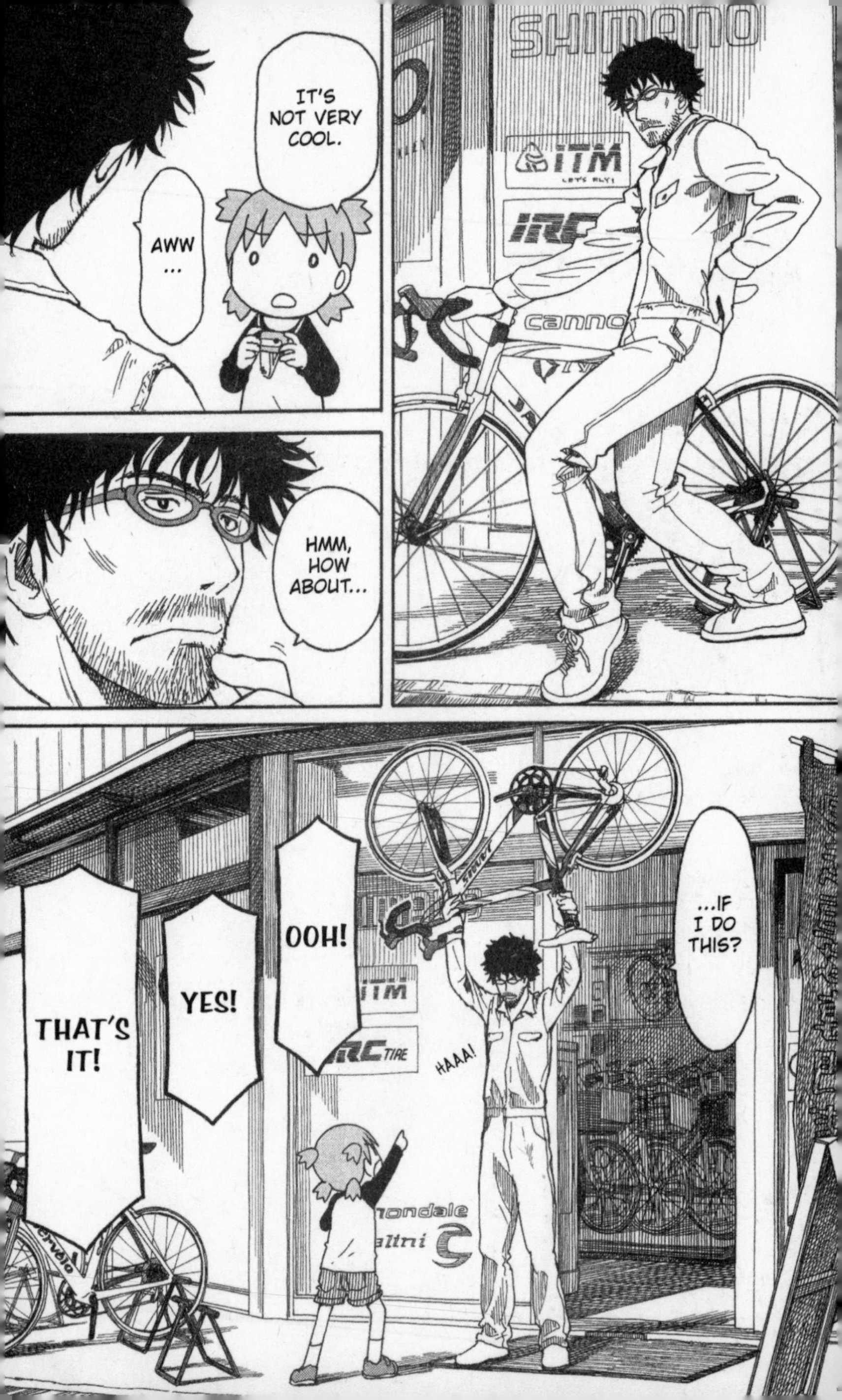
IT'S NOT VERY COOL.
AWW ...
HMM, HOW ABOUT...
...IF I DO THIS?
HAAA!
OOH!
YES!
THAT'S IT!

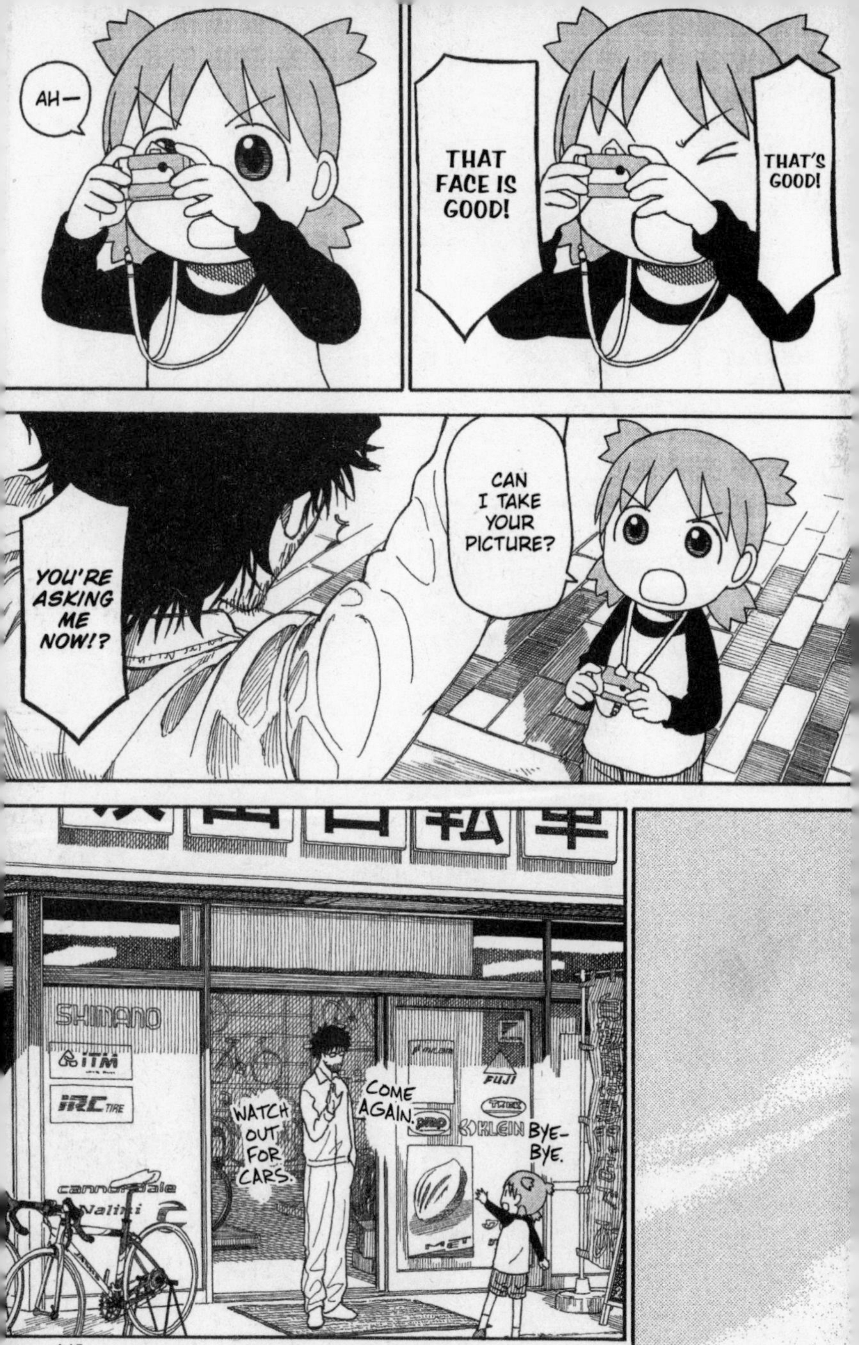
THAT'S GOOD!
THAT FACE IS GOOD!
AH—
CAN I TAKE YOUR PICTURE?
YOU'RE ASKING ME NOW!?
BYE-BYE.
COME AGAIN.
WATCH OUT FOR CARS.
SHIMANO
IRC TIRE
FUJI
KLEIN

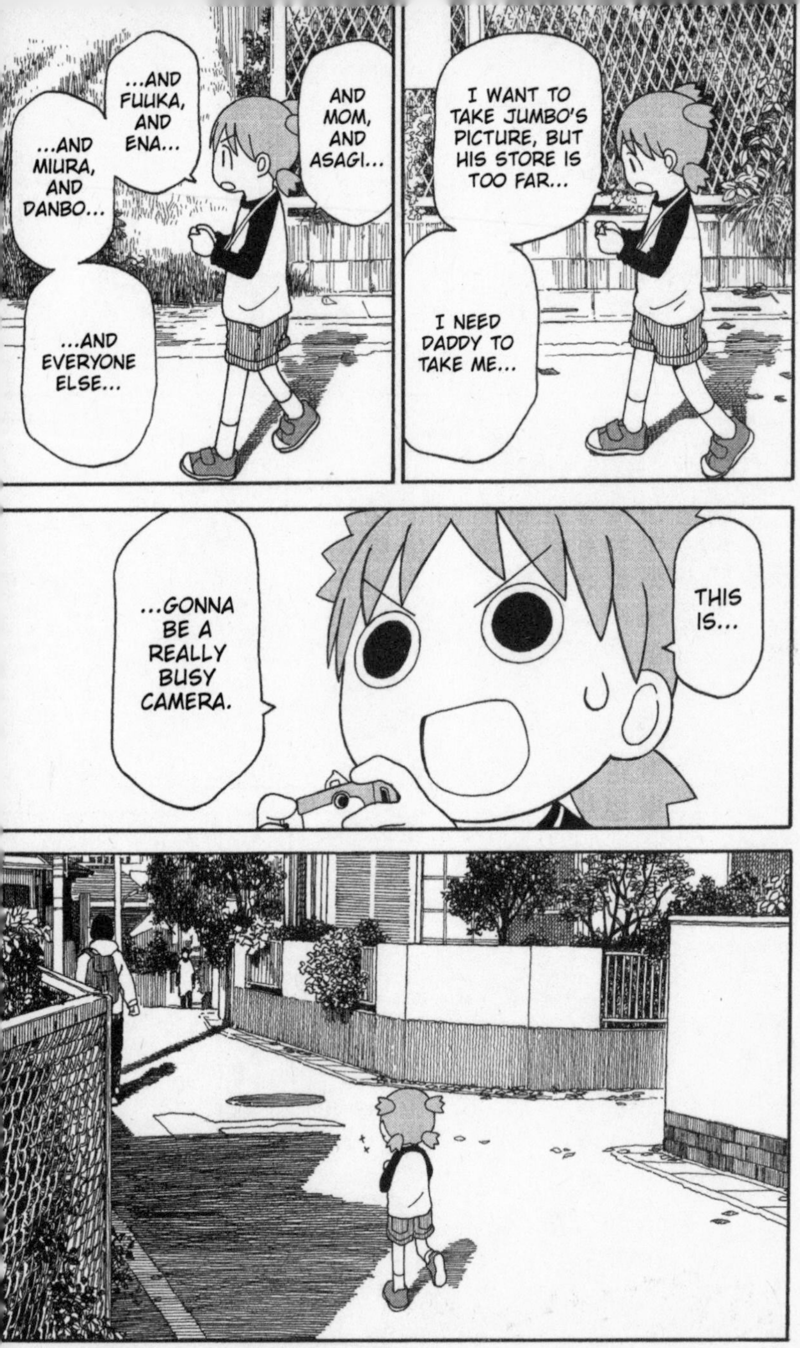
I WANT TO TAKE JUMBO'S PICTURE, BUT HIS STORE IS TOO FAR...
I NEED DADDY TO TAKE ME...
AND MOM, AND ASAGI...
...AND FUUKA, AND ENA...
...AND MIURA, AND DANBO...
...AND EVERYONE ELSE...
THIS IS...
...GONNA BE A REALLY BUSY CAMERA.

YOTSUBA&!

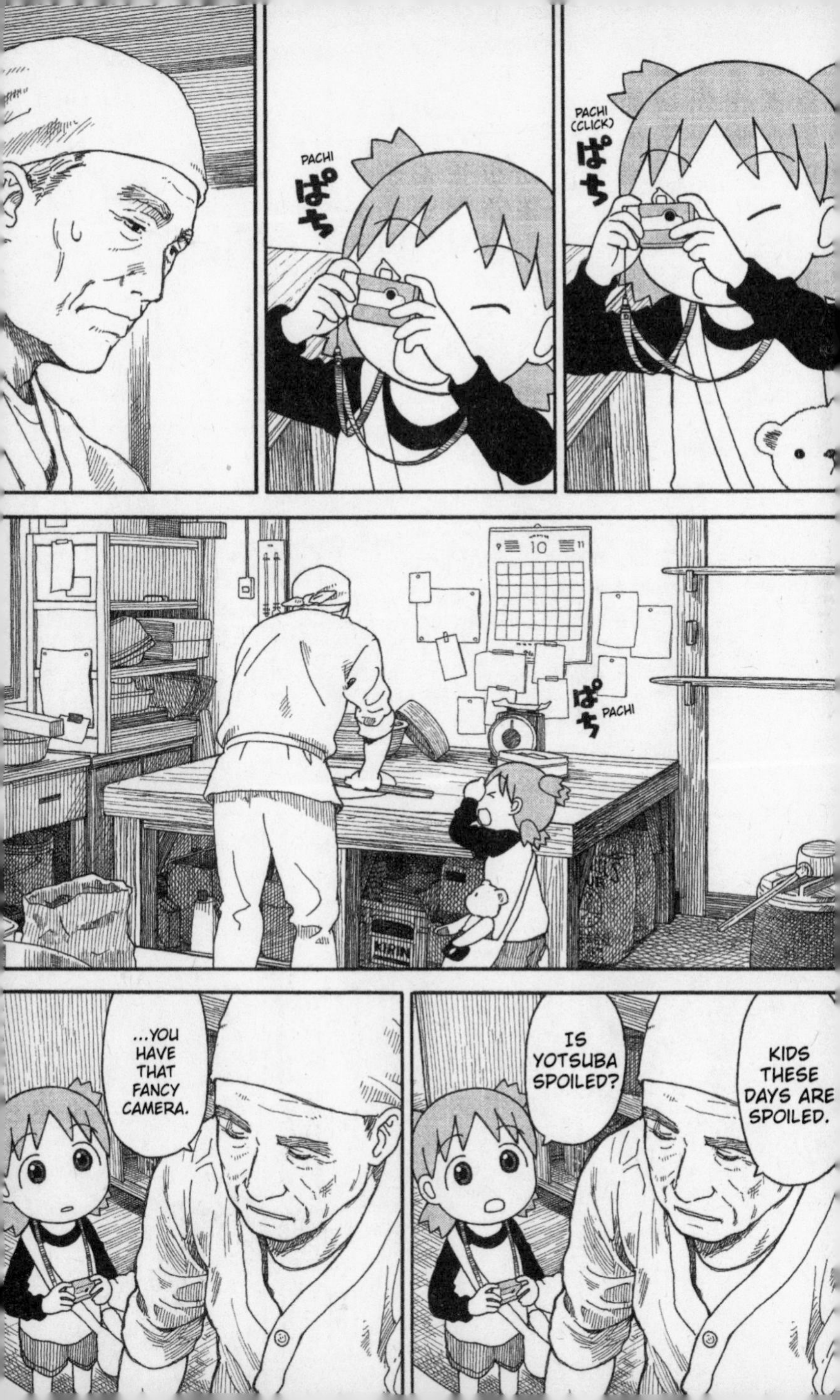
PACHI (CLICK)
ぱち
PACHI
ぱち
ぱち
PACHI
KIDS THESE DAYS ARE SPOILED.
IS YOTSUBA SPOILED?
...YOU HAVE THAT FANCY CAMERA.

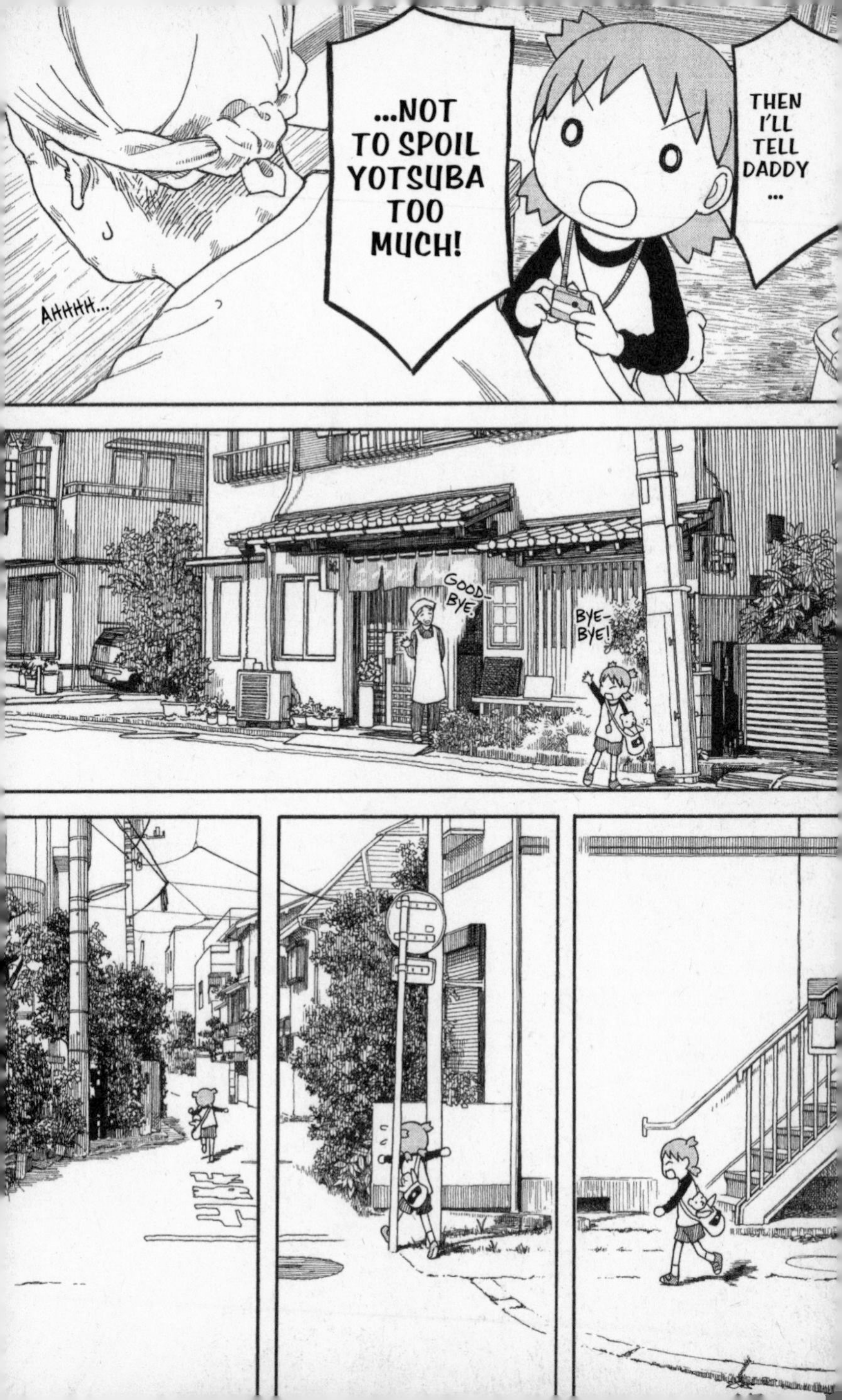
THEN I'LL TELL DADDY ...
...NOT TO SPOIL YOTSUBA TOO MUCH!
AHHHH...
GOOD-BYE.
BYE-BYE!

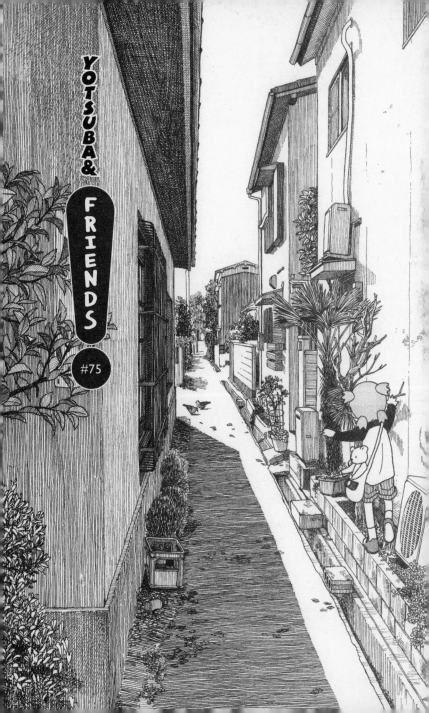

YOTSUBA&

FRIENDS!

#75

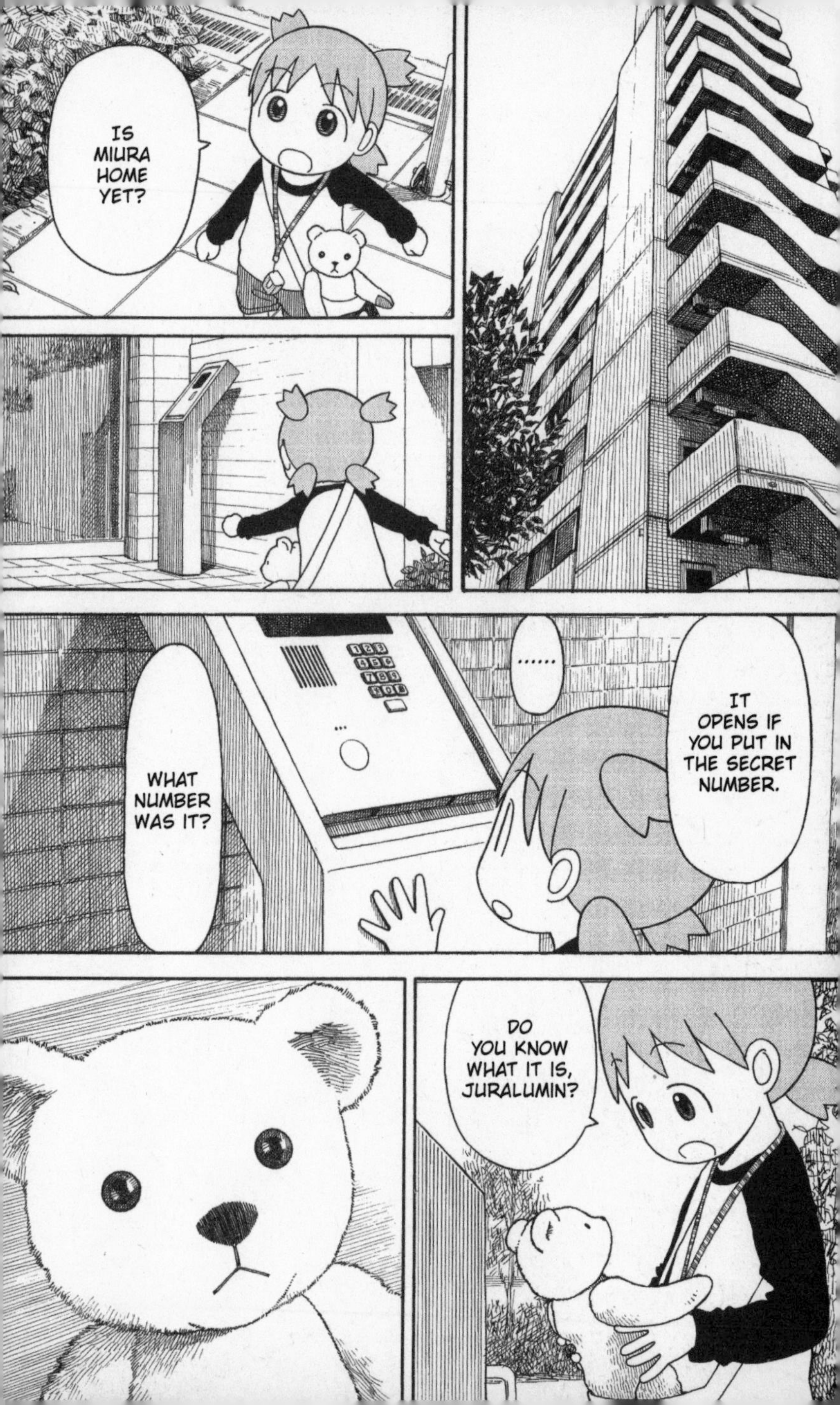
IS MIURA HOME YET?
IT OPENS IF YOU PUT IN THE SECRET NUMBER.
......
WHAT NUMBER WAS IT?
DO YOU KNOW WHAT IT IS, JURALUMIN?

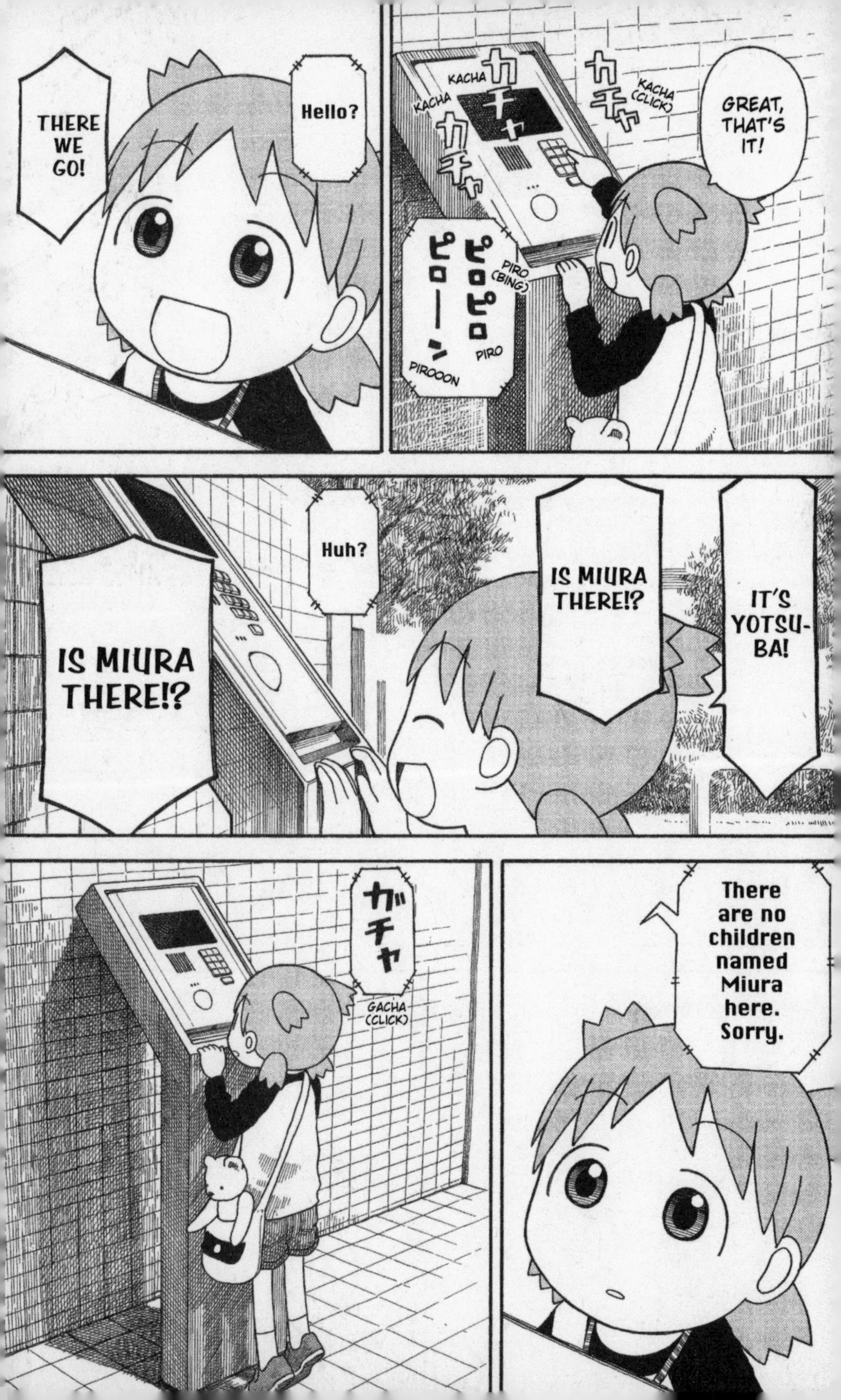
GREAT, THAT'S IT!
カチャカチャ
KACHA KACHA (CLICK)
カチャカチャ
KACHA KACHA
ピロピロピローン
PIRO (BING) PIRO PIROOON
Hello?
THERE WE GO!
IT'S YOTSU-BA!
IS MIURA THERE!?
Huh?
IS MIURA THERE!?
There are no children named Miura here. Sorry.
ガチャ
GACHA (CLICK)

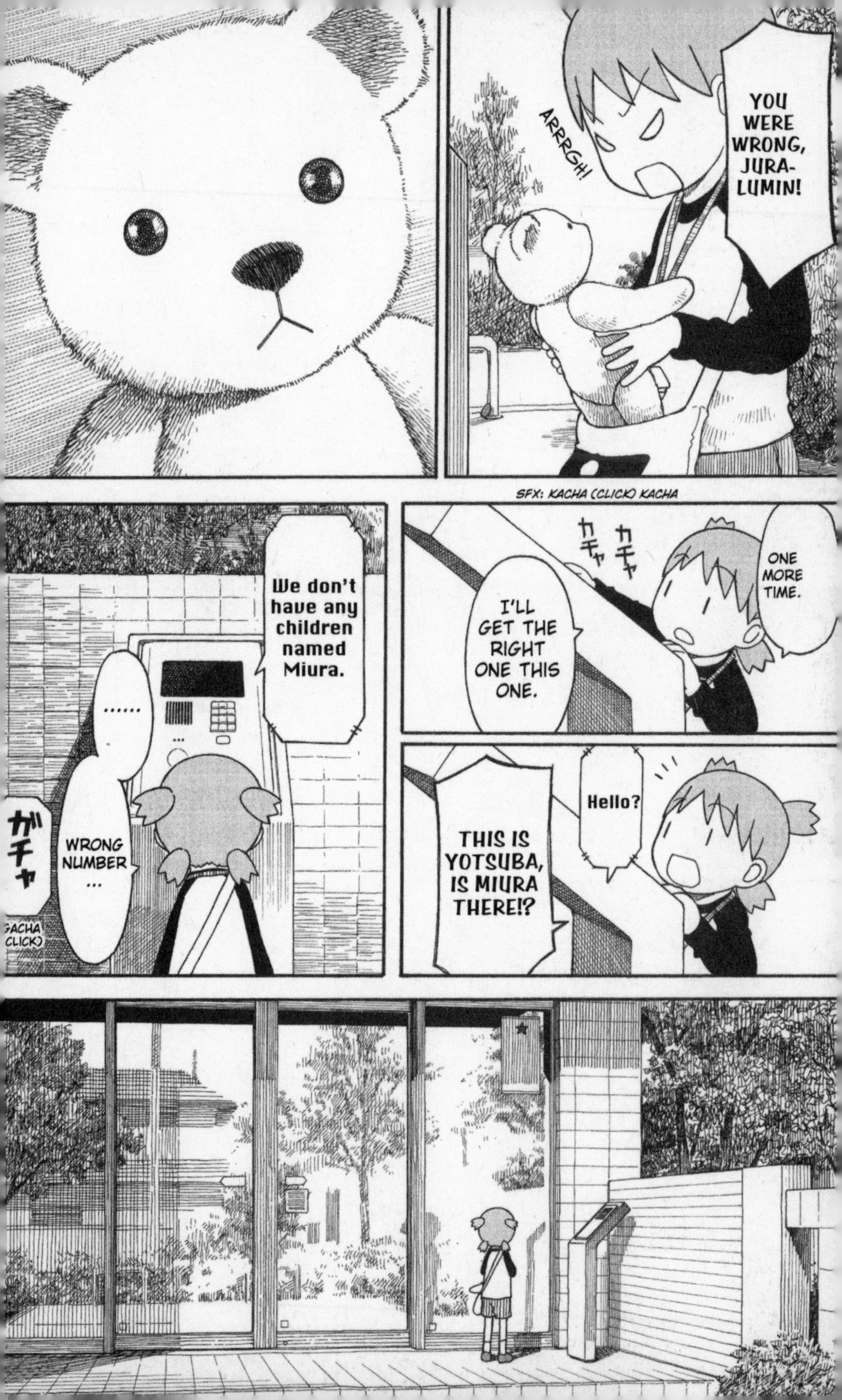
YOU WERE WRONG, JURA-LUMIN!
ARRRGH!
SFX: KACHA (CLICK) KACHA
ONE MORE TIME.
カチャ
カチャ
I'LL GET THE RIGHT ONE THIS ONE.
Hello?
THIS IS YOTSUBA, IS MIURA THERE!?
We don't have any children named Miura.
......
WRONG NUMBER ...
ガチャ
GACHA (CLICK)

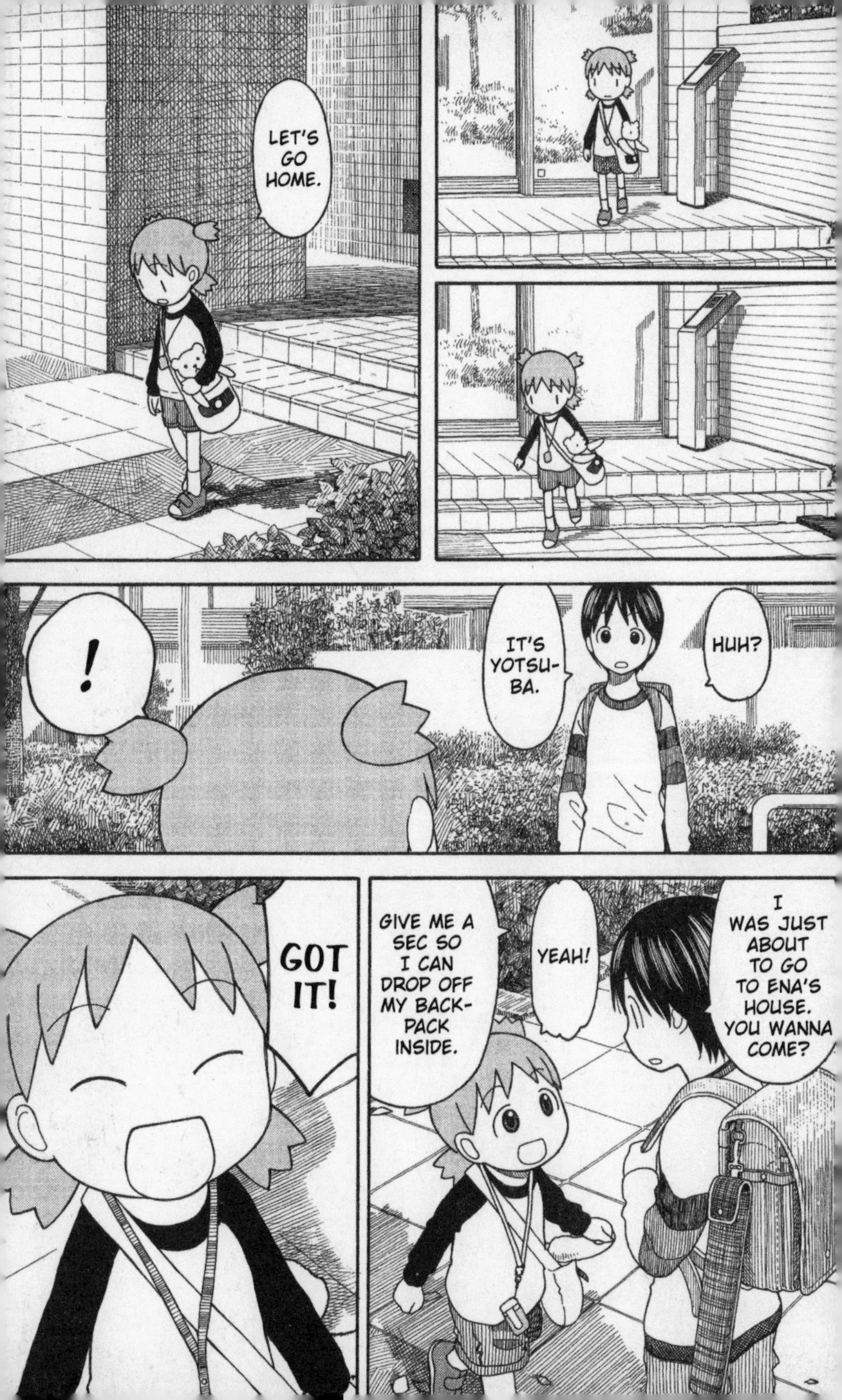
LET'S GO HOME.
HUH?
IT'S YOTSUBA.
!
I WAS JUST ABOUT TO GO TO ENA'S HOUSE. YOU WANNA COME?
YEAH!
GIVE ME A SEC SO I CAN DROP OFF MY BACK-PACK INSIDE.
GOT IT!

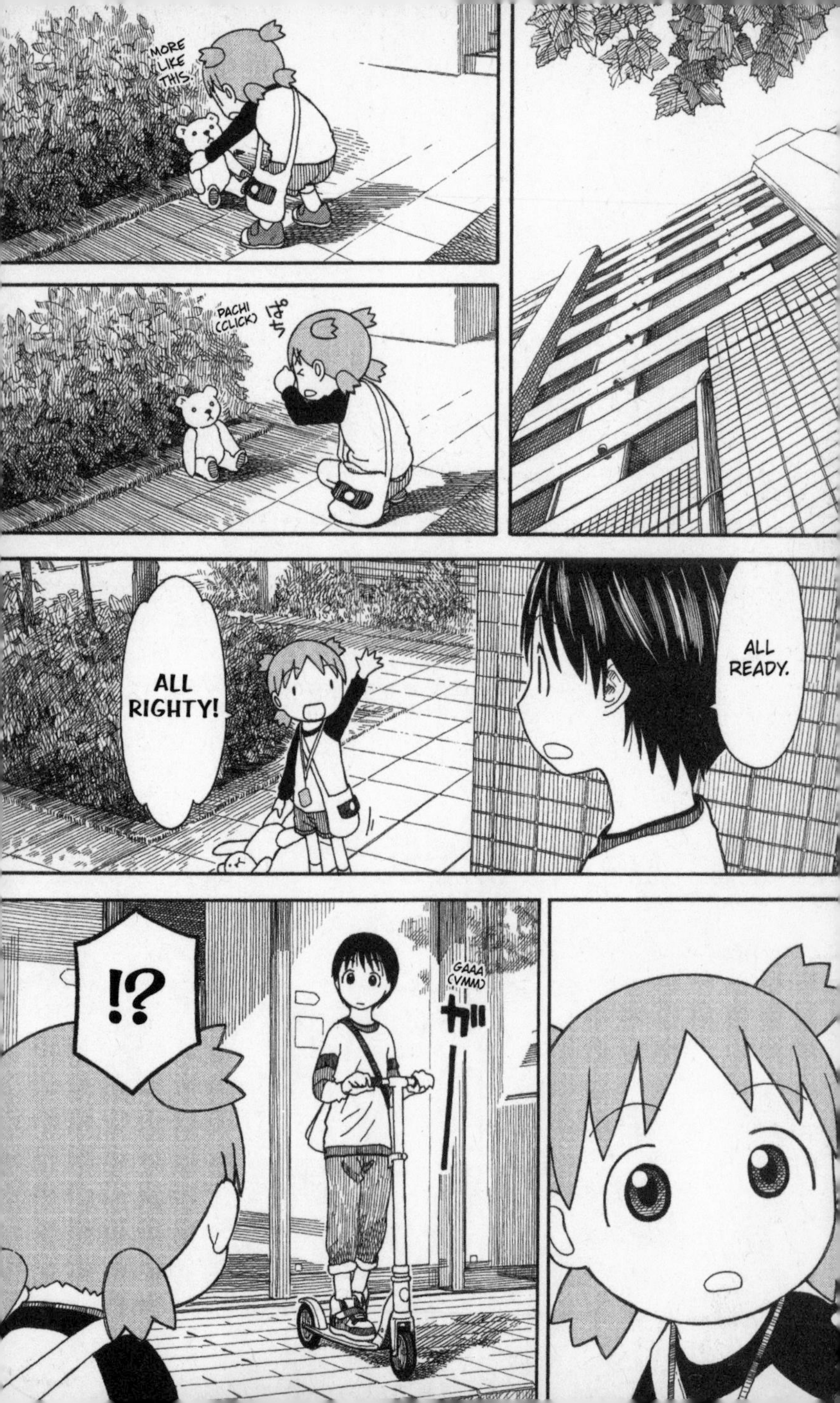
MORE LIKE THIS.
PACHI (CLICK) ぱち
ALL READY.
ALL RIGHTY!
!?
GAAA (VMM) ガー

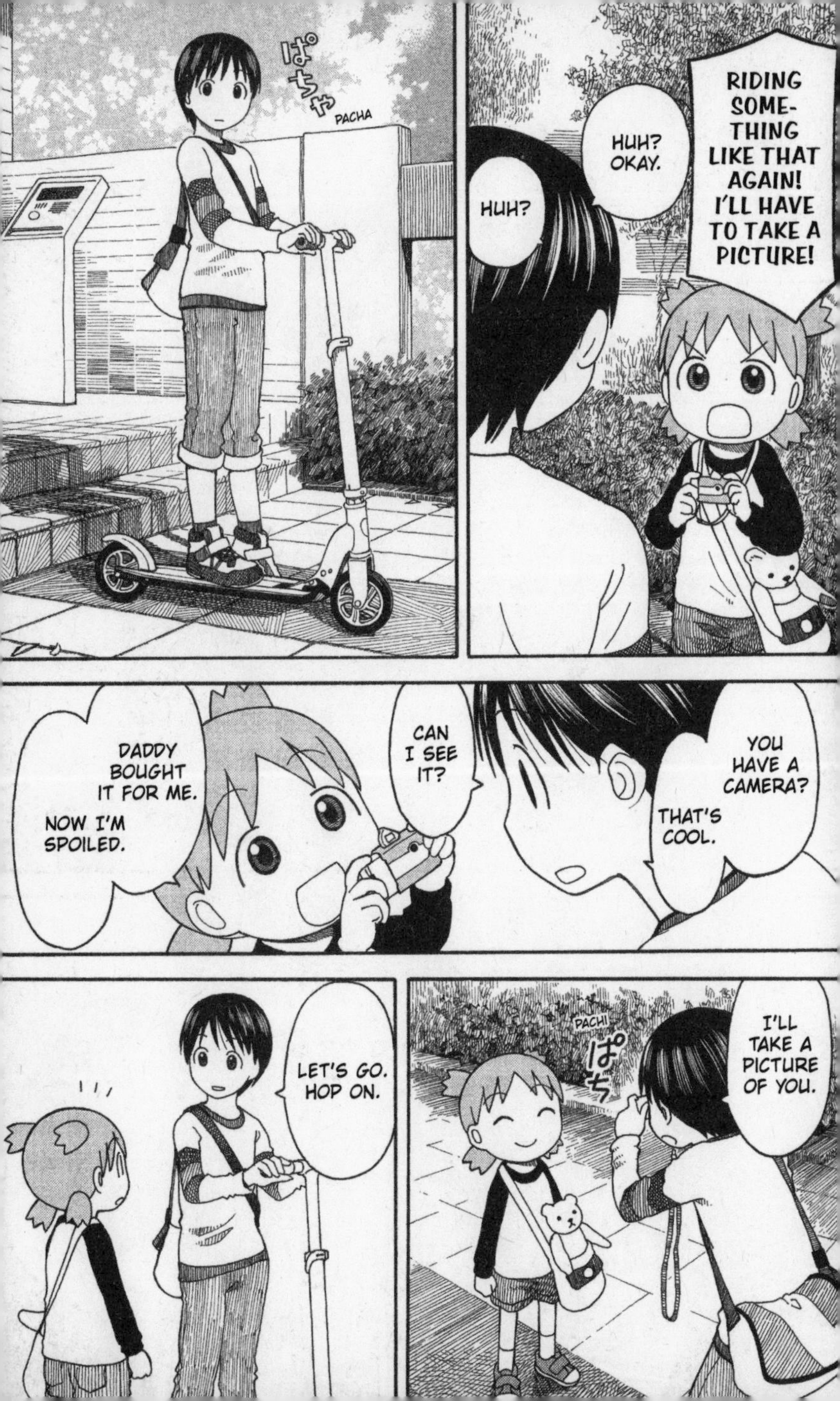

RIDING SOME-THING LIKE THAT AGAIN! I'LL HAVE TO TAKE A PICTURE!
HUH? OKAY.
HUH?
ぱちゃ
PACHA
YOU HAVE A CAMERA?
THAT'S COOL.
CAN I SEE IT?
DADDY BOUGHT IT FOR ME.
NOW I'M SPOILED.
I'LL TAKE A PICTURE OF YOU.
ぱち
PACHI
LET'S GO. HOP ON.

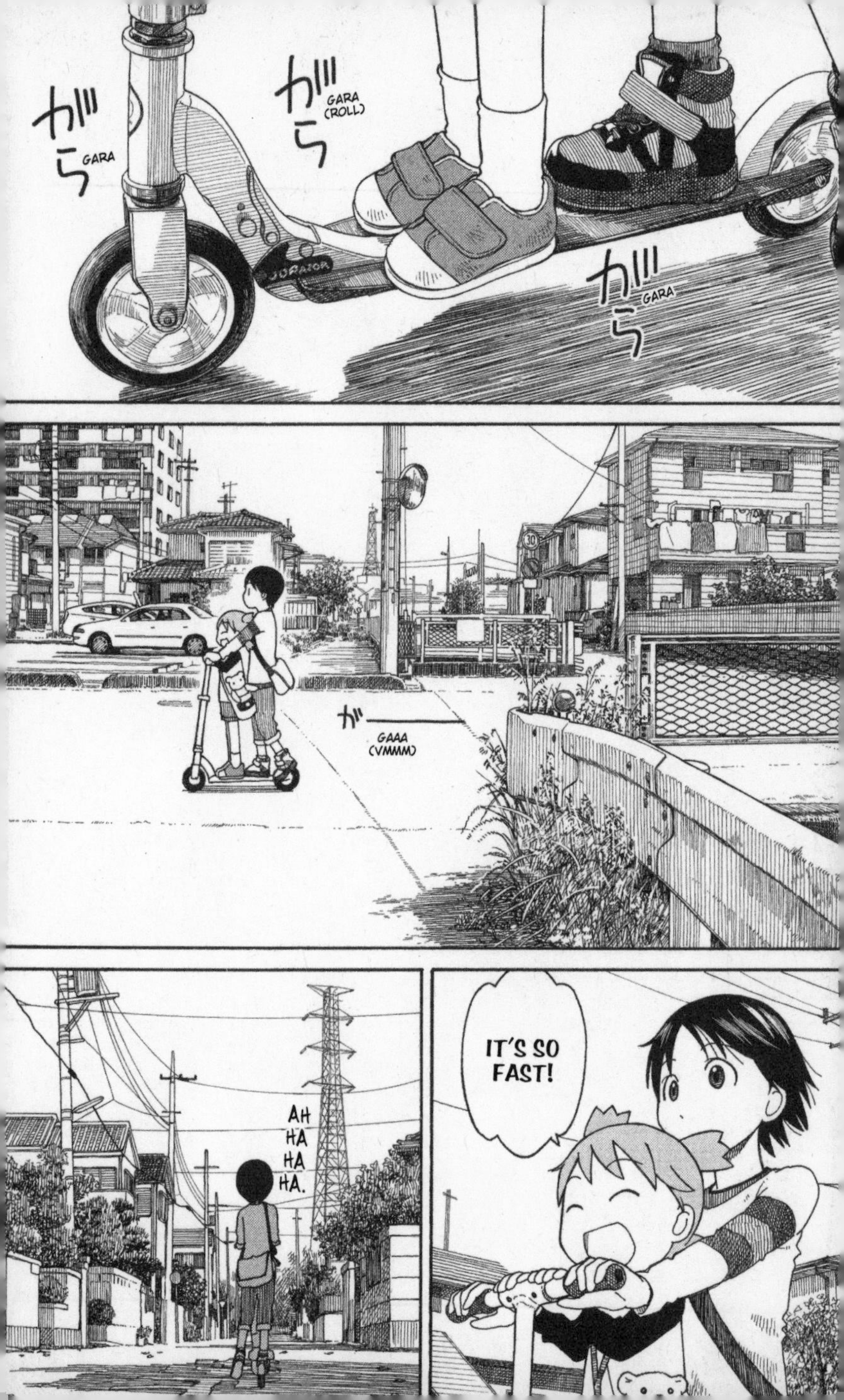

ガ
ら
GARA (ROLL)
ガ
ら
GARA
ガ
ら
GARA
ガ———
GAAA (VMMM)
IT'S SO FAST!
AH HA HA HA HA.

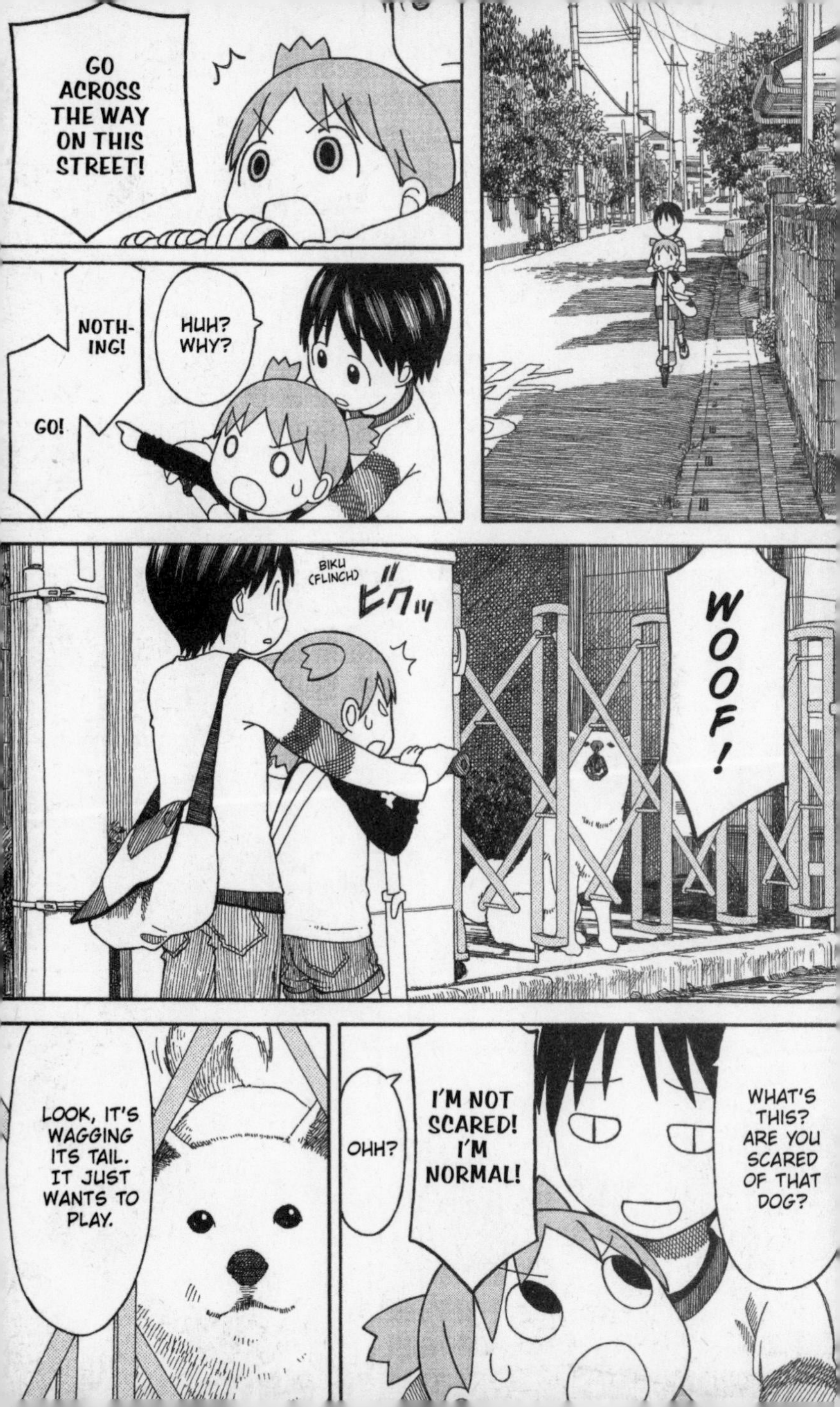
GO ACROSS THE WAY ON THIS STREET!
HUH? WHY?
NOTH-ING!
GO!
BIKU (FLINCH)
ビクッ
WOOF!
WHAT'S THIS? ARE YOU SCARED OF THAT DOG?
I'M NOT SCARED! I'M NORMAL!
OHH?
LOOK, IT'S WAGGING ITS TAIL. IT JUST WANTS TO PLAY.

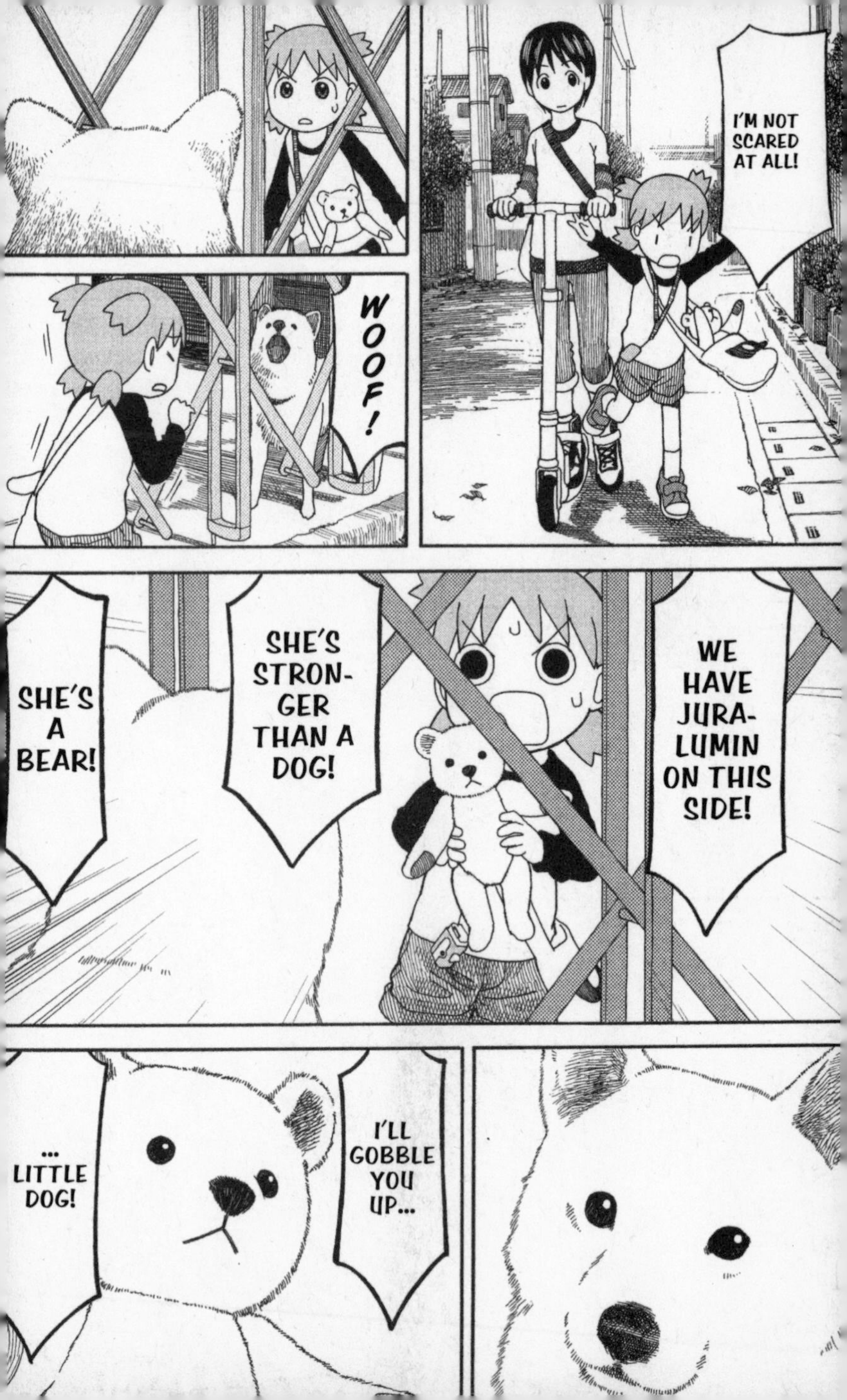
I'M NOT SCARED AT ALL!
WOOF!
WE HAVE JURA-LUMIN ON THIS SIDE!
SHE'S STRON-GER THAN A DOG!
SHE'S A BEAR!
I'LL GOBBLE YOU UP...
... LITTLE DOG!

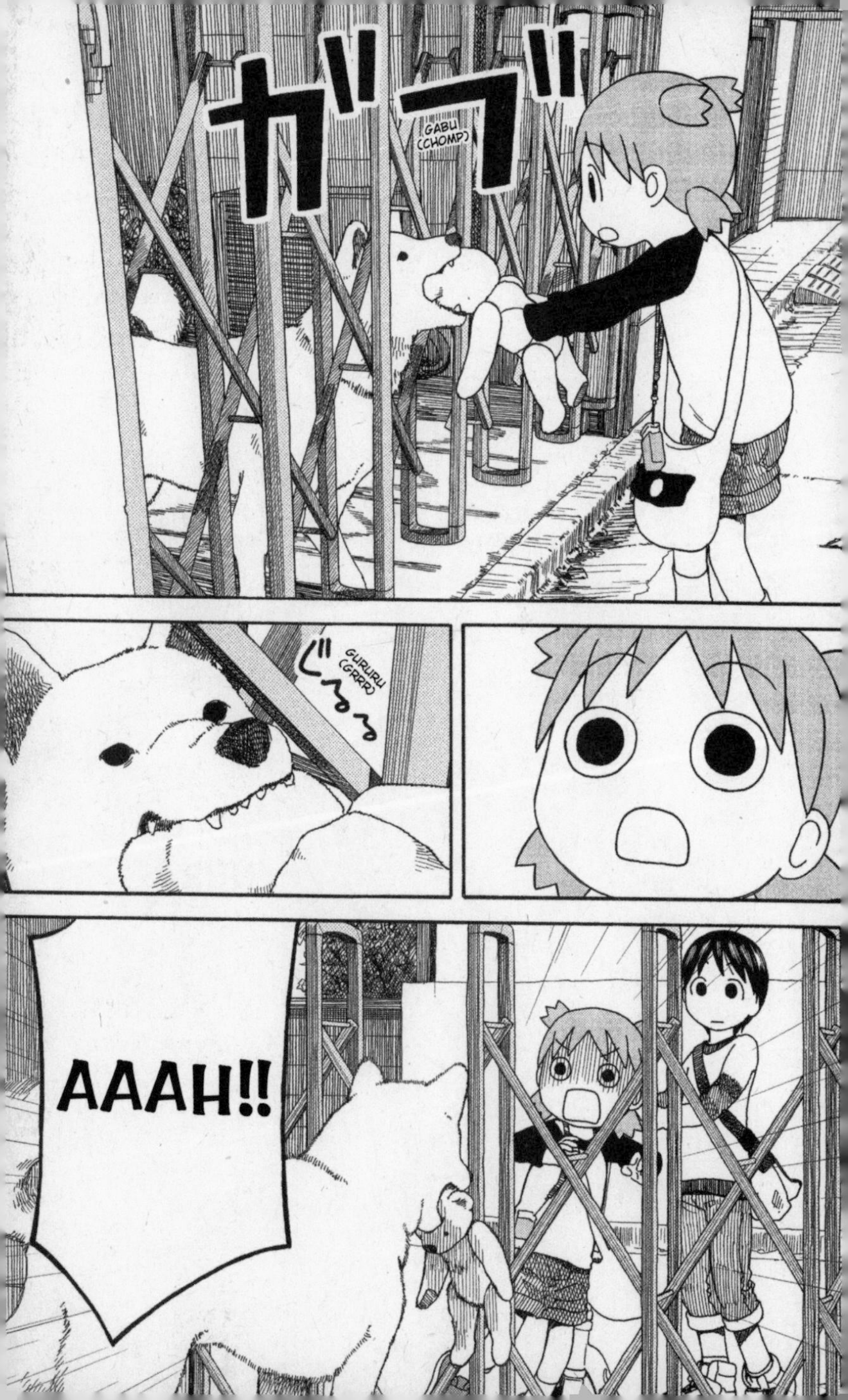
ガブ
GABU (CHOMP)
ぐるる
GURURU (GRRR)
AAAH!!

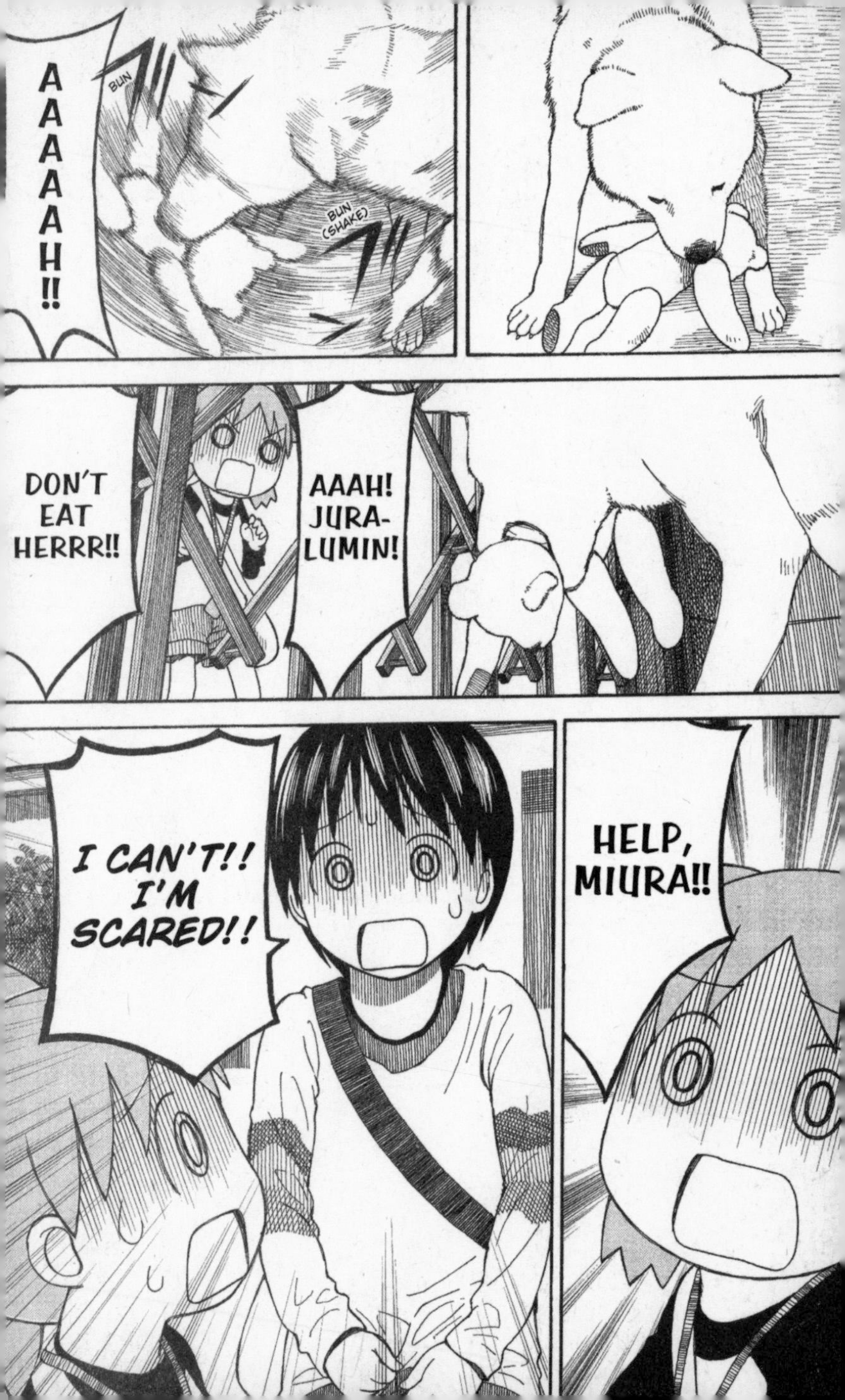
BUN
BUN (SHAKE)
AAAAAAH!!
AAAH! JURA-LUMIN!
DON'T EAT HERRR!!
HELP, MIURA!!
I CAN'T!! I'M SCARED!!

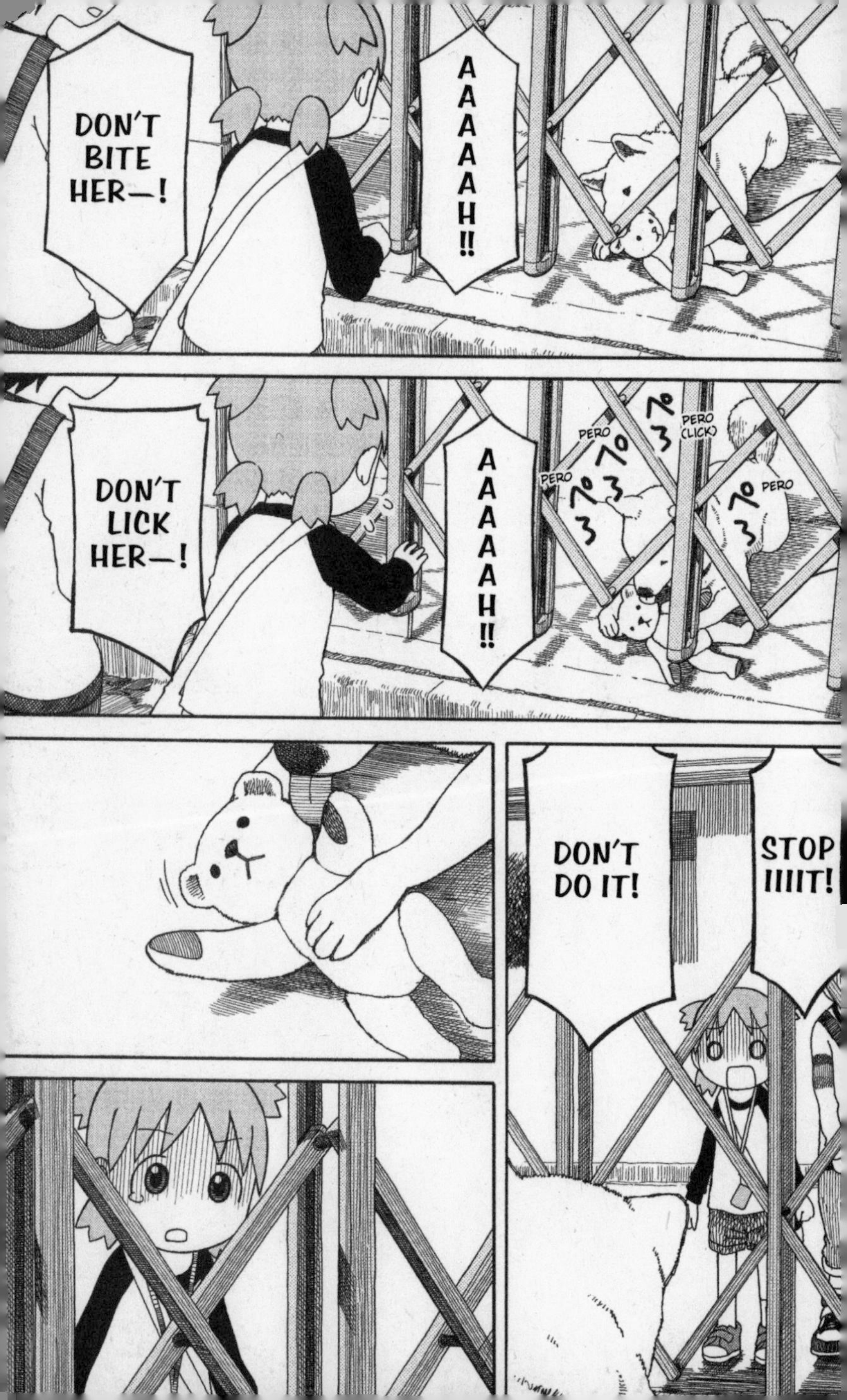
AAAAAAH!!
DON'T BITE HER—!
PERO (LICK)
PERO
PERO
PERO
AAAAAAH!!
DON'T LICK HER—!
STOP IIIIT!
DON'T DO IT!

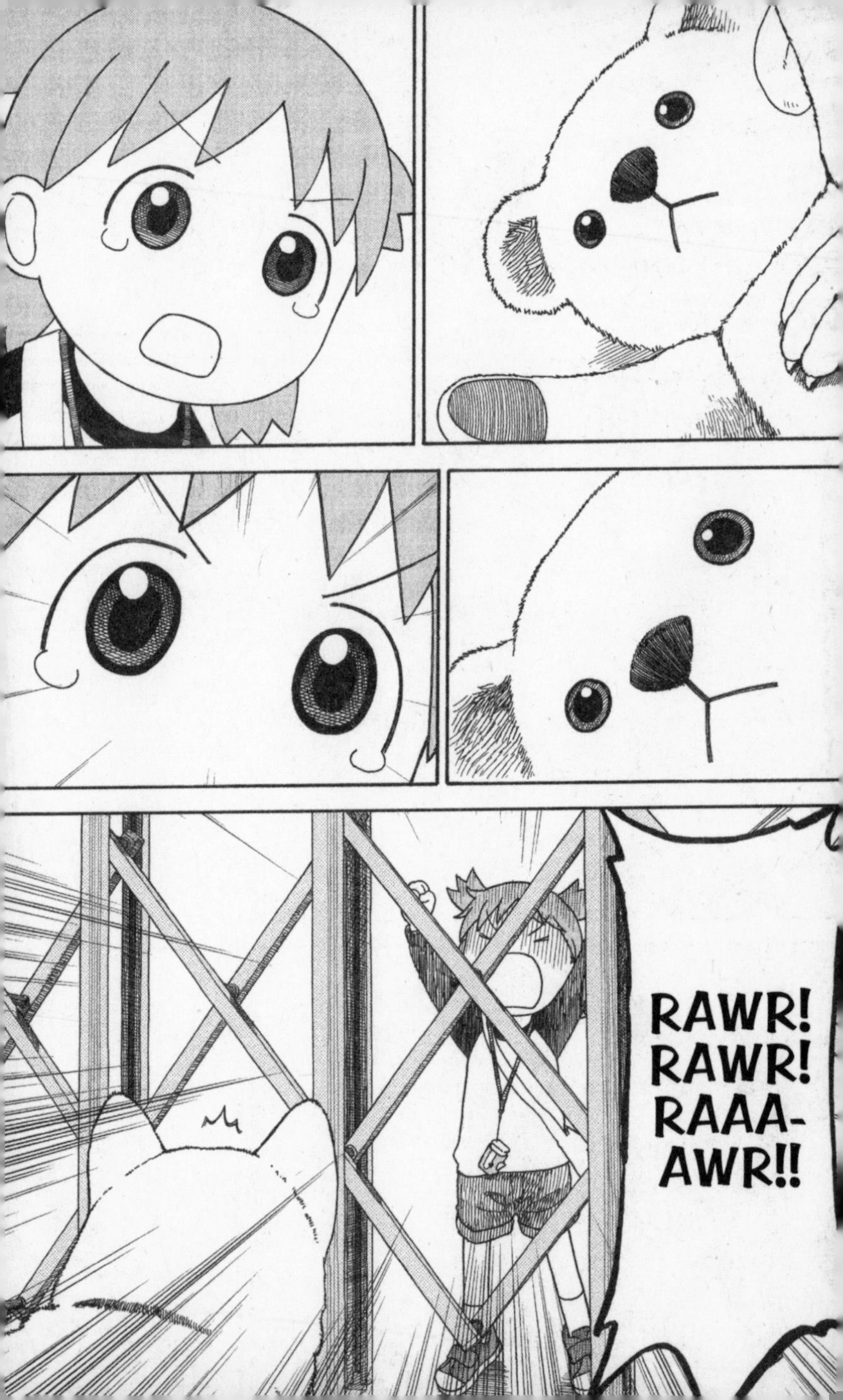
RAWR!
RAWR!
RAAA-
AWR!!

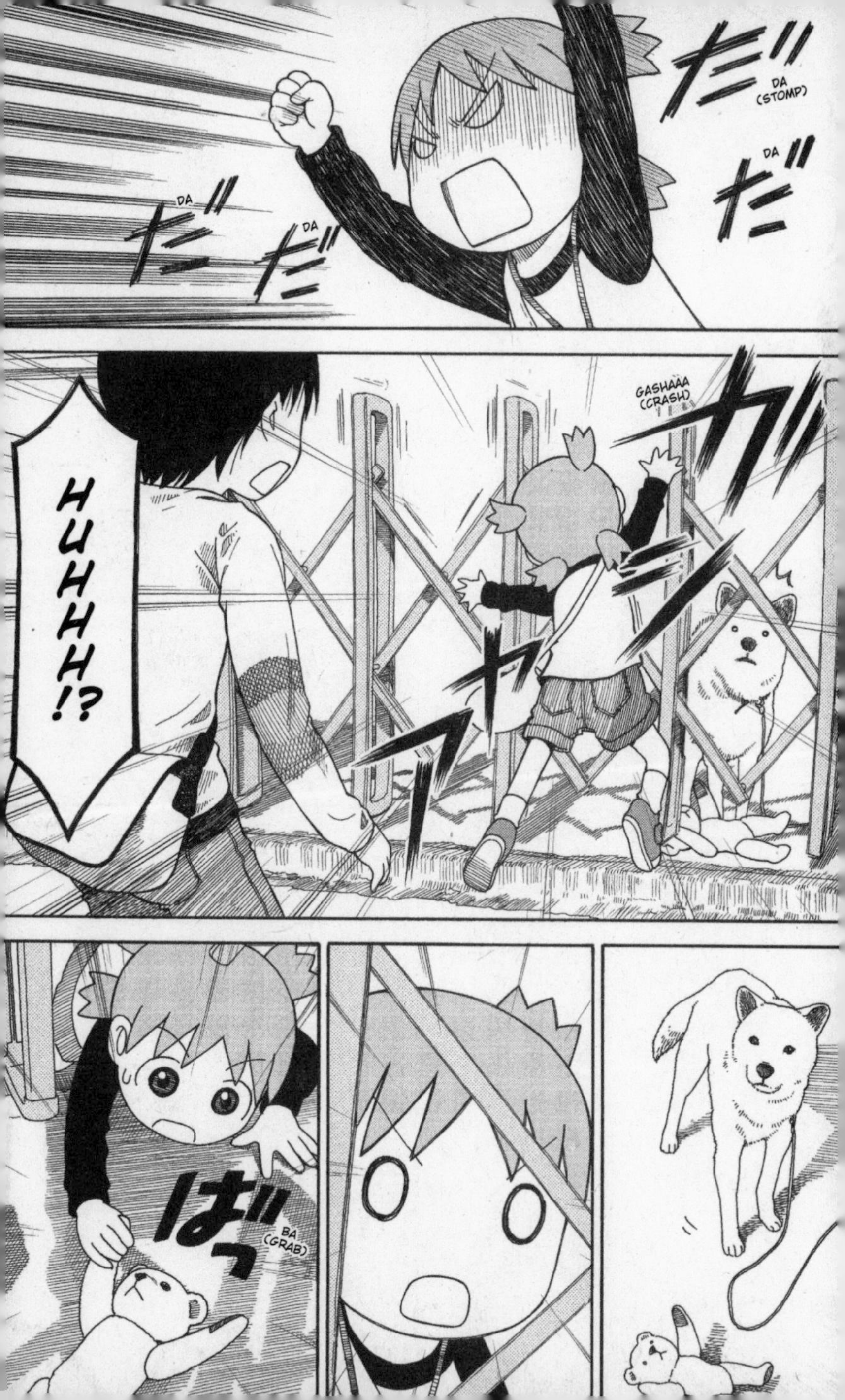
DA (STOMP)
DA
DA
DA
GASHAAA (CRASH)
HUHHHH!?
BA (GRAB)

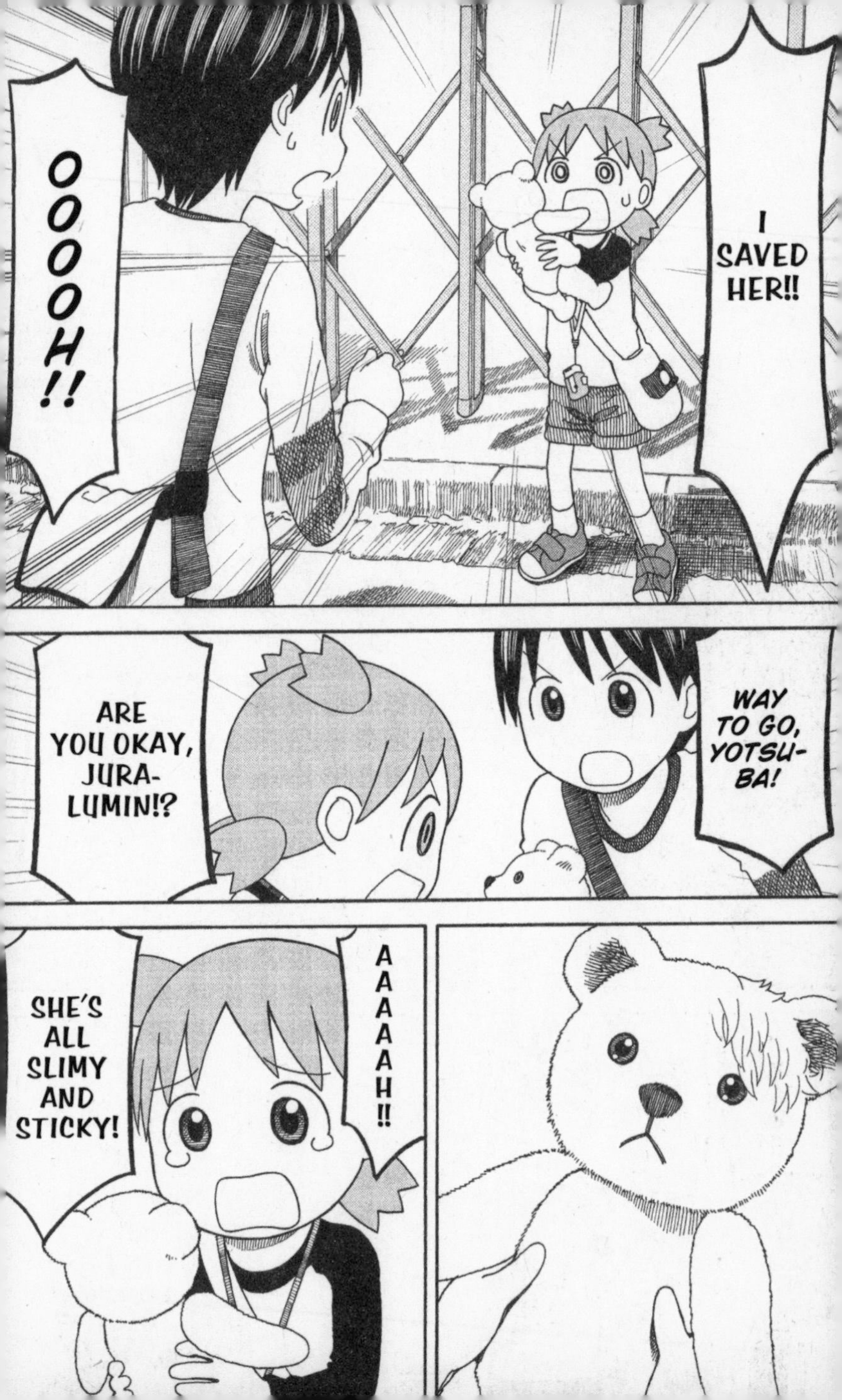
I SAVED HER!!
OOOOOH!!
WAY TO GO, YOTSU-BA!
ARE YOU OKAY, JURA-LUMIN!?
AAAAAH!!
SHE'S ALL SLIMY AND STICKY!

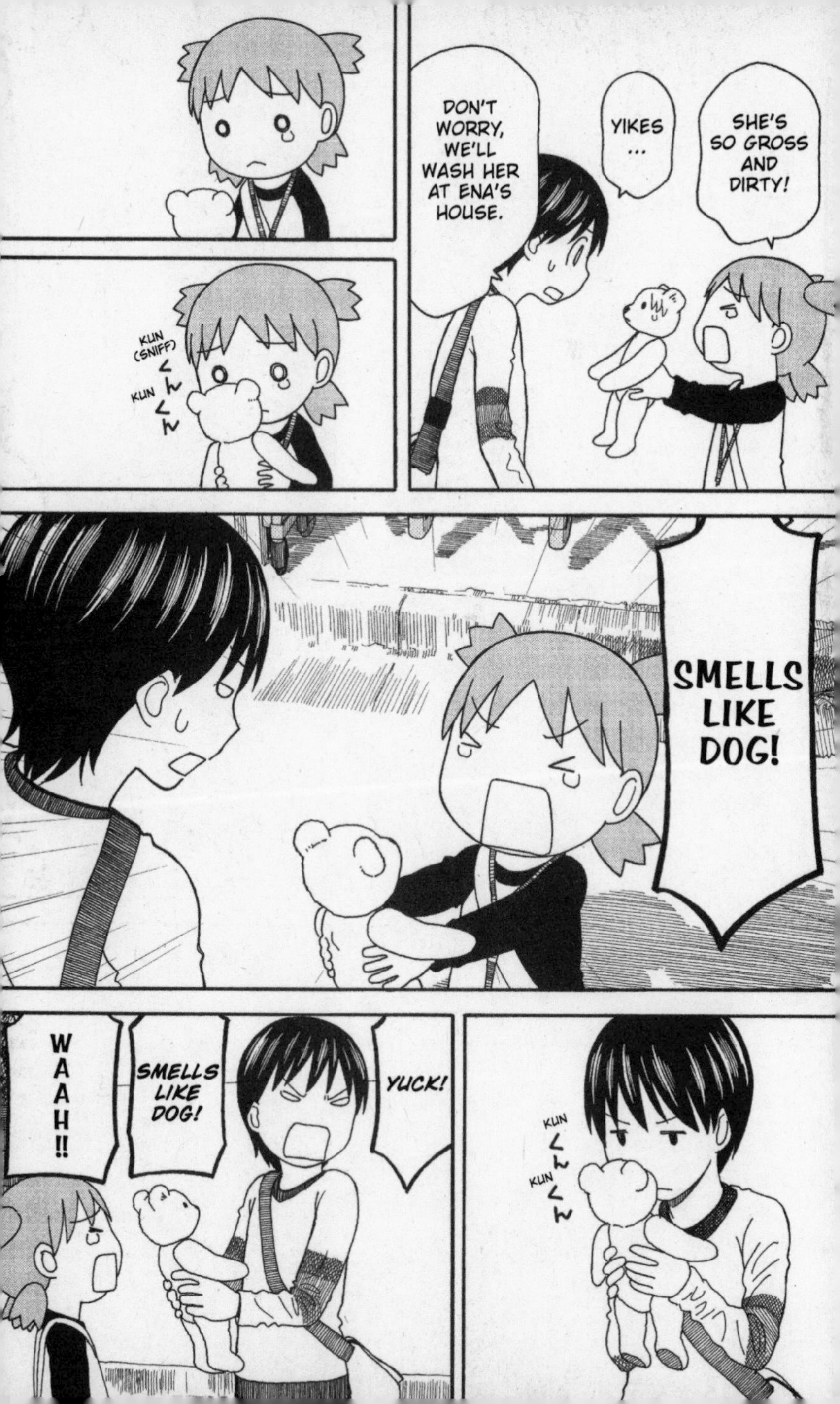
SHE'S SO GROSS AND DIRTY!
YIKES ...
DON'T WORRY, WE'LL WASH HER AT ENA'S HOUSE.
KUN (SNIFF) くん
KUN くん
SMELLS LIKE DOG!
KUN くん
KUN くん
YUCK!
SMELLS LIKE DOG!
WAAH!!

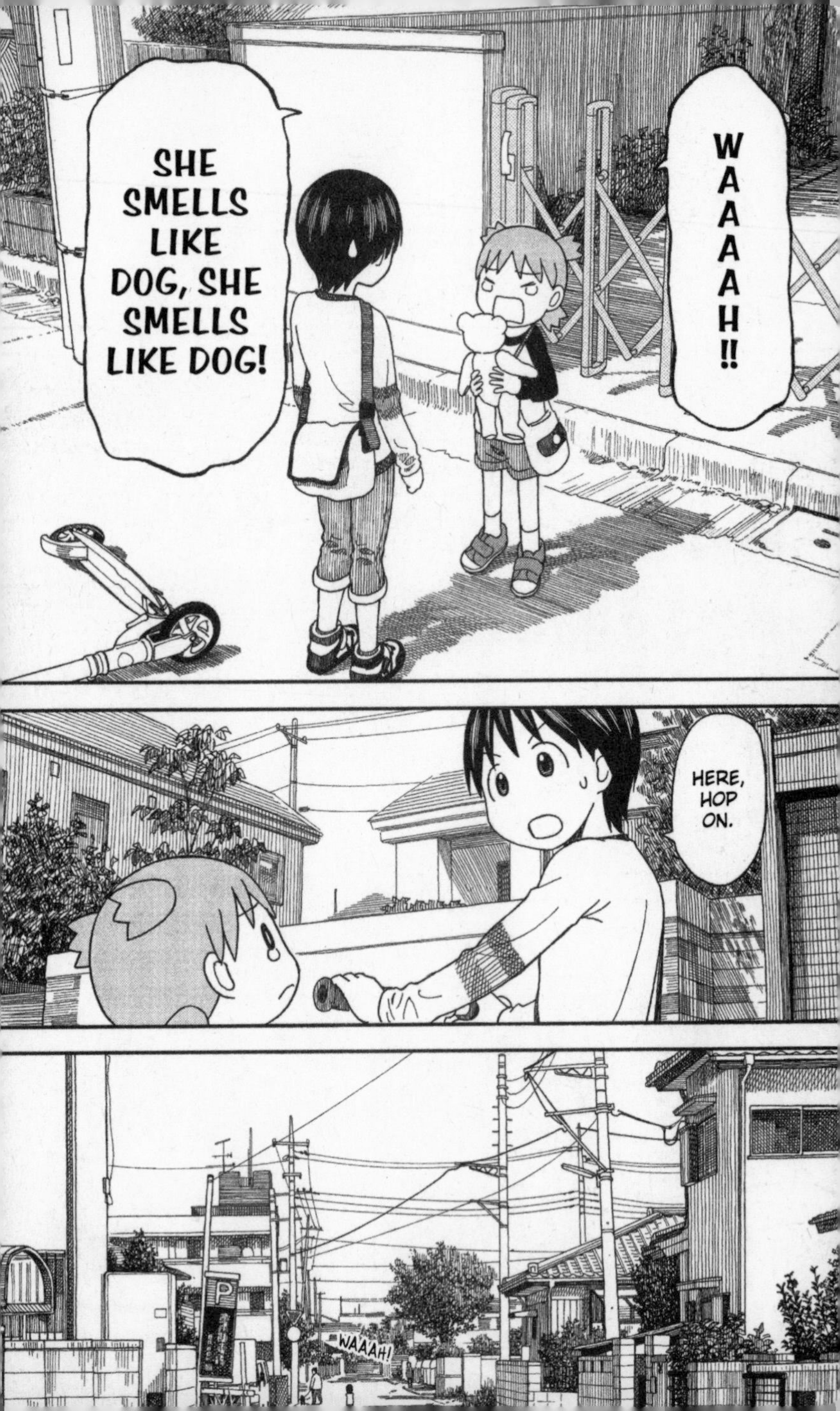
WAAAAAH!!
SHE SMELLS LIKE DOG, SHE SMELLS LIKE DOG!
HERE, HOP ON.
WAAAH!

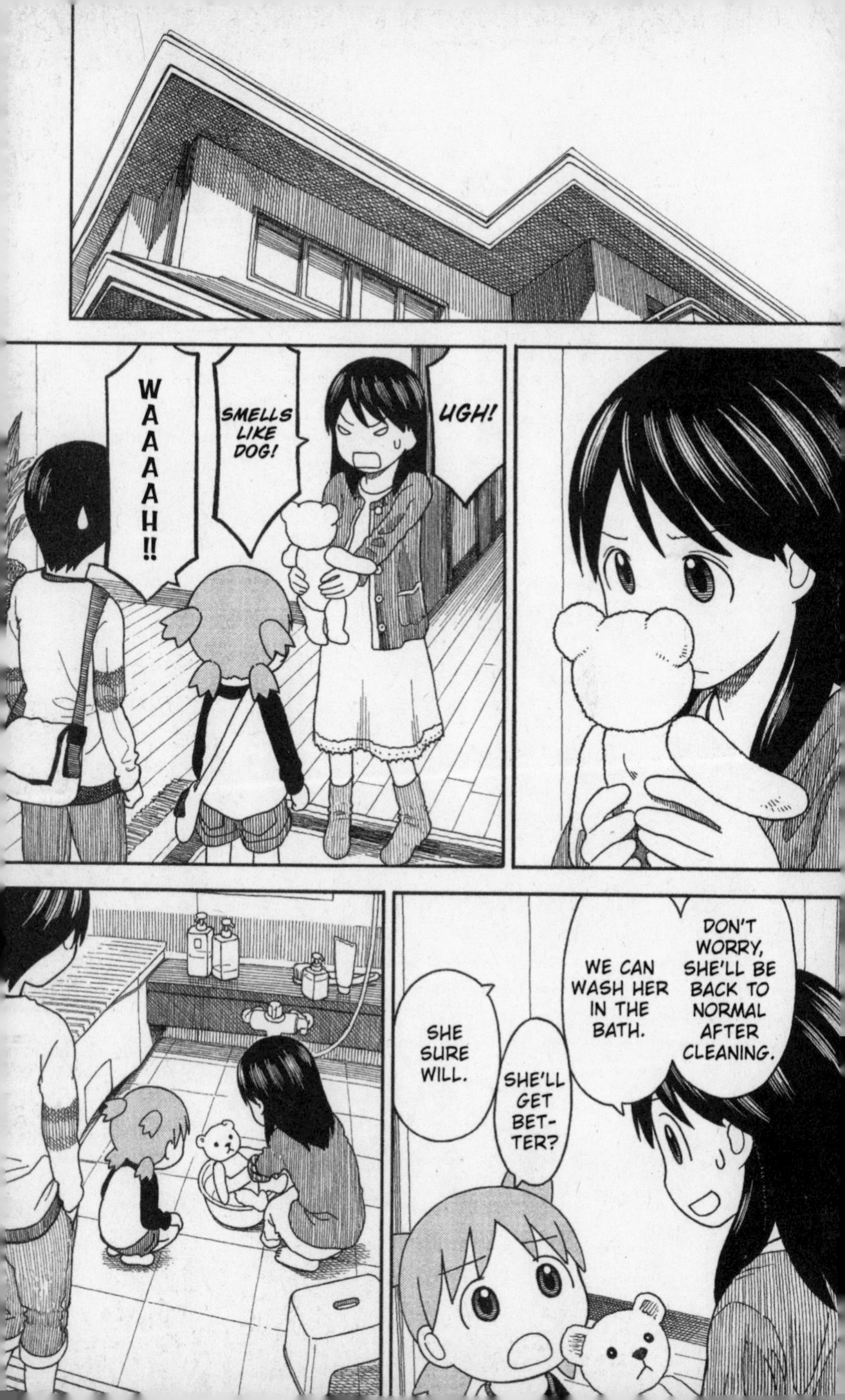
UGH!
SMELLS LIKE DOG!
WAAAAAH!!
DON'T WORRY, SHE'LL BE BACK TO NORMAL AFTER CLEANING.
WE CAN WASH HER IN THE BATH.
SHE'LL GET BET-TER?
SHE SURE WILL.

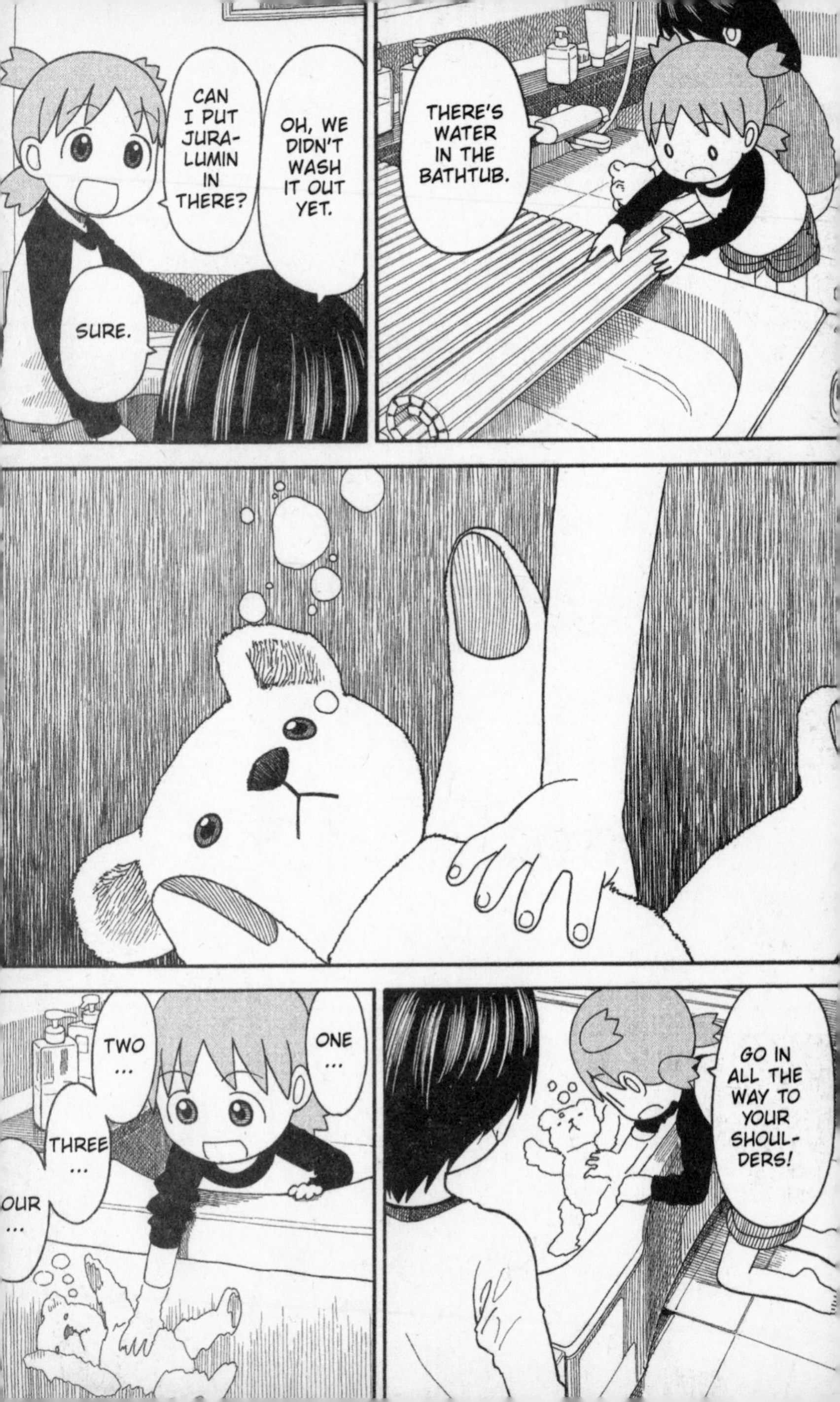

THERE'S WATER IN THE BATHTUB.
OH, WE DIDN'T WASH IT OUT YET.
CAN I PUT JURA-LUMIN IN THERE?
SURE.
GO IN ALL THE WAY TO YOUR SHOUL-DERS!
ONE ...
TWO ...
THREE ...
OUR ...

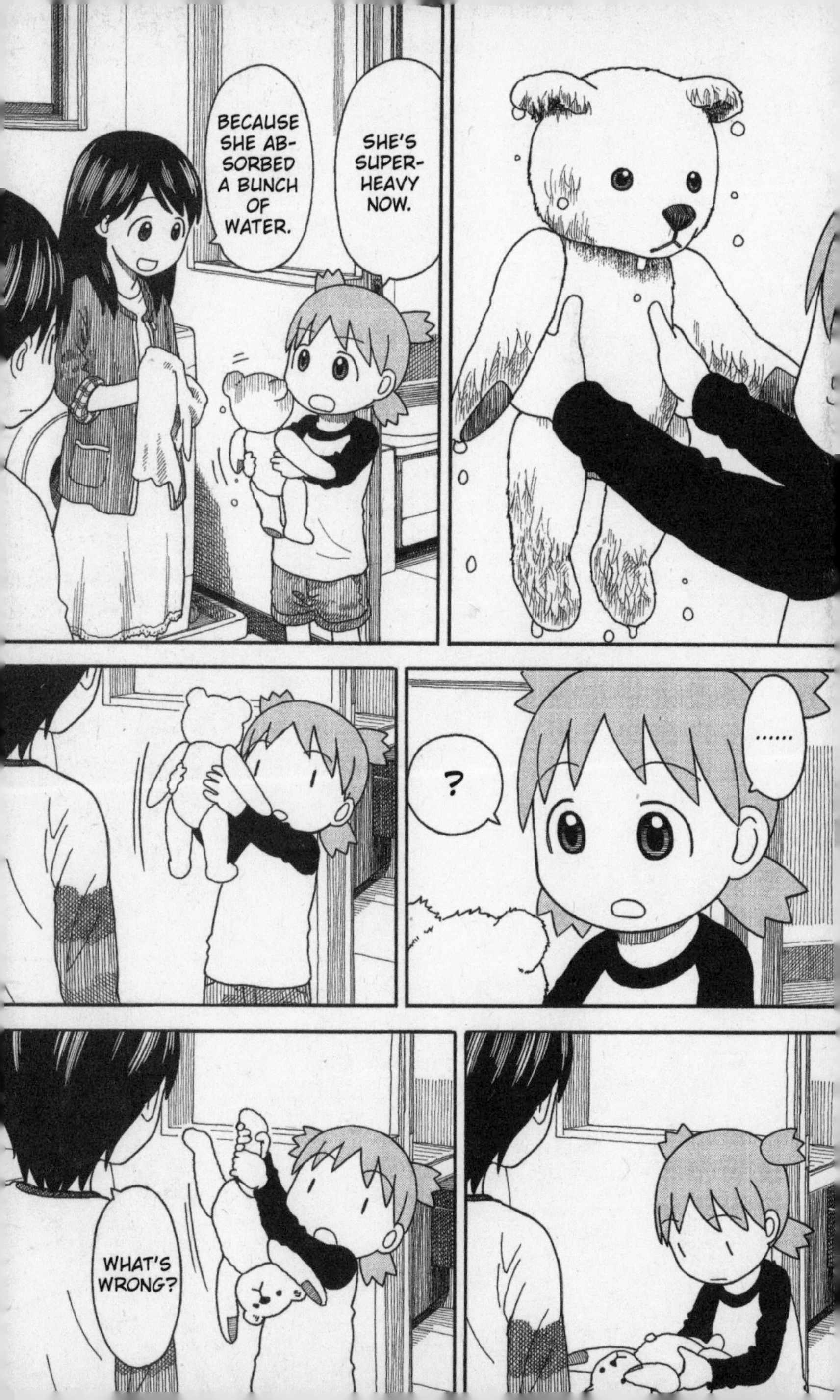
SHE'S SUPER-HEAVY NOW.
BECAUSE SHE AB-SORBED A BUNCH OF WATER.
......
?
WHAT'S WRONG?

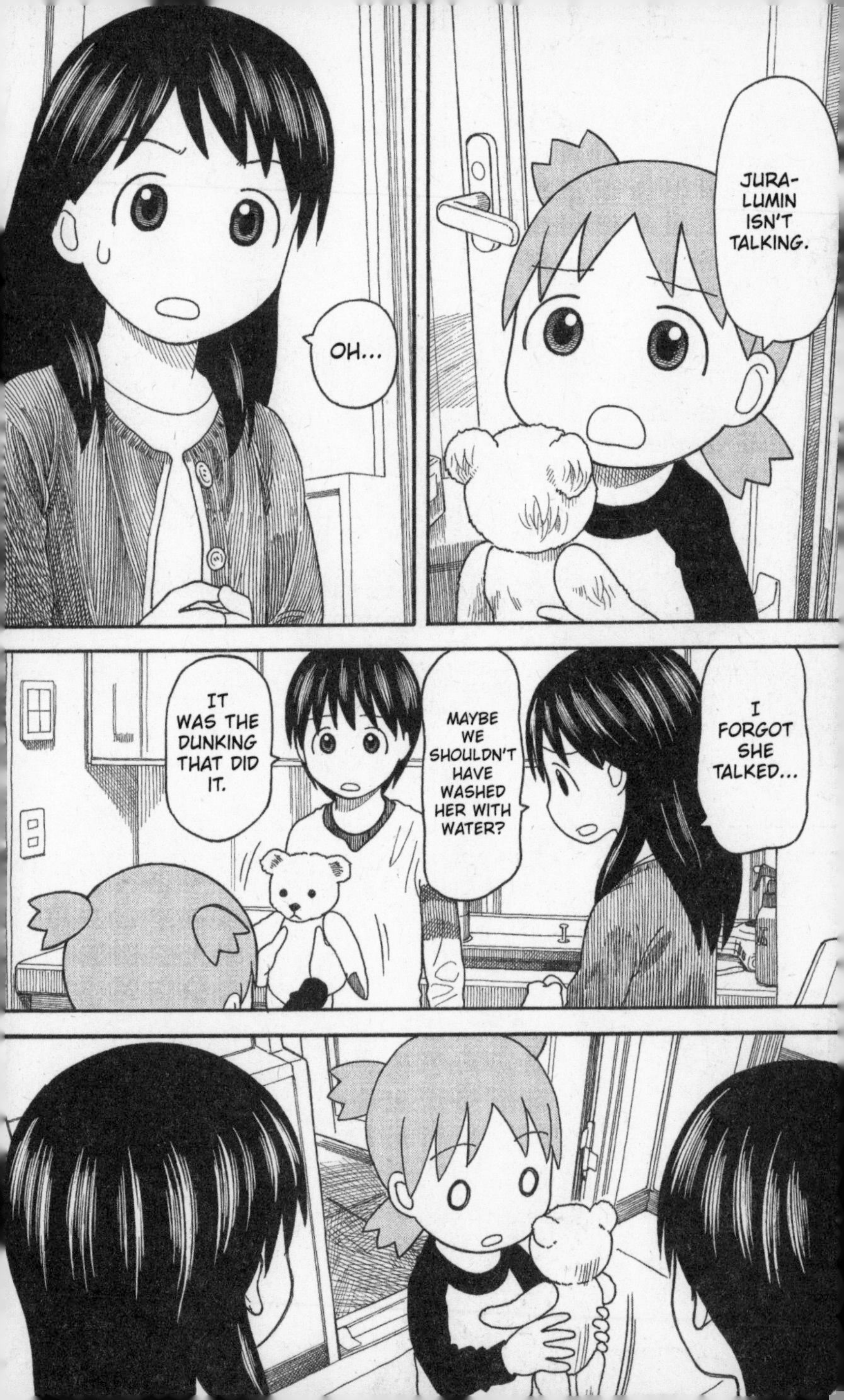
JURA-LUMIN ISN'T TALKING.
OH...
I FORGOT SHE TALKED...
MAYBE WE SHOULDN'T HAVE WASHED HER WITH WATER?
IT WAS THE DUNKING THAT DID IT.

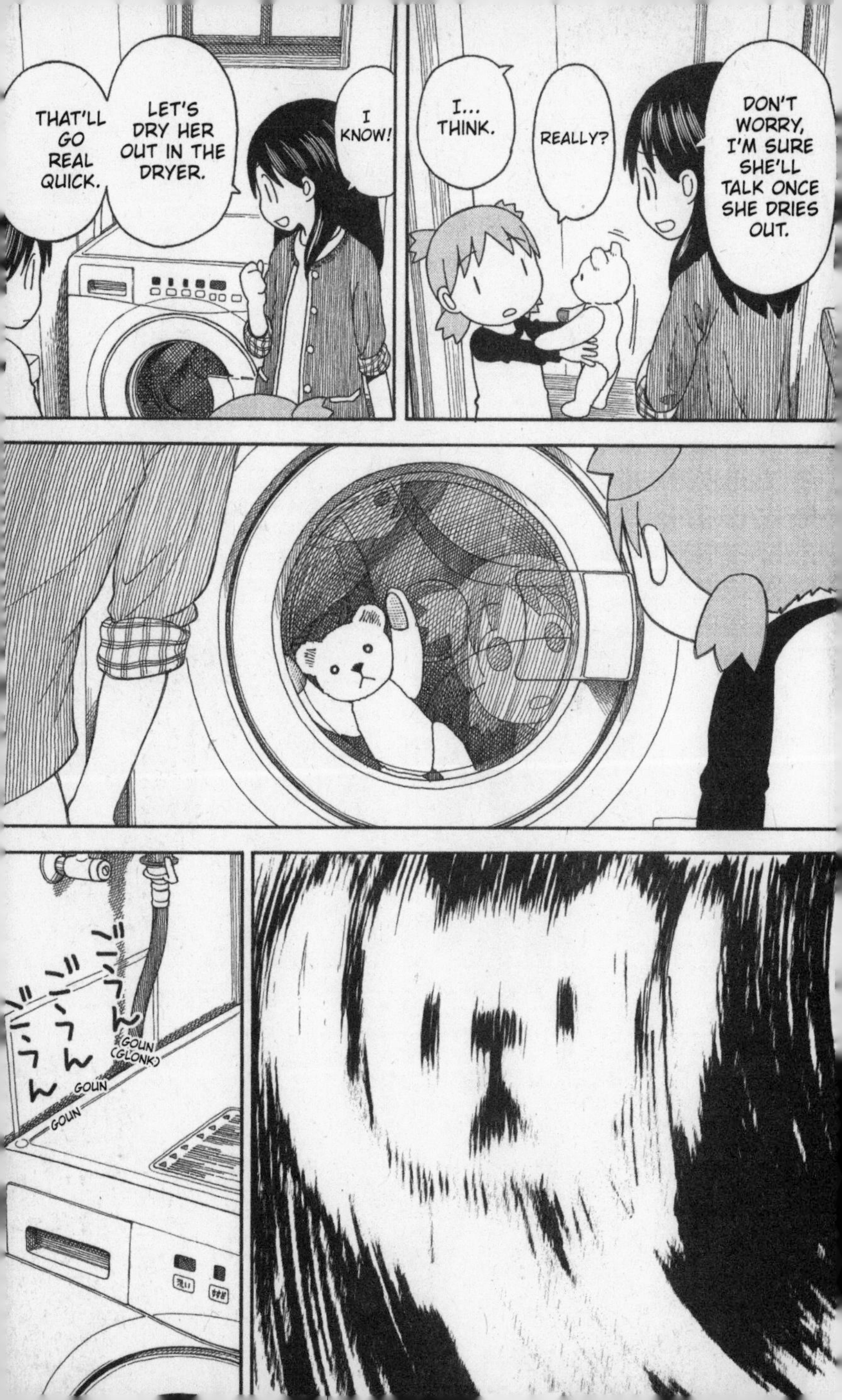
DON'T WORRY, I'M SURE SHE'LL TALK ONCE SHE DRIES OUT.
REALLY?
I... THINK.
I KNOW!
LET'S DRY HER OUT IN THE DRYER.
THAT'LL GO REAL QUICK.
GOUN (GLONK)
GOUN
GOUN

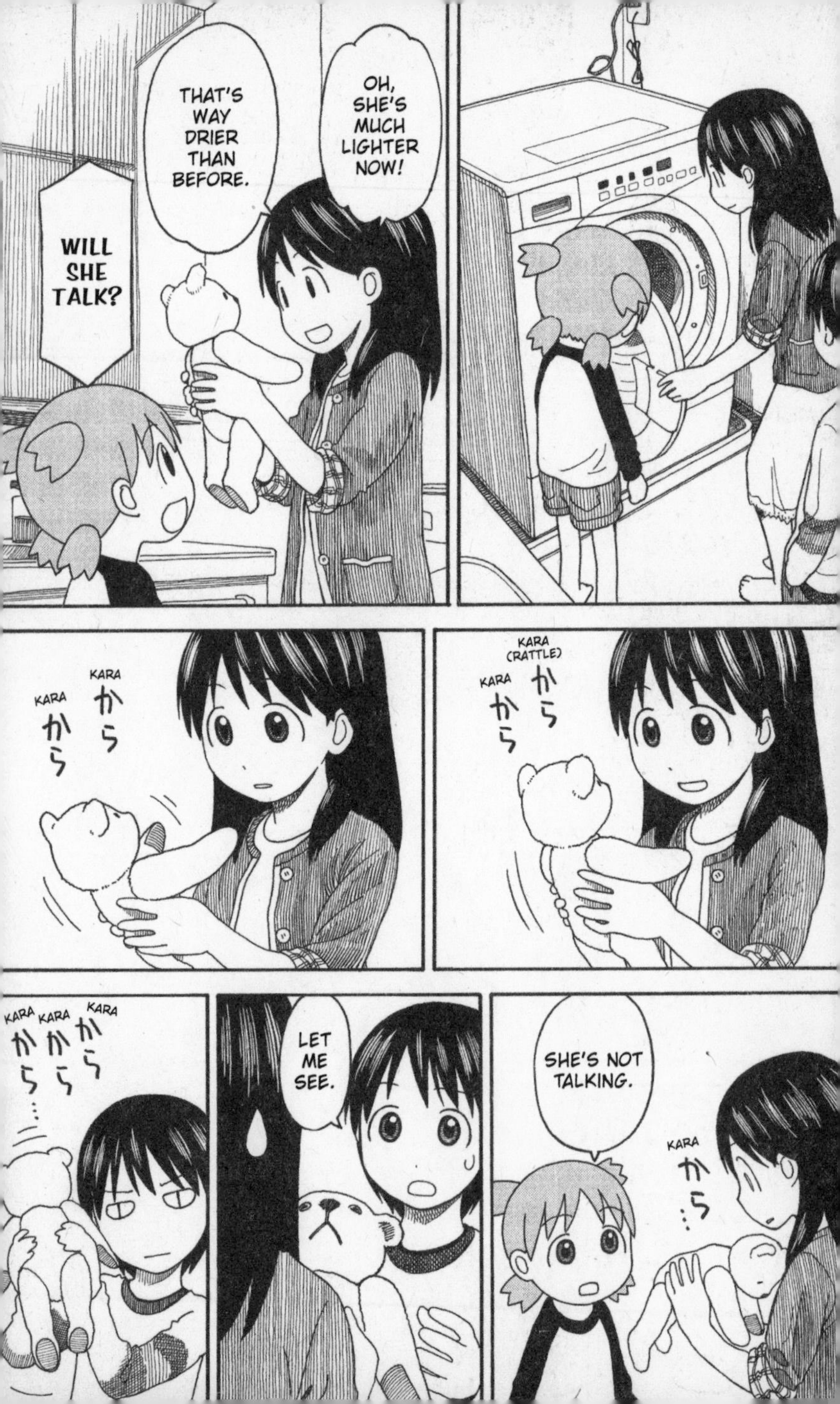
OH, SHE'S MUCH LIGHTER NOW!
THAT'S WAY DRIER THAN BEFORE.
WILL SHE TALK?
KARA (RATTLE) から
KARA から
KARA から
KARA から
SHE'S NOT TALKING.
KARA から…
LET ME SEE.
KARA から
KARA から
KARA から…

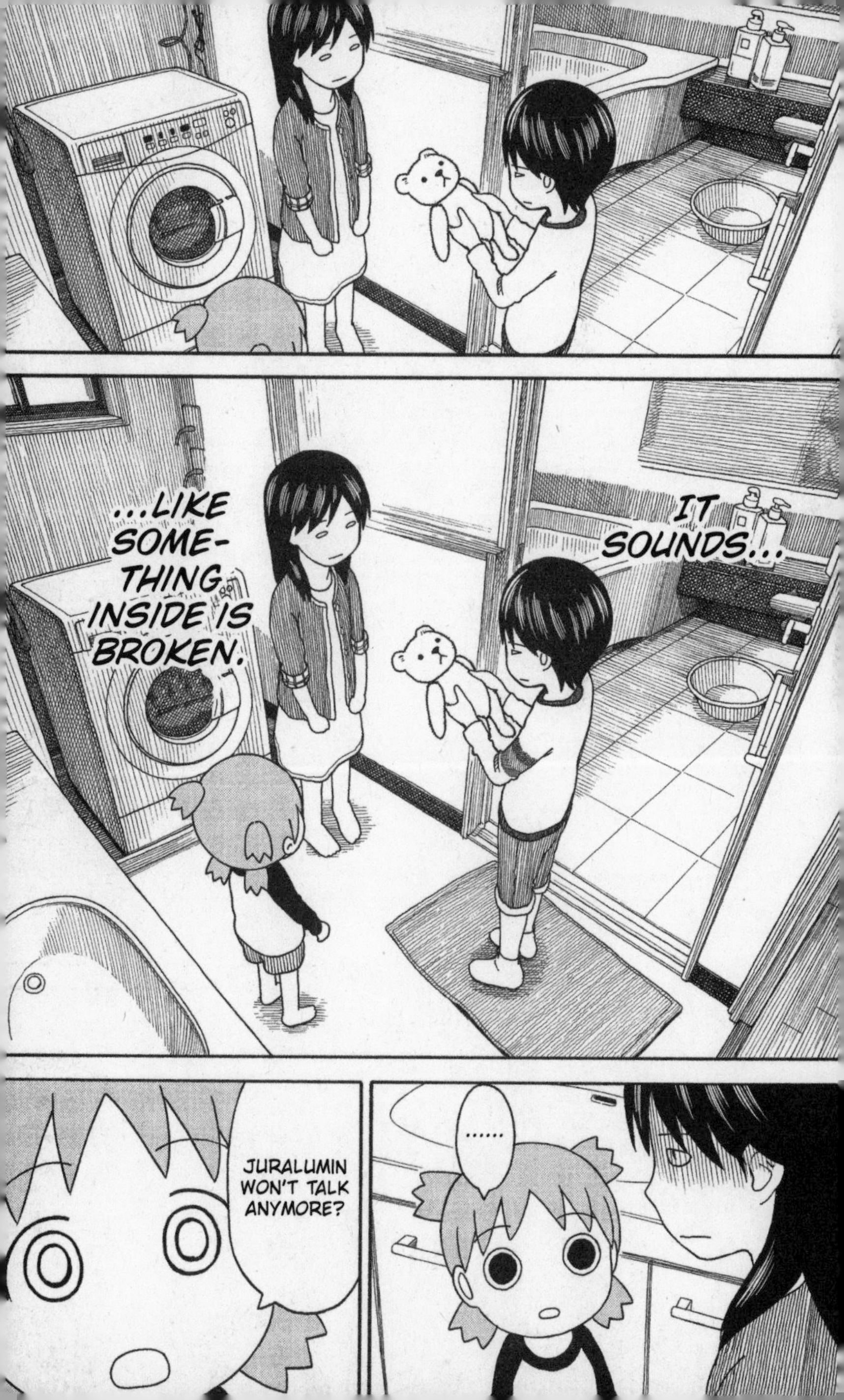
IT SOUNDS...
...LIKE SOMETHING INSIDE IS BROKEN.
......
JURALUMIN WON'T TALK ANYMORE?

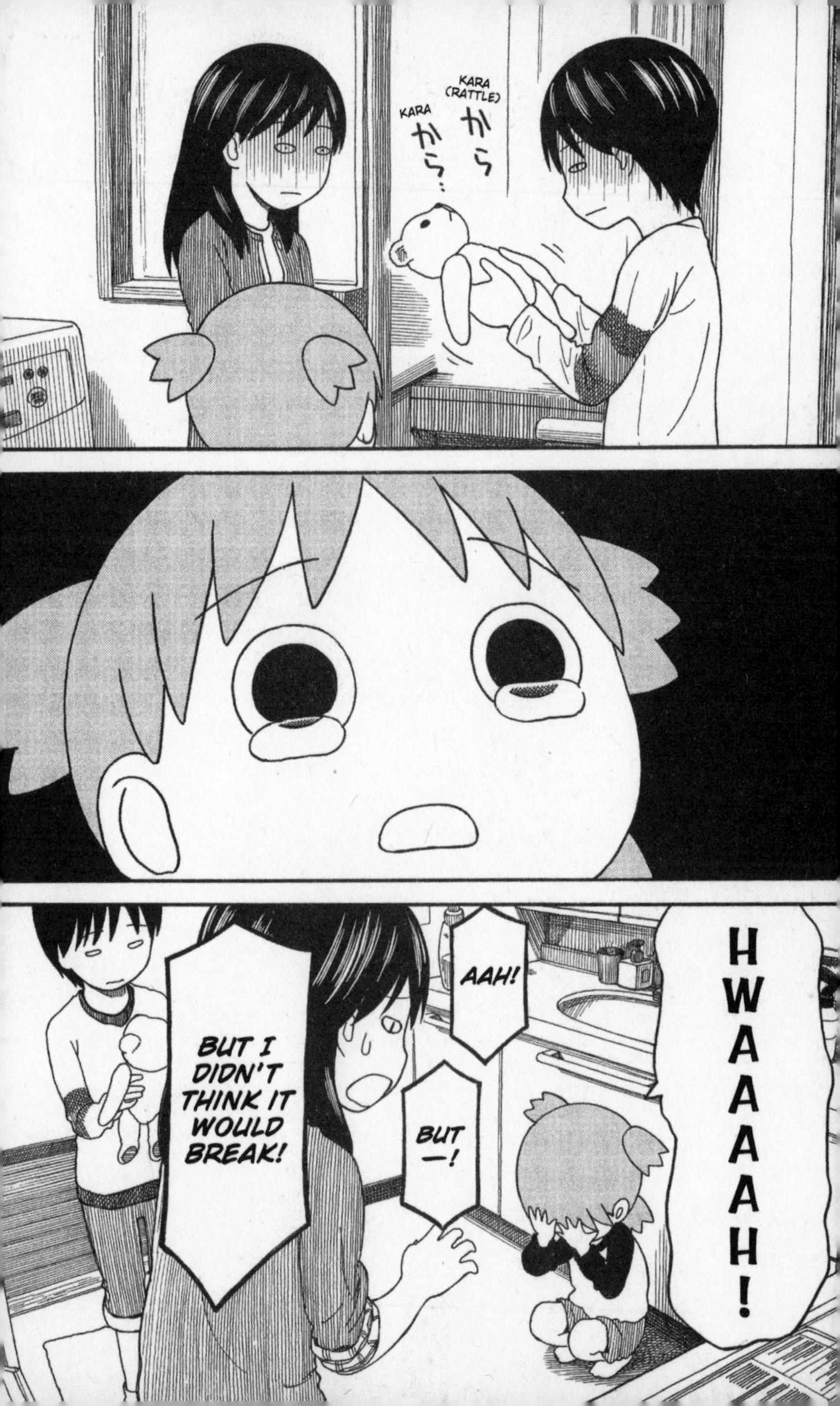
KARA (RATTLE)
から
KARA
から…
HWAAAAAH!
AAH!
BUT —!
BUT I DIDN'T THINK IT WOULD BREAK!

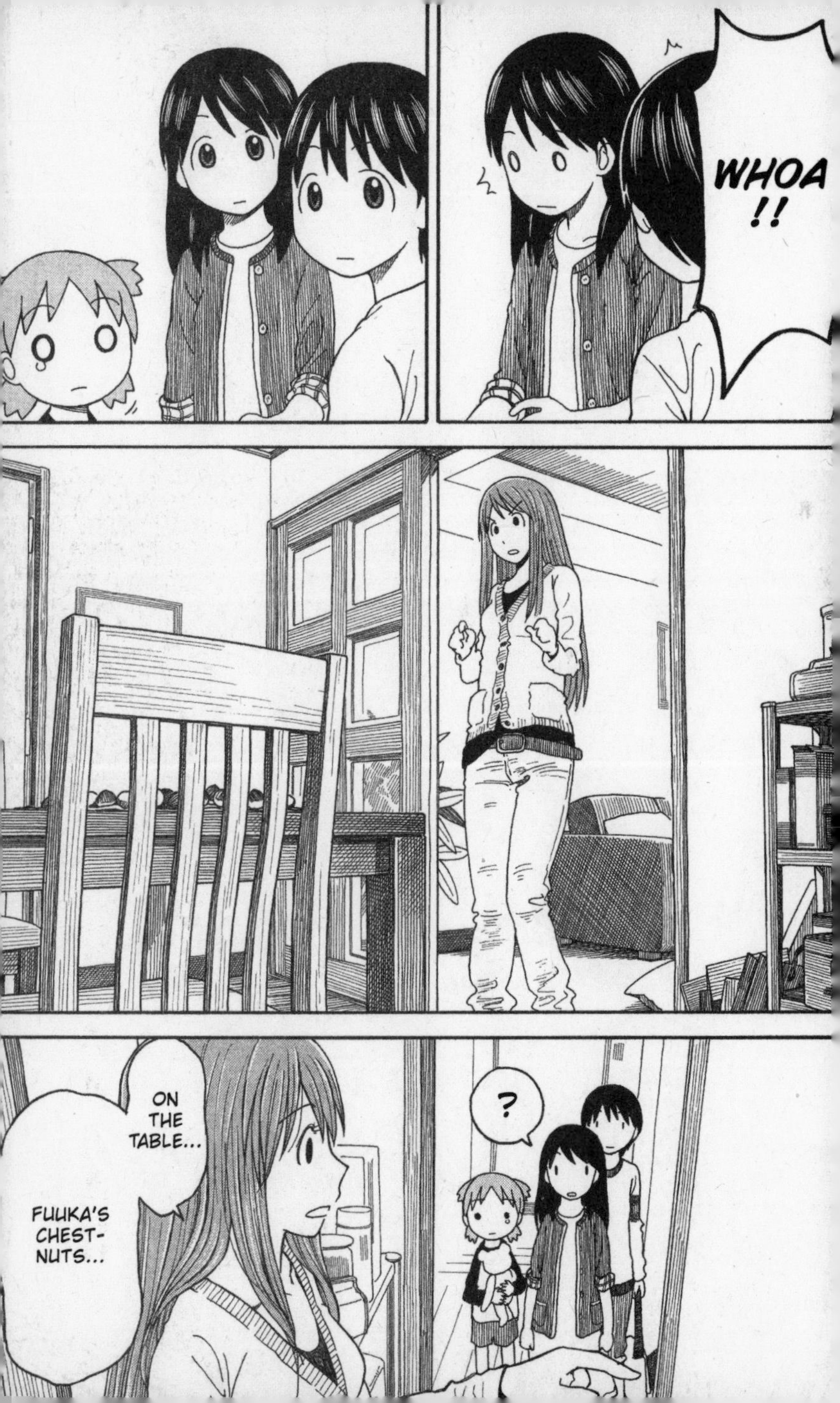

WHOA !!
?
ON THE TABLE...
FUUKA'S CHEST-NUTS...

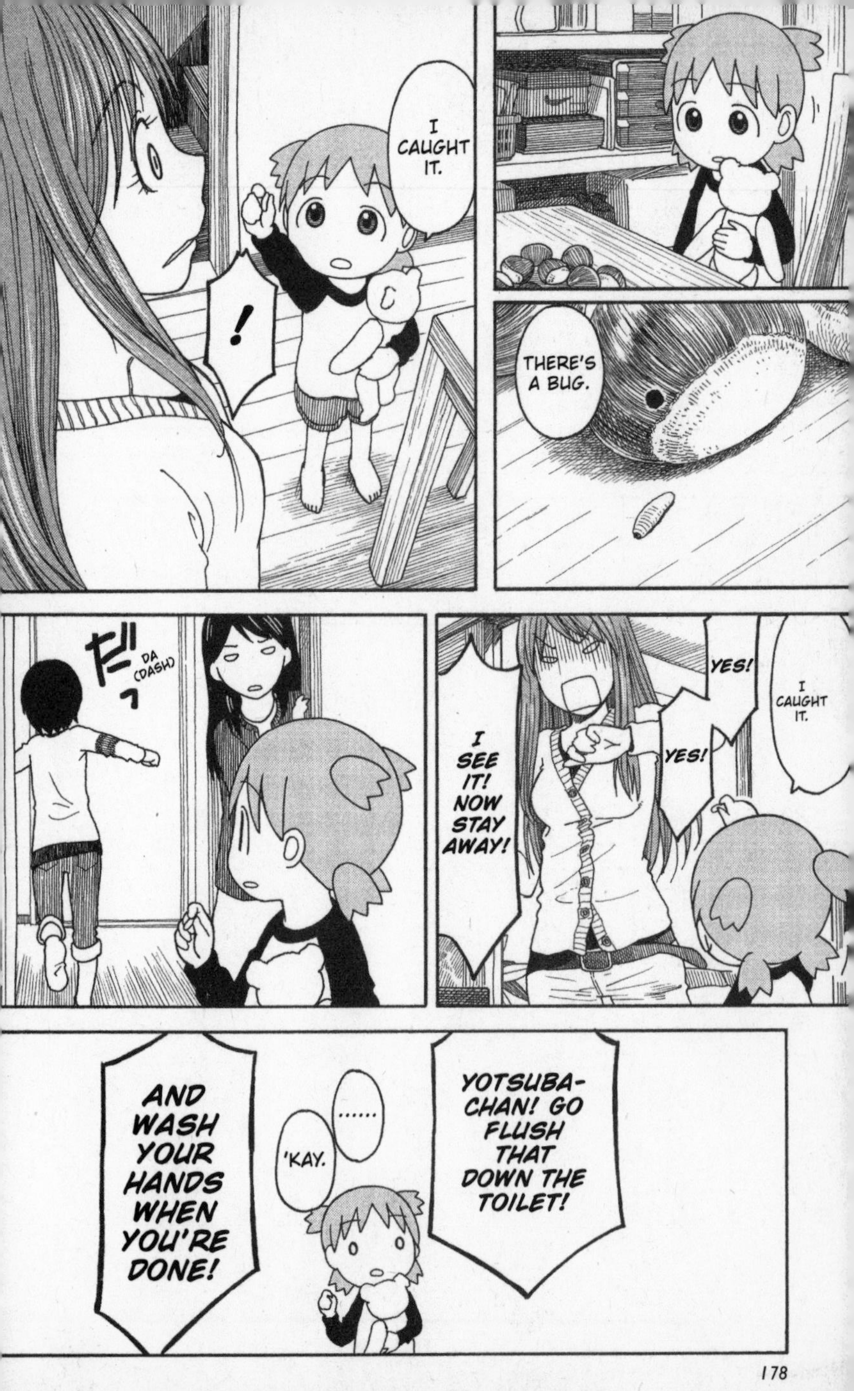
THERE'S A BUG.
I CAUGHT IT.
!
I CAUGHT IT.
YES!
YES!
I SEE IT! NOW STAY AWAY!
DA (DASH)
YOTSUBA-CHAN! GO FLUSH THAT DOWN THE TOILET!
......
'KAY.
AND WASH YOUR HANDS WHEN YOU'RE DONE!

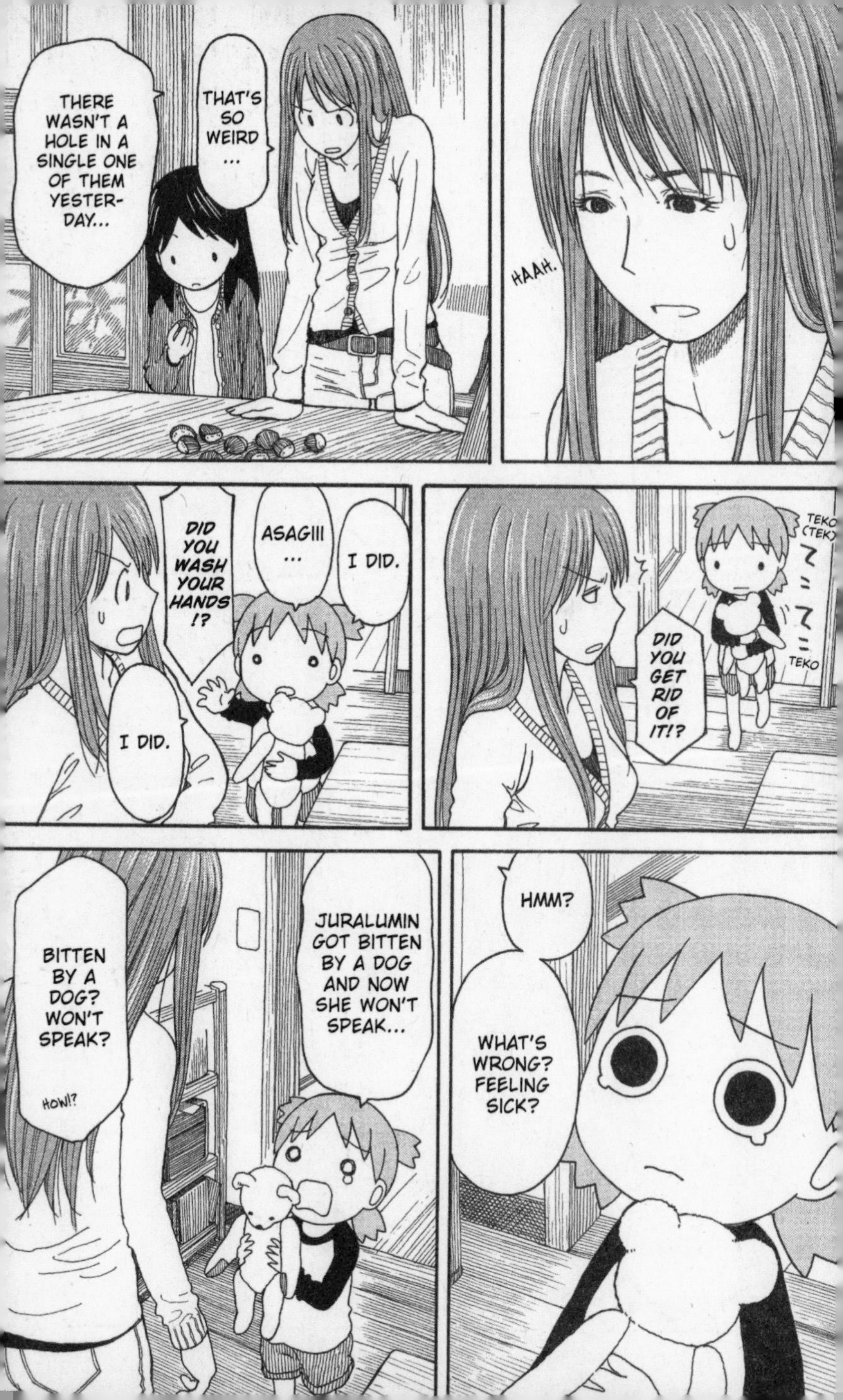
THERE WASN'T A HOLE IN A SINGLE ONE OF THEM YESTER-DAY...
THAT'S SO WEIRD ...
HAAH.
DID YOU WASH YOUR HANDS !?
ASAGIII ...
I DID.
I DID.
DID YOU GET RID OF IT!?
TEKO (TEK)
てこてこ
TEKO
BITTEN BY A DOG? WON'T SPEAK?
HOW!?
JURALUMIN GOT BITTEN BY A DOG AND NOW SHE WON'T SPEAK...
HMM?
WHAT'S WRONG? FEELING SICK?

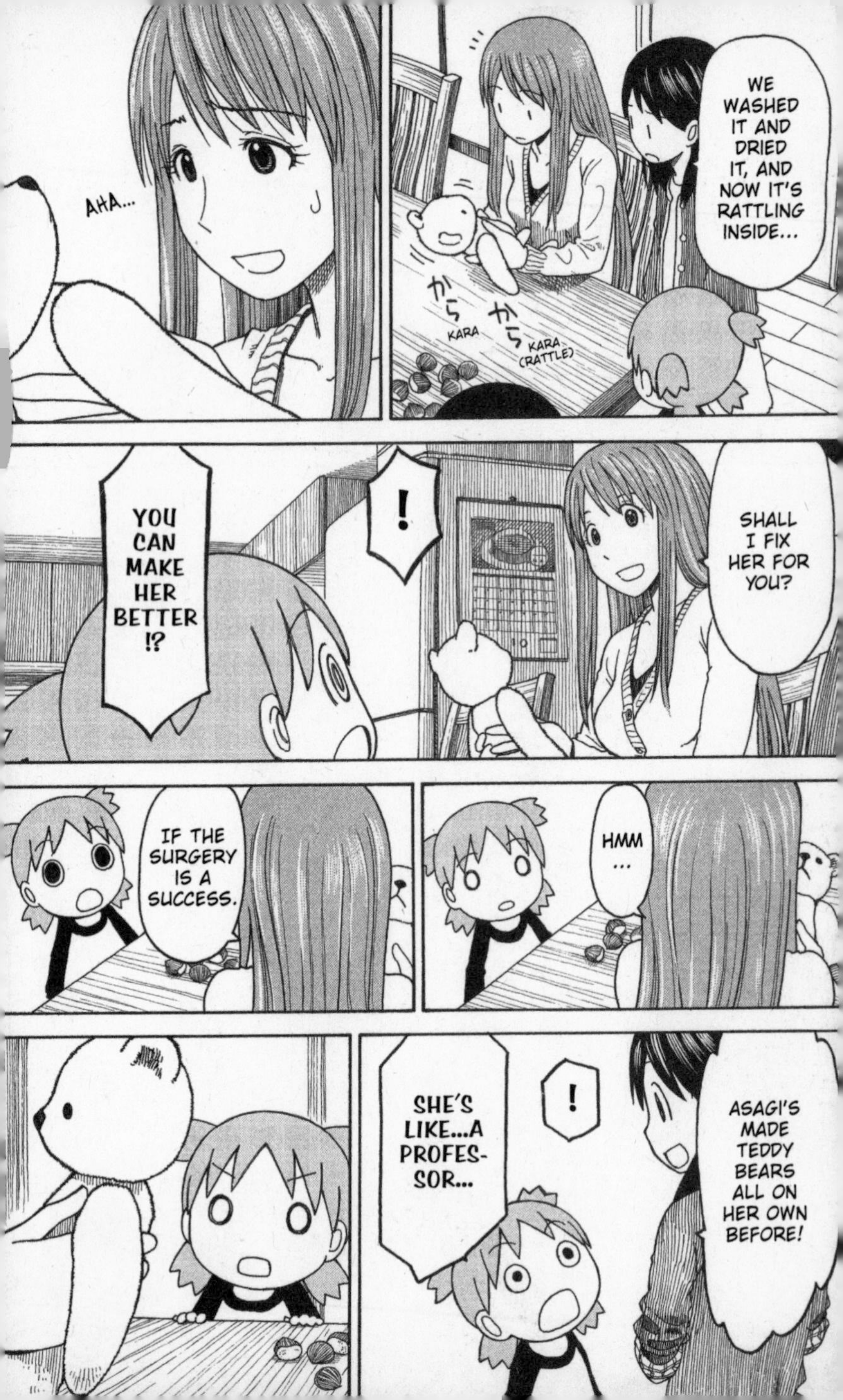
WE WASHED IT AND DRIED IT, AND NOW IT'S RATTLING INSIDE...
から から
KARA KARA (RATTLE)
AHA...
SHALL I FIX HER FOR YOU?
!
YOU CAN MAKE HER BETTER!?
HMM...
IF THE SURGERY IS A SUCCESS.
ASAGI'S MADE TEDDY BEARS ALL ON HER OWN BEFORE!
!
SHE'S LIKE...A PROFES-SOR...

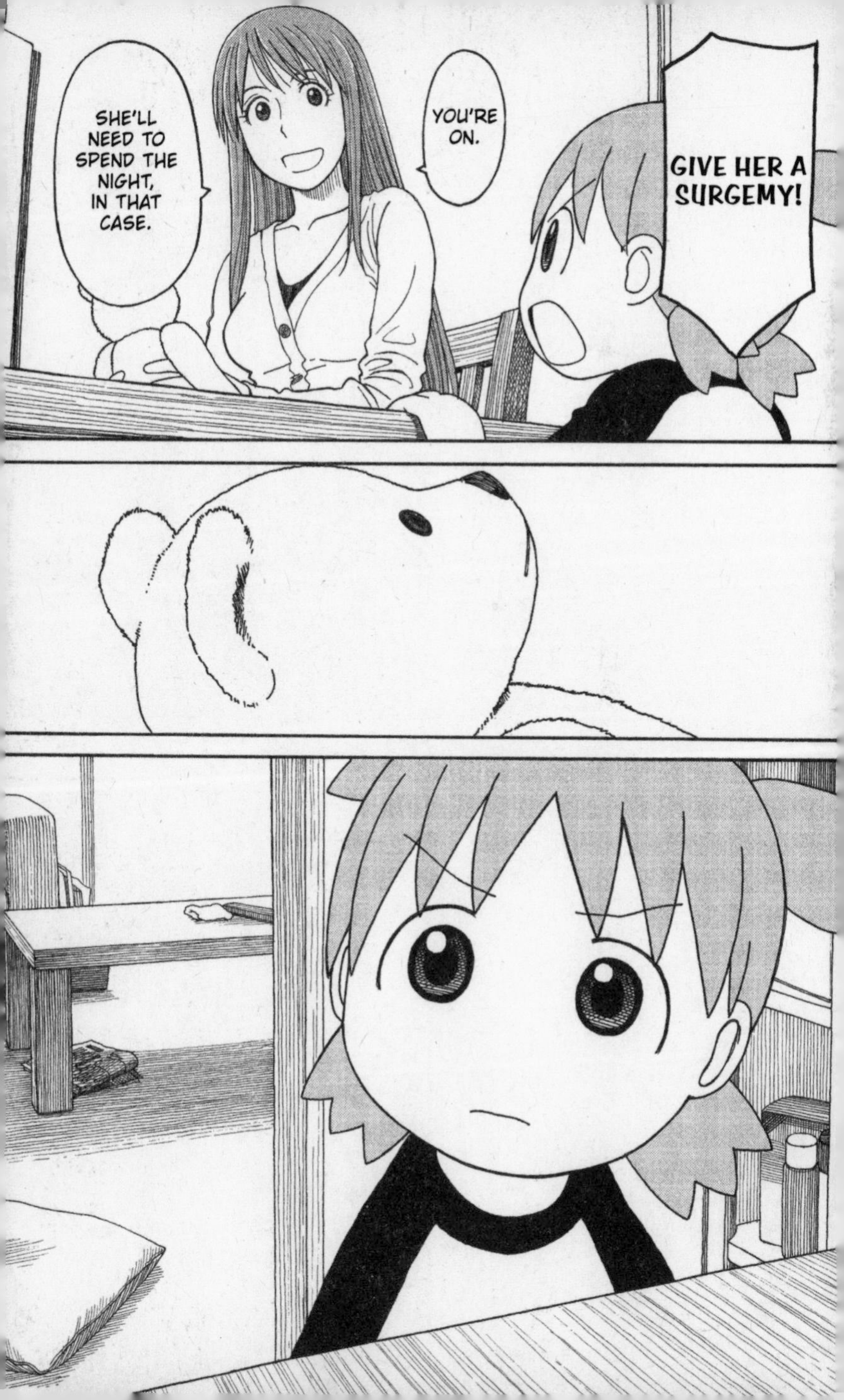
GIVE HER A SURGEMY!
YOU'RE ON.
SHE'LL NEED TO SPEND THE NIGHT, IN THAT CASE.

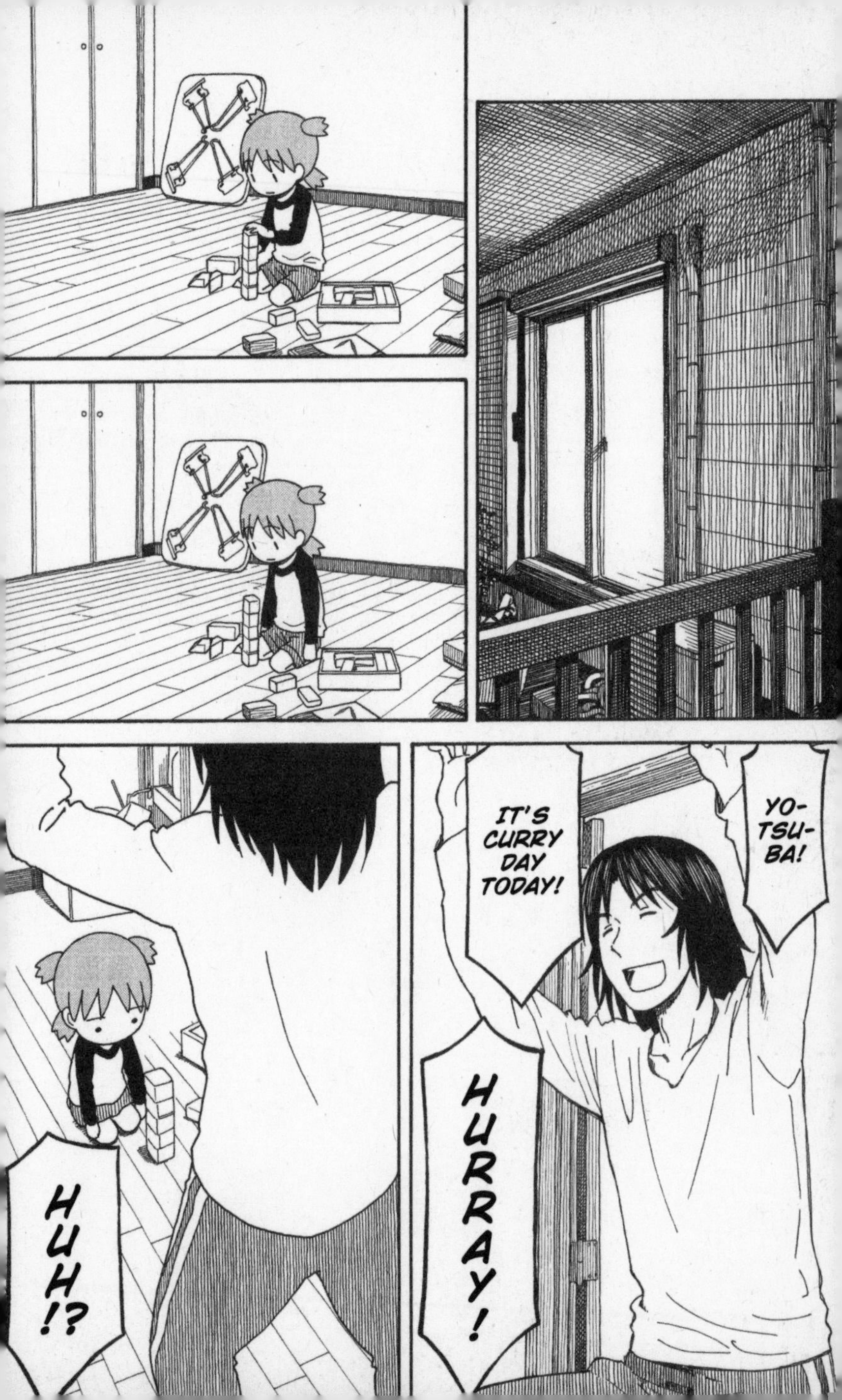
YO-
TSU-
BA!
IT'S
CURRY
DAY
TODAY!
HURRAY!
HUH!?

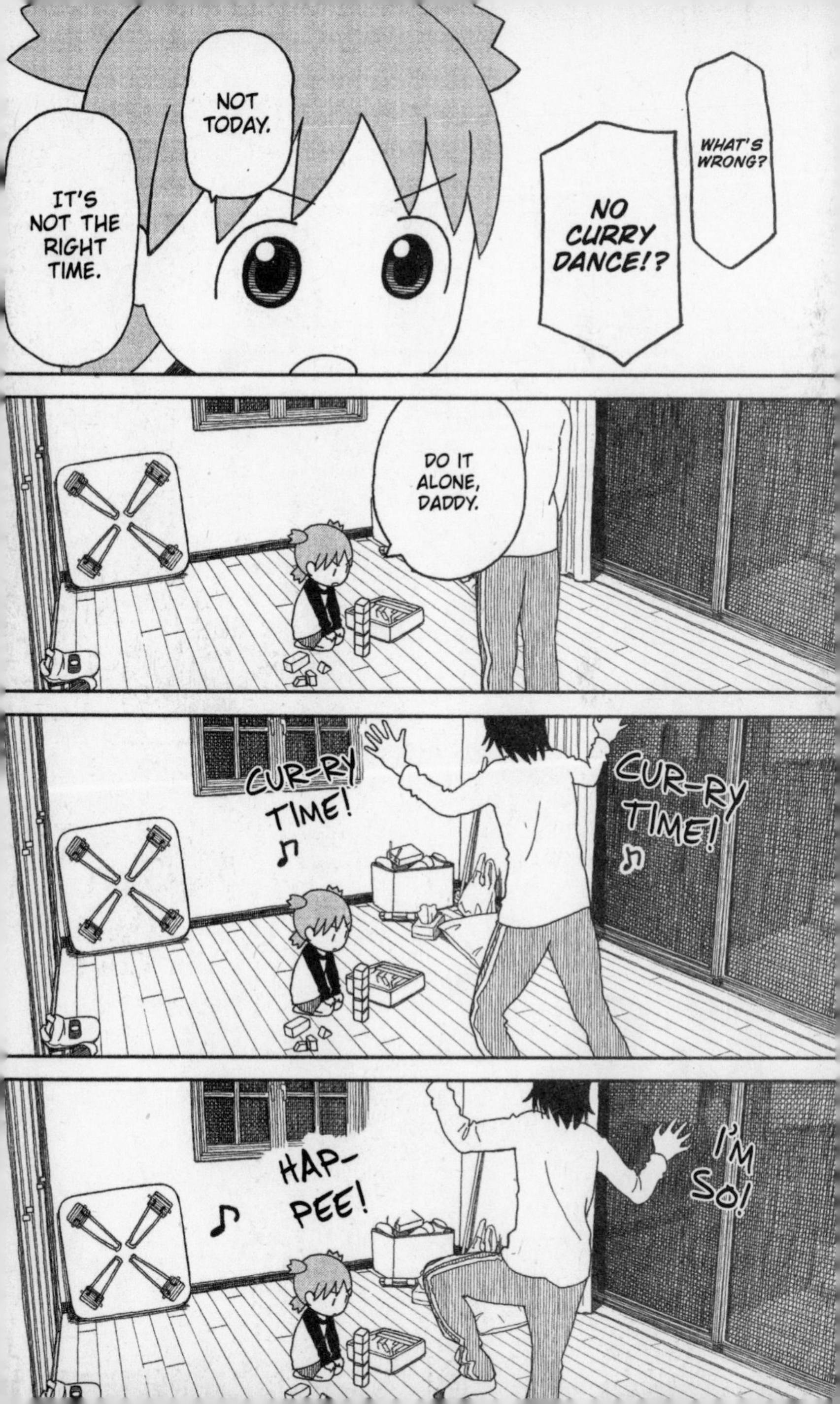
WHAT'S WRONG?
NO CURRY DANCE!?
NOT TODAY.
IT'S NOT THE RIGHT TIME.
DO IT ALONE, DADDY.
CUR-RY TIME! ♪
CUR-RY TIME! ♪
I'M SO!
HAP-PEE! ♪

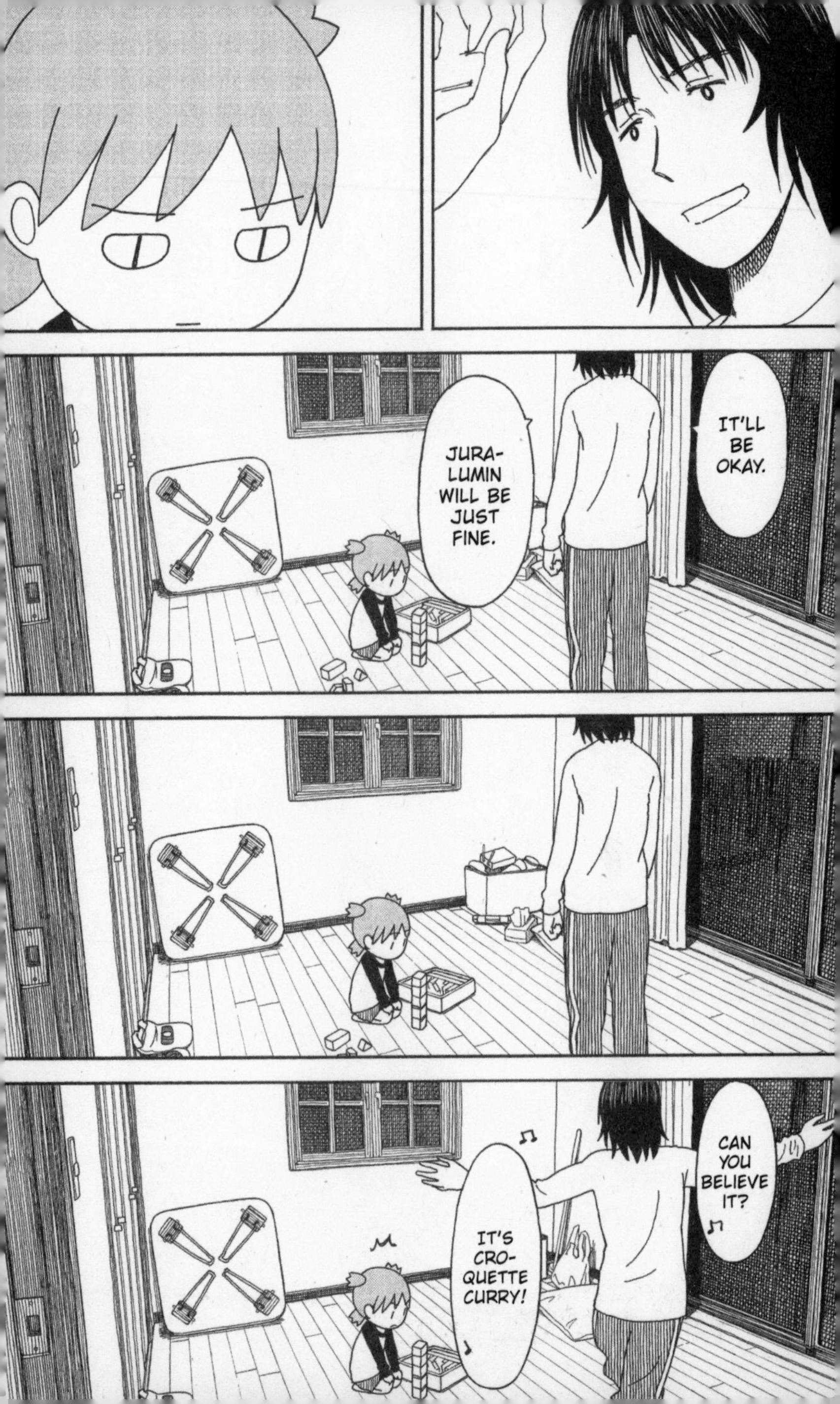

IT'LL BE OKAY.
JURA-LUMIN WILL BE JUST FINE.
CAN YOU BELIEVE IT?
IT'S CRO-QUETTE CURRY!

YOTSUBA&!

• • • • • •

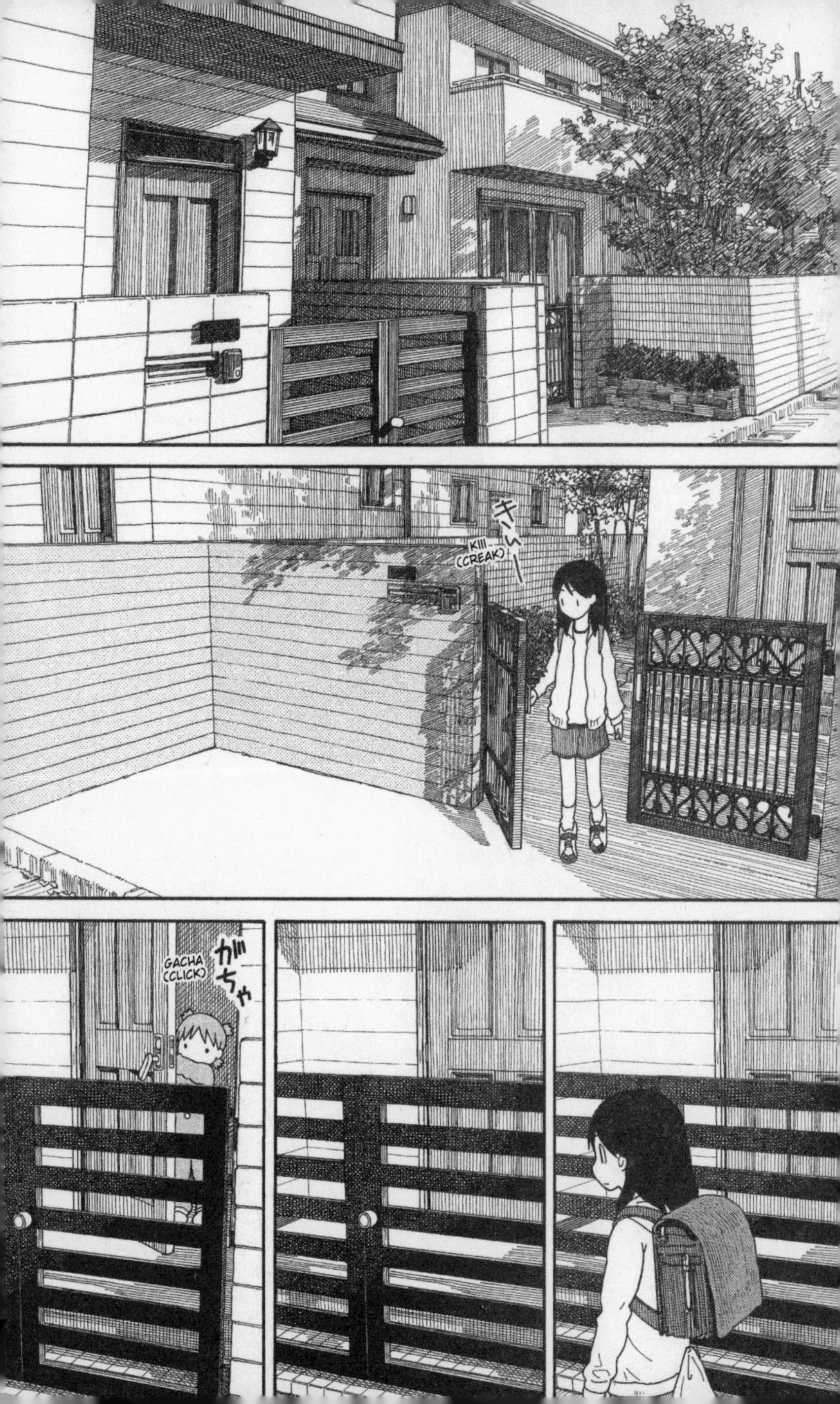

キぃー
KIII (CREAK)
がちゃ
GACHA (CLICK)

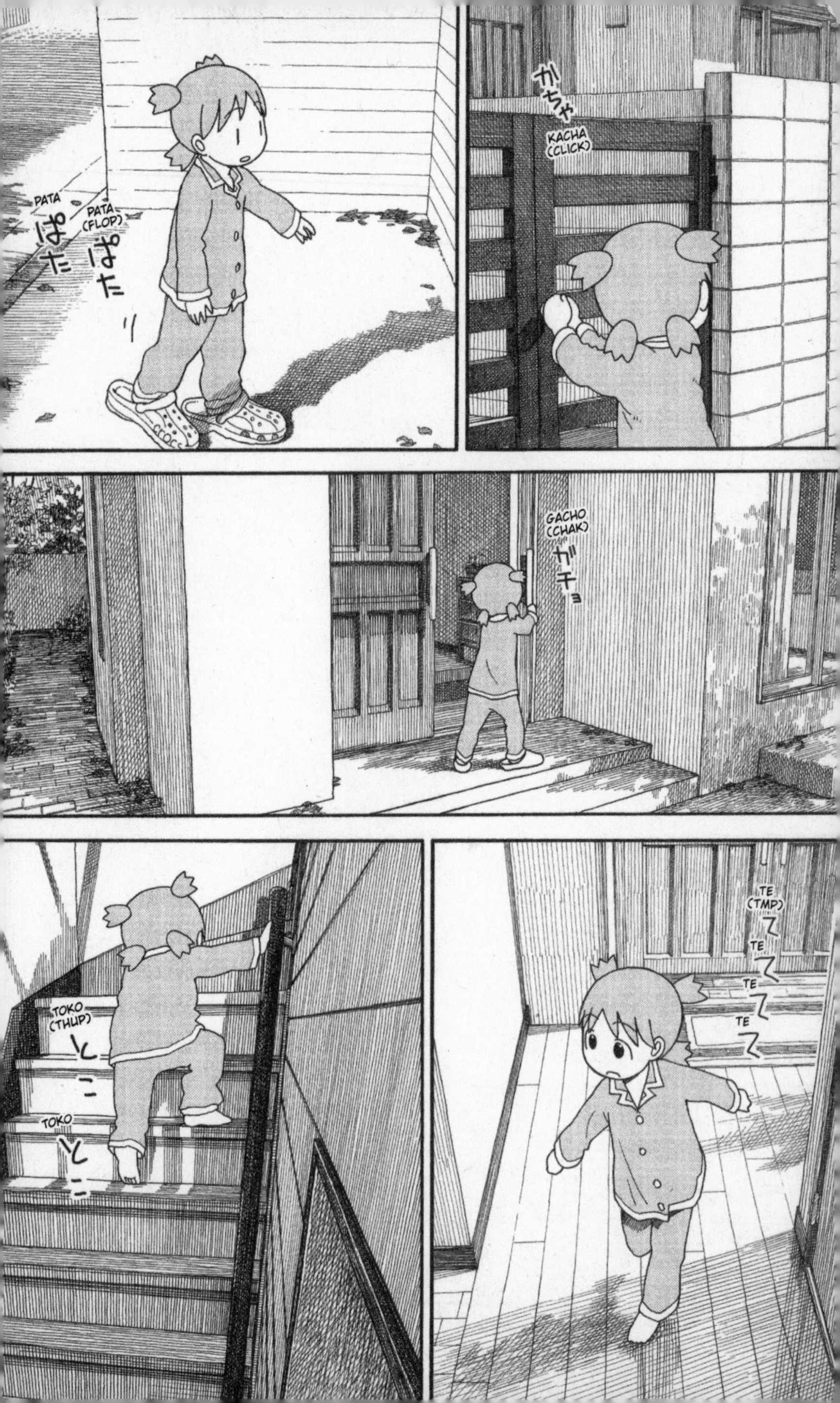

かちゃ
KACHA (CLICK)
PATA
ぱた
PATA (FLOP)
ぱた
GACHO (CHAK)
ガチョ
TE (TMP)
て
TE
て
TE
て
TE
て
TOKO (THUP)
とこ
TOKO
とこ

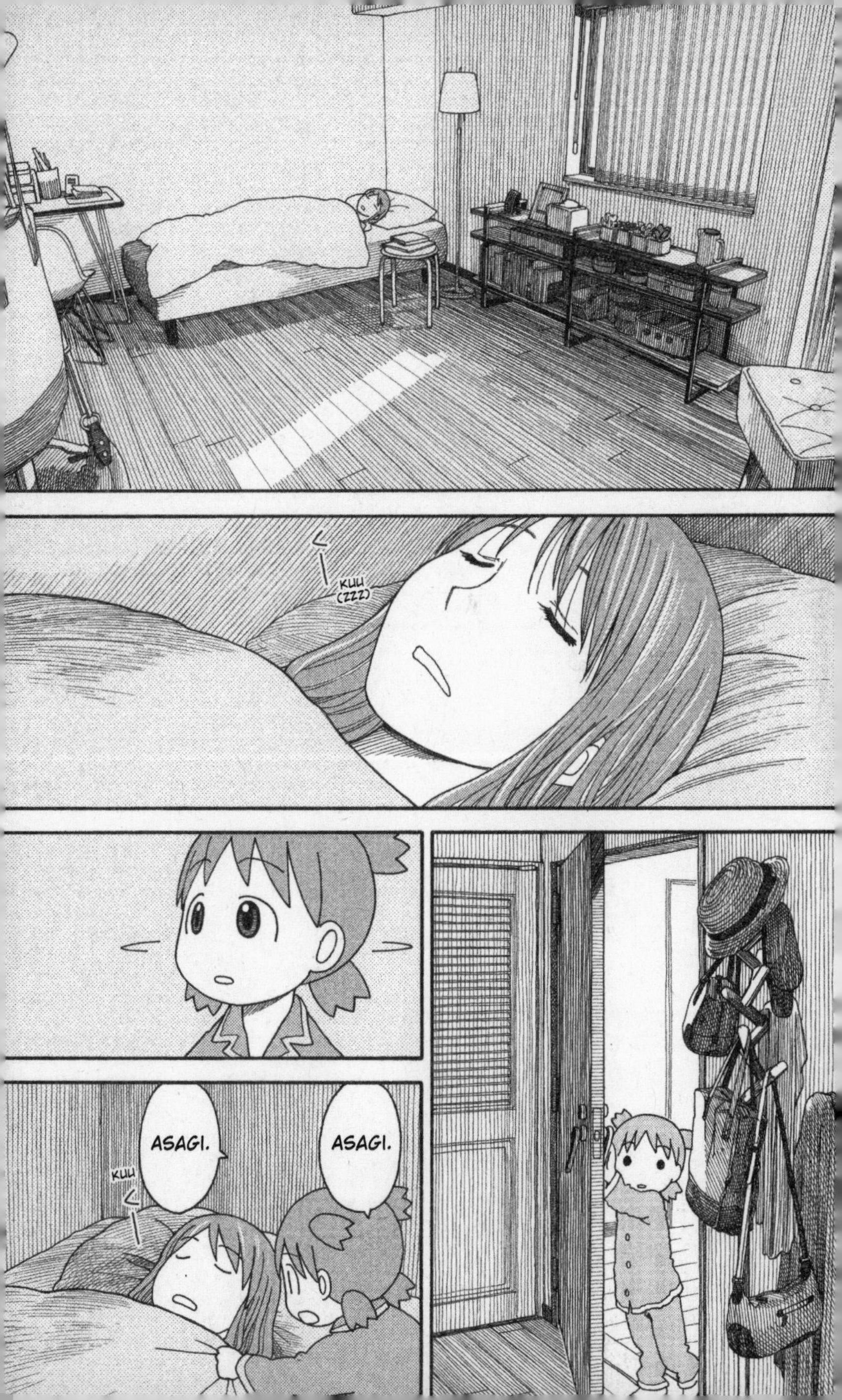

KUU (ZZZ)
ASAGI.
ASAGI.
KUU

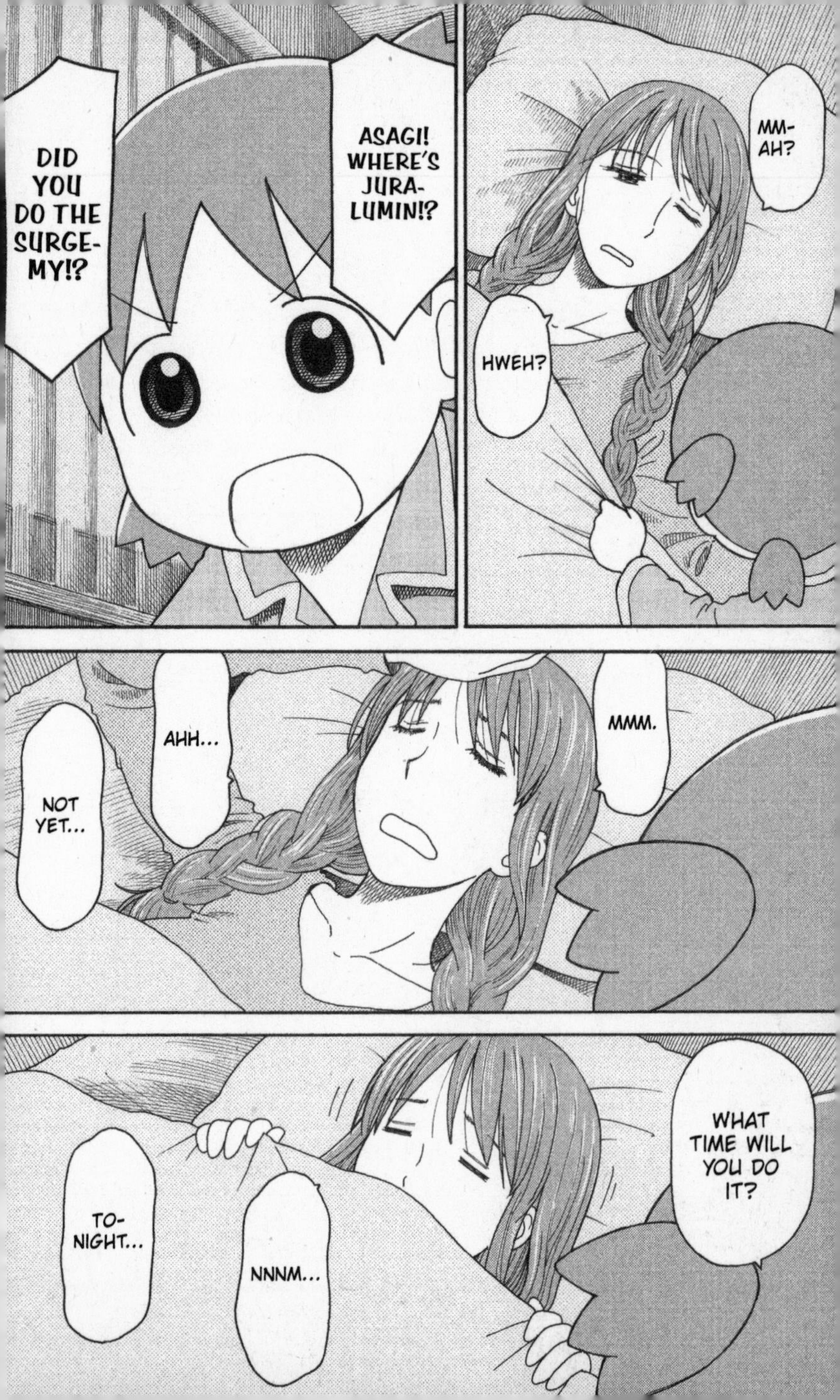
ASAGI! WHERE'S JURA-LUMIN!?
DID YOU DO THE SURGE-MY!?
MM-AH?
HWEH?
MMM.
AHH...
NOT YET...
WHAT TIME WILL YOU DO IT?
NNNM...
TO-NIGHT...

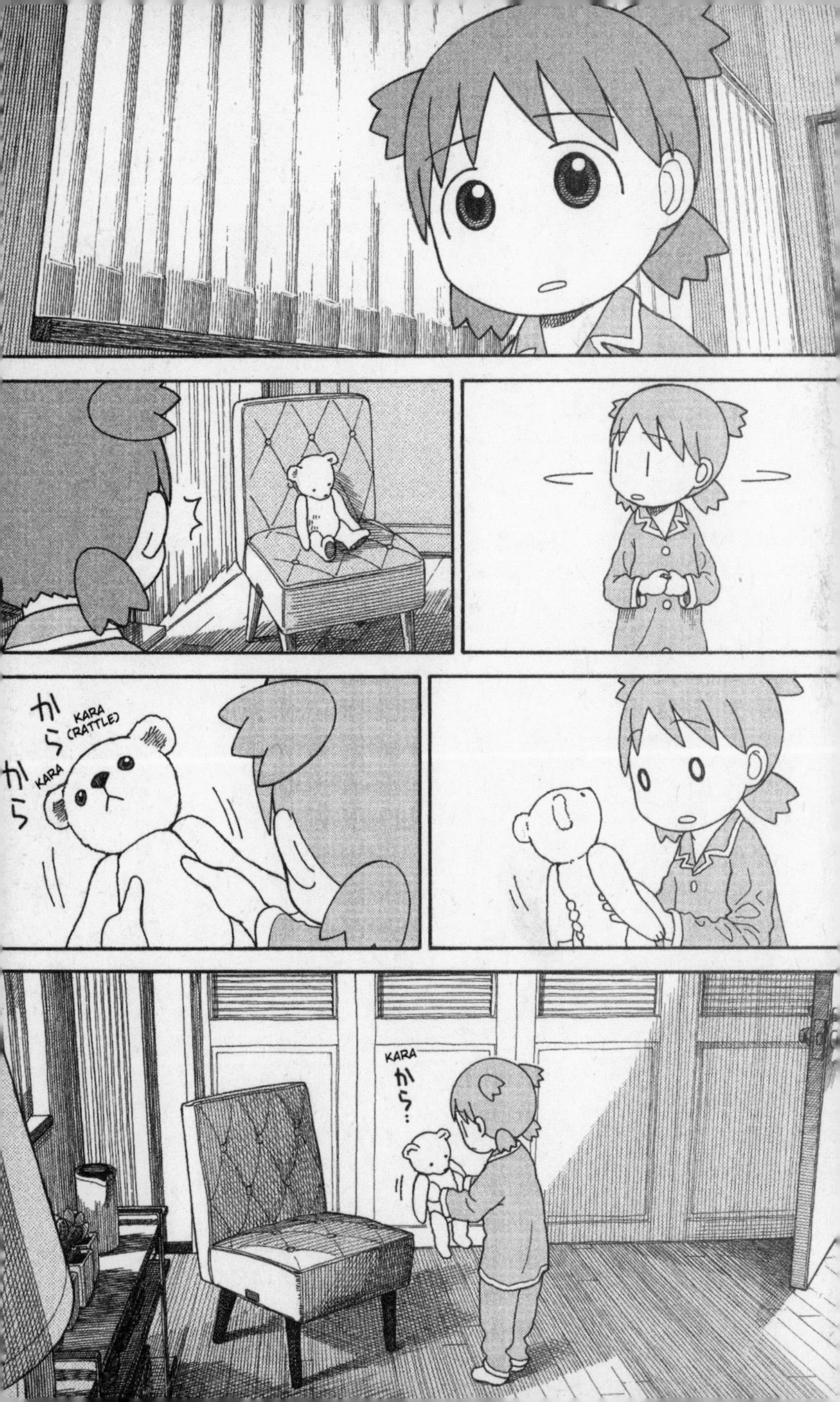
から
KARA (RATTLE)
から
KARA
KARA
から…

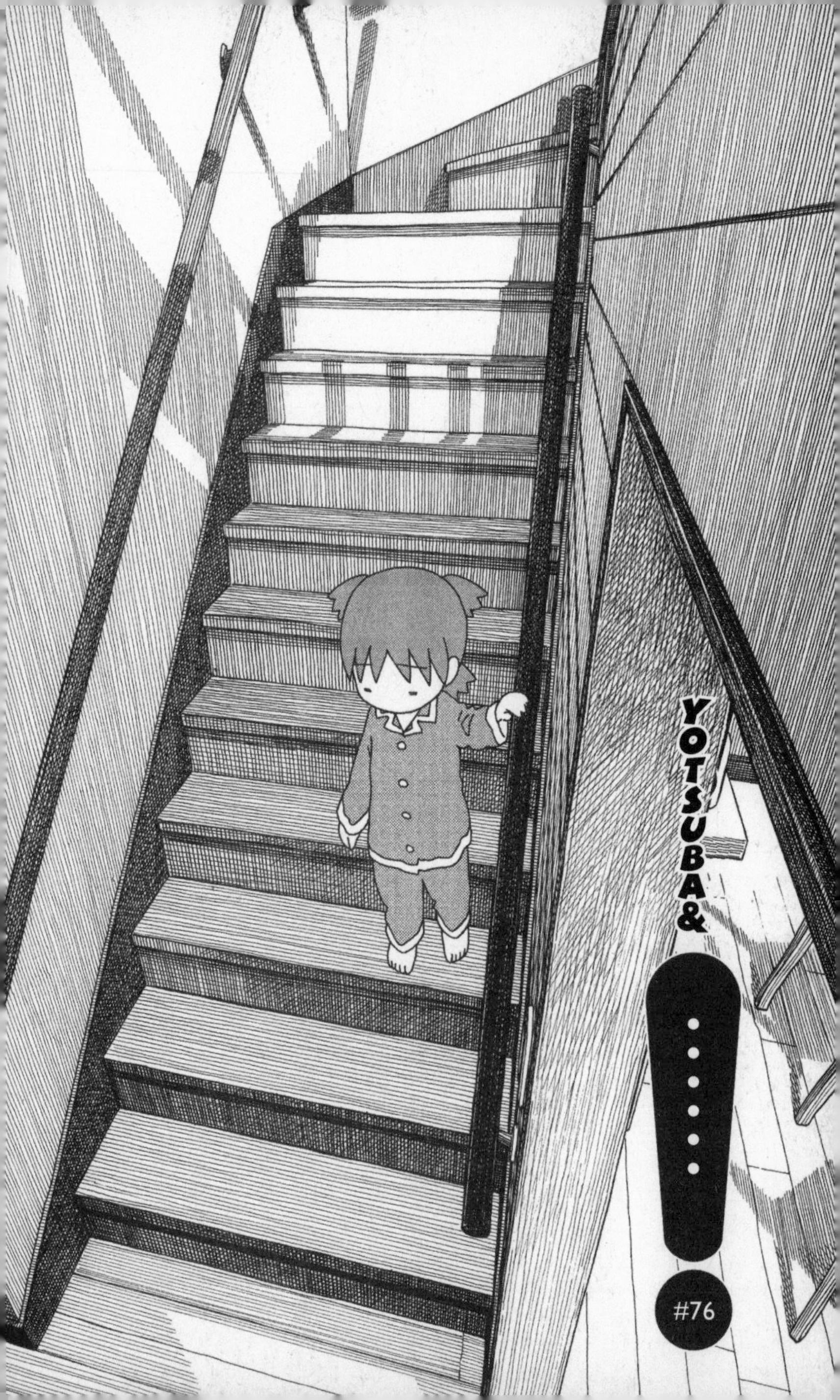
YOTSUBA&
!
#76

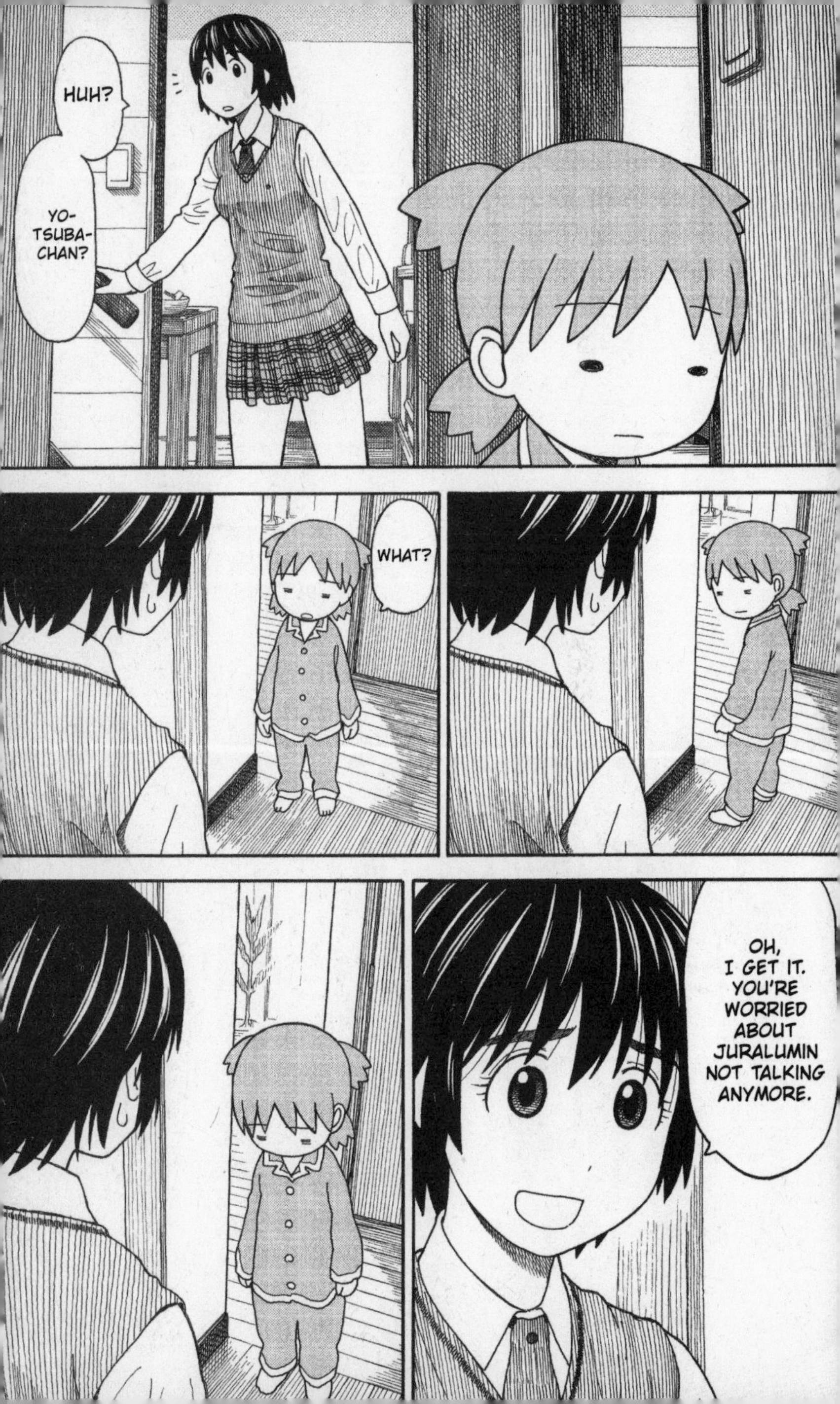
HUH?
YO-TSUBA-CHAN?
WHAT?
OH, I GET IT. YOU'RE WORRIED ABOUT JURALUMIN NOT TALKING ANYMORE.

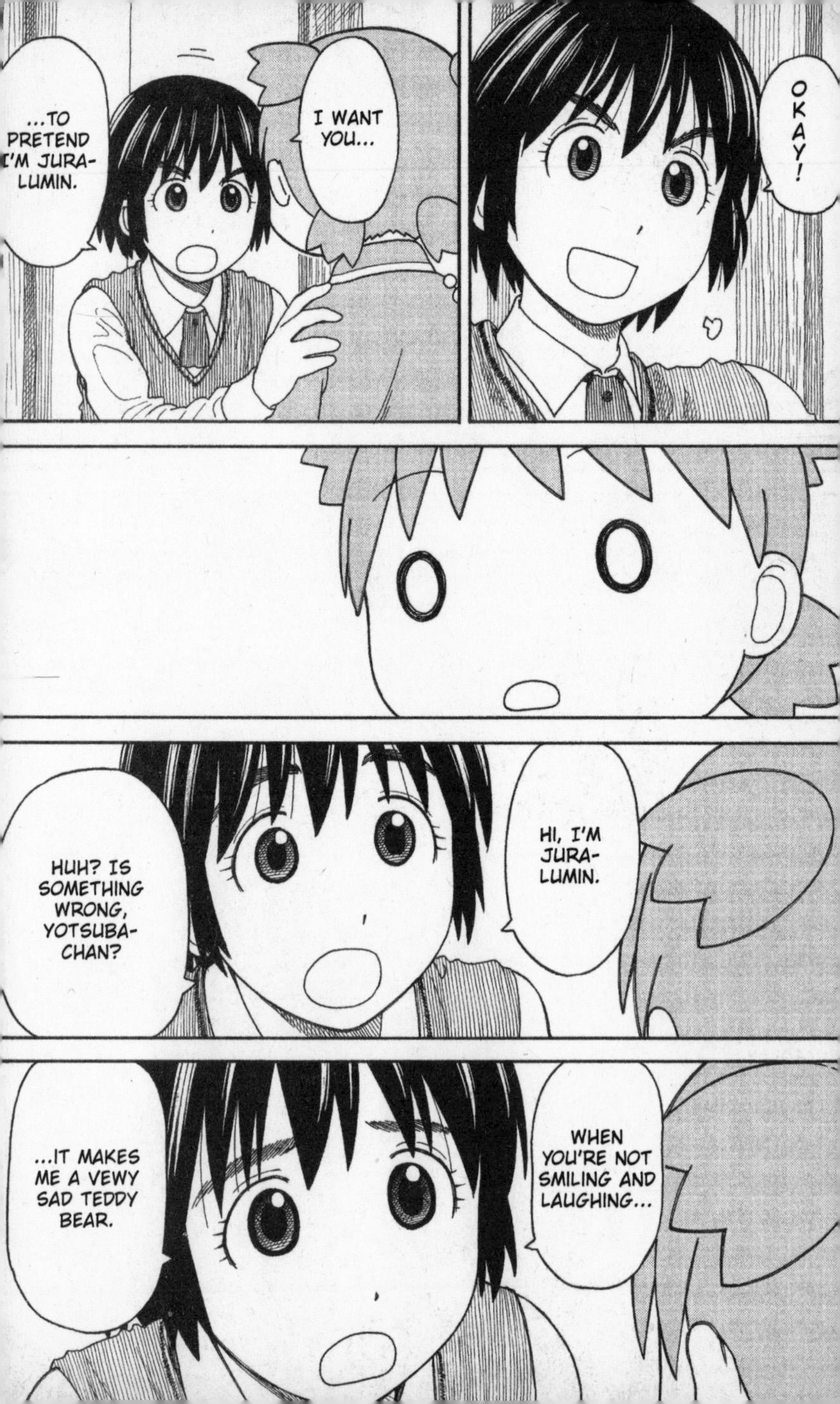
OKAY!
I WANT YOU...
...TO PRETEND I'M JURA-LUMIN.
HI, I'M JURA-LUMIN.
HUH? IS SOMETHING WRONG, YOTSUBA-CHAN?
WHEN YOU'RE NOT SMILING AND LAUGHING...
...IT MAKES ME A VEWY SAD TEDDY BEAR.

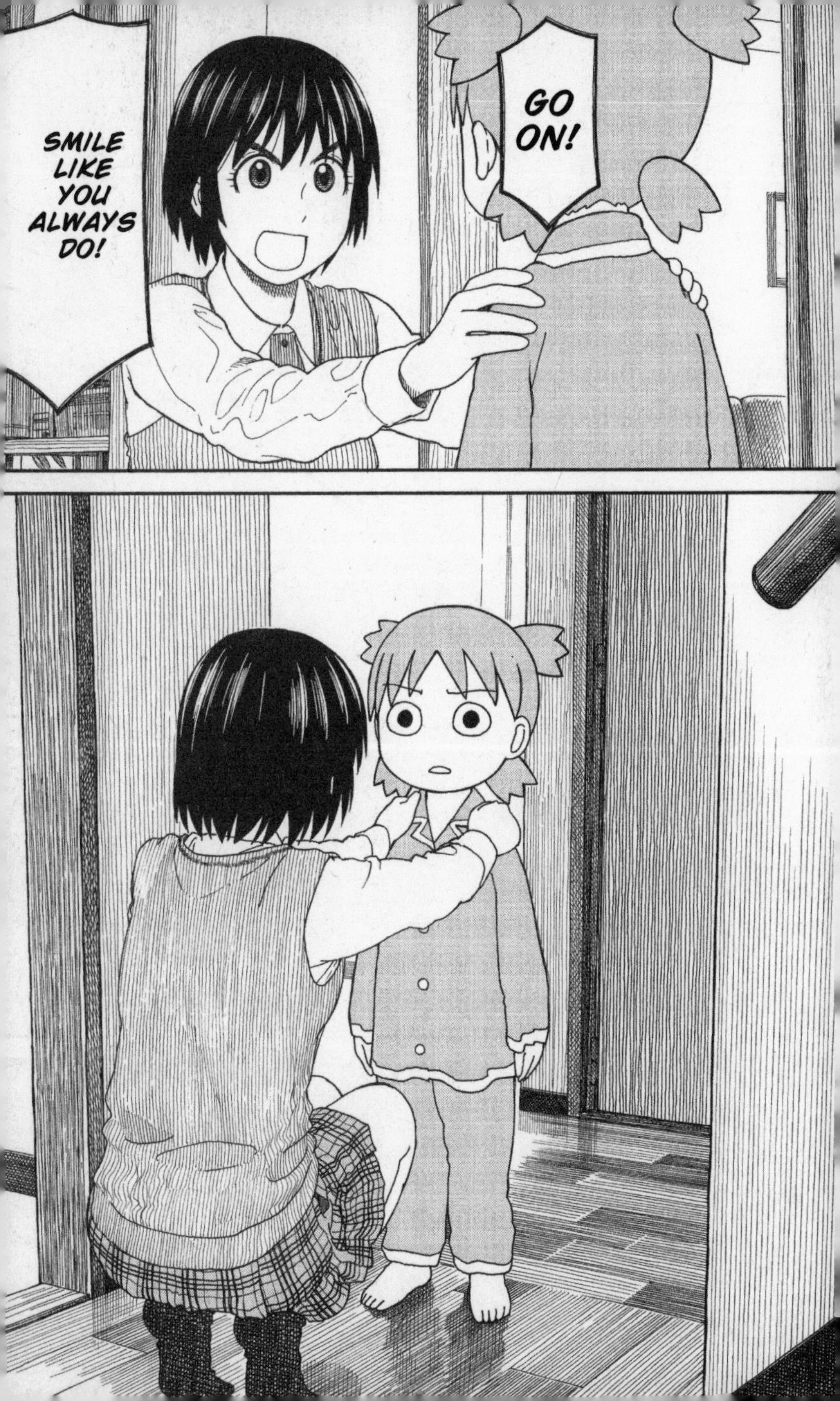
GO ON!
SMILE LIKE YOU ALWAYS DO!

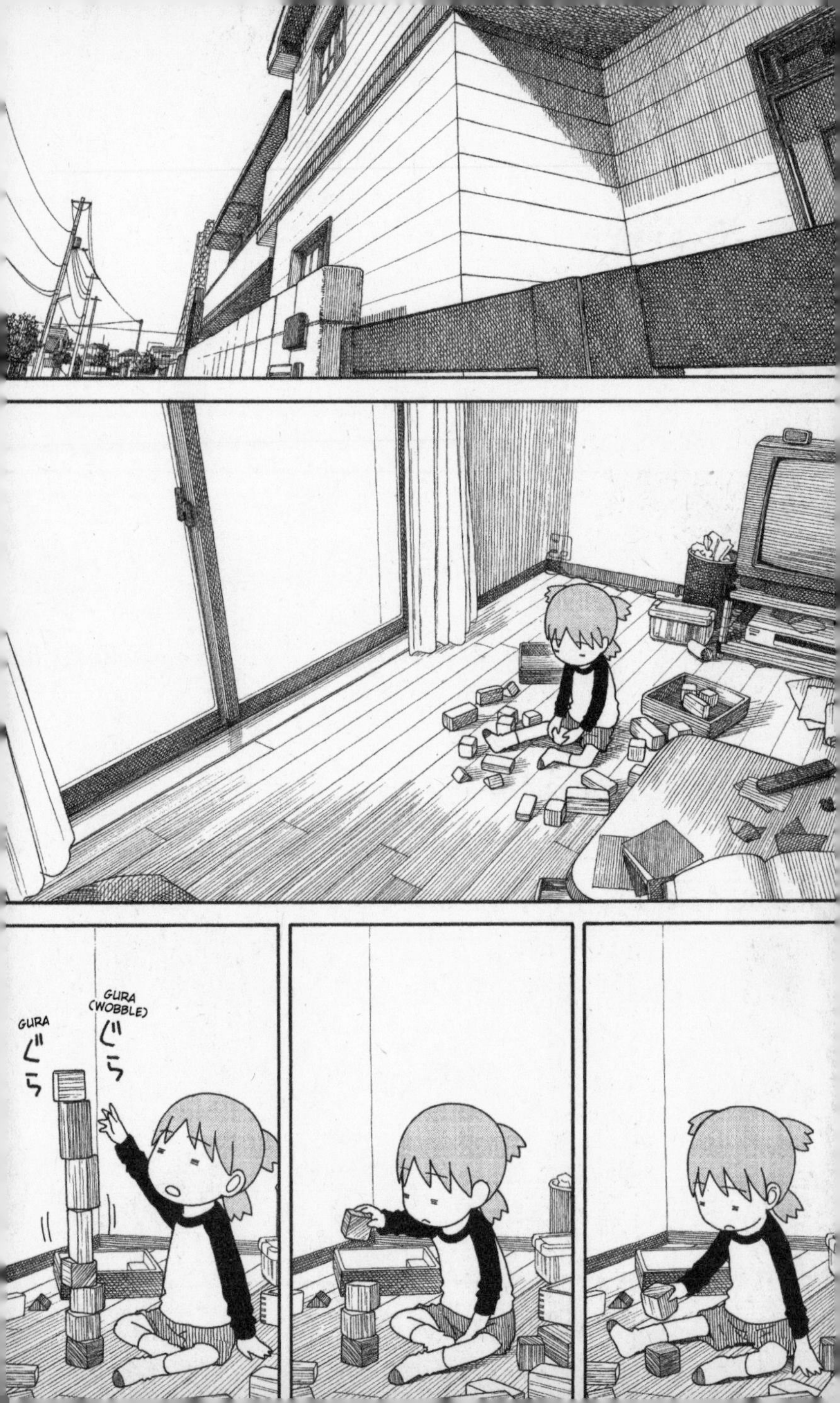
GURA
ぐら
GURA (WOBBLE)
ぐら

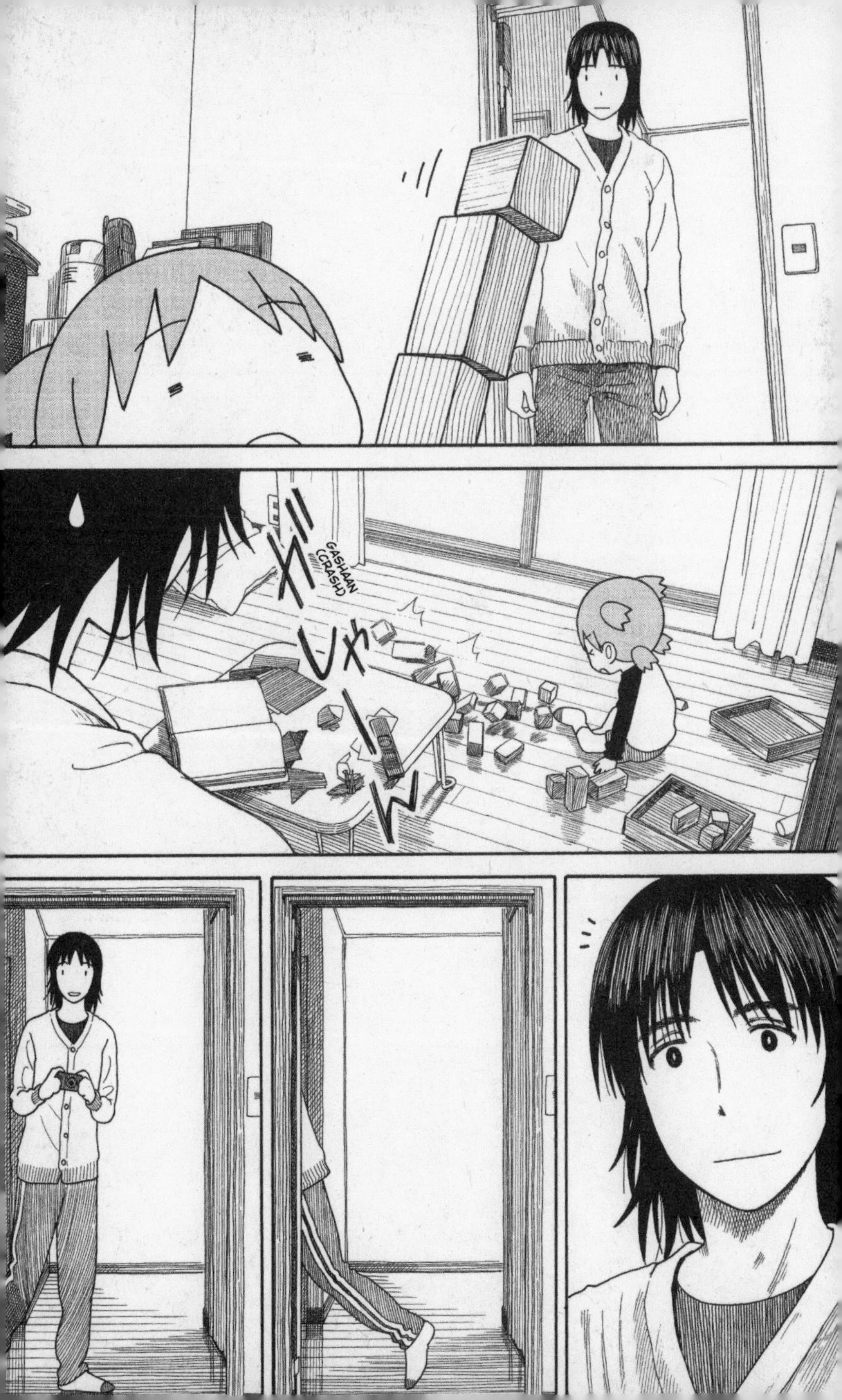
GASHAAN (CRASH)

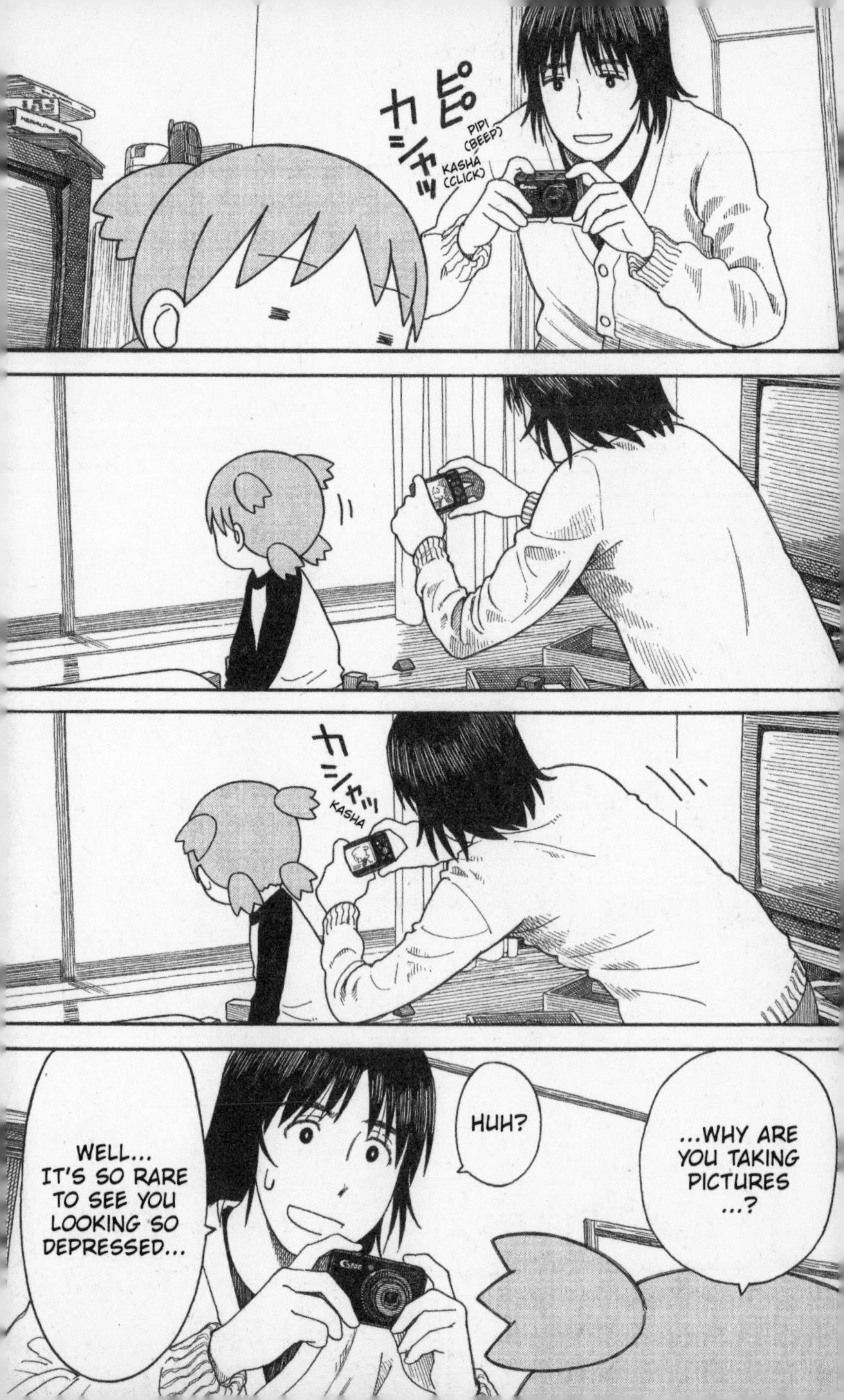
PIPI (BEEP)
KASHA (CLICK)
カシャッ
KASHA
...WHY ARE YOU TAKING PICTURES ...?
HUH?
WELL... IT'S SO RARE TO SEE YOU LOOKING SO DEPRESSED...

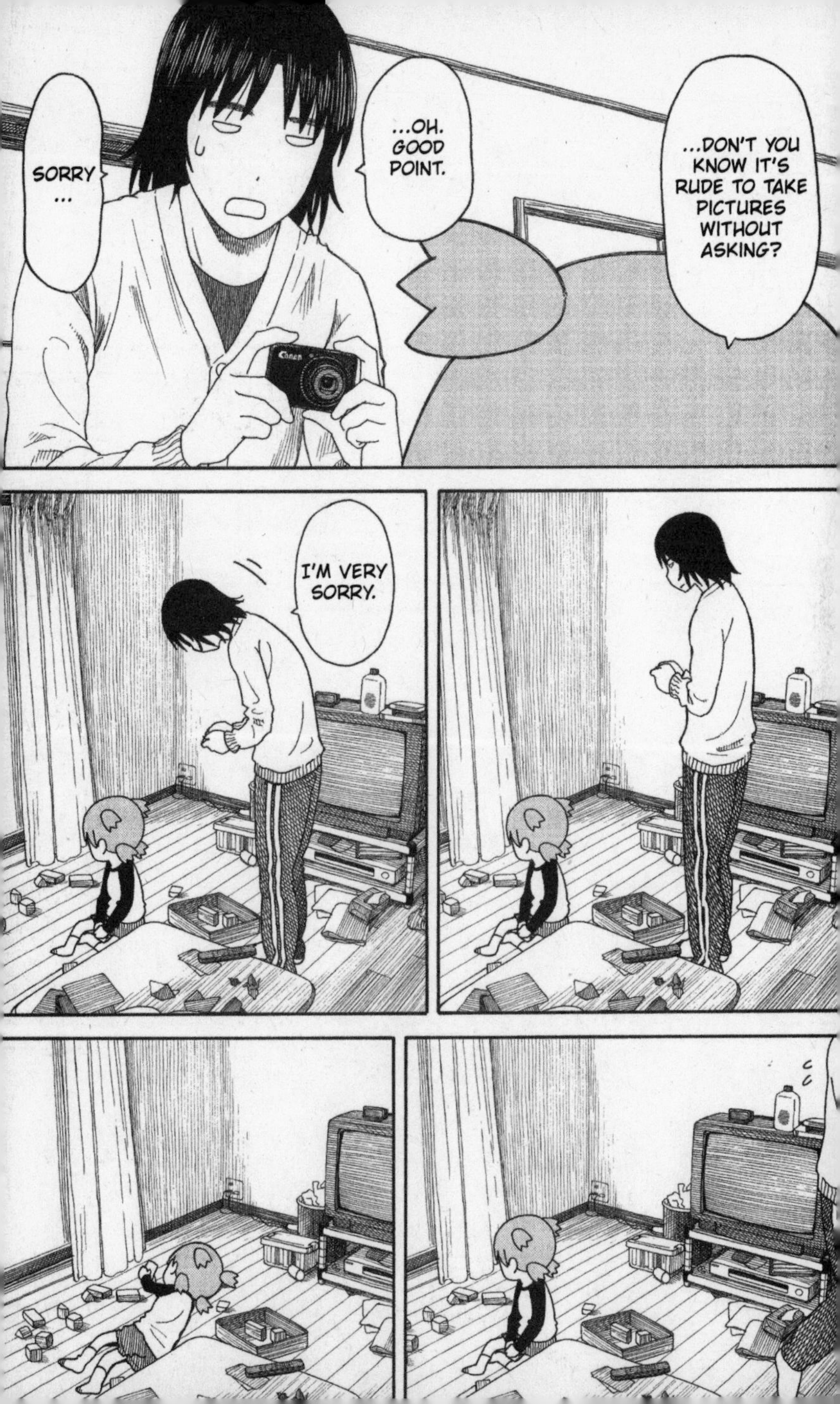
...DON'T YOU KNOW IT'S RUDE TO TAKE PICTURES WITHOUT ASKING?
...OH. GOOD POINT.
SORRY ...
I'M VERY SORRY.

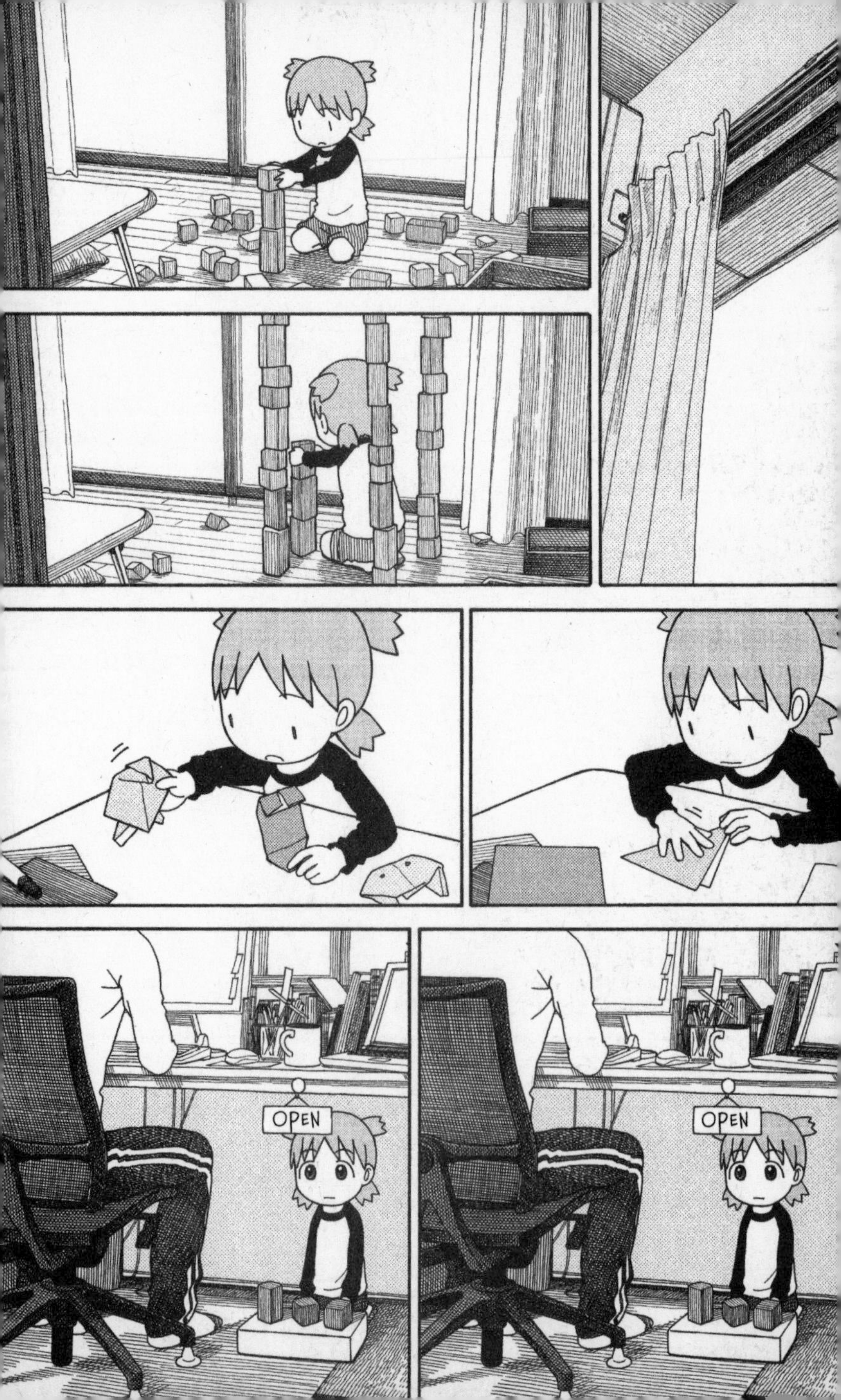
OPEN
OPEN

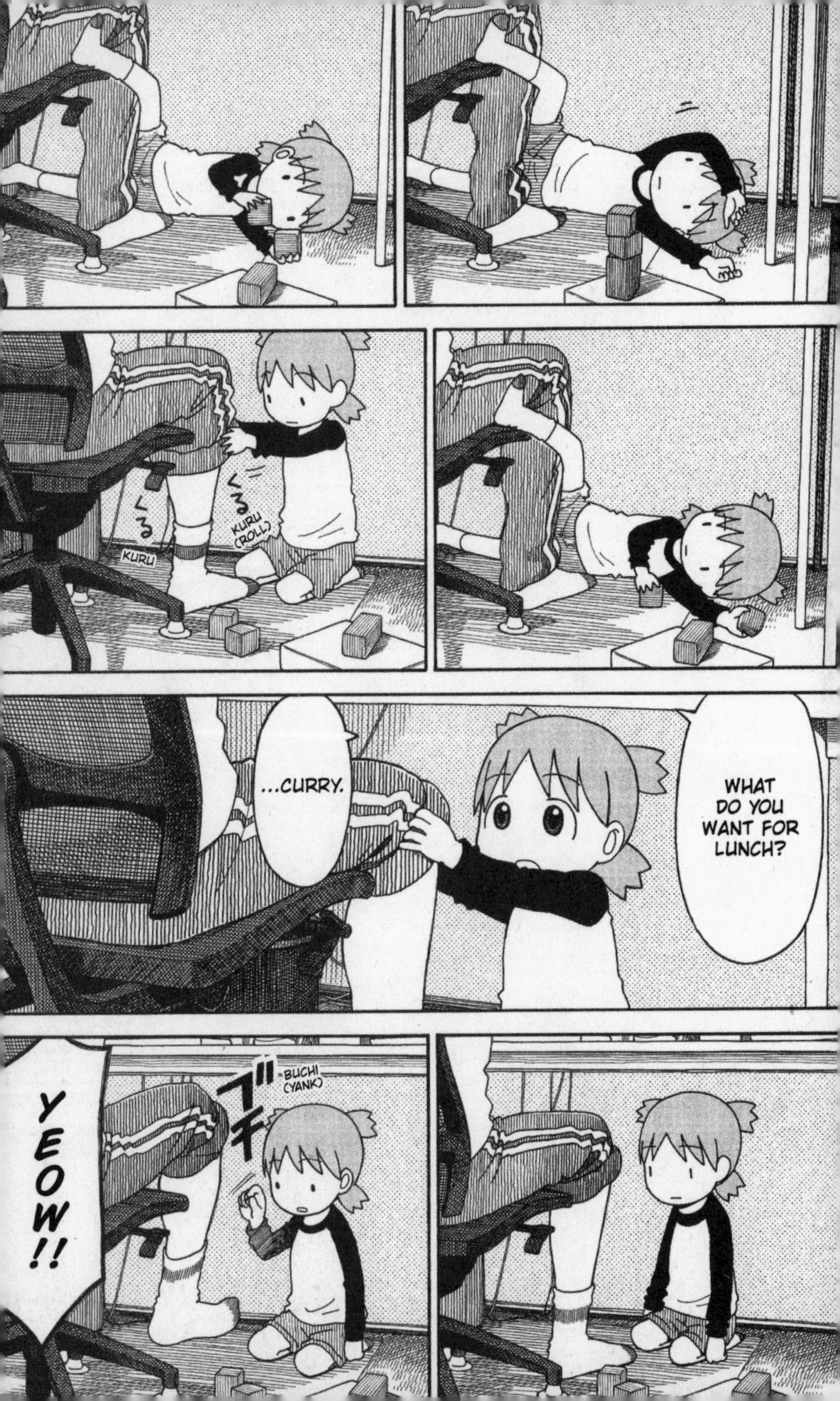

くる
KURU (ROLL)
くる
KURU
WHAT DO YOU WANT FOR LUNCH?
...CURRY.
ブチ
BUCHI (YANK)
YEOW!!

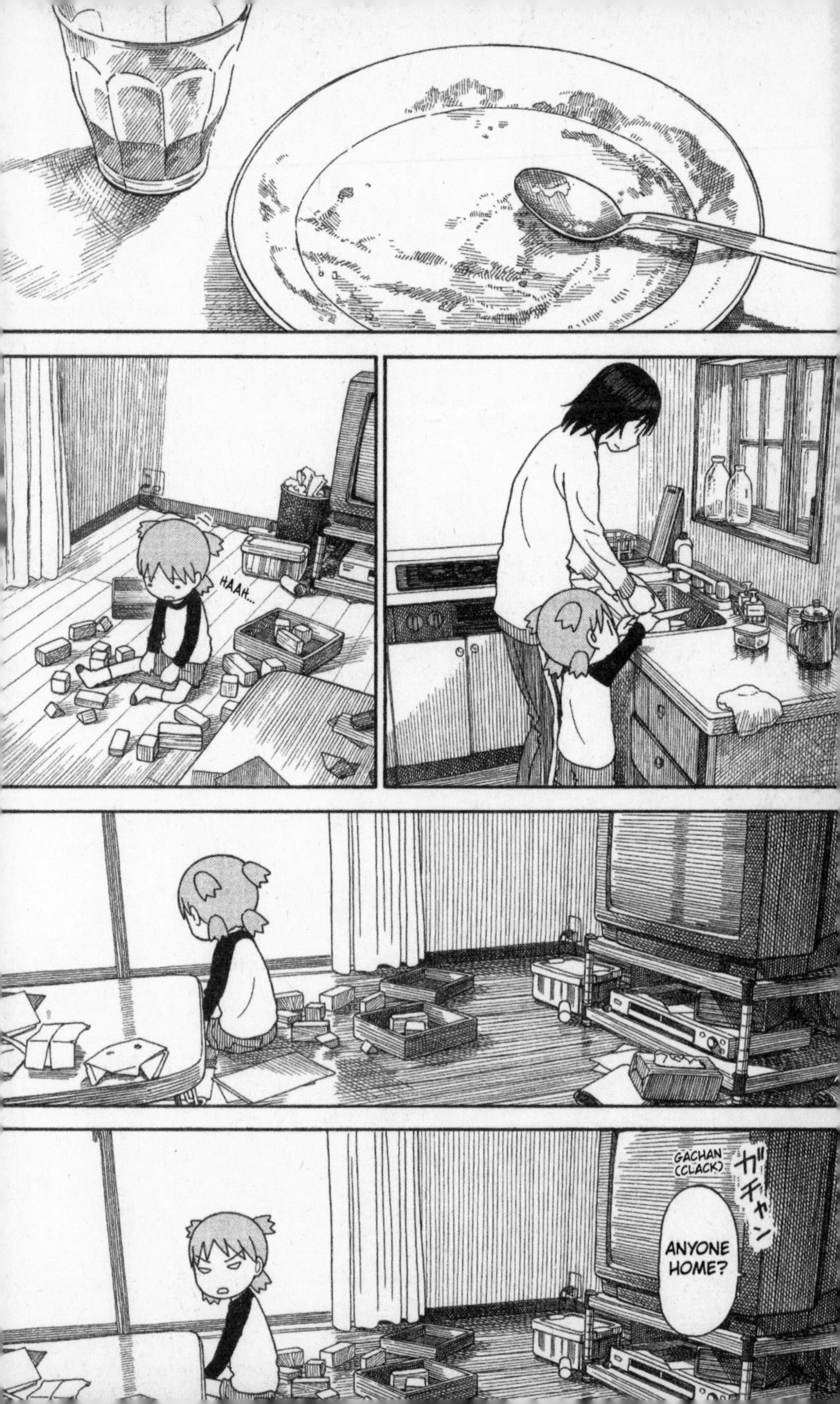
HAAH...
ガチャン
GACHAN (CLACK)
ANYONE HOME?

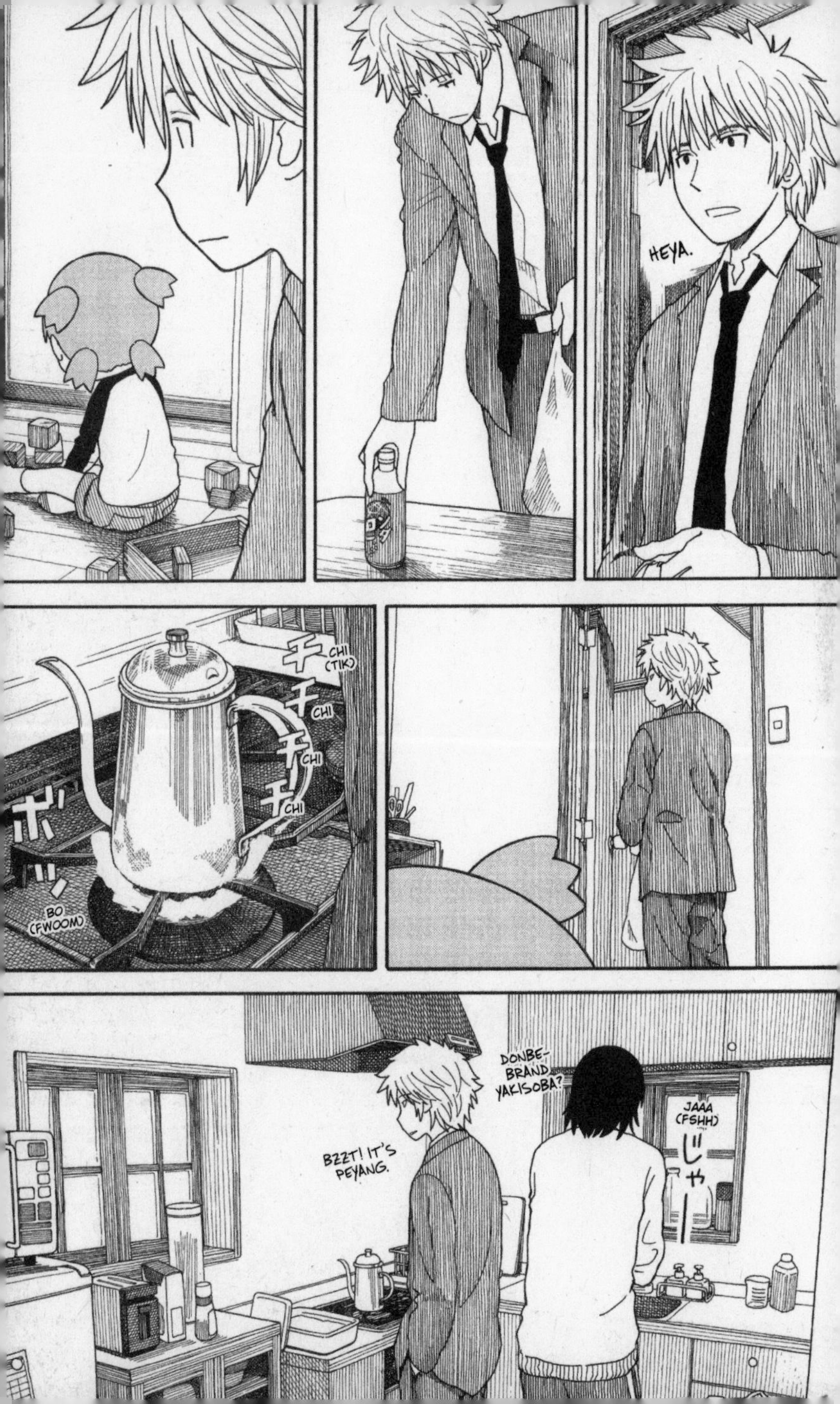

HEYA.
チ CHI (TIK)
チ CHI
チ CHI
チ CHI
ボッ BO (FWOOM)
DONBE-BRAND YAKISOBA?
じゃー JAAA (FSHH)
BZZT! IT'S PEYANG.

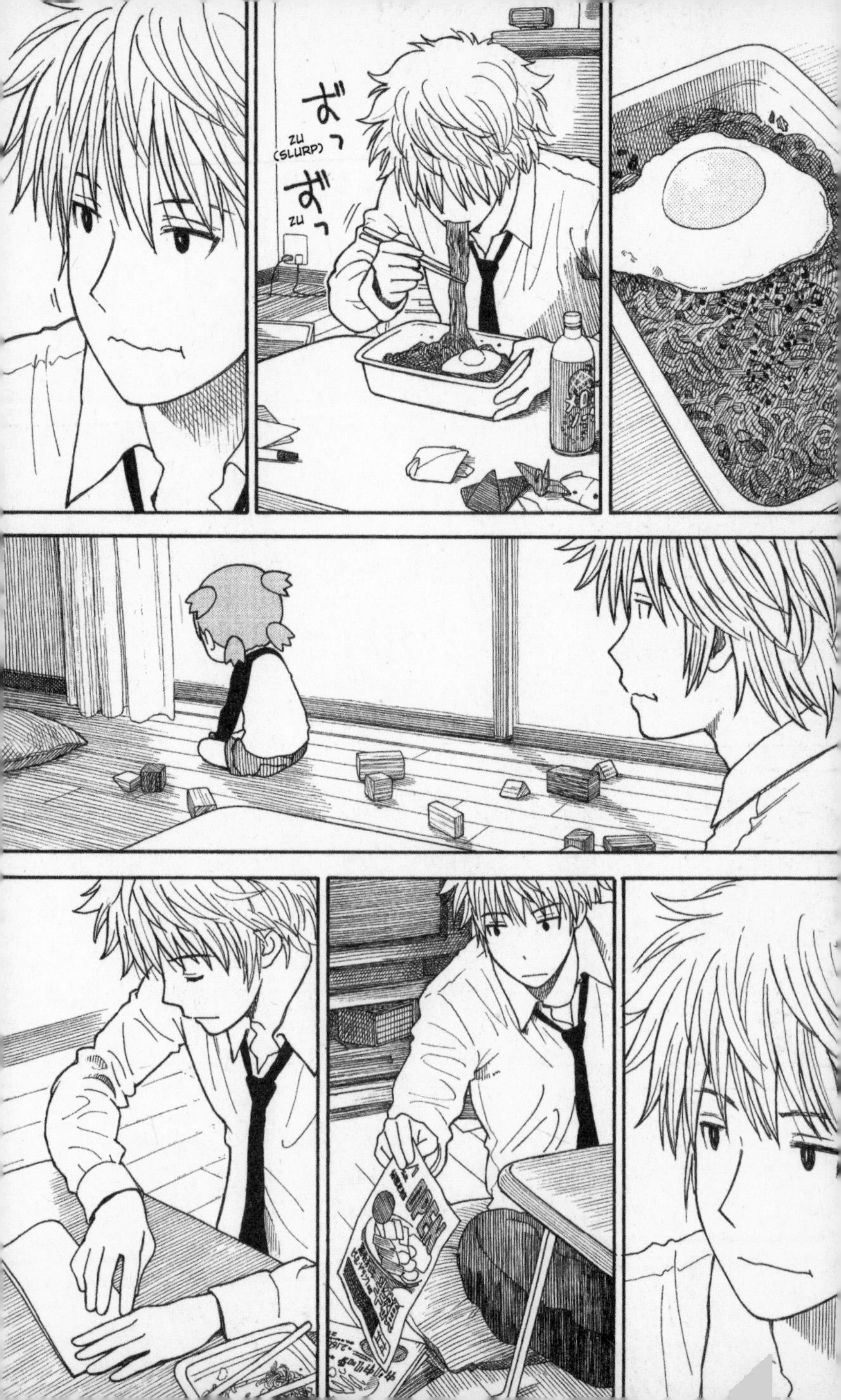
ずっ
ZU (SLURP)
ずっ
ZU

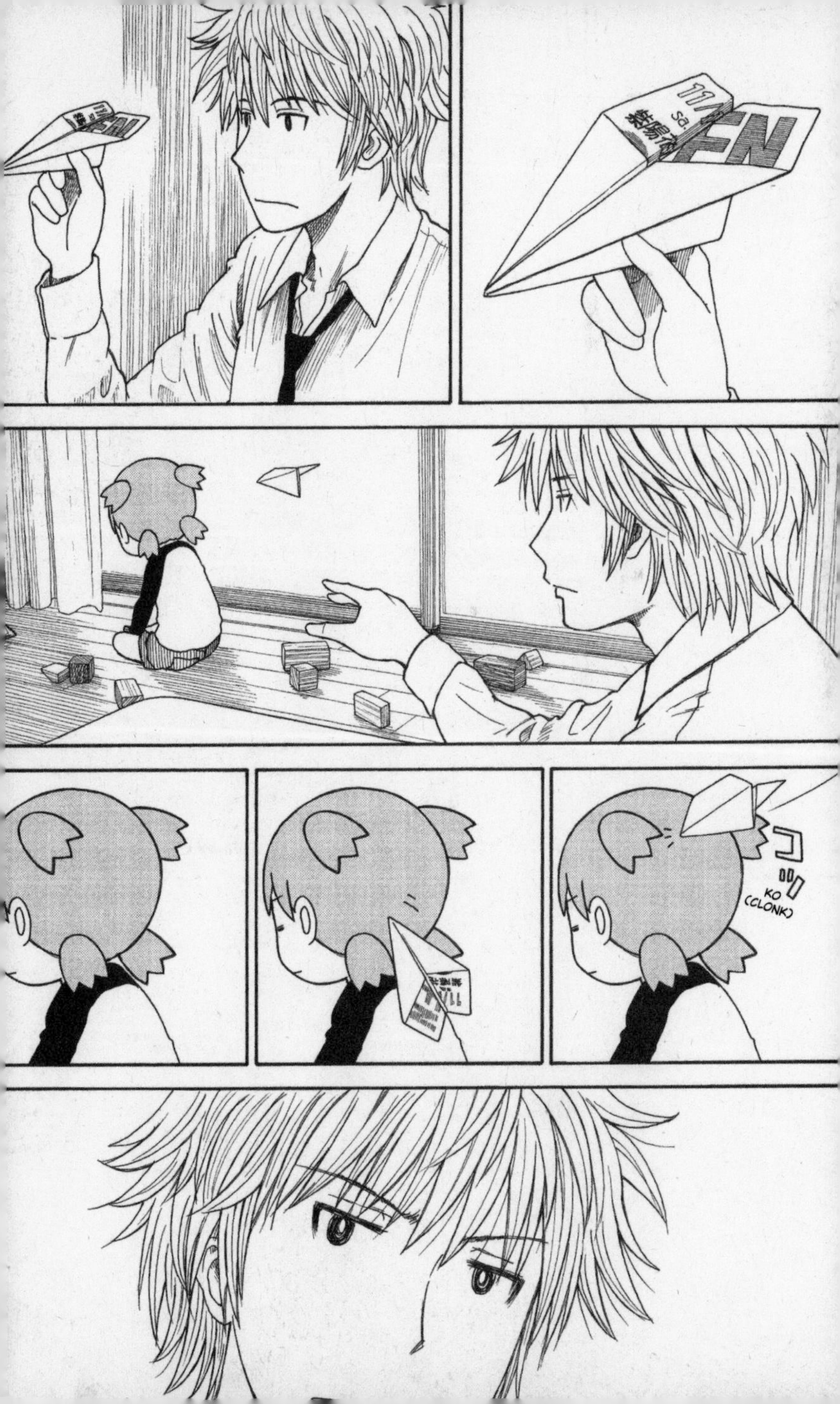
コッ
KO (CLONK)

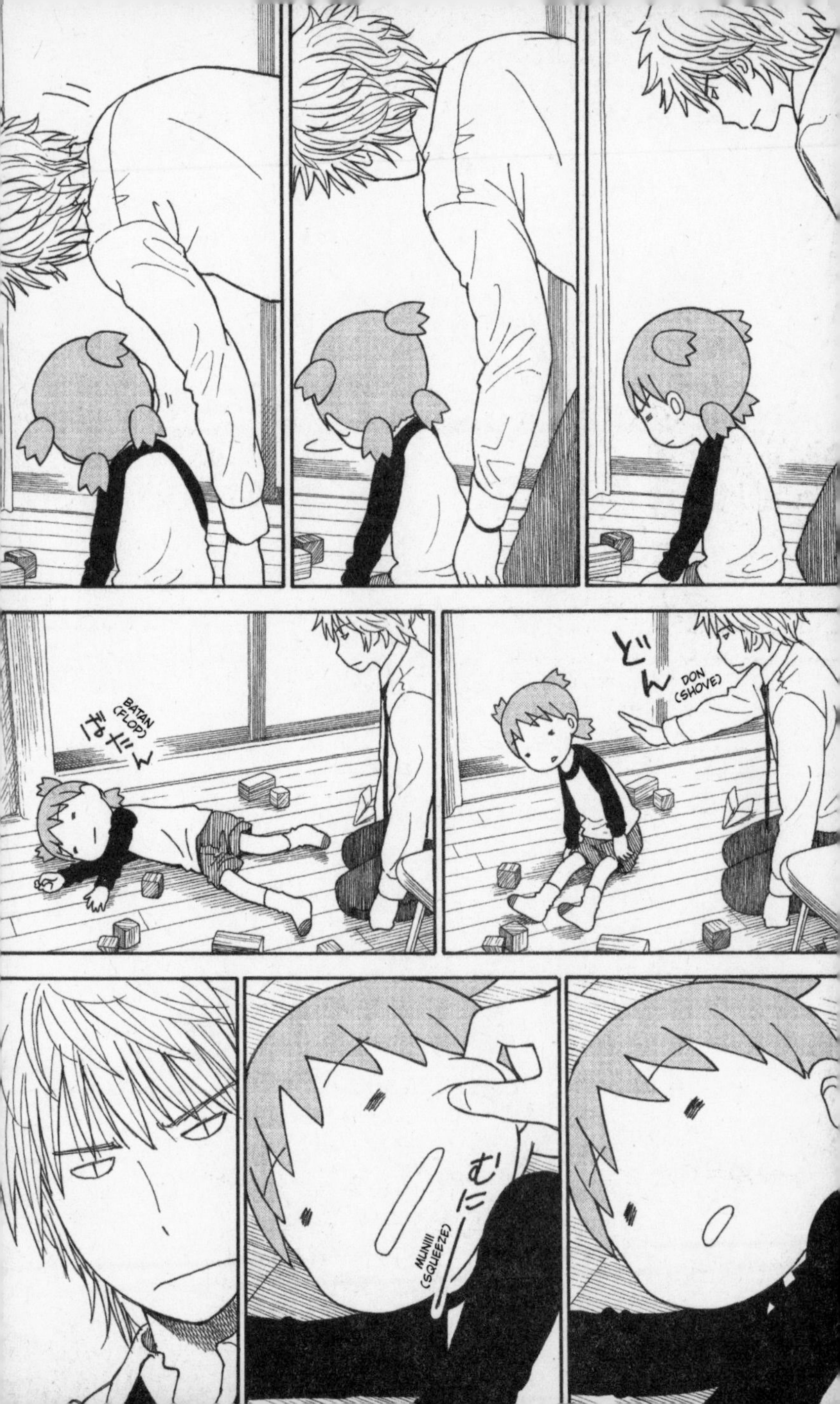

ばたん
BATAN (FLOP)
どん
DON (SHOVE)
むに
MUNIII (SQUEEZE)

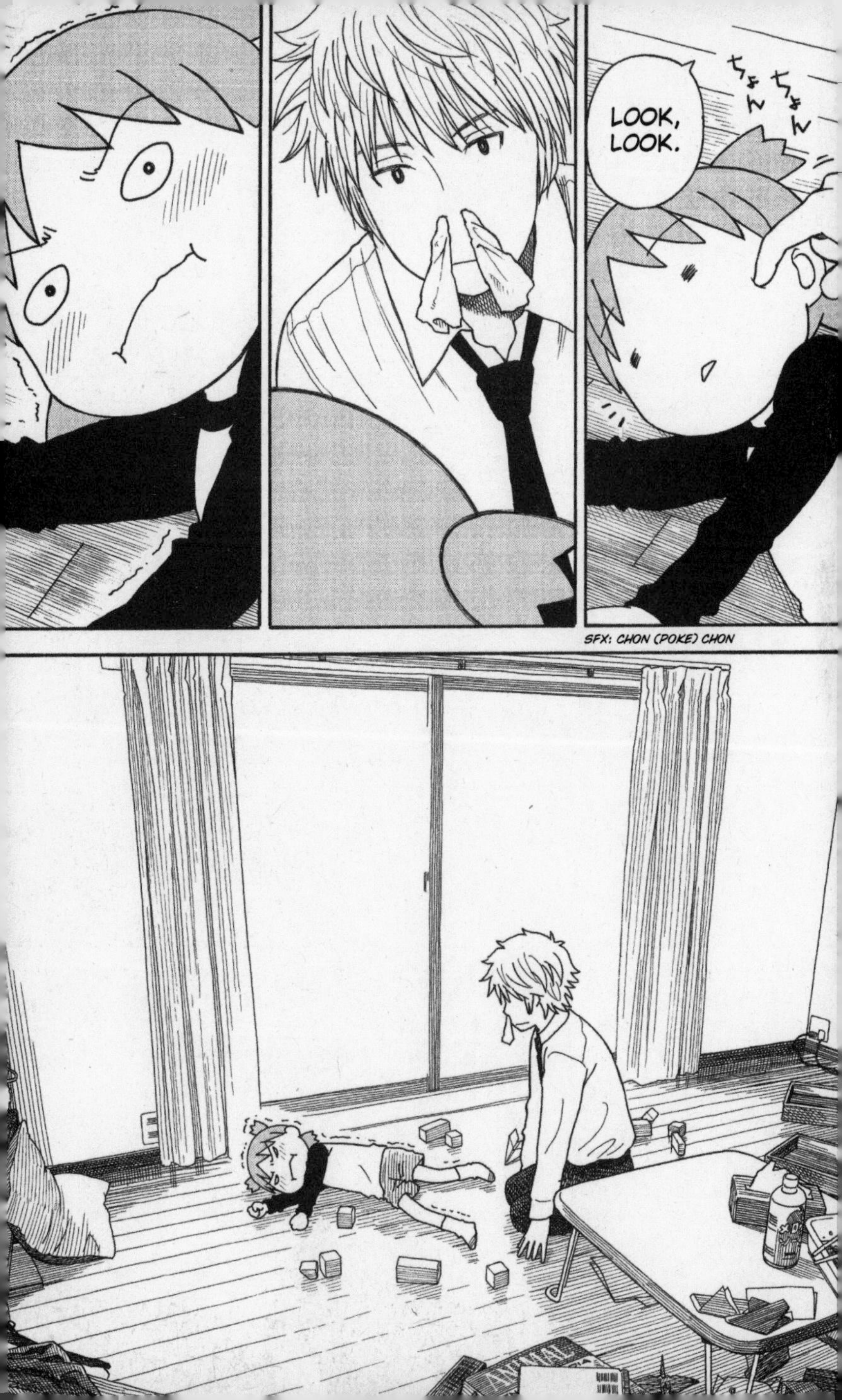
ちょん ちょん
LOOK, LOOK.
SFX: CHON (POKE) CHON

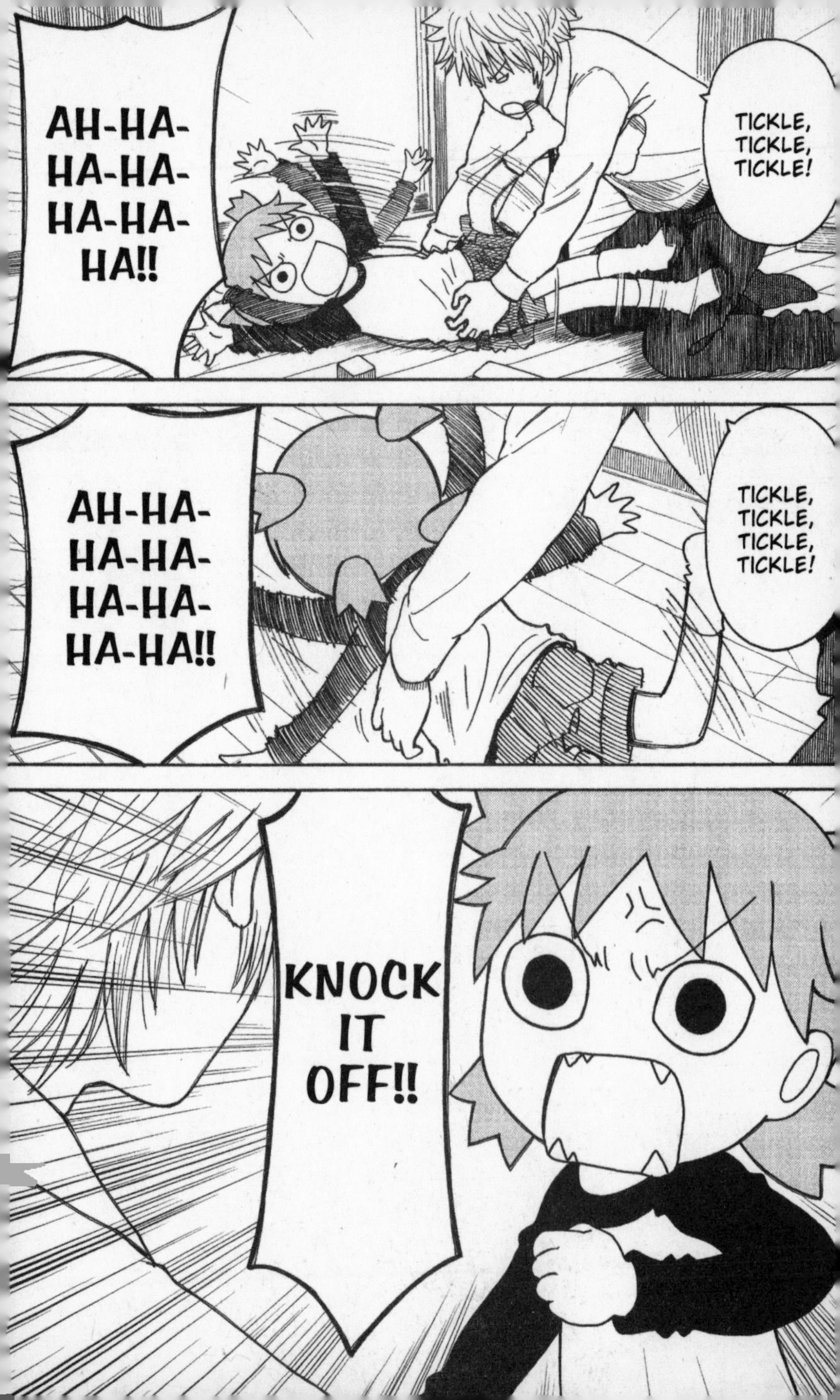
TICKLE, TICKLE, TICKLE!
AH-HA-HA-HA-HA-HA-HA!!
TICKLE, TICKLE, TICKLE, TICKLE!
AH-HA-HA-HA-HA-HA-HA-HA!!
KNOCK IT OFF!!

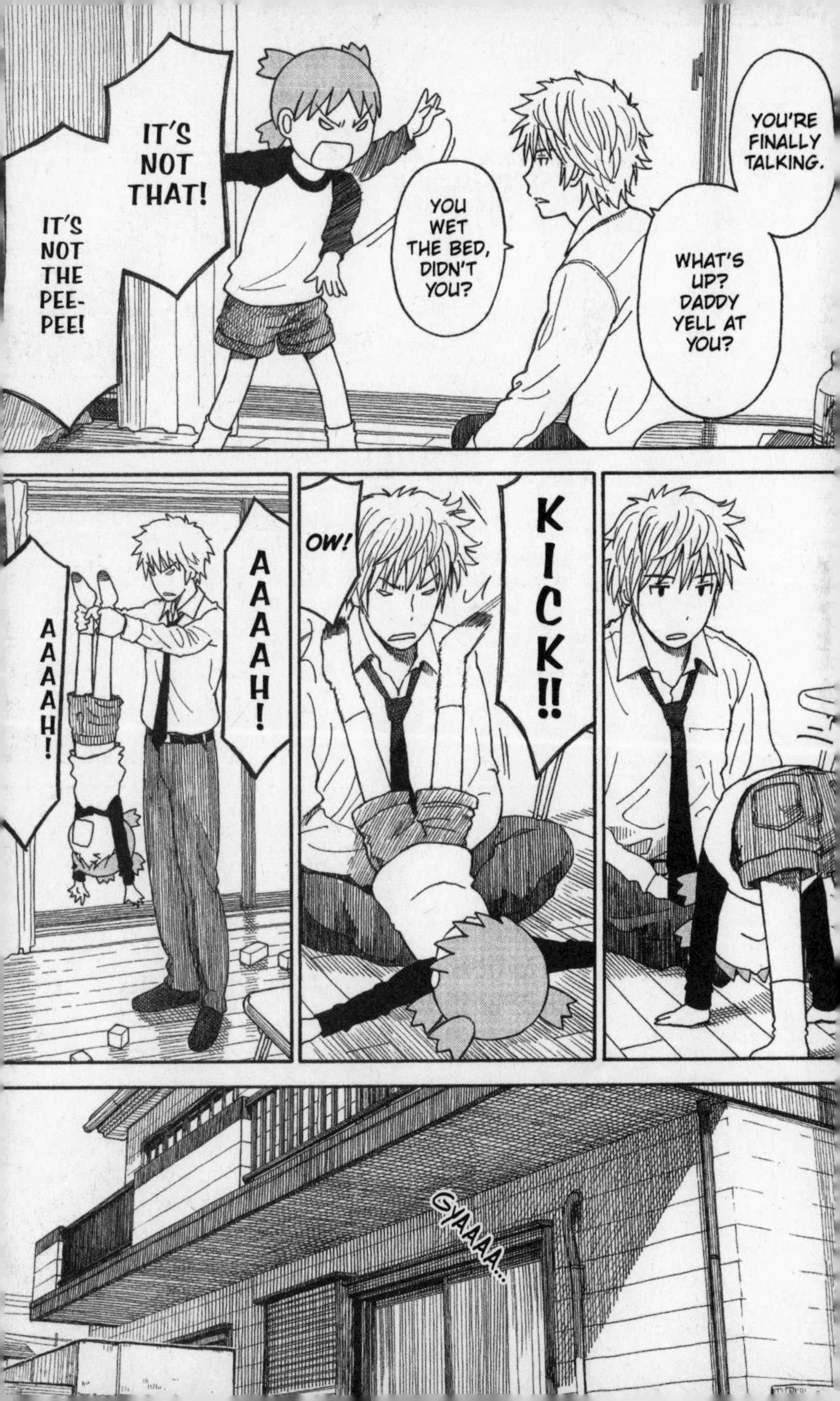
YOU'RE FINALLY TALKING.
WHAT'S UP? DADDY YELL AT YOU?
YOU WET THE BED, DIDN'T YOU?
IT'S NOT THAT!
IT'S NOT THE PEE-PEE!
KICK!!
OW!
AAAAAH!
AAAAAH!
GYAAAA...

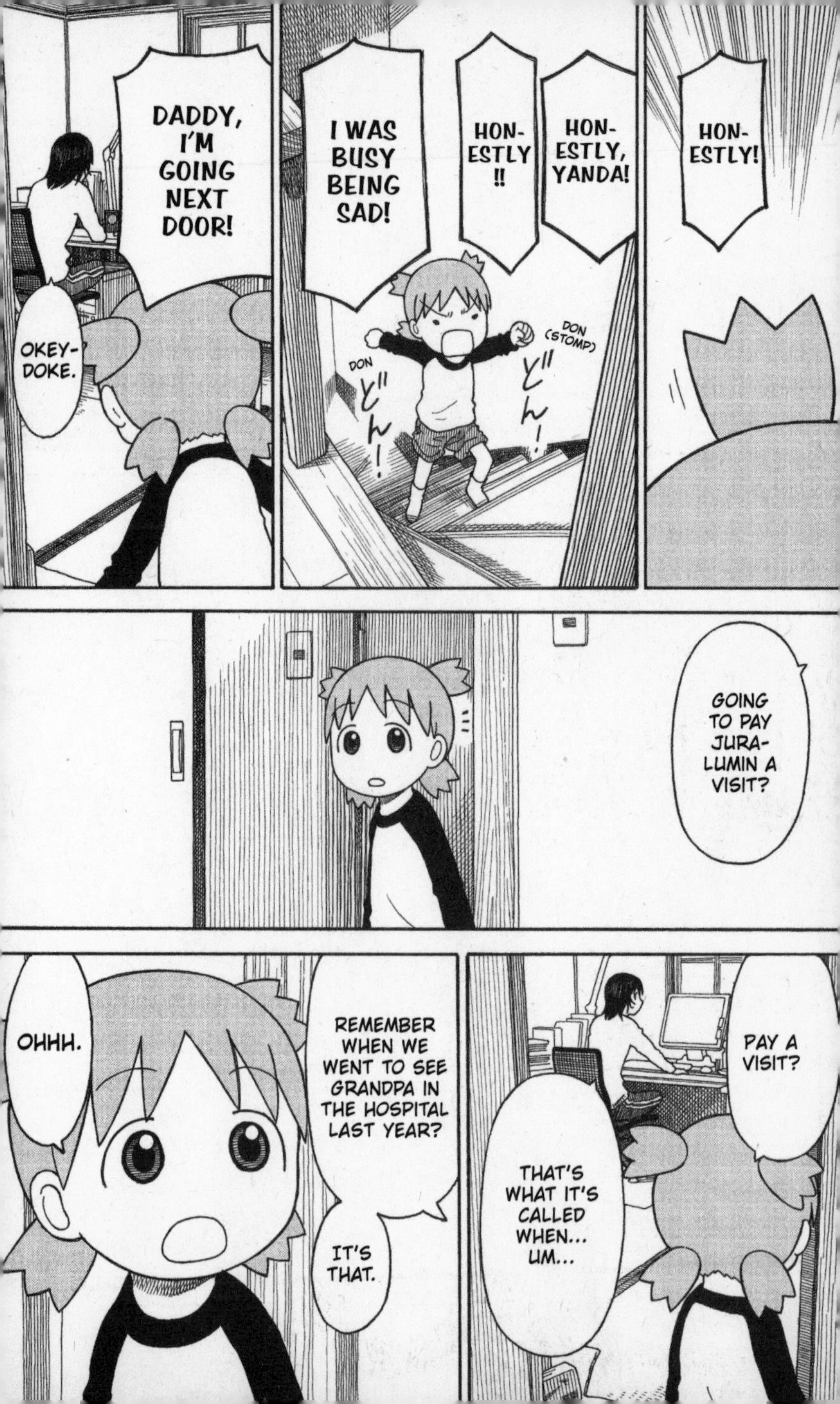
HON-ESTLY!
HON-ESTLY, YANDA!
HON-ESTLY !!
I WAS BUSY BEING SAD!
DON (STOMP)
DON
DADDY, I'M GOING NEXT DOOR!
OKEY-DOKE.
GOING TO PAY JURA-LUMIN A VISIT?
PAY A VISIT?
THAT'S WHAT IT'S CALLED WHEN... UM...
REMEMBER WHEN WE WENT TO SEE GRANDPA IN THE HOSPITAL LAST YEAR?
IT'S THAT.
OHHH.

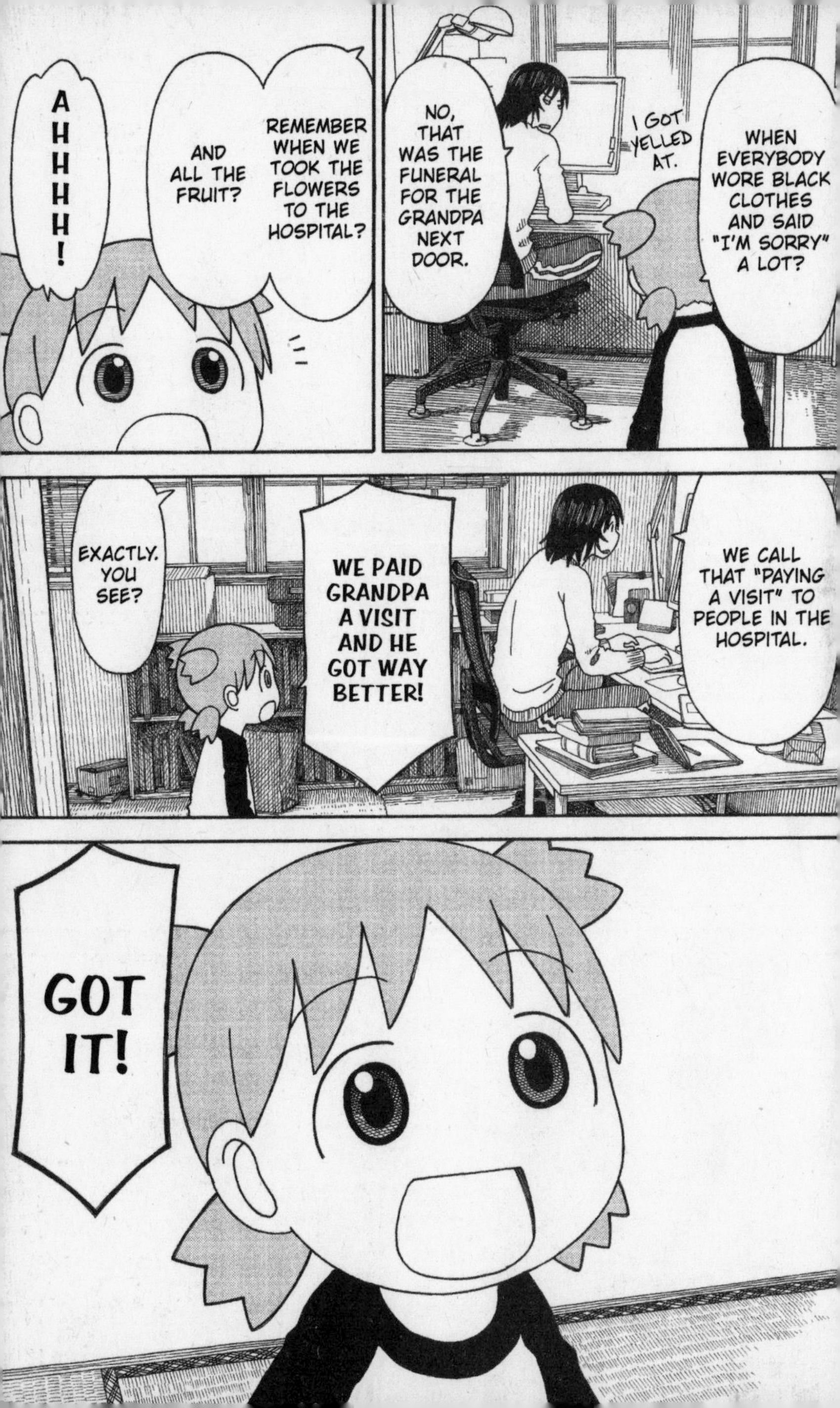
WHEN EVERYBODY WORE BLACK CLOTHES AND SAID "I'M SORRY" A LOT?
I GOT YELLED AT.
NO, THAT WAS THE FUNERAL FOR THE GRANDPA NEXT DOOR.
REMEMBER WHEN WE TOOK THE FLOWERS TO THE HOSPITAL?
AND ALL THE FRUIT?
AHHHHH!
WE CALL THAT "PAYING A VISIT" TO PEOPLE IN THE HOSPITAL.
WE PAID GRANDPA A VISIT AND HE GOT WAY BETTER!
EXACTLY. YOU SEE?
GOT IT!

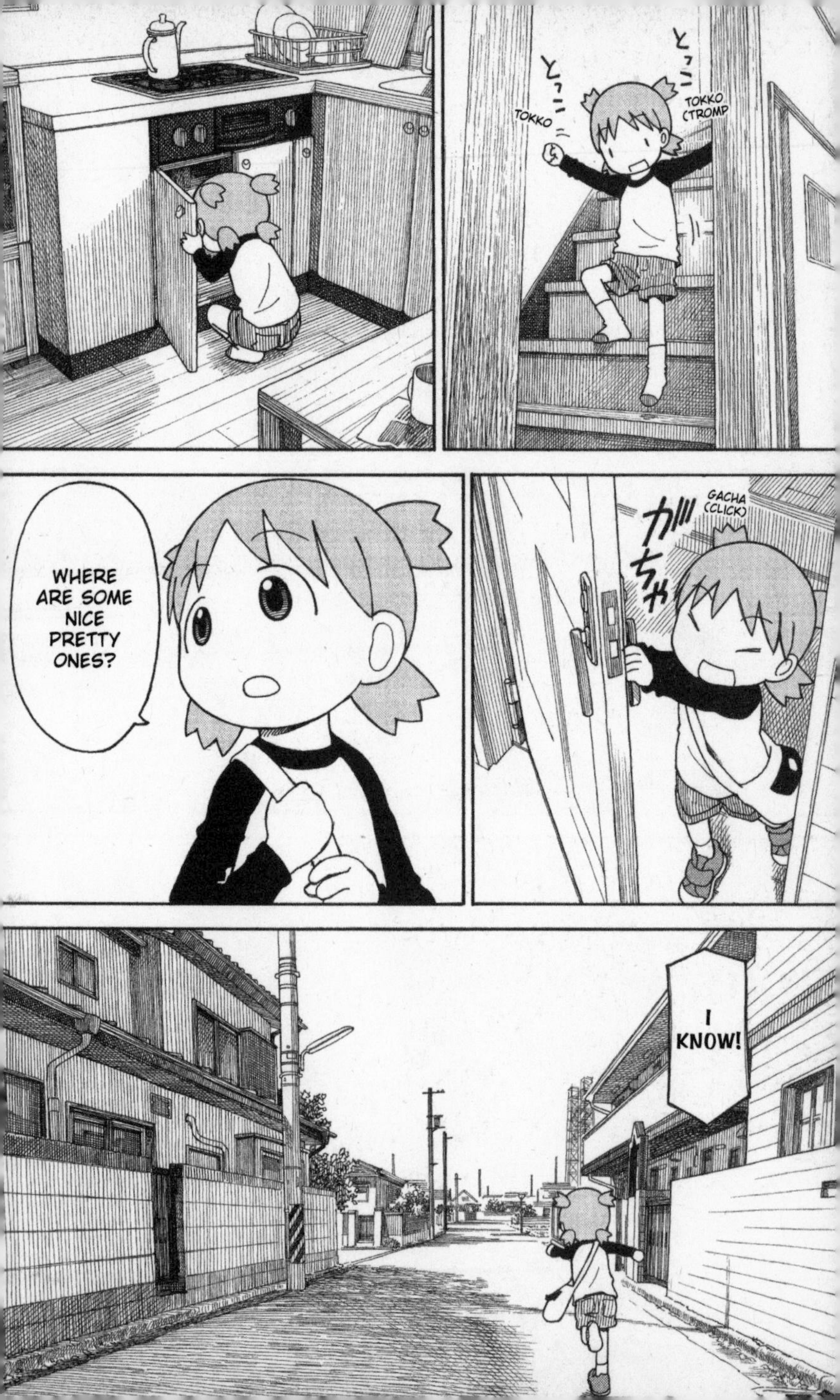
TOKKO (TROMP
TOKKO
GACHA (CLICK)
WHERE ARE SOME NICE PRETTY ONES?
I KNOW!

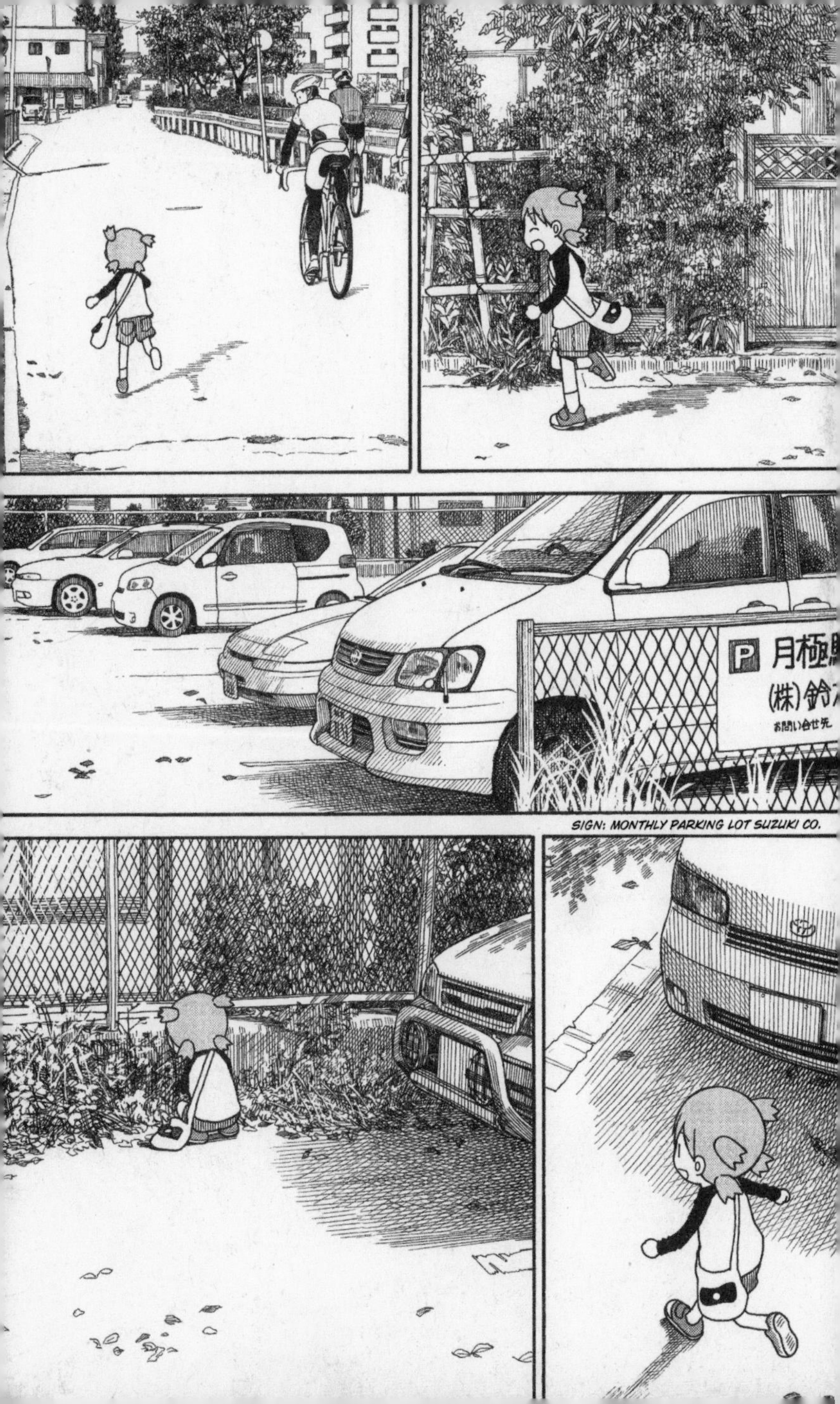
P 月極
(株)鈴
お問い合せ先

SIGN: MONTHLY PARKING LOT SUZUKI CO.

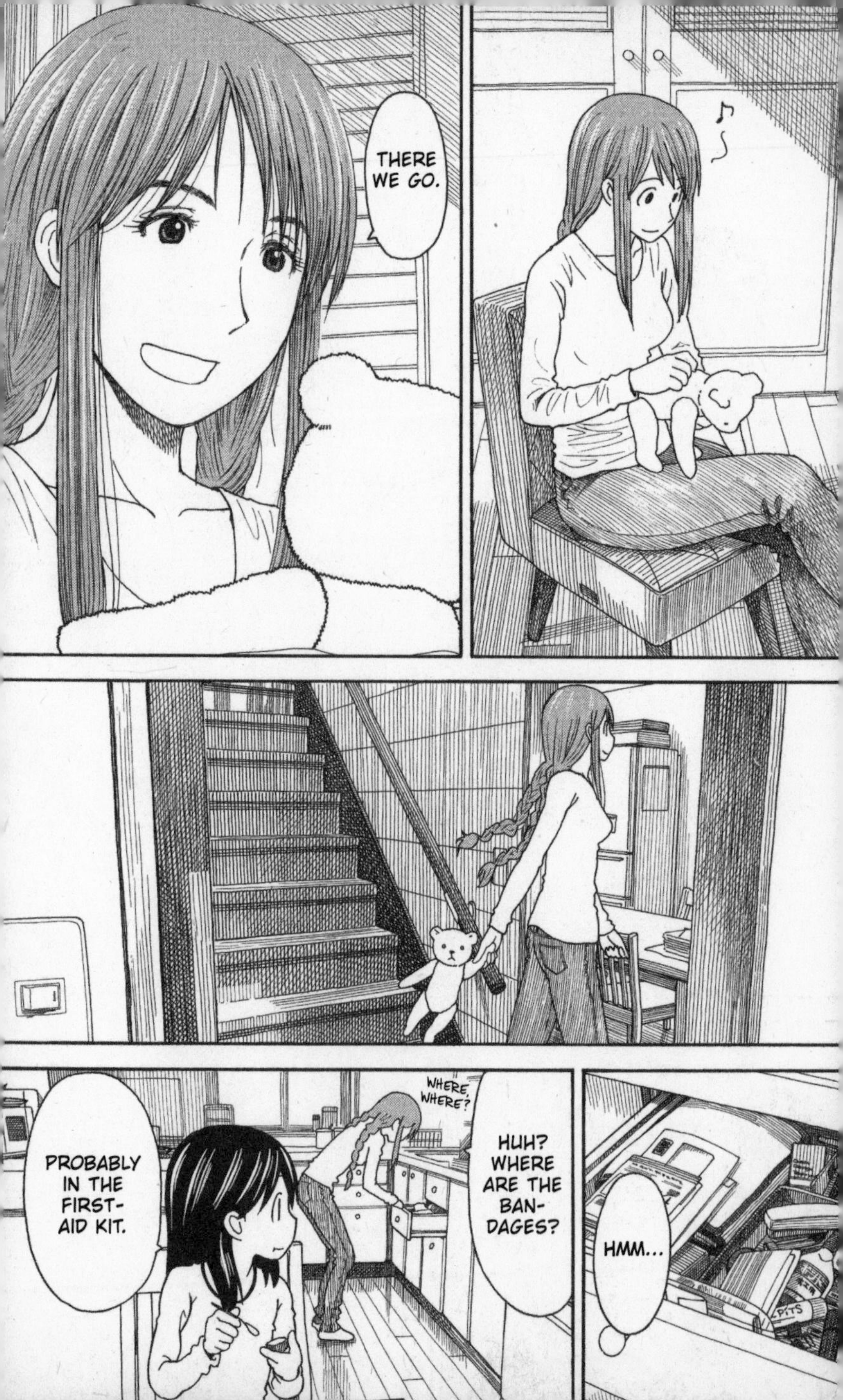
THERE WE GO.
HMM...
HUH? WHERE ARE THE BAN-DAGES?
WHERE WHERE?
PROBABLY IN THE FIRST-AID KIT.

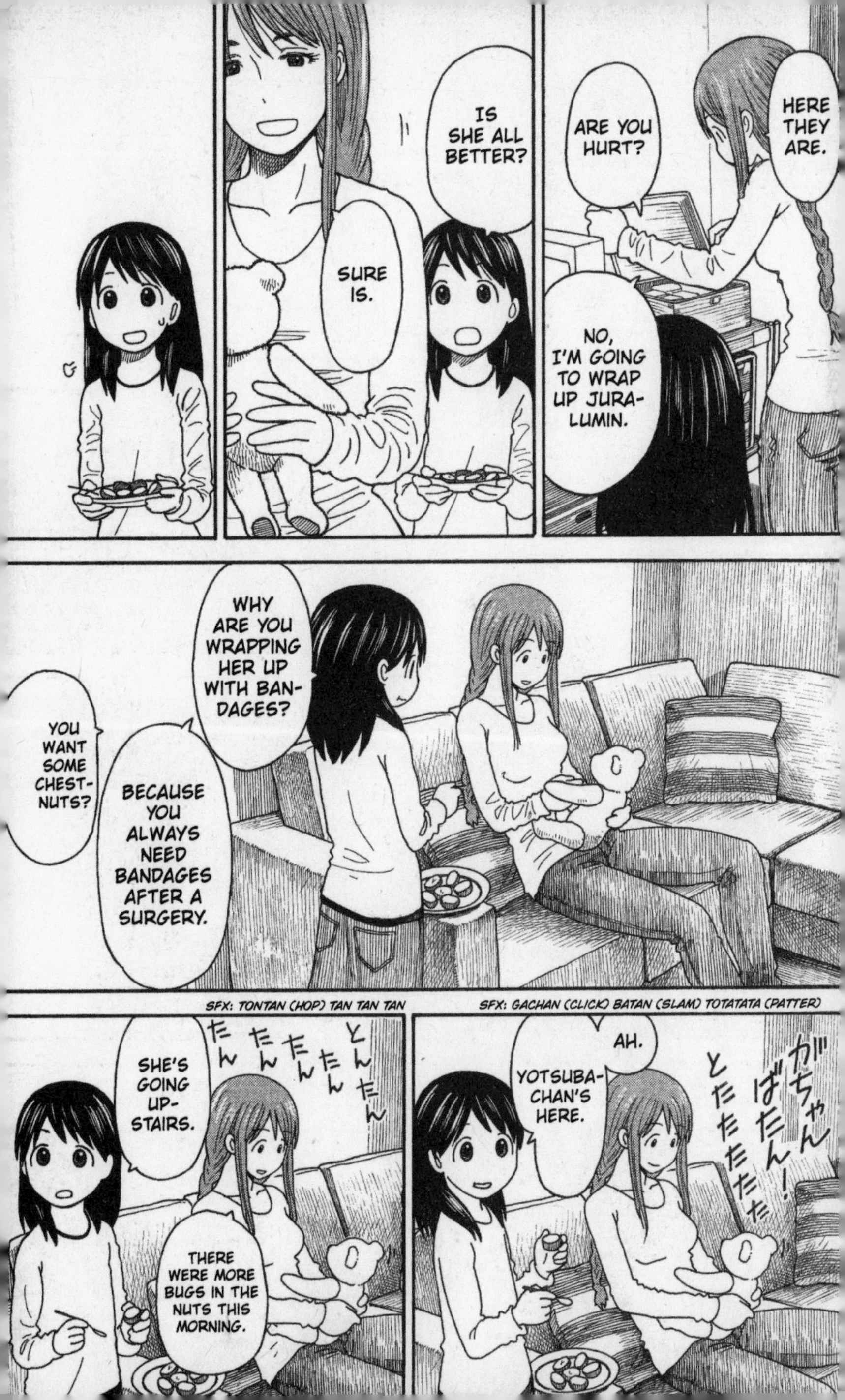
HERE THEY ARE.
ARE YOU HURT?
NO, I'M GOING TO WRAP UP JURA-LUMIN.
IS SHE ALL BETTER?
SURE IS.
WHY ARE YOU WRAPPING HER UP WITH BAN-DAGES?
BECAUSE YOU ALWAYS NEED BANDAGES AFTER A SURGERY.
YOU WANT SOME CHEST-NUTS?
SFX: GACHAN (CLICK) BATAN (SLAM) TOTATATA (PATTER)
がちゃん ばたん! とたたたた
AH.
YOTSUBA-CHAN'S HERE.
SFX: TONTAN (HOP) TAN TAN TAN
とんたん たん たん たん
SHE'S GOING UP-STAIRS.
THERE WERE MORE BUGS IN THE NUTS THIS MORNING.

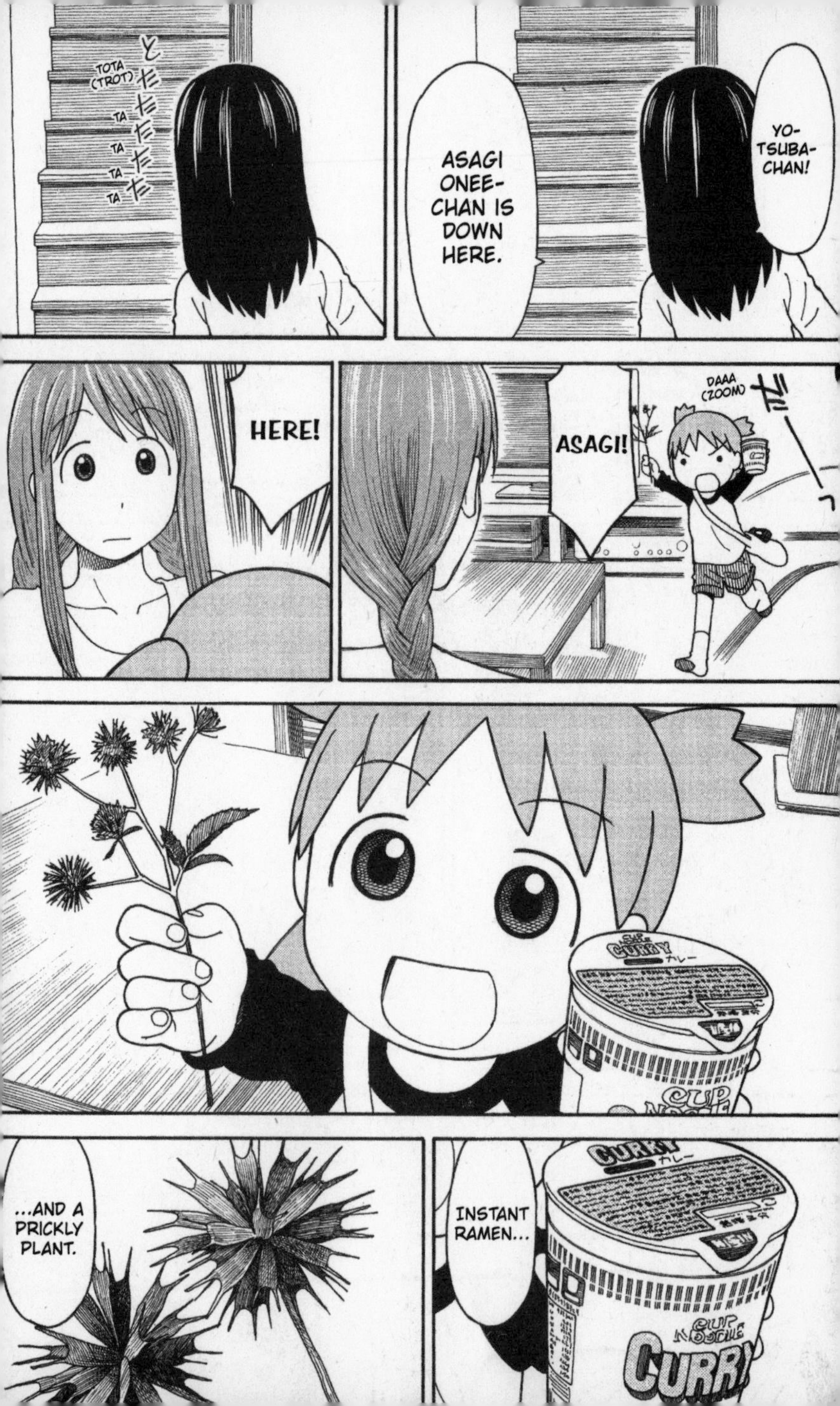
YO-TSUBA-CHAN!
ASAGI ONEE-CHAN IS DOWN HERE.
TOTA (TROT) TA TA TA TA
DAAA (ZOOM)
ASAGI!
HERE!
INSTANT RAMEN...
...AND A PRICKLY PLANT.

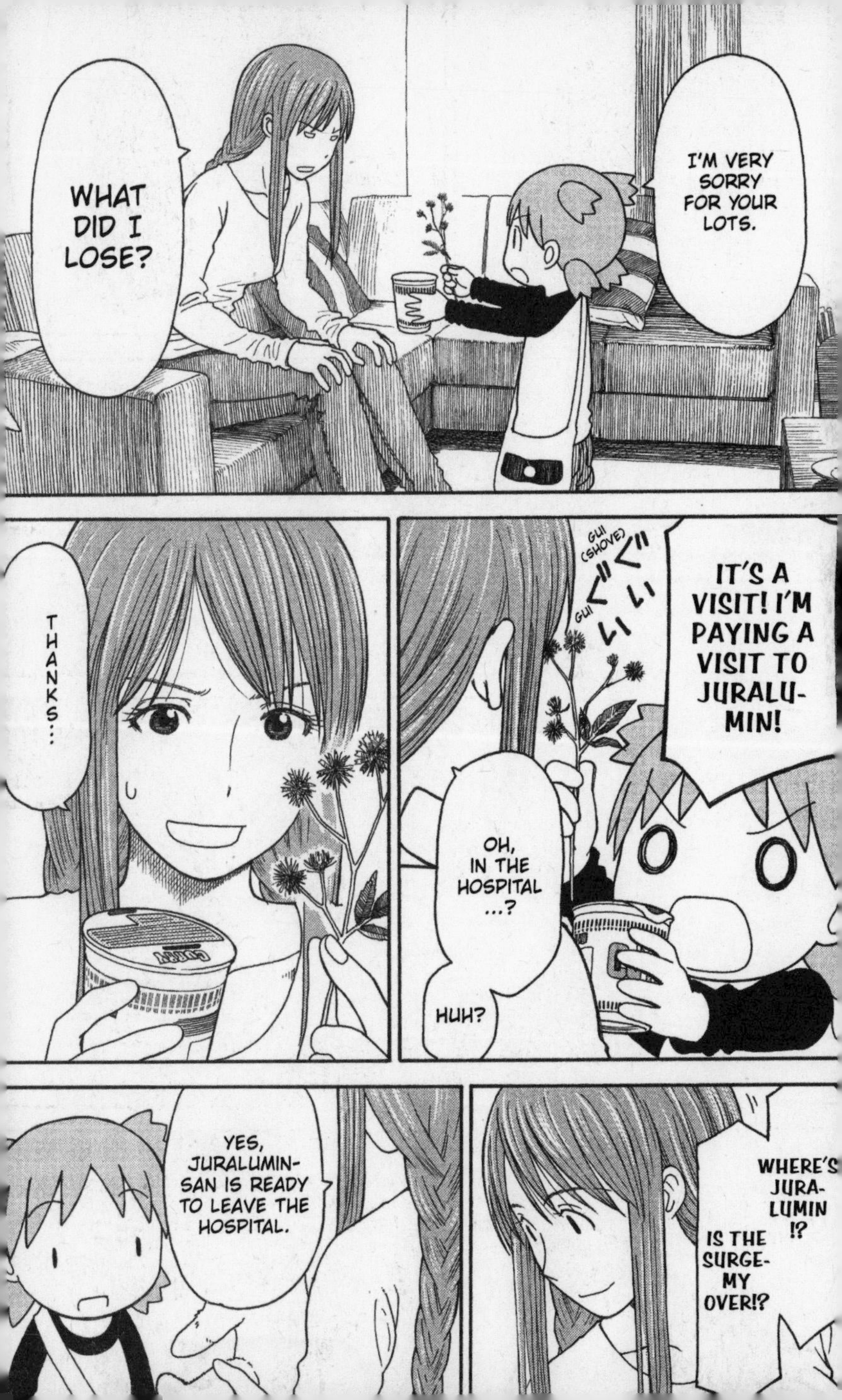
I'M VERY SORRY FOR YOUR LOTS.
WHAT DID I LOSE?
GUI (SHOVE)
GUI
IT'S A VISIT! I'M PAYING A VISIT TO JURALU-MIN!
OH, IN THE HOSPITAL ...?
HUH?
THANKS...
WHERE'S JURA-LUMIN !?
IS THE SURGE-MY OVER!?
YES, JURALUMIN-SAN IS READY TO LEAVE THE HOSPITAL.

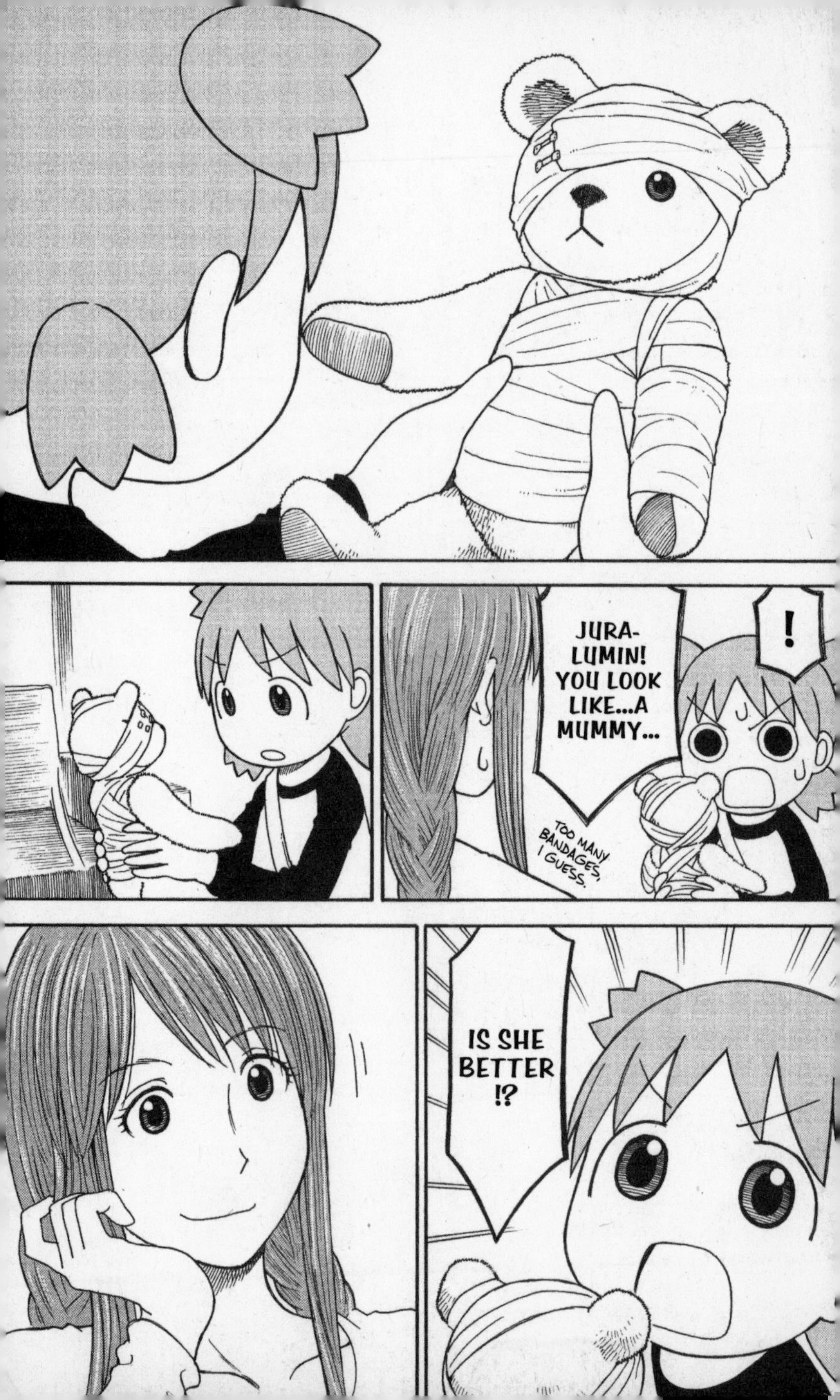
JURA-LUMIN! YOU LOOK LIKE...A MUMMY...
!
TOO MANY BANDAGES, I GUESS.
IS SHE BETTER !?

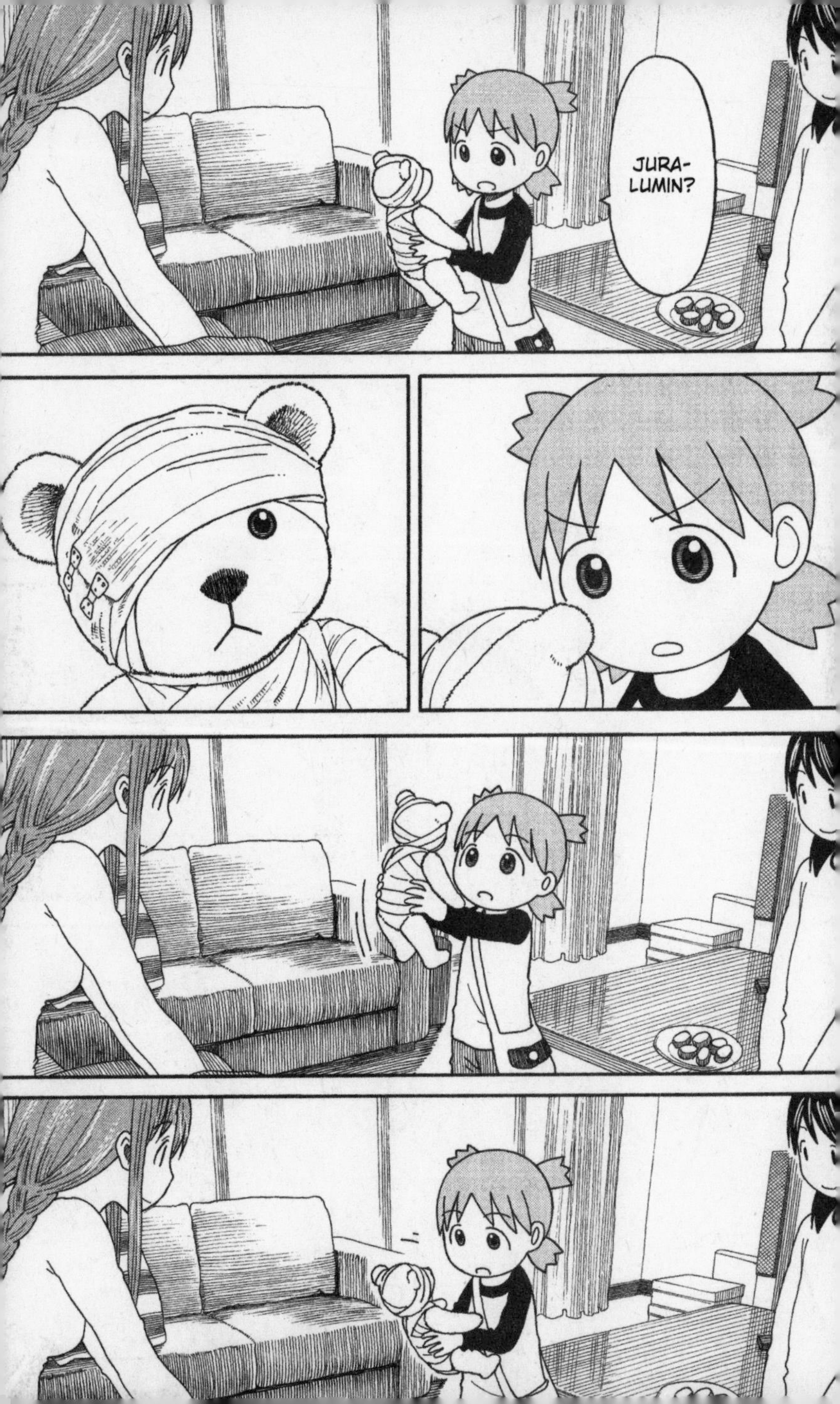
JURA-
LUMIN?

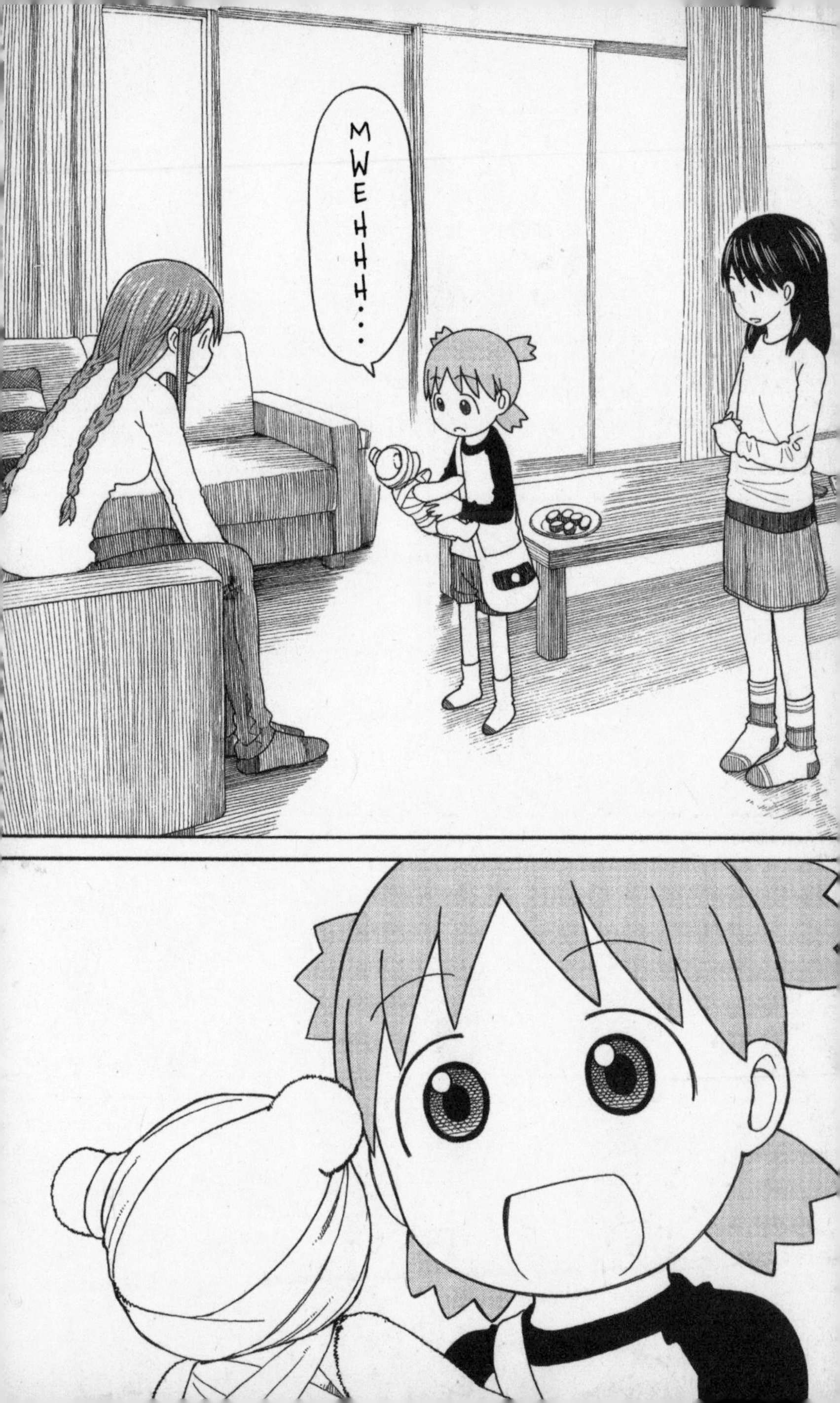
MWEHHH...

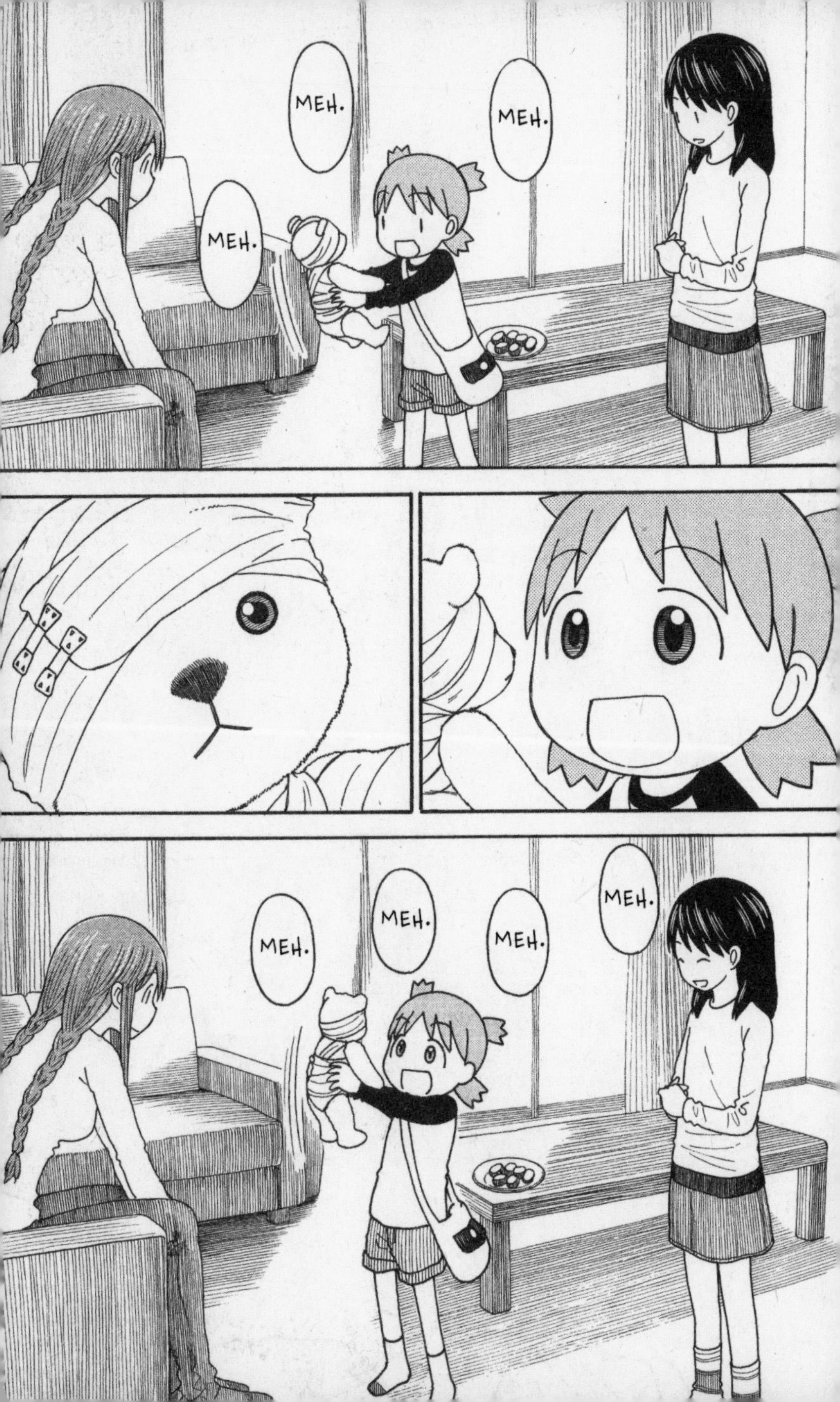
MEH.
MEH.
MEH.
MEH.
MEH.
MEH.
MEH.

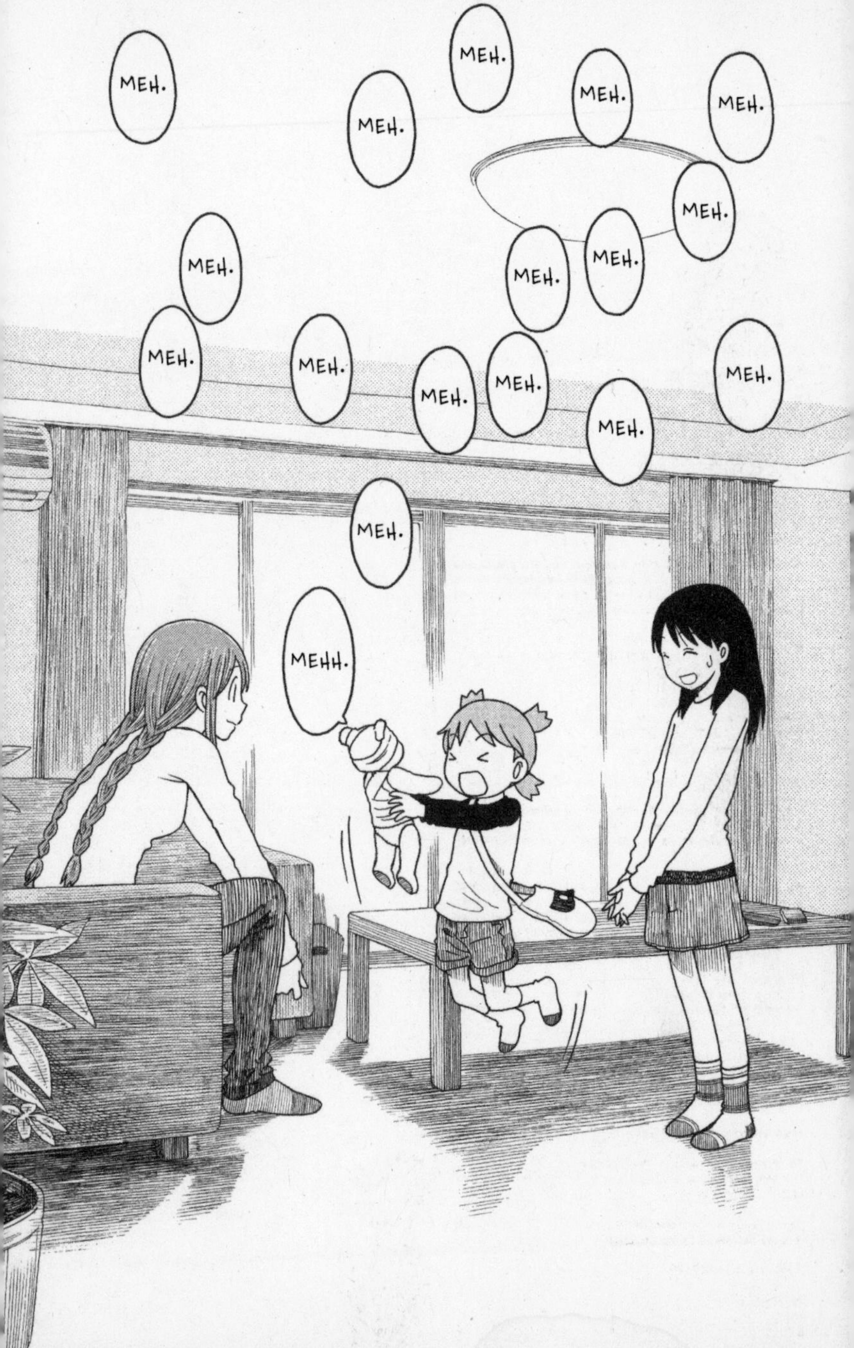

MEH.
MEH.
MEH.
MEH.
MEH.
MEH.
MEH.
MEH.
MEH.
MEH.
MEH.
MEH.
MEH.
MEH.
MEH.
MEH.
MEHH.

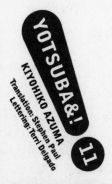

YOTSUBA&! 11

KIYOHIKO AZUMA

Translation: Stephen Paul
Lettering: Terri Delgado

YOTSUBA&! Vol. 11

Edited by ASCII MEDIA WORKS
First published in Japan in 2011 by
KADOKAWA CORPORATION, Tokyo.
English translation rights arranged with
KADOKAWA CORPORATION, Tokyo,
through Tuttle-Mori Agency, Inc., Tokyo.

Yen Press
1290 Avenue of the Americas
New York, NY 10104

Visit us at yenpress.com
facebook.com/yenpress
twitter.com/yenpress
yenpress.tumblr.com
instagram.com/yenpress

First Yen Press Edition: September 2012

Yen Press is an imprint of Yen Press, LLC.
The Yen Press name and logo are trademarks of Yen Press, LLC.

ISBN: 978-0-316-22539-7

10 9 8 7 6

BVG

Printed in the United States of America

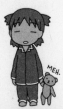

MEH.

YOTSUBA&!

ENJOY EVERYTHING.

TO BE CONTINUED!